THE BLACK PUBLIC SPHERE

BLACK LITERATURE AND CULTURE

A series edited

by Houston A. Baker, Jr.

THE BLACK PUBLIC SPHERE

A PUBLIC CULTURE BOOK

EDITED BY THE BLACK PUBLIC SPHERE COLLECTIVE

THE UNIVERSITY OF CHICAGO PRESS / CHICAGO AND LONDON

The essays in this volume originally appeared in the journal *Public Culture*. Original publication data can be found on the first page of each essay.

The University of Chicago Press, Chicago, 60637
The University of Chicago Press, Ltd., London
© 1995 by The University of Chicago
All rights reserved. Published 1995
Printed in the United States of America
99 98 97 96 95   5 4 3 2 1
ISBN (cl.) 0-226-07190-1
ISBN (pa.) 0-226-07912-8

Library of Congress Cataloging-in-Publication Data

The Black public sphere/edited by the Black Public Sphere Collective.
    p.   cm. — (Black literature and culture)
  Includes bibliographical references and index.
  ISBN 0-226-07190-1. — ISBN 0-226-07192-8 (pbk.)
  1. Afro-Americans — Social conditions — 1975- 2. Popular culture — United States. 3. Afro-Americans — Politics and government.
I. Black Public Sphere Collective. II. Series.
E185.86.B533   1995
305.896'073 — dc20   95-21303
                                                                                CIP

The paper used in this publication meets the minimum requirements of American National Standard for Information Sciences — Permanence of Paper for Printed Library Materials, ANSI Z39.48-1984. ∞

Contents

Cover: Photograph taken by Charles Martin of the televised appearance of Nelson Mandela at Yankee Stadium in New York City in June 1990. The worldwide support for the struggle for freedom in South Africa is one example of the global reach and composition of the Black public sphere.

Preface

The black public sphere can be seen as both a question and an answer. It is a question because it is not clear whether critical public spheres — and none is more critical than the black public sphere — can survive the contemporary political onslaught on compassion and public criticism in the United States. But the black public sphere is also an answer insofar as it is a transnational space whose violent birth and diasporic conditions of life provide a counternarrative to the exclusionary national narratives of Europe, the United States, the Caribbean, and Africa. Thus the black public sphere is one critical space where new democratic forms and emergent diasporic movements can enrich and question one another.

This Public Culture Book first appeared in the Fall of 1994 as a special issue of the journal *Public Culture*. The collaboration that yielded this issue is part of a larger project of the Black Public Sphere Collective. And it drew in part upon contributions made at two conferences: the first, "Toward an Ethnography of the Institutions of Caring in the Black Community" in the Spring of 1993 was organized by the Africana Studies Program of New York University under the directorship of Manthia Diawara; and the other, "The Black Public Sphere in the Reagan-Bush Era" in the Fall of 1993 was organized by the Chicago Humanities Institute of the University of Chicago under the directorship of Arjun Appadurai and in conjunction with the Center for Transcultural Studies (Chicago) under the directorship of Benjamin Lee. These initiatives importantly benefited from the inspiration, counsel, and commitment of John Brenkman, Dilip Gaonkar, Thomas

Holt, Carla Kaplan, Kenneth Warren, and the staff of the respective supporting institutions.

Only some of the essays in this collection derived from the above two conferences and only some of the presentations from the two conferences yielded essays in this volume. Those from the conferences included here are by Regina Austin, Elsa Barkley Brown, Michael Dawson, Manthia Diawara, Michael Hanchard, and Elizabeth Maguire. Other essays which became part of the project to advance a discussion of black publicity include those by Elizabeth Alexander, Houston A. Baker, Jr., Todd Boyd, Rosemary Coombe and Paul Stoller, Reebee Garofalo, Paul Gilroy, and Steven Gregory. An afterword by Thomas Holt that draws on his statement of purpose for the Chicago conference is included here, but did not appear in the *Public Culture* issue. The conceptual and intellectual responsibility for the special issue of *Public Culture* lies with Carol A. Breckenridge and Manthia Diawara who benefited from the support of Lauren Berlant. And authors benefited from the constructive comment by anonymous reviewers who engaged them on a range of critical issues. The responsibility of overseeing the production process lay with Lise McKean, the managing editor of *Public Culture*, assisted by Caroline Cleaves, Ora Gelley, Shao Jing, and Janelle Taylor, members of the editorial office. They were flexible and imaginative in seeing an unusually large issue of the journal through to its completion.

This intellectual project represents transdisciplinary collaboration on matters of contemporary import. Authors speak from a variety of perspectives including those that derive from law (Regina Austin and Rosemary Coombe), anthropology (Steven Gregory and Paul Stoler), history (Elsa Barkley Brown and Thomas Holt), political science (Michael Dawson and Michael Hanchard), sociology (Paul Gilroy), literature (Elizabeth Alexander and Houston A. Baker, Jr.), film and music (Todd Boyd, Manthia Diawara, and Reebee Garofalo), and publishing (Elizabeth Maguire). Collaborative visions like this one have their special coordinates. There are the material practicalities of deadlines and fund-raising, the organizational realities of xeroxing and distribution, issues of hospitality and publication rhythms, matters of overextended lives, and moments of vulnerability. The question of who can speak for the black public sphere and who is willing to speak on behalf of those who do, remains.

The black public sphere — as a critical social imaginary — does not centrally rely on the world of magazines and coffee shops, salons and highbrow tracts. It draws energy from the vernacular practices of street talk and new musics, radio shows and church voices, entrepreneurship and circulation. Its task is not the provision of security for the freedom of conversation among intellectuals, as was the case with the bourgeois public spheres of earlier centuries. Rather, it marks a wider sphere of critical practice and visionary politics, in which intellectuals can join with the energies of the street, the school, the church, and the city to constitute a challenge to the exclusionary violence of much public space in the United States. This Public Culture Book is a contribution to that collective work. The vitality of the black public sphere is a necessary condition for the vitality of the dominant public sphere. It extends the horizon of generosity, the politics of well-being, and the deepening of democratic values.

The Black Public Sphere Collective
April 1995

The Black Public Sphere

Critical Memory and the Black Public Sphere

Houston A. Baker, Jr.

Temporally, modernity is always situated before or after the revolution. Black modernity in the United States—like modernity in general—is articulated through the twin rhetorics of *nostalgia* and *critical memory*. Nostalgia does not here mean arrested development, a distraught sentimentality ever pining for "ole, unhappy, far-off things, and battles long ago." Rather it suggests *heimweh* or homesickness. Nostalgia is a purposive construction of a past filled with golden virtues, golden men and sterling events. Nostalgia plays itself out in two acts. First, it writes the revolution as a well-passed aberration. Second, it actively substitutes allegory for history.

Critical memory, by contrast, is the very faculty of revolution. Its operation implies a continuous arrival at turning points. Decisive change, usually attended by considerable risk, peril or suspense, always seems imminent. To be critical is never to be safely housed or allegorically free of the illness, transgression and contamination of the past. Critical memory, one might say, is always uncanny; it is also always in crisis. Critical memory judges severely, censures righteously, renders hard ethical evaluations of the past that it never defines as well-passed. The essence of critical memory's work is the cumulative, collective maintenance of a record that draws into relationship significant instants of time past and the always uprooted homelessness of now.

Public Culture 1994, 7: 3–33

Black modernity is figured in the textural and textual interweavings of nostalgia and critical memory. Hence, it is ceaselessly dependent upon the peculiar light and responsiveness brought to bear on it. Black modernity's stylistic and political resonances are ever-varying in their appearances. With respect to the politics of style, only a sweet and beautiful reasonableness of future expectations can nostalgically write the past. Reason pats the present on the back for its good intentions. With this optimistic gesture of good cheer occurs the primal scene of black conservative modernity. Absent from this beautifully constructed scene — normally marked by black-and-white social and professional camaraderie of a discreet, controlled temper — is the noise or even a fleeting memory of the black masses.

The masses should not be taken as a code phrase, but should be conceived in terms of the cultural style or lifeworld of the overwhelming majority of black people in the Americas. In relation to the black public sphere, it is this majority and its interests that make the work of critical memory so crucial. Black conservative nostalgia offers an exclusively middle-class beautification of history designed to erase the revolution, pray blessings upon the heads of white people and give a rousing cheer for free enterprise individualism. The time frames of conservatism are a congratulatory present and a shamelessly revisionist past in which the black masses play, at best, a boisterously misguided role.

But the black majority and its institutions have always provided the only imaginable repository for the formation of a self-interested and politically engaged black public sphere in the United States. Furthermore, the resources of the black majority have enabled both the emergence of effective (self-, or better, community-interested) leadership and radical redefinitions of black publicness itself. Critical memory works to illustrate the continuity, at a black majority level, in the community-interested politics of black publicity in America. It also seeks to reclaim from conservative revisionism and nostalgia the organic interconnections between black leadership such as that of the Reverend Dr. Martin Luther King, Jr. and the black majority.

Critical memory operates to save Dr. King from arrest in a golden allegory of the past. In so doing, it sets in motion a critique of the very notion of the public sphere, and calls black conservative nostalgia to serious scholarly account. The following discussion is excerpted from a larger work in progress. It commences at a primary site of public sphere scholarship and proceeds to a critical reading of King and the black public sphere.

No matter how critical the topic, a discussion of blacks in the public sphere might start out in a somewhat lighthearted way. The following comes to mind:

Be eloquent in praise of the very dull old
   days which have long since passed away,
And·convince'em if you can, that the reign
   of good Queen Anne was Culture's palmiest day.
Of course you will pooh-pooh whatever's
   fresh and new, and declare it's crude and mean,
For Art stopped short in the cultivated court
   of the Empress Josephine.
   And everyone will say,
   As you walk your mystic way,
"If that's not good enough for him which is
   good enough for *me*,
Why, what a very cultivated kind of youth
   this kind of youth must be!"

This is from Bunthorne's song in Gilbert and Sullivan's *Patience*, a wonderful light opera parody of 1890s English aestheticism. Bunthorne is the opera's arch aesthete, appearing on stage dressed in the style of Oscar Wilde. The stanza's time frame—from the ascension of Anne in 1702 to the close of Josephine's reign in 1809—coincides with the valorized moment specified by Jürgen Habermas for the development of the bourgeois public sphere as an historical category.

Bunthorne's privileging of "Art" and cultivation of a bygone era strikingly represents a conscious, simultaneous mystification of the actual "dullness" of the "old days." It also expresses the aesthete's mystification of himself. His "eloquent praise" is meant precisely to distance him from the common sense, the politics of everyday life, and newly emergent phenomena of his times. He, thus, ransacks the past for gold. Moreover, he engages in a purposive self-fashioning, including that of sexual orientation, which enables him to be singularly at home amidst the militarism and revolutionary incumbencies of his age. In the world of Gilbert and Sullivan, public opinion rewards Bunthorne with the sincerest form of flattery: imitation.

Habermas's work in that monumental moment of critical social theory titled, *The Structural Transformation of the Public Sphere: An Inquiry into a Category of Bourgeois Society*, sets forth an intriguing valorization of a bygone era along with a peculiarly anachronistic self-fashioning in the vein of the Frankfurt School. Habermas can be as much a detractor of the culture industry as his friend Adorno. Like Bunthorne, he also sometimes seems far too elaborate in his praise of dull old days when distinctive structures and relationships of the conjugal family, economic markets and state authority allowed the emergence of a bourgeois public sphere. Habermas writes:

> The bourgeois public sphere may be conceived above all as the sphere of private people come together as a public; they soon claimed the public sphere regulated from above against the public authorities themselves, to engage them in a debate over the general rules governing relations in the basically privatized but publicly relevant sphere of commodity exchange and social labor. The medium of this political confrontation was peculiar and without historical precedent: people's public use of their reason (*offentliches Rasonnement*). (1993:27)

Habermas elaborates further:

> A public sphere that functioned in the political realm arose first in Great Britain at the turn of the eighteenth century. Forces endeavoring to influence the decisions of state authority appealed to the critical public in order to legitimate demands before this new forum. (1993:56)

At a specifiable historical moment, then, a rational public forms itself out of a congeries of structural arrangements. These arrangements produce public debate in sites such as coffee houses, reading societies, clubs and salons. The public formed in these locations takes, as grist for its conversational mills, legitimate, subjective, rational responses to issues of the day as they occur to participants (votaries of coffee houses) from their scrutiny of the press and literature. Bourgeois subjectivity is created, according to Habermas, in the intimate sphere of the family. But it is projected or mirrored in literary genres such as letters and diaries. It is also reflected in the commodification of both of these genres when Samuel Richardson combines them into his bestseller *Pamela*. The press, in Habermas's view, is represented by public organs like the *Tattler, Spectator* and *Guardian*.

What ultimately emerges as Habermas's ideal of the early public sphere is an associational life of male property-owners gathered to exchange rational arguments and critical opinions shaped and mirrored by novels and the press. This translates into an influential bourgeois public sphere. And what is the outcome? Habermas answers:

Because it turned the principle of publicity against the established authorities, the objective function of the public sphere in the political realm could initially converge with its self-interpretation derived from the categories of the public sphere in the world of letters; the interest of the owners of private property could converge with that of the freedom of the individual in general. (1993:56)

Hence, the democracy of the bouregois public sphere became normative because:

The cliches of "equality" and "liberty," not yet ossified into revolutionary bourgeois propaganda formulae, were still imbued with life. The bourgeois public's critical public debate took place in principle without regard to all preexisting social and political rank and in accord with universal rules . . . intrinsic to the idea of a public opinion born of the power of the better argument was the claim to that morally pretentious rationality that strove to discover what was at once just and right. (1993:54)

Habermas implies that while the sphere of the market was called private, and the sphere of the conjugal family was called intimate, the scene of private, rational persons gathered in contestatory (vis-à-vis the State) argumentation and exchange was actually a public sphere. The publicness of this sphere was, of course, dependent upon both (male) ownership and (male) literacy.

This reading of *The Structural Transformation of the Public Sphere* finds Habermas eager to enter a time machine and return to the good old days of London coffee houses and literary societies: things long ago and far away. Once the structural outlines and historical contours of the bourgeois public sphere's emergence and effects are fully drawn, Habermas proceeds to detail a lamentable decline and fall that brings the reader up to the "pseudo-public sphere" consumerism of postindustrial modernism. (His characterization is enough to make even Gilbert and Sullivan's Captain of the Dragoons weep!) About today's arrangements of life in a welfare-state economy, Habermas writes:

The disappearance of publicity inside large organizations, both in state and society, and even more their flight from publicity in their dealings with one another results from the unresolved plurality of competing interests; this plurality in any event makes it doubtful whether there can ever emerge a general interest of the kind to which a public opinion could refer as a criterion. A structurally ineradicable antagonism of interests would set narrow boundaries for a public sphere reorganized by the social-welfare state to fulfill its critical function. (1993:234)

"Structural transformation," thus, manifests itself not so much as objective historiography as an affective epic, a wish-fulfillment narrative of now and then, of decline and fall . . . the golden nostalgia of once upon a time.

Habermas certainly does *not* suffer from either methodological sleight-of-hand or an ideological narrative zeal. *Structural Transformation* deftly anticipates qualifications, corrections and criticism. It adduces far too many caveats for us to interpret it as simply a valorization of the bourgeois public sphere. Habermas understands fully that his most valued notion of "publicity" (*Offtenlicheit*) is exclusionary, overdetermined both ideologically and in terms of gender, overconditioned by the market and by history, and utopian in the extreme.

He notes, in great detail therefore, that the bourgeois in the pursuit of his private (market) interests never left behind "the unfreedom of the property owner." Hence, the bourgeois was never able to develop into that actual and authentic human being in whose capacity the bourgeois wanted to assume the function of the *citoyen*. In brief, a patriarchal "family" dominated by a property-owning male, who claims exclusive rights via literacy, to both rationality and argumentation in coffee houses and reading societies may importantly challenge some authority. It scarcely qualifies, however, as a realization of the most valuable associational life for a universal *homme* in quest of a pluralistic and egalitarian world.

The very idea of the bourgeois public sphere is shot through with contradictions. Habermas's *Structural Transformation* dutifully records these contradictions:

the equation of "property owners" with "human beings" was untenable; for their interest in maintaining the sphere of commodity exchange and of social labor as a private sphere was demoted, by virtue of being opposed to the class of wage earners, to the status of a particular interest that could only prevail by the exercise of power over others. (1993: 124–125)

Theoretically, and with a certain willing suspension of disbelief, the idea of a bourgeois public sphere, one compelled by reason alone, free of class and status distinctions and resolutely challenging state authority, is tremendously attractive. Even in a discussion of Habermas's model, however, it is obvious that the *idea* of such an apparatus is far more compelling than its shadowy, exclusive manifestations in history.

If Marx, in the nineteenth century, was so brilliantly clear about the limitations of the model, how can black Americans of the 1990s take it up as a serious analytical construct? Marx regarded the seductions of the idea of the bourgeois public sphere as false consciousness. For black America, the attraction of the idea may result not so much from false consciousness as from, to invoke Gilbert and Sullivan, aesthetic consciousness. Habermas's bourgeois public sphere, *in situ*, is a beautiful idea. It is grounded in a historiography that claims universal men were once golden citizens, rationally exchanging arguments in a realm between the family and the market—regardless of race, creed, color, annual income or national origin. But insofar as the emergence and energy of Habermas's public sphere were generated by property ownership and literacy, how can black Americans, who like many others have traditionally been excluded from these domains of modernity, endorse Habermas's beautiful idea?

Black Americans arrived on New World shores precisely as *property* belonging to the bourgeoisie. They were strategically and rigorously prevented from acquiring literacy. And they were defined by Thomas Jefferson and his compeers among America's Founding Fathers, as devoid of even a germ in their minds that might be mistaken for reason. Historically, therefore, nothing might seem less realistic, attractive or believable to black Americans than the notion of a black public sphere. Unless, of course, such a notion was meant to symbolize a strangely distorting chiasma: a separate and inverted opposite of a historically imagined white rationality in action. Such a black upside-down world could only be portrayed historically as an irrational, illiterate, owned, nonbourgeois community of chattel—legally barred from establishing even conjugal families—sitting bleakly in submissive silence before the state. It would be precisely what white America has so frequently represented in blackface: the "b," or negative, side of a white imaginary of public life in America.

◆◆◆

Yet, it is exactly because black Americans have so aptly read this flip side that they are attracted to a historically imagined "better time" of reason. They are drawn to the possibilities of structurally and affectively transforming the founding notion of the bourgeois public sphere into an expressive and empowering self-fashioning.

Fully rational human beings with abundant cultural resources, black Americans have always situated their unique forms of expressive publicity in a complex set of relationships to other forms of American publicity (meaning here, paradoxically enough, the sense of publicity itself as authority). The sorrow songs, as expressed and marketed by the Fisk Jubilee Singers, which W. E. B. Du Bois treats so eloquently, became a global currency of black spirituality. In the nineteenth century they *materially* purchased both a building for a Negro college in Nashville, and affective changes-of-the-human-heart to set against the racist imaginary in American courts of power. What was publicized in the voice, presence, global migratory movements of the Jubilee Singers was a black counter-authority of interpretation. This black authority and montaged composition removed the songs as decisively from an imagined circle of primitive, incoherent, subhuman noise as did the brilliantly contestatory reading of the spirituals by the great Frederick Douglass in his 1845 *Narrative of the Life of Frederick Douglass*.

The public sphere, then, expressively conceived as *black*, can suggest a nostalgic, purely aestheticized fascination with the narrative of a beautiful "time past." Or, in the more critical vein of Habermas himself, it can make its way through the interruptions and fissures of an idealized notion of universal man without class, racial and gender distinctions. Habermas's own analyses portend a critique of any claim that public can legitimately be confined to a singular sphere, rather than read as a plurality of spheres. From his own critique evolve such clear-eyed readings as the following observation by Bruce Robbins: "Within the concept of the public sphere, there is an unresolved and perhaps unresolvable tension, between a tight, authoritative singleness (the public as object of a quest for a universal collective subject or a privileged arena of struggle) and a more relaxed, decentered pluralism (public as something spread liberally through many irreducibly different collectivities)" (1993:xxi).

Robbins's assumption of plurality rather than singularity is, in some ways, like the simple lemon juice that children learn to spread across the invisible ink on a page. His assumption casts light on a variety of "invisible publics": the secret message of social plurality comes to view. We come to see, for example, not simply The (white male) Abolitionists, but The (Plural) Abolitionist Movement, replete with Women Abolitionist Organizers, Black Abolitionist Orators and Ethnic Immigrant Abolitionist Sympathizers on the Underground Railroad. The publicness of abolitionism, thus, becomes less a golden narrative of white male New England Brahmins than a site of montage. A space where a variety of forms of "talk," to paraphrase Nancy Fraser, come together to constitute "political participation" (1993:2).

Out of critique and modulation, alteration and adjustment, the analytical instrument of the public sphere suggests revised notions of how human interactive modes — other than reason alone — bear on publicity. The "wishes," "desires" and "fantasies," again invoking the work of Fraser, of a subaltern counterpublic always help to shape their appropriation of even the most subliminally resonant mass media propaganda.

We might, therefore, following Fraser's lead, regard the politics, or publicity of the wish as a conversion process that characterizes inter- or post-media moments of personal, face-to-face interaction and display.

Such wishful publicity is the postmodern, immediate response of black everyday life to, for example, the dominant media culture's attempt to institute black role models for purposes of consumption. Even when Charles Barkley says "I'm not a role model," black publicity responds with: "You are intended as a role model of media/consumer culture, Sir Charles. You are meant to convince us that you are not role-modelling, so that we, who have thoroughly discredited the notion of role models, will buy the product that you, Sir Charles, are being paid to hustle." The commercial may be regarded as "dope" on the street, but nobody black is buying the product simply because of Sir Charles's slickness in relationship to role-modelling. This shortlived commercial is simply one result. The actual wish for real forms of power can be thought of as a desire for counterauthority. Reading through the commercial is a form of rational and emotional resistance by marginal groups. There are also insiders' envious critiques of such commercially motivated productions. Recently, the star of the Chicago Bulls, Scottie Pipin viciously said of Barkley: " 'He walks around thinking he's the ambassador of the league, but he's a phony person. Until he gets a [National Basketball Association Championship] ring, he's not the ambassador of the league. Until then, I'm considering myself the ambassador' " (*Philadelphia Inquirer*, 13 March 1994, D5). Taking apart reigning commercial models by using the very signs and emblems of publicity, Pippin clearly knows how to "Change the joke, and slip the yoke." Outrageous dress—the implicitly "gay oriented" blue jeans advertisement converted to a public "acting up," or the industry-controlled kinesthetics of MTV's Rap music converted to insurgent forms of black walking and talking in the city—constitute "reading through." What then seems passively consumed as culture as a whole, whether popular, high, commercial, mass or otherwise, may be psychologically and affectively appropriated as merely a base/bass line for wildly fanciful counterpublic performances. (Even if they are only "talking-the-talk" like Pippin.)

Seizing the critical possibilities of Habermas's analyses in their evolving forms of 1990s cultural studies, black Americans are surely in tandem with Arjun Appadurai's suggestion:

The image, the imagined, the imaginary—these are all terms which direct us to something critical and new in global cultural processes: *the imagination as a social practice.* No longer mere fantasy (opium for the masses whose real work is elsewhere), no longer simple escape (from a world defined principally by more concrete purposes and structures), no longer elite pastime (thus not relevant to the lives of ordinary people) and no longer mere contemplation (irrelevant for new forms of desire and subjectivity), the imagination has become an organized field of social practices, a form of work . . . and a form of negotiation between sites of agency ('individuals') and globally defined fields of possibility. (1993:274)

◆◆◆

Certainly, the white American imaginary's view of public with respect to blackness has made abundantly necessary an agential, black imaginative work of the kind suggested by Appadurai. A different, sometimes invisible, black cultural work can be conceived as ceaselessly inventing its own modernity. In the concrete instance of southern Jim Crow legality, for example, it had to fashion a voice, songs, articulations, conversions of wish into politics. This creative agency enabled hundreds of thousands of black men, women and children to gain access to basic public accommodations. The black civil rights struggle, and particularly during the decade from 1955–1965, exemplifies the active working of the imagination of a subaltern, black American counterpublic.

In so many ways, the language, the voice, the articulation of Martin Luther King, Jr. captures the peculiar agency of civil rights and the movement's effort to recapture and recode all existing American arrangements of publicness. King's voice and language made fully visible and audible the black public sphere in America. He is, in fact, the King of the public sphere.

His was also a double work: simultaneously making visible this sphere, and expanding the black public's expression, experience and influence in globally significant ways. King reached back and took hold of the Reconstruction moment of American defaulted debt concerning forty acres . . . and a mule. His was a *critical* act, and it brought all of the implications of Du Bois's modern and informed "laborer" to full black, and ultimately, to American consciousness. What black folks most needed, Du Bois had long ago insisted, were opportunities and resources for dignified labor.

King put a black imagination and the resources of its public sphere to work in order to structurally transform the virtually feudal South of the 1950s. His southern efforts eventually led to an ambitious attempt to rewrite completely the inequitable rearrangements of a late-capitalist global order. His goal, like Du Bois's, was a dignified labor; it is not yet a black reality in America, or elsewhere, as the twentieth century rushes to an ending. By 1968, the public status of Memphis sanitation workers in their sphere of labor became for King an icon of American injustice. The struggle of these workers alone signaled for him the desperate requirements, in a post-industrial world, for new and effective forms of counter-hegemonic publicity.

The historian Taylor Branch (1988) in his magnificent historical account, *Parting the Waters: America in the King Years 1954–63*, captures the creation of a new black *publicness*. Branch's work demonstrates how any consideration of the American public sphere in recent years must account for this new form of black social and imaginative work. Branch suggests that beginning with the famous bus boycott in Montgomery, Alabama in 1955, Martin Luther King, Jr. increasingly realized and enhanced the most important of his gifts for leadership: oratory. Of the huge church rally that followed the first successful day of the Montgomery boycott, Branch writes:

> King would work on his timing, but his oratory had just made him for-
> ever a public person. In the few short minutes of his first political ad-
> dress, a power of communion emerged from him that would speak inex-
> orably to strangers who would both love and revile him, like all
> prophets. He was twenty-six, and had not quite twelve years and four
> months to live. (1988:142)

In fascinating detail, *Parting the Waters* chronicles the national print media's captivation with King, a media that only began to report seriously on a black American general public with the emergence of the Montgomery Improvement Association.

By 1957 when *Time* magazine published a cover story devoted to the popular leader of the Montgomery boycott, Martin Luther King had displaced in the American press's imagination all of the traditional faces and roles of "Negro Leadership" in America. The familiar space of Negro Leadership associated with the Executive Director's office of the National Association for the Advancement of Colored People (NAACP) was all but cast into the shadows. Comfortably situated in his Northern importance, NAACP Director Roy Wilkins was seriously annoyed about the success of the powerful upstart down in Montgomery.

Young, charismatic and intensely sincere in his commitment to nonviolent direct action in the service of a black collective, King became a national sensation. He also became an international figure, a model for emerging Third World leaders and nations of color. In the same year that the *Time* story appeared, one American magazine estimated that King's annual travel was 780,000 miles. This would have amounted to his speaking in public at the rate of four events per week: two hundred talks a year! (Branch 1988: 225). One of King's close advisors suggested, even at this early moment, that the Montgomery leader had achieved the global recognition and praise that a younger generation would come stridently to berate him for. He had, in fact, become a media star.

Oratory and nonviolent direct action; commitment to, and reliance upon the power of the southern black American masses; charismatic appeals to racial and religious coalition; organizational merging of the Southern Christian Leadership Conference with the struggles of the youth-led sit-ins and Freedom Rides—all of these King-endorsed strategies produced a new black American publicity. Branch describes the movement:

> From the Montgomery bus boycott to the confrontations of the sit-ins, then on to the Rock Hill jail-in and now to the mass assault on the Mississippi prisons, there was a "movement" in both senses of the word—a moving spiritual experience, and a steady expansion of scope. The theater was spreading through the entire South. One isolated battle had given way to many scattered ones, and now in the Mississippi jails they were moving from similar experiences to a common experience. Students began to think of the movement as a vocation in itself. (1988: 485)

Early in the Montgomery struggle, black preachers realized the only way to unify their efforts was to follow King wherever the struggle led him, including jail. This was the beginning of the ironic creation of a new space of black freedom: the entire criminal justice system of the American South. With the sit-ins, the most thunderous cry of black public resistance was "jail, no bail." This cry indisputably defined a new southern black public consciousness that instituted a body-on-the-line revolution.

Suddenly, the entire apparatus of white policing and surveillance, which had evolved from the "patter-rollers" in the armed camp of slavery, was converted, mostly by young black students, into a vocational site for liberation. The white-controlled space of criminality and incarceration was transformed into a public arena for black justice and freedom. When, in Rock Hill, South Carolina, black youth were given the option of a one hundred dollar fine or a sentence of hard labor for their protest activities, they chose hard labor. Jail, thus, became a primary associational and communicative site for the freedom struggle. The Rock Hill Nine were, in fact, joined by four members of the Student Non-Violent Coordinating Committee (SNCC) who made their way to Rock Hill with the goal of being jailed. A new moment of the black public sphere had been instituted. About Rock Hill, Branch writes:

> It was an unforgettable vicarious triumph for thousands of sit-in veterans . . . because the thirteen Rock Hill prisoners set a new standard of psychological commitment to be debated and matched. More important, they introduced the idea of roving jail-goers and mutual support. As students began to think of any jail in any town as potentially their own, a new kind of fellowship took hold on the notion that the entire South was a common battlefield. (1988:393)

Neither anomalous nor accidental, one of Martin Luther King's most poignant and effective civil rights documents was, in fact, inscribed from within the new black public sphere of the jail. It was a letter from Birmingham, Alabama. Furthermore, after witnessing the communicative effect, the "group-identity-formation effect" of the white American site of incarceration, how can one be surprised by the emergence of a post-civil-rights-era "prison" consciousness in black America? From George Jackson to the hyper-success of Sanyika Shakur's *Monster*, there is a continuity in the development of black publicity rather than a recurrent novelty. The Black Muslims, Black Panthers and such "independents" as Eldridge Cleaver, all contributed, as did an accomplished poet like Etheridge Knight, to the resonances of this black public sphere of incarceration.

If there was a paradox in the southern jail as a rallying place for freedom, there also was an amazing twist of expressive-cultural irony in the fact that music became its own form of cultural and leadership capital during the struggle. In so many historical writings of black America, music is portrayed as the source of spirited religious reverie, or, an inspiration for the most outrageous forms of secular escapism—in dives, jukes and speakeasies, from Memphis to Mobile, from Atlanta to Los Angeles. But in the moment of the creation of the new black publicity of civil rights, sacred and secular traditions coalesced in the office of struggle. Traditional gospels and hymns were rewritten to fit the mounting struggle and spectacle of the movement. A final word from Branch:

At first, the SNCC leaders accepted the songleader role because of their appreciation for movement singing, and the elders conceded them the role because music was of marginal importance to the normal church program. But the SNCC leaders soon developed a manipulative guile about the music. Their *a capella* singing took the service away from established control by either the preachers or the organist. The spirit of the songs could sweep up the crowd, and the young leaders realized that through song they could induce humble people to say and feel things that otherwise were beyond them. (1988:532)

This was a reshaping of black American media in the service of liberation; song became the expressive mode in which the struggle attracted the voices of the young across the nation. They helped to create a completely different set of associative and communicative norms within black America. School cafeterias and after-school church rallies alike resounded with the new harmonies and lyrics of traditionally black religious songs. These songs were preludes and spurs to committed action in streets, towns and cities across the American South.

Civil rights, then, signifies black cultural work of a mass movement: oratory, songs, new and surprising sites of resistance. The movement, in its mass energies and vernacular harmonies, unequivocally pulled the rug out from under the traditional, high *bourgeois*, conservative black leadership in the United States. The majority black church did not support King's leadership; indeed, the multi-million-member National Baptist Convention relentlessly *opposed* a civil rights agenda. Similarly, the NAACP did all in Director Roy Wilkins's and his regional agents' power to keep the spotlight off King and on the organization's own program of legal-defense gradualism. The courts were, in Wilkins's opinion, the best public place for black American advancement. Politicians such as Adam Clayton Powell were cynically opposed to King, refusing during the mid-1960s to allow SCLC leaders actively to support social reform in Harlem.

King did not find at his beck and call an established leadership or a visible public that was in any way ready to make the leap into black modernity which occurred between 1955 and 1965. The insightful historian Clayborne Carson cautions us about encomia for King:

Although King biographies and King-centered studies of the black struggle continue to appear, serious writers have moved beyond hagiography and have challenged the notion of King as the modern black struggle's initiator and indispensable leader. This reflects a general historiographical trend away from the notion of Great Men either as decisive elements in historical processes or as sole causes, through their unique leadership qualities, of major historical events. (1993:244)

Carson's reminder is sound and timely. At the grassroots level the struggle had extraordinary leaders such as E. D. Nixon, Amzie Moore, Ella Baker, Septima Clarke, Robert Moses, Fred Shuttlesworth and so many others.

Yet, at the same time, any adequate reading of the black public sphere during the decade between 1955 and 1965 is unthinkable without, the "indispensable" and unique leadership of Martin Luther King. A struggle, and indeed a successful one, may well have occurred, but without King, it could never have been as significantly informed or profoundly inscribed as a modern form of black publicity. For King's oratory was absolutely emblematic of his genius for identifying with a black public constituted in the poverty and exclusion of a Jim Crow system. King felt this economically impoverished public's history, spirit, local knowledge and leadership like the very beating of his heart. His voice was always tuned by and attuned to its deepest registers. King's goal, therefore, was to transform the invisible deprivations of black day-to-day life into a national *scene*.

A scene such as Birmingham in 1963, with its black masses, white fire hoses and vicious dogs, became through King's presence and agency a national media *spectacle*. Internationally, Birmingham was read as an American moral scandal. The famous March on Washington of the same year, surely, qualifies as spectacle in the office of black publicity and liberation. And only King's voice metaphorically and expansively imagined could have achieved such publicity. To analyze King's oratorical engagement enhances understanding of his role in specific forms of black modernity.

In a sermon delivered shortly before his death, King suggested terms for his eulogy. He asked to be remembered not as a Nobel Laureate, nor as the recipient of more than 300 other distinguished awards. Rather, he wanted to be remembered as a Christian practitioner who had fed the hungry, clothed the naked and refreshed the thirsty. These terms of remembrance were meant to document a harmony between King's life and the New Testament preachments of Christ, specifically those found in *Mark* 10:35–45. King chose a striking metaphor for this harmony, asking to be eulogized as a "drum major for justice."

The drum major leads a marching band of followers, sometimes with highly unique style. One might say a unique, black cultural style if one recalls the high-stepping, smoothly coordinated Florida State A and M Marching Band of *the public thru its literary & cinematic dimension!*

the 1960s. This Florida band, in the tradition of Marcus Garvey's remarkable drill teams with sparks flying from taps on their heels as they paraded summer streets of Harlem, combined the precision of military drill teams, the flair of black fraternity step shows and the choreography of black, post-funeral gyrations in New Orleans. The result was, at least, a revolution in halftime entertainment. The band's drum major fronted and guided a dazzling display with baton-wielding, deep-bowing, downright magical grace. If the field of reference for King's drum major includes such grace and synthesizing energy, then surely it is more than a common metaphor. It can be read as both a vibrant *conceit* and a type of mounting or performative trope for an aesthetics of *montage*.

Conceit is the trade name given by literary critics to figurative language that combines dissimilar images and, in the words of the eighteenth-century lexicographer Samuel Johnson, "discovers occult resemblances in things [that are] apparently unlike." Johnson and his successors have traditionally culled the poetry of writers like John Donne and George Herbert, the Metaphysical Poets, for examples of the conceit. Donne's comparison of sorrowfully parting lovers to "stiff twin compasses" and his writing of love's most enduring memorial as "a bracelet of bright hair about the bone" are frequently cited as conceits par excellence.

Conceits negotiate between mental and material worlds. They are designed to make even the most philosophically and theologically complicated thought as immediately present, in the words of T. S. Eliot, "as the odor of the rose." Indeed, Eliot speaks of the conceit as a poetical sign that produces a "direct sensuous apprehension of thought, or a recreation of thought into feeling." The conceit, like the Florida State A and M drum major, makes cultural style and its philosophical implications as palpable as the smell of black southern cooking at a church homecoming during a week of successful voter-registration activity.

The verbal resourcefulness that produced Martin Luther King's drum major conceit is often viewed by his biographers as a direct outcome of the civil rights leader's family background. He was, after all, the product of three generations of black Baptist ministers; he knew the language of the black church and its traditions in their full emotional and metaphorical brilliance. To explain King's verbal dexterity as a family matter is surely correct. Yet, this explanation is incomplete unless we realize that the drum major conceit and, indeed, King's entire repertoire of sparkling oratory are not products of a Christian familial background alone. The language and effectiveness of his civil rights leadership also point to a specific habit of mind. This habit of mind enabled him to convert the torturous, complex, heterogeneous lines and images of United States race relations into a strategically conceived and brilliantly articulated program of

American social reform that led directly to a new and modern black publicity in America.

The conceit is the linguistic correlative of a mind that imaginatively combines the most seemingly dissimilar things and orders of existence. King's sensibility was metaphysical. It was one of montage, or after the example of Romare Bearden in the graphic arts, collage. It was capable of both effecting and expressing a peculiar synthesis between seemingly disparate walks of American life. Ultimately, King's mind seems to survey a world where the Lord may be the undisputed owner of the field, but He still needs the shrewd, secular drum major to move forward His designs for black liberation.

The bare linguistic bones of conceit may have come to King from Baptist forbearers. But the habit of mind that put flesh on the bones was surely a developmental outgrowth of King's participation in and astute understanding of the wider black public sphere in which the Baptist church itself is located. Having come of age and graduated from an historically black college in the deep south of the 1950s, King shared a legacy of black collectivity that is virtually inconceivable amidst the fragmentation and rubble of today's black American world.

Without romanticizing or minimizing the brutal realities of America's deep-south apartheid, it is still possible to acknowledge that racial segregation in the United States both necessitated and gave birth to a remarkable black southern public sphere. This definitively separate and putatively equal black public sphere of American life comprised a world of civic responsibility, commercial duty and professional obligations shared by southern blacks. These behaviors and values were sheltered and nurtured in institutions like the black family and church, and at historically black colleges and universities. In its codes of class, patriotism, respectability, dissent, consensus, tolerance, justice and ethics, the black public sphere offered a sometimes radical critique of the dominant white society with which it coexisted. For example, the Constitution of the United States and the American national flag were valued sites of patriotism and pride for the black public sphere.

Which of us, for example, who attended those awesomely-scrubbed black urban public southern schools of the 1950s that always smelled of disinfectant, can forget the pride and solemnity with which each school day began in recitation of the "Pledge of Allegiance" to the flag of the United States of America?

How sharply this *Black Federalism*, as it were, contrasts with and critiques the state sovereignty and Confederate nostalgia of, say, 1950s Mississippi. Woven into the very warp and woof of the Mississippi state flag, waving over the capital in Jackson, were then, and still are, the stars and bars of the Confederacy. Southern

State Sovereignty meant, in effect, a resolve by the dominant society of the deep south to preserve southern whiteness as a separate public sphere.

In *The Souls of Black Folk*, W. E. B. Du Bois captures the spirit and consequences of coexisting black and white public spheres when he analyzes the black church. The church, says Du Bois in his chapter "Of the Faith of the Fathers," is effectively a government of men, reproducing "in microcosm, all that great world from which the Negro is cut off by color-prejudice and social condition" (1965: 340). Du Bois does not intend to characterize black religion as a poor substitute for black participation in the American macrocosm. Rather, he seeks to convey the magnificent originality and signal importance of the black Americans' institutionalization of "his higher life." In the black public sphere, the church sustains and expresses the tensions of black American group life. It is at once a social and a religious center, a site of material ownership, a place of frenzied spiritual regeneration, a mecca for intellectual leadership and a bright oasis for the musical ministry of those who cannot read and write.

The black church negotiates vigorously between the concrete need for black freedom and opportunity in this world, and a black theological and philosophical desire for the glories of the infinite. Hence, its mission might be described as psychosocial. Its "twin-compassed" institutionalization is bound to require and produce a special brand of leadership as Du Bois asserts: "The [black] Preacher is the most unique personality developed by the Negro on American soil." Similarly, the music of the church and its "frenzy" (animated black congregational responses) are seen by Du Bois as significant aspects of its unique, public being-in-the-world. Sociologist Aldon D. Morris astutely notes that when Martin Luther King began his work in black America, "the black church was the only popularly based institution within the black community that was, for the most part, economically and politically independent of the white community. This independence allowed it to serve as the staging ground for the black protest movement" (1993: 39–40).

Black colleges and universities also offer, in the view of Du Bois, prime examples of a creative convergence between black expressivity such as the "Sorrow Songs" of the Fisk Jubilee singers and unique forms of leadership such as the black Talented Tenth. Like that of the church, the mission of black colleges and universities combines or, better, holds in intricate tension, the curriculum for a liberating black economics, and programs geared to the "higher life" of black intellectual speculation. Especially significant for the black intellectual, as discussed earlier, is that activism and speculation are seldom mutually exclusive.

In the flourishing days of the black university, intellectual speculation was generally held to be a means to a liberatory social end.

Given Du Bois's passionate analyses of black institutions, it seems fair to say he is less interested in condemning the existence of a segregated black public sphere "behind the veil" than in locating the *sui generis* material and spiritual strengths of that sphere. Insofar as these strengths exist in institutional form, Du Bois hopes to decipher their special codes and unique angles of vision. He wants both to read their institutional conceits, one might say, and to present them in his own powerfully figurative language. Du Bois's narrative conceit in *Souls* is that of a black intellectual speaking from "behind the veil." This image provides just the double edge and second sight of verbal mastery that Du Bois required to make his collection of fugitive essays into a black public intellectual document of record. During the 1930s, James Weldon Johnson astutely proclaimed that Du Bois created what had never existed before—a "Negro intelligentsia."

When Martin Luther King was growing up in the deep south, the truths of black folk, their collective sense of responsibility and their pride in their public institutions, were matters of history and record. In part, this was so because Du Bois had achieved the montaged style to take them public. By the time of King's youth in black Atlanta, where Du Bois accomplished some of his most outstanding intellectual work, self-evident truths of the black public sphere rolled trippingly off the tongues of King's Baptist progenitors every Sunday. Such truths were the mainstay of Sunday morning rituals in polished assembly halls of southern churches from Richmond to New Orleans. The great civil rights leader, thus, learned at home in the black public sphere of church, college and community in a segregated South the contrasting codes and conceits of black American critique.

King came to know that in order to be a drum major, one has first to be touched by the frenzy of black spiritual existence. Du Bois describes this experience: "Finally, the Frenzy or 'Shouting,' when the Spirit of the Lord passed by, and, seizing the devotee, made him mad with supernatural joy, was the last essential of Negro religion and the one more devoutly believed in than all the rest" (1965:339). The words belong to Du Bois, but King's oratorical performances and leadership during the years between Montgomery and Memphis prove that he fully appreciated their wisdom. He understood that before one can be a successful leader in the black public sphere, one must first be instructed in the spirit. This alone allows one to become an instrument of the Lord. The proof of such instrumentality is in the rhetorical effectiveness of the person who, it is provisionally agreed, has been touched. A frenzied style makes one recognizable and resonant before a spirited mass audience. In black public sphere shorthand: King knew that he had to self-consciously model himself as one of "God's Trombones."

Yet his leadership language and development were not simply black recapitulations of, say, Saul's scriptural journey along the road to Damascus. Christian spirituality was preeminent in King's life. But this spirituality did not allow him to be satisfied by a simple call to local ministry or clownishly to bellow homespun truths before a gullible audience. Those sacred, black, university ideals expounded by Du Bois at the turn of the nineteenth century motivated King. These ideals were as present in the black public sphere of the 1950s as the calling of the black church and King was fortunate enough to stand intellectually and generationally at the fragile cusp between a closed, nearly feudal South and its inevitable entry into twentieth-century modernity.

In the black public sphere the idea of advanced graduate degrees beyond bachelor's of arts and science credentials was gaining currency. Furthermore, a new black ecumenical spirit was at least as well grounded in the 1950s black American public sphere as the drive to independence by various African nations and the anticolonial struggles of India. Global work awaited, and it seemed in the 1950s there were global economic possibilities for the black American. New media and communications technologies provided greater access to the world for the South via television and improved telephone services. Conversely, the South and its everyday realities were destined to be internationally telecast.

Finally there were generational differences that have always marked the black public sphere. Thrust into leadership at twenty-six years of age, King found himself amidst a congeries of competing black age groups, mind sets, ethical orientations and reform agendas. He was compelled to speak as convincingly to Rosa Parks and her cohort of adult wage earners and domestic laborers as to an adolescent, advanced guard of newly-middle-class, high-school and college sit-in participants. He had to make as much sense to James Lawson of Vanderbilt University as to Reverend Ralph Abernathy and the Southern Christian Leadership Conference.

King was equal to the challenge. His legacy from the black public sphere, in combination with his graduate theological training in eastern and western philosophy, enabled him to articulate a new conceit of black moral leadership. His performances before mass audiences made his strategies of leadership irresistible. The pulpit, the podium and the premiere place in nonviolent protest marches became sites of King's drum-major leadership. He adjusted and keyed his voice and vision to the music of the church and its new SNCC variations, to the values of a southern black collectivity and to the social and spiritual rhetoric of the black public sphere at large.

Ultimately, King's leadership was a performative occasion. He used it to declare war on American injustice. His performances always combined, after the fashion of the conceit, enormously varied tropological energies. The combinations or montages which seemed to flow, to be moving images, as naturally fluid as the pulsing of the blood were powerfully persuasive. On any single occasion, he might move from an explanation of the history of a local protest action, to citations (in layman's terms) of the Constitutional supports for the protest, to a parable drawn perhaps from children's literature, to the rollicking exegesis of a scriptural passage relevant to the protest. He then would conclude with a rousingly applauded quotation, half-chanted and half-sung, from a repertoire that ranged from Aristotle's *Logic* to "The Battle Hymn of the Republic."

◆◆◆

King proclaimed clearly and repeatedly that words were not enough. Action—nonviolent, direct action—was the goal of his performances. He was intent on an active gospel designed to correct centuries of American injustice. He knew that his performances would first have to erase a traditional image of black religion that had ruled the white imaginary for decades.

James Baldwin was surely correct when he suggested in his 1955 essay, "Everybody's Protest Novel" that the most valorized image of black religion in the white imagination is Harriet Beecher Stowe's title character from her 1852 novel, *Uncle Tom's Cabin.* "Uncle Tom," writes Baldwin, "is jet-black, wooly-haired, illiterate; and he is phenomenally forbearing. He has to be; he is black; only through this forbearance can he survive or triumph . . . [and] his triumph is metaphysical, unearthly" (1955:17). For Baldwin, Uncle Tom is indisputably a "category" that white America has substituted for black humanity. Stowe's character represents, in Baldwin's account, a divestiture of both the black American's humanity and his sex.

Stowe's divestiture attempts to nullify evil. According to Baldwin, this New England author's theology is a "theology of terror," and is widely shared by Americans. It asserts a clear equivalence between blackness and evil; only clothing blackness in the white robes of salvation will redeem America. However, salvation's bright, smothering mantle chokes to death the black personality—and possibilities for a new and liberating publicity. This theology of terror and the

Isn't the performative always linked to the public?

protest novel that it spawns, reduce black humanity to a cipher; a will-less, Christian thing incapable of resisting even its own denigration. Baldwin writes:

> This tableau [of Stowe's Uncle Tom], this impossibility, is the heritage of the Negro in America: *Wash me*, cried the slave to his Maker, *and I shall be whiter, whiter than snow!* For black is the color of evil; only the robes of the saved are white. (1955:16)

Baldwin's terrifying vision of white American Christianity's effect on black America is precisely the image that King designed his own performances and conceits to eradicate.

The genius of King's campaign was its radical, active, uncompromising transformation of the solacing American space occupied by Uncle Tom. Mrs. Stowe's medieval, Christian grotesquerie yields figurative right-of-way to King's black public sphere conceits. King's performance of such conceits — working them into his oratory and living them as a drum-major leadership style — produced a new national scene. It was a scene of sharp and ineluctable moral crisis. It was the scene, without a shadow of a doubt, of critical memory in the office of new black publicity and liberation.

◆◆◆

King understood that he was compelled to walk and talk in the ways of a southern, rurally oriented, black community that transmitted wisdom as often through oral/aural means as by "the book." He realized that he must carry the church itself and its manifold congregation out of comfortable conservative structural alignments with southern Jim Crow such as his own father's Republican ministry. They had to collectively move onto a new national political stage. "Forbearance" and "death," which in Baldwin's account of Uncle Tom serve merely to make Mrs. Stowe's character a quiet casualty of theology, were converted by King's leadership into mass, public, moral weapons.

Weapons were mandatory. King was convinced, from his first engagement at Montgomery, that he had entered a fight, a battle, a war. And he intended to win. "Don't be afraid," he counselled during one memorable speech. "Don't even be afraid to die. . . . For I submit to you tonight that no man is free, if he fears death. But the moment you conquer this fear, you are free." According to King, the "capacity to die" without fear and in the knowledge that you have confronted — without money, power or the law's protection — the dread, beauty and rights of your own black humanity is a mighty weapon against injustice. Furthermore, he proudly, and with the glad endorsement of his constituency, assured his adversaries: "We will wear you down by our capacity for suffering."

King reclaimed those imaginary racial traits of Uncle Tom that caused Mrs. Stowe's "thing" to virtually commit suicide for Christianity. Indeed, he dramatically and performatively refigured them. They were metaphysically refigured in terms of the will, daring, spirit and institutional strengths of a new black public sphere in formation. King brought this sphere to an intense consciousness of the immediate necessity to achieve full citizenship rights *now*, in *this* world. Economic impoverishment and social segregation had to be eliminated. Only tension and crisis, as King declared in his "Letter From Birmingham Jail," could produce first, negotiation, and then, new laws offering new opportunities for the black public sphere.

cf. Albert Murray

Thus, the conceit of the drum major is far more than a common metaphor or a simple figure for a humble Good [black] Samaritanism. In its black public sphere resonances from the world of King's more than twelve-year battle to open the American South to the sounds of modern justice, the conceit of the drum major assumes a military signification. It gestures toward the point man for a drumming corps of followers. The uniquely black rhythms of such a corps may well guide the stylish strut of a leader. Ultimately, however, King's constituency and its leader were closely akin to the Lord's chosen thousands, in ancient times, across the Jordan, as described in *Joshua* 6:20.

On the seventh day of their occupation, the priests of Joshua sounded their trumpets of rams' horns seven times and

> So the people shouted when the priests blew with the trumpets: and it came to pass, when the people heard the sound of the trumpet, and the people shouted with a great shout, that the wall fell down flat, so that the people went up into the city, every man straight before him, and they took the city.

By transfiguring mortality, forbearance and white America's theology of terror with the intellectual and imaginative resources of the black public sphere, King led his followers in the brilliant (might one say conceited?) sounds of struggle that tumbled the walls of injustice—like the walls of Jericho—and drove the wicked from their seats of power.

◆◆◆

Martin Luther King's leadership was so firmly rooted in a black southern public sphere that it became virtually impossible for King himself, or for America at large, to separate his work from this "publicity." It is a mistake, however, to see the coming of Black Power into the black liberation struggle of the 1960s as a fateful rupture in the work of King's corps that was drumming evil out of the land.

In the far too allegorical historiography of black conservatism, Stokeley Carmichael and the field secretaries of SNCC are charged with substituting a gospel of (evil) armed self-defense and black separatist empowerment for what are held to be Martin Luther King's (good) preachments of integration. But since Jamestown in 1619, notions of black separatism (e.g., emigration) and community empowerment have always coexisted with other orientations in the black public sphere. However, such notions as Carmichael's and H. "Rap" Brown's have only sporadically gained currency with the masses of black America. Their strength of appeal relates to peculiar convergences of American social and economic opportunities with the necessary black leadership to articulate a black power agenda.

By the mid-1960s in the United States such a convergence had come to fullness in the North with the organization of the Black Muslims and the charismatic leadership of Malcolm X. Moreover, the necessity for a new agenda beyond nonviolent, direct action protest in the South had been made clear by the suddenness and ferocity of the Los Angeles Watts Riot of 1965. Suddenly visible to national and international publicity was the black urban ghetto, where migration had brought so many former black southerners in quest of a promised industrial land. But the new land has all too often left these immigrants from the South abandoned, victims of the death of smokestack industries. They turned to the meager doles of the welfare state.

Carmichael, Brown and a black power cohort of the 1960s, with King's unhappy agreement, imported "northern" notions into the black southern struggle. But the appeal of black power was surely as much generational as regional. If one watches carefully videos of the Black Sanitation Workers Strike in Memphis which was King's last point of struggle, one sees *young*, southern black men brandishing sturdy clubs in the camera's eye and shouting "Black Power!" When the youth of the corps begin to drum a different cadence, what choice does the drum major have but to rethink his work?

Though Martin Luther King was enveloped in the imagery of the black South at his death — his funeral cortege was led by a mule-drawn wagon — even by 1965 he had moved to a conception of global economic justice and anti-imperialism that forced him to oppose the war in Vietnam and to call for a Poor People's Campaign to be spectacularly staged in Washington, D.C. He had realized during his nonviolent 1966 summer campaign in Chicago just how difficult and dangerous urban modernism made the struggle for black liberation, saying, "I've never seen mobs, even in Alabama and Mississippi, as hostile as mobs in Chicago."

In the South, the scene had altered from medieval morality to legally civil, twentieth-century premodernity. Blacks could vote in Lownes County, Mississippi, eat at the Woolworth lunch counter in Greensboro, North Carolina and ride a Greyhound bus from Durham to Birmingham without being murdered. The South had opened up from feudalism. But the real stakes of modernism were in the ethnically divided cities of the north and west, where there were jobs, economic security, gleaming cars, and sturdy homes: symbols of a fulfilled American dream. In these cities young, black urban dwellers were confronting the forces of racism with combative strategies that they deemed far more appropriate than moral suffering or a courageous capacity to die.

King himself had said that the mobs of northern and western cities were more hostile than those of Alabama and Mississippi. Furthermore, as James R. Ralph reminds us in his fine study of the Chicago Freedom Movement: "By 1965, as Chicago's black population approached one million and accounted for almost a third of the city's residents, more blacks lived there than in the entire state of Mississippi" (1993: 45). The scene of black modernity had to be staged, if it was to be meaningful, where most of black America lived.

The black novelist Richard Wright had indeed been prescient in his best-selling work of 1940, *Native Son*, which is set in Chicago. The scene of modernism for blacks was to be a Chicago of the intellect and imagination, an urban space in which an archetypal "Bigger" black consciousness was to find itself caught in a nightmare of acquisitive real estate owners, callous labor leaders, corrupt political officials and morally blind social welfare workers. Bigger in the electric chair might well have been emblematically and realistically enacted by the Black Panthers' leader, Fred Hampton, who was murdered by the State's Attorney office in 1969.

Suddenly, the task before young black activists of the mid-1960s, whether in Chicago or Memphis, was to create a new conceit for modernism. It required a figure that could move an urban black public sphere to consciousness and action.

The black writer Amiri Baraka states the theme for such modernity in his poem, "Return of the Native" (Jones 1969:108):

> Harlem is vicious
> modernism. BangClash.
> Vicious the way its made.
> can you stand such beauty?
> So violent and transforming.

[handwritten note:] cf. November, The Melody Never Stops

> Each thing, life
> we have, or love, is meant
> for us in a world like this.
> Where we may see ourselves
> all the time. And suffer
> in joy, that our lives
> are so familiar.

Isolated, spatially confined, abandoned by industry, marked by crumbling schools and indifferent teachers, cruelly defined by wretched public housing, the ghetto is its own unique arrangement of black American life. In the 1960s it brought forth from the black publicity of the prison and the ranks of the Black Muslims not only the leadership of a Malcolm X, but also minimalistic, modern black poetic cadences such as those of a fiery Amiri Baraka.

King had already realized by the mid-1960s that his familiar conceits would have to take account of a far more expansive and complex geographical and imaginative territory than he had previously envisioned. The tragedy for the 1990s is that he did not live long enough to guide us – in the fine energy of his drum major leadership and black public sphere brilliance – through straits of the past quarter century. Can anyone doubt that had King lived, moral tawdriness and black nostalgia would scarcely be as all consuming as they are in our era?

[handwritten note in margin: much too cryptic or perhaps unfounded]

King's continuing and always transformative leadership might have stood as a bulwark against the disingenuous, conservative black revisionism of the 1990s that seeks to return Mrs. Stowe's Christian martyr to where a mighty drum major of the public sphere lived and had his being-in-the-world. Martin Luther King was the master of conceit. He understood, even as he drew his last breath on that balcony in Memphis, that the language of the black public sphere en masse is the leader's only source of regeneration.

In 1968, that language was Black Power.

Aldon Morris writes of King, the civil rights movement and the media:

> Throughout much of American history blacks were exploited, beaten,
> and oppressed while most Americans and people around the world went
> about their daily affairs barely aware of the situation. Indeed, racial seg-
> regation and oppression isolated blacks from the American mainstream,
> making their wretched conditions invisible. The media, however, played
> an important role in bringing King's leadership and the civil rights move-
> ment to national and international attention. (1993:46)

The liberation struggle under King's leadership moved from "invisibility" to legal
civil rights victories. It also brought black rights a recognition by the highest
legislative body in the land. King managed to recuperate a numerical and ideological black public that had been violently erased by the post-Reconstruction South.

The new visibility achieved by civil rights was no more than a "recuperation,"
a small payment of interest on that vast debt noted by Du Bois in 1903. Blacks
in 1965 had, in effect, returned to Reconstruction, hoping once again that civil
and voting rights would enable them to get ahead with daily life in America
without being summarily lynched. The new black visibility scarcely constituted
a gain sufficient to satisfy a black majority. This was made abundantly clear as
early as 1964 when the "long hot summers" of ghetto rioting began. Black urban
uprisings became normative publicity in the very heart of the Great Society that
had been declared by President Lyndon Johnson. New social welfare initiatives
designed to end poverty in America were, thus, made more urgent by the international visibility of American cities on fire. King himself realized that a paradoxical
return to the future constituted by yet another bestowal of black southern voting
rights was scarcely more than a Pyrrhic victory. Late in his leadership he angrily
declared:

> "I am appalled that some people feel that the civil rights struggle is over
> because we have a 1964 civil rights bill with ten titles and a voting
> rights bill. Over and over again people ask, What else do you want?
> They feel that everything is all right. Well, let them look around at our
> big cities." (Cone 1993:206)

Radically new forms of visibility, or black publicity, were required. Black residents of big cities had decided the only way to gain the nation's attention was
by rebellious community action. The theologian James Cone reports that King

[handwritten marginal notes:]
) hence the uncertainty of a public institution driven by profit — which is only in favor of blacks

\ hence my point about the essential feudalism of the movement

) *And yet perhaps for some people the struggle wasn't over but perhaps the civil right struggle was, for the moment)*

was shocked after surveying the destruction of the Watts riot to hear community residents claiming a victory. How could they think they had won in the face of such wreckage? They answered: "We won because we made them pay attention to us."

Attention, a publicity quite different from any attained by noble sacrifice, was desperately needed if a genuine black modernity was ever to occur. This modernity called for an urban liberation of black America, and for its movement to cultural and economic independence. In July of 1967 King proclaimed: "The movement must address itself to restructuring the whole of American society. The problems that we are dealing with . . . are not going to be solved until there is a *radical* redistribution of economic and political power" (Garrow 1993: 28–29; emphasis added).

King, thus, moved into harmony with Du Bois by making national indebtedness to the black and the poor a matter of radical American structural concern. Early in the century, Du Bois had outlined the necessities for such structural work. He speculated that had a "permanent" network of government social organizations and arrangements been established during Reconstruction, then the newly emancipated freedmen would have been assured long-term "equal opportunity" and parity in American citizenship with their white brothers and sisters. Instead, the freedmen were handed nothing more than the ballot: "The Freedmen's Bureau died, and its child was the Fifteenth Amendment" (Du Bois 1965: 239). The amendment was completely unenforceable in a South where "there was scarcely a white man . . . who did not honestly regard emancipation as a crime, and its practical nullification as a duty" (Du Bois 1965: 238). King knew enough history to know that a Voting Rights Act was scarcely enough for black modernity.

◆◆◆

Though a fascinating project, I cannot trace here the complex outcomes of what can tentatively be called a "Black Power Agenda," which accompanied the final years of King's life and work. Nevertheless, it is possible to specify results such as the establishment of Black Studies in American colleges and universities, the birth of nationwide programs designed to foster black business and economic development, the emergence of a new Black Theology circulating in economically independent and popularly based black churches, the exponential increase in new and well-heeled black middle-class professionals, the national recognition and acknowledgment of a new Black Arts and its creativity and criticism, the emergence of a flourishing and internationally influential Black History movement.

To these might be added the growth of groups such as the National Bar Association, the National Medical Association, the African Heritage Studies Association—all imbued with cultural and racial pride summed up in the phrase "Black Is Beautiful."

In brief, Black Power led the way and established guidelines for the upsurge in marginal constituency politics in the United States during the last twenty-five years. Black Power decisively broke, sometimes in problematic ways, the lock on national definitions of AMERICA and AMERICAN that had been held for centuries by wealthy, academically and socially privileged white males. The possibilities of a new and structurally significant visibility became an empowering model for initiatives by women, gay and lesbian, Chicano and Chicana, Puerto Rican, Native American, Asian American and other groups in the United States. All followed Black Power's lead into a radical politics of visibility, as that politics has already been defined.

In focus and goals the later leadership of Martin Luther King was commensurate with this Black Power agenda. Only a colossal act of historical forgetting allows envisioning the King of 1967 as anything but *a black political radical of the first order*. He had become a man temperamentally inclined to radical restructuring rather than slow and noble reform.

and thus ahead of his own civil rights initiating

◆◆◆

In the matter of black modernity, critical memory focuses the historical continuities of black-majority efforts, strategies and resources for leadership and liberation. Furthermore, it demonstrates the ever-renewing promise inherent in the contiguity between majority and "leadership" remembrance. Black intellectual and political self-interest, therefore, demands emphasis on an integrity of critical recall. By integrity, I am suggesting a historically verifiable emphasis on how the black public sphere has always been restructured through contiguity: the closeness of King to the black majority, the inevitable segue of civil rights into Black Power, the convergence of SNCC activists' secular versions of black church Jubilees and the minimalistic poetics of Black Arts modernism.

The critically imagined closeness of our black-majority selves and the birth of black radical modernism must be continually foregrounded. Re-membering King on the far side of the Reagan-Bush era is necessarily a critical and imaginative act. It requires sharp resistance to nostalgia. To the extent that black conservatism dedicates itself to a nostalgic fissuring of continuity and the erasure of contiguity between black majority and black leadership interests, it must be seriously challenged. Such historical revisionism — one that reads King as aloof from or majestically out-of-touch with the majority at *any* time during his leadership — offers a false reading of the past. Moreover, at this complex moment of late-capitalism, such revisionism woefully limits majority interests in a black public sphere, an arena that requires perhaps more urgently than ever before, the good offices of critical memory.

Houston A. Baker, Jr. is Professor of English and the Director of the Center for the Study of Black Literature and Culture at the University of Pennsylvania. He has published numerous studies of Afro-American literature and culture; the most recent is *Black Studies, Rap, and the Academy* (Chicago: University of Chicago Press, 1993). His latest volume of poetry is *Blues Journeys Home* (Lotus Press).

Literature Cited

Abrams, M. H. 1962. *A Glossary of Literary Terms.* New York: Holt, Rinehart and Winston.

Albert, Peter J. and Ronald Hoffman, eds. 1993. *We Shall Overcome: Martin Luther King, Jr. and the Black Freedom Struggle.* New York: De Capo Press.

Appadurai, Arjun. 1993. "Disjuncture and Difference in the Global Cultural Economy." In *The Phantom Public Sphere*, edited by Bruce Robbins. Minneapolis: University of Minnesota Press, 269–295.

Baldwin, James. 1955. "Everybody's Protest Novel." In *Notes of a Native Son.* Boston: Beacon Press, 1955, 13–23.

Branch, Taylor. 1988. *Parting The Waters: America In The King Years, 1954–63.* New York: Simon & Schuster.

Carson, Clayborne. 1993. "Reconstructing the King Legacy: Scholars and National Myths." In *We Shall Overcome*, 239–248.

Cone, James H. 1993. "Martin Luther King, Jr., and the Third World." In *We Shall Overcome*, 197–221.

Douglass, Frederick. 1982. *Narrative of the Life of Frederick Douglass.* New York: Penguin.

Du Bois, W.E.B. 1965. *The Souls of Black Folk.* In *Three Negro Classics*, edited by John Hope Franklin. New York: Avon Books, 207–389.

Eliot, T.S. 1950. "The Metaphysical Poets." In *Selected Essays.* New York: Harcourt, Brace, and Company, 241–250.

Fraser, Nancy. 1993. "Rethinking the Public Sphere: A Contribution to the Critique of Actually Existing Democracy." In *The Phantom Public Sphere*, 1–32.

Garrow, David J. 1993. "Martin Luther King, Jr. and the Spirit of Leadership. In *We Shall Overcome*, 11–34.

Habermas, Jürgen. 1993. *The Structural Transformation of the Public Sphere: An Inquiry Into a Category of Bourgeois Society*. Trans. Thomas Burger with the assistance of Frederick Lawrence. Cambridge: MIT Press.

Jones, LeRoi. *Black Magic: Collected Poetry 1961–1967*. Indianapolis: Bobbs-Merrill.

Knight, Etheridge and other inmates of Indiana State Prison. 1970. *Black Voices From Prison*. With an introduction by Roberto Giammanco. New York: Pathfinder Press.

Morris, Aldon. 1993. "A Man Prepared for the Times: A Sociological Analysis of the Leadership of Martin Luther King, Jr." In *We Shall Overcome*, 35–58.

Ralph, James R., Jr. 1993. *Northern Protest: Martin Luther King, Jr., Chicago, and the Civil Rights Movement*. Cambridge: Harvard University Press.

Robbins, Bruce. 1993. "Introduction." In *The Phantom Public Sphere*, vii–xxvi.

Malcolm X and the Black Public Sphere: Conversionists versus Culturalists

Manthia Diawara

C ulture, defined as a whole way of life, is that which the passenger both brings to a destination, and carries back home, in an altered shape, from the places visited. In other words, cultures and their attendant attires, names, customs and ideologies are always influenced by commercial, religious, and political relations between insides and outsides. This broader definition of culture, which animates the best work in contemporary Cultural Studies, is eclipsed in Black Studies by a narrower and purist definition which sees culture as a people's nostalgic relations to images of themselves or, as the best achievements and thoughts of a people. Furthermore, Black intellectuals, be they apostles of Afrocentricity, Black Conservatism, Islam or Liberation Theology, tend to discredit and categorize as pathological certain cultural practices that challenge their ideal of Blackness. I shall provisionally call culturalists those practitioners that work with the broader definition of culture, and conversionists those that reserve an elitist and exclusionary domain for it.

This essay discusses Black conversionist and culturalist discourses and their relation to the life world, politics and economics in *The Autobiography of Malcolm X* by Alex Haley and Malcolm X.[1] The analysis focuses on the battle for custody between the conversionists and the culturalists over the first part of the autobiogra-

1. Alex Haley and Malcolm X, *The Autobiography of Malcolm X* (New York: Ballantine Books, 1992), 150.

Public Culture 1994, 7: 35–48

phy which includes such pivotal chapters as "Homeboy," "Harlemite," "Detroit Red" and "Hustler." I argue that, in spite of the conversionist discourse of the second half of the book, which warns the reader against embracing the early chapters, these chapters constitute the appeal of the book today, giving significance to the inner-city youth's identification with Malcolm X as a Homeboy, and making Detroit Red the archetype of Rap songs and new Black male films in the 1980s and 1990s. A culturalist reading, which resists the definition by the second part of the book of the first part of the book as Black pathology, is better able to account for the popularity of Malcolm X among the youth, who see a mirror image of their own lives in the experience of Detroit Red.

The Autobiography's detailed description of Black life in Harlem—and its vibrant nightlife—is particularly compelling. Malcolm X provides a cultural, political and economic setting for Harlem in the 1940s. Harlem's nightlife attracts Blacks as well as soldiers recruited to fight in World War II, Whites from midtown and tourists. The constitution of audiences around Black good life institutions, clubs, bars, theaters, dance halls and entertainers in Harlem affects interracial relations during a climate of war. Harlem's culture in *The Autobiography* defies the ban on interracial relations, and subverts the code of morality imposed on Black and White soldiers during World War II. Crucially, Detroit Red's relation to, and fascination with this Black culture in Harlem, the ways that he cultivates his personal appearance and takes pleasure in the institutions and entertainers, are grounds for identifying with him and the text. These grounds are not convincingly deconstructed in the last part of *The Autobiography*.

The Conversionists

How ridiculous I was! Stupid enough to stand there simply lost in admiration of my hair now looking "white," reflected in the mirror in Shorty's room.

The Autobiography of Malcolm X

Conversionist discourses deploy narratives about the worst sinners to justify the need for transformation. In *The Autobiography*, at the end of the chapter entitled "Caught" Malcolm X confesses, "I have never previously told anyone my sordid past in detail. I haven't done it now to sound as though I might be proud of how bad, how evil, I was" (150). Malcolm X tells the story of his perdition which leads to his discovery of Allah and Islam as proof that he has been there, so to speak, down with the rest of the people, and that they, too, can join him on the other side. He states that once motivated, "no one can change more completely than the man who has been at the bottom. I call myself the best example of that" (261). Malcolm X does not stress the difficulty of conversion here; he emphasizes instead the superiority of his new world over the old one. Conversionist discourses, whether they are motivated by religion, science or politics, always underestimate culture or regard it as pathological. Conversionists, whether they are politicians or religious leaders, appeal to their audiences by blaming the culture of the people they are trying to convert. They always expect people to come to a revolutionary consciousness or a spiritual awakening, and walk out of their culture, shedding it like a shell or a cracked skin, in order to change the world.

to convert one must abandon one's culture

The rhetoric of the second half of *The Autobiography* seems to move too rapidly to its conclusion, condemning Black culture through the demise of Detroit Red. Malcolm X uses alienation as an analytic tool for denigrating the Harlem culture he so vividly describes earlier in the book. He depicts Detroit Red's passage from observer of culture to participant, underlining Black people's consumption and their relation to style as major manifestations of estrangement. Malcolm X's critique of the conked hair style as an unnatural desire for Black people to look white (54) is consistent with the position of other conversionists on Black hair, and it informs the decision by many Black youth to abandon the conked hair styles for so-called natural styles such as the Afro.[2] Malcolm X also detects symptoms of alienation in patterns of Black consumption: "I was really a clown, but my ignorance made me think I was 'sharp.' My knob-toed, orange-colored 'kick-up' shoes were nothing but Florsheims, the ghetto's Cadillac of shoes in those days. (Some shoe companies made these ridiculous styles for sale only in the black ghettoes where ignorant Negroes like me would pay the big-name price for something that we associated with being rich)" (78).

The metamorphosis from Detroit Red to Malcolm X requires the protagonist to deny one part of himself for every piece of knowledge gained from the Nation of Islam: "'You don't even know who you are,' Reginald said. 'You don't even know, the white devil has hidden it from you, that you are of a race of people of ancient civilizations, and riches in gold and kings. You don't even know your true family name, you wouldn't recognize your true language if you heard it'" (160). Religious or political conversionists are particularly prone to self-denial.

2. For a critique of hair and alienation see Kobena Mercer, "Black Hair/Style Politics," *New Formations* 3 (Winter 1987), and Robin Kelley, "The Riddle of the Zoot: Malcolm Little and Black Cultural Politics During World War II," *Malcolm X: In Our Own Image*, ed. Joe Wood (New York: St. Martin's Press, 1992).

Once in Ghana, at a party given for his birthday, Malcolm X says: "'You wonder why I don't dance? Because I want you to remember twenty-two million Afro-Americans in the U.S.!'" And, as an afterthought, he adds, "But I sure felt like dancing! The Ghanaians performed the high-life as if possessed. One pretty African girl sang 'Blue Moon' like Sarah Vaughan. Sometimes the band sounded like Milt Jackson, sometimes like Charlie Parker" (358).

Through conversion, Malcolm X not only attempts to abandon expressive styles in language, dress and hair associated with the way of life of some Black ghetto people, he also speaks of Detroit Red as if he were a different person: "I still marvel at how swiftly my previous life's thinking pattern slid away from me, like snow off a roof. It is as though someone else I knew of had lived by hustling and crime. I would be startled to catch myself thinking in a remote way of my earlier self as another person" (170). Malcolm X views Detroit Red as a menace to society who is likely to die young or age into a hardened criminal: "Awareness came surging up in me—how deeply the religion of Islam had reached down into the mud to lift me up, to save me from being what I inevitably would have been: a dead criminal in a grave, or, if still alive, a flint-hard, bitter, thirty-seven-year-old convict in some penitentiary, or insane asylum" (287).

The first part of *The Autobiography* is carefully crafted to lead up to Detroit Red's transition from unemployed hick to hustler to hardened criminal and drug addict. Even the linear progression of the chapters—"Detroit Red," "Hustler," "Trapped" and "Caught"—presupposes an inevitable descent that, for Malcolm X, can only be reversed through conversion: "Today, when everything that I do has an urgency, I would not spend one hour in the preparation of a book which had the ambition to perhaps titillate some readers. But I am spending many hours because the full story is the best way that I know to have it seen, and understood, that I had sunk to the very bottom of the American white man's society when—soon now, in prison—I found Allah and the religion of Islam and it completely transformed my life" (150). Malcolm X attempts to account for the rough edges in the text, such as the places where the reader identifies with Detroit Red's love for Black culture, by ascribing to them a state of alienation. About Detroit Red he cautions: "what makes the ghetto hustler yet more dangerous is his 'glamour' image to the school-dropout youth in the ghetto" (311).

Toward the end of the first part of *The Autobiography*, Detroit Red sinks to the bottom, and the narrator with him, as if Black culture has died with them. Of the Black cultural figures in the chapter, "Trapped," Billie Holiday looms largest. Her end as a drug addict resembles Detroit Red's last days in Harlem. The placement of Billie Holiday and other tragic figures at the end of the first part of the book works as a narrative device to endorse the conversionists' position that culture is a dead end. Malcolm X traps Detroit Red in a hole and leaves him only the choice to convert, inducing the reader, too, to identify with the sermon of change. Crucially, when Detroit Red returns to Harlem as Malcolm X, he wants to change it completely. This also coincides with the time when the jazz clubs moved from Harlem to 52nd Street, leaving hustlers and prostitutes without customers.

Malcolm X makes an important contribution to the art of autobiography through his use of alienation, a trope which enables him to distance himself from Detroit Red. Malcolm X often refers to Detroit Red as another person in the text; this produces an autobiographical narrative that sounds like a sermon. Malcolm X and Alex Haley shaped *The Autobiography* as a preacher shapes a sermon: they do not intend that readers be entertained by Detroit Red's story; they want readers to understand the symbolism behind it, and let it serve as a lesson. Malcolm X and Alex Haley transform an intimate and personal story into a public and conversionist essay.

The recourse to change in conversionist discourse coincides with the modernist impulse toward the constant renewal of things. Every conversionist discourse addresses an epistemological crisis which requires the author's contemplation for a solution. Malcolm's *Autobiography* includes moving scenes where he reflects on crisis situations and imagines how to get out of them. His reflections mark him as an outsider to culture, as a philosopher charged with the desire to change things, as a utopian reconstructionist.

The most frequently quoted lines in *The Autobiography* dealing with an epistemological crisis are from the passage in which Malcolm's English teacher, Mr. Ostrowski, tells him: "A lawyer—that's no realistic goal for a nigger. You need to think about something you can be. You're good with your hands—making things. Everybody admires your carpentry shop work. Why don't you plan on carpentry?" (36). The young Malcolm is asked to accept a stereotype of himself and his people as a reality. His reaction embodies the reasons why young Blacks question the system's fairness, and identify with a lawbreaker ideology through which they feel that they can overcome the obstacles they face living in a society full of people like Mr. Ostrowski.

In my view, Malcolm X describes his epistemological crises more effectively when he delineates them as a coming into consciousness from a state of innocence, as new knowledge displaces business-as-usual and enables movement forward. These are the moments of discovery in *The Autobiography*, moments when Malcolm X is with the group but feels the most lonely, lost in contemplation of a *this is loneliness?*

better future for Black people. For instance, in a lovely reflexive passage in the book's opening chapter Malcolm X refers to the satisfaction he derives from working in the family garden: "I loved especially to grow peas. I was proud when we had them on our table. I would pull out the grass in my garden by hand when the first little blades came up. I would patrol the rows on my hands and knees for any worms and bugs and I would kill and bury them. And sometimes when I had everything straight and clean for my things to grow, I would lie down on my back between two rows, and I would gaze up in the blue sky at the clouds moving and think all kinds of things" (8).

Clouds moving across the sky is a leitmotif for change in *The Autobiography*. Years later, during his trip to Mecca, Malcolm pictures his new predicament, after the break with Elijah Muhammad, with the sky as a tableau: "I remember one night at Muzadalifa with nothing but the sky overhead I lay awake amid sleeping Muslim brothers and I learned that pilgrims from every land—every color, and class, and rank; high officials and the beggar alike—all snored in the same language" (344). This leitmotif occurs a third time when Malcolm X returns to the United States: "I remember there in the holy world how I used to lie on the top of Hector's Hill, and look up at the sky, at the clouds moving over me, and daydream, all kinds of things. And then, in a funny contrast of recollection, I remember how years later, when I was in prison, I used to lie on my cell bunk— this would be especially when I was in solitary: what we convicts called 'The Hole'—and I would picture myself talking to large crowds" (365).

We are in 1965 when Malcolm X makes this last allusion to the sky and the clouds during an epistemological crisis concerning how to build a Black nationalist organization that interpellates Christians, Jews, Buddhists, Hindus, agnostics, and atheists. Malcolm X recalls that time: "I have friends who are called capitalists, Socialists, and Communists! Some of my friends are moderates, conservatives, extremists—some are even Uncle Toms! My friends today are black, brown, red, yellow and white!" (375). Malcolm X was a complex man who constantly revised his thinking. As the recurring cloudy sky tableau suggests, he was very American in his dreams. That is, he was impatient with the obstacles placed in front of Black people. Like the "founding fathers" of the United States he was prepared by all means necessary to remove these obstacles in order to progress into better and better societies. Malcolm X's reflexive gazing at the changing sky also suggests his modernism: he kept revising his style in order to build larger audiences for his ideas. *maybe "*

Other conversionists since Malcolm X have resorted to Marxism, Afrocentrism, Liberation Theology and Black Nationalism as themes for building a Black public sphere. In fact, Malcolm X's *The Autobiography* is exemplary and inspirational for other conversionist schools, with its detailed discussions of identity politics, class struggle, Black self-determination and religion. Conversionists continue to ring the wake-up-bell for Black people, and, much in the manner of Malcolm X, treat Black culture as pathological (312–314).

Yet, Malcolm the modernist also appears to be conflicted about his ardent conversionist position. He emphasizes that his success as a public speaker depends on the fact that he is a homeboy who "never left the ghetto in spirit, . . . could speak and understand the ghetto's language" (310) and has been schooled as a hustler like most ghetto kids (296). But it is possible to argue that Malcolm X's purist philosophy is too demanding because it can only incorporate Black people who have left their culture behind. To use a statement from the Black Arts Movement, Malcolm X's philosophy in the second part of *The Autobiography* does not "address itself to the mythology and lifestyle of Black people."[3] Malcolm X ponders several times over this shortcoming of his purist philosophy through statements such as "my old so-called 'Black Muslim' image, kept blocking me" (375), and "numerous people said that the Nation of Islam's stringent moral restrictions had repelled them—and they wanted to join me" (316). Nonetheless, Malcolm X remains a conversionist who believes that "it was a big order—the organization I was creating in my mind, one which would help to challenge the American black man to gain his human rights, and to cure his mental, spiritual, economic, and political sicknesses" (315).

Culturalists

> Then, suddenly, we were in the Roseland's jostling lobby. And I was getting waves and smiles and greetings. They shouted 'My man!' and 'Hey, Red!' and I answered "Daddy-O."
>
> *The Autobiography of Malcolm X*

An understanding of the epistemological crisis Malcolm shared with other Black people does not require reverting to a view of Black culture as pathological. It is informed by partisan identification with culture, a belief that *culture* knows, and that it can be channelled to create and capitalize on epistemological breaks. My culturalist approach stipulates that—contrary to the conversionists' view of

---

3. See Phillip Brian Harper, "Nationalism and Social Division in Black Arts Poetry of the 1960s," *Critical Inquiry* 19:2 (Winter 1993), 248.

"authentic Black culture" as an emanation of the Black church, or of a truly revolutionary consciousness or of a separatist gesture toward Africa — religion, revolutionary theories, and the political economy are all specifications of Black culture.[4]

The view that conversionist discourses are enunciations of *particular* theories of Black culture, enables us, first of all, to distinguish culture from its specific manifestations in the church, in arts or politics. I define culture here as a way of life aimed at reproducing the Black good life. Much of Black culture in America is created through attempts to liberate the life world from colonizing systems. Blacks often derive the good life from repressive institutions by systematically reversing the signification of those institutions. They test the limits of modern institutions for inclusion and emancipation of multicultural lifeworlds. Hence, Black culture is the last frontier of American modernism.

A view of culture as that which encompasses the church, the Black nationalist tradition and other ideological movements liberates us from the monopoly that these institutions place on Black culture. It also legitimizes other specifications of culture such as economic narratives, art in the context of international politics, as well as other cultural forms engendered through Black peoples' relation to more and more complex systems. In other words, we can no longer afford to locate and fix Black culture in a specific ideological institution, without the risk of overlooking newer manifestations of culture which more effectively engender a Black good life society and ethics in the context of the political economy of transnational capitalism. Malcolm's popularity today resides as much in the specification of Black culture through his personal transformation and his description of the economics of Harlem high life in the 1940s, as in his conversionist discourse in favor of Black self-determination.

Homeboy

I still was country, I know now, but it all felt so great because I was accepted.

The Autobiography of Malcolm X

4. The reversal I have in mind bears resemblance to poststructuralists' reversal of the relation between linguistics and semiotics. For Roland Barthes, who turns Ferdinand de Saussure up-side-down, semiotics can no longer be considered as an extension of linguistics, it becomes the definition of linguistics. See *Essais Critiques* (Paris: Seuil, 1964), 257.

But people would watch for clues from Bird and Dizzy, and if they smiled when you finished playing, then that meant that your playing was good. They smiled when I finished playing that first time and from then on I was on the inside of what was happening in New York's music scene.

Miles: The Autobiography

The young Malcolm's flight from Lansing, Michigan to Boston and later to Harlem points toward a rift between the country and the city, which Malcolm X, himself, characterizes as a protest against White racism and Black petit-bourgeois ideals of order and respectability. Malcolm Little makes his break with the country after the crisis wrought by an encounter with Mr. Ostrowski, his school teacher. He says, "If I had stayed on in Michigan, I would probably have married one of those Negro girls I knew and liked in Lansing. I might have become one of those state capitol building shoeshine boys, or a Lansing Country Club waiter, or gotten one of the other menial jobs which, in those days, among Lansing Negroes, would have been considered 'successful'" (38).

By 1940, when Malcolm Little leaves Lansing to go to Boston, his image of cities has come from his half-sister, Ella and from Black music. Ella's visit to Lansing helps shape the phantasmagoria of city life for the young Malcolm because she instills in him a sense of pride, freedom and mobility: "A commanding woman, maybe even bigger than Mrs. Swerlin, Ella wasn't just black, but like her father, she was jet Black. The way she sat, moved, talked, did everything, bespoke somebody who did and got exactly what she wanted. This was the woman my father had boasted of so often for having brought so many of their family out of Georgia to Boston. She owned some property, he would say, and she was in 'society'" (32).

Jazz music and musicians are the other forces beckoning Malcolm Little to the city. In the 1940s, as James Naremore puts it, some people associated jazz "with flappers, skyscrapers, and the entire panoply of the twentieth century modernity."[5] Malcolm Little, too, used music to contemplate the city, and to detach himself from the country: "Sometimes, big bands from New York, out touring the one-night stands in the sticks, would play for big dances in Lansing. Everybody with legs would come out to see any performer who bore the magic name 'New

[handwritten marginalia: Negro / Country / City / block]

5. James Naremore, *The Films of Vincente Minnelli* (Cambridge: Cambridge University Press, 1993), 52.

York.' Which is how I first heard Lucky Thompson and Milt Jackson, both of whom I later got to know well in Harlem" (28).

By the time he leaves Michigan, Malcolm Little has already developed a resentment toward the Jim Crow system that places obstacles in the way of Black peoples' movements into modernity, secularism and progress. Malcolm's arrival in the city can be compared to Walter Benjamin's description of the *Boheme* in his classic book, *Charles Baudelaire: A Lyric Poet in the Era of High Capitalism*: "The brutal, starved, envious, wild Cain . . . has gone to the cities to consume the sediment of rancour which has accumulated in them and participate in the false ideas which experience their triumph there. This characterization expresses exactly what gave Baudelaire solidarity with Dupont. Like Cain, Dupont had 'gone to the cities' and turned away from the idyllic."[6]

Malcolm Little, too, has gone to the city to get even with the modernists. The chapter dealing with Malcolm's arrival in Boston is appropriately entitled "Homeboy," and it opens with the following remarks: "I looked like Li'l Abner. Mason, Michigan was written all over me. My kinky, reddish, hair was cut hick style, and I didn't even use grease in it" (39). At one level in *The Autobiography* a homeboy is understood as someone, usually from the country, who has come to the city through a network of migration, in search of the American dream. Living among other migrants from the same region, a new form of kinship develops between the homeboys which leads members of the group to empathize with one another, to help each other find work and prepare for life in the city. To put it in the words of Malcolm's homeboy, Shorty, "Man, this is a swinging town if you dig it. . . . You're my homeboy – I'm going to school you to the happenings" (44).

Malcolm Little the homeboy is both hustler and cosmopolitan artist. A homeboy is a *boheme* who is angry at the world for not getting his fair share. Malcolm Little joins other similarly positioned homeboys to take revenge on the system for standing between them and the American dream. The homeboys, as today's Rap music and the resurgence of *film noir* made by Black directors reveal to us, form a group of professional conspirators who believe that the most important thing in life is to be paid in full. Today's homeboys, like Malcolm Little, are impatient with the system, and more prone to take power than receive it from a public sphere they perceive as hostile to them. They believe, as one homeboy

6. Walter Benjamin, *Charles Baudelaire: A Lyric Poet in the Era of High Capitalism* (London: Verso Press, 1983), 25.

tells Malcolm Little, "The main thing you got to remember is that everything in the world is a hustle" (48).

Empathy with homeboys who are hustlers relates to Black cultural criticism of the colonization of the Black lifeworld by modern systems. Several places in *The Autobiography* Malcolm identifies with lawbreakers on the grounds that racism prevents homeboys from developing their skills in such productive areas as the sciences, linguistics and the arts. About an old pickpocket in Small's Paradise, he says: "to wolves who still were able to catch some rabbits, it had meaning that an old wolf who had lost his fangs was still eating" (90).

Identification with lawbreakers, however, is not the only way Black structures of feeling are expressed in *The Autobiography*. Malcolm's cosmopolitan artistic sensibility is another way Black culture is felt in the book. Malcolm Little is a *flaneur* looking for modernism in the ballrooms, bars and streets frequented by the world's greatest and hippest musicians. His search for musical specifications of Black culture in the 1940s parallels the quest of Miles Davis. In his autobiography, Davis states that he enrolled in Julliard School of Music in order to be in New York, near Charlie Parker. Later, Davis travels from New York to Los Angeles, and back to New York, looking for Bird. He considers these years as studying for the "master's degrees and the Ph.D.'s from Minton's University of Bebop under the tutelage of professors Bird and Diz. Man, they was playing so much incredible shit" (61).

Malcolm Little spends a good deal of his time looking at and soaking up the styles and world views of great musicians like Duke Ellington, Count Basie and Lionel Hampton: "They'd be up there in my chair, and my shine rag was popping to the beat of all their records, spinning in my head. Musicians never have had, anywhere, a greater shoeshine-boy fan than I was" (50). It is easy to see why the young Malcolm admires these musicians. They appear to be free, to be in control of their lives at a time when the only lifestyles available to Black people are those imposed on them. The musicians, with their zoot suits, conked hair and music that fascinate Blacks and Whites alike, seem to have more power than other people; most of all, like a popular commodity, they appear to be desired by everyone and to enjoy an enviable position in the marketplace. Of course, Malcolm X as conversionist criticizes this situation in the second half of the book, describing it as alienation from the true spiritual, economic and political course.

Detroit Red, on the other hand, wants to lose himself in the musicians' specification of Black culture: "Sometimes I would be down there standing inside the door jumping up and down in my gray jacket with the whiskbroom in the pocket, and the manager would have to come and shout at me that I had customers upstairs" (51). In his secular imagination, Detroit Red considers musicians such as Duke Ellington, Lionel Hampton and Billie Holiday as leading Black people toward spiritual, economic and political fulfillment. If it were true that the revolution presupposed by Malcolm X, in which Black people would resist commodification and take control over the modes of production, was out of the reach of the musicians, for Detroit Red, music helped people pass the time. As Detroit Red's reading of a song by Lionel Hampton reveals, the musicians provided the public sphere with philosophical narratives which defined the culture and the reality of the time: "The people kept shouting for Hamp's 'Flyin' Home,' and finally he did it. (I could believe the story I'd heard in Boston about this number — that once in the Apollo, Hamp's 'Flyin' Home' had made some reefer-smoking Negro in the second balcony believe he could fly, so he tried — and jumping — and broke his leg, an event later immortalized in song when Earl Hines wrote a hit tune called "'Second Balcony Jump'" (74).

Detroit Red is a homeboy who wanted to be intoxicated by the city, and its nightlife was where he found Black cosmopolitan culture. Unlike the 1920s when Black writers exemplified the best of culture, in the 1940s, the energy was located in the music scene. Detroit Red surveyed the scene and soaked up the Harlem nightlife like a sponge. When he was completely modernized, he posed the way "hipsters" wearing their zoots "cool it," and took a picture to send home, with "hat dangled, knees drawn close together, feet wide apart, both index fingers jabbed toward the floor. The long coat and swing chain and the Punjab pants were more dramatic if you stood that way" (52).

The Periodization of 1940s Harlem

Malcolm's story operates on several levels. It tells the story of the development of the Black public sphere and the creation of audiences for Black culture in Harlem in the 1940s. It is a personal account of his own growth and decline and a narrative of how Black art was channeled toward greater economic well-being for Blacks and how that channeling came to an end. Malcolm X portrays the 1940s as a period when new doors opened for Black people in America: "Old Man Roundtree, an elderly Pullman porter and a friend of Ella's had recommended the railroad job for me. He had told her the war was snatching away railroad men so fast that if I could pass for twenty-one, he could get me on" (70). The war years saw nightlife flourish in Harlem when good-time-loving servicemen crowded the streets and the bars: "Up and down along and between Lenox and

Seventh Avenues, Harlem was like some technicolor bazaar. Hundreds of Negro soldiers and sailors, gawking and young like me, passed by" (74).

It is important to distinguish this attempted resurgence of a Black entertainment industry in Harlem, during the war, from the Harlem Renaissance and its nightlife which came to an end in 1929, after the stock market crash. Some clubs and ballrooms like the Savoy, Small's Paradise and Minton's and theaters like the Apollo were still around. But the most obvious difference between the Black public sphere in the 1920s and the 1940s involves the decreased influence of writers and political figures such as W.E.B. Du Bois, Langston Hughes, Marcus Garvey and Alan Locke and the increased popularity of entertainers such as Duke Ellington, Dizzy Gillespie, Billy Eckstine, Billie Holiday, Ella Fitzgerald and Diana Washington.

from writing
to
musicians
(writing
to
orality)

Detroit Red derives his cultural and political formation from the bars and streets of Harlem, or, to paraphrase Miles Davis, from the universities of Small's Paradise and the Bradock Hotel, where the bars were jam-packed with famous Black entertainers. Today, our own situation bears similarities with the 1940s, with Rap music, the films of Spike Lee and such popular novelists as Terry McMillan providing dominant definitions of Black culture.

Finally, like Detroit Red, I too am fascinated by the Harlem of the 1940s, when arts and entertainment were interwoven with economic activity in the community. It is still not clear to me why the jazz clubs moved to 52nd Street around 1945, leaving many Harlemites without jobs in the formal and informal sectors. Maybe it relates to the imminent end of the war and the desire to return to the status quo. Maybe it was racism and greed as Miles Davis states in his autobiography: "If it's one thing white people are united on it is that they all hate to see black people making the money they think belongs to them. They were beginning to think that they owned these black musicians because they was making money for them" (73).

According to Malcolm X, hustlers like Detroit Red may have turned to armed robbery after the 1943 Harlem riot and the move of the music scene from Uptown to 52nd Street. He writes, "Things had grown so tight in Harlem that some hustlers had been forced to go to work. Even some prostitutes had gotten jobs as domestics, and cleaning office buildings at night. The pimping was so poor, Sammy had gone on the job with me" (114–115). Malcolm's deteriorating economic status coincides with a decline in the audience for Black culture and a decline in the solidity and activity of the Black economic sphere in Harlem.

The argument of this essay focuses on a comparison of culturalist discourse with conversionist discourse. First of all, I reversed the relations between culture and materialist and ideological systems such as economics, religion and politics in order to extricate culture from the pathological spaces that these systems reserve for it. By turning these systems upside down as parts of Black cultural specifications, it becomes obvious how conversionists enunciate culture while calling it something else, how they embrace it even as they denigrate it.

This argument aims to open the door to criticism, not to formulate or espouse a grand theory. A more inclusive view of culture empowers us to criticize any Black church's monopoly on ethics while recognizing its historical importance to Black people. The definition of ethics should be tied to culture-building and to the creation of audiences. Malcolm's embrace of the Nation of Islam and then Islam itself constituted a move beyond Christian morality, toward a secularization of the just and the true; and beyond "Black culture is bad," to a more inclusive ethics. Even as his text disavows the enchantments of Black metropolitan modernity in themselves, their centrality to generating an imaginative and material horizon of possibility for Black people is crucial to his understanding and his practice. In other words, Black people do not divorce ethics from the material conditions that reproduce the Black good life. We should be unafraid to embrace a multiplicity of cultural expressions as we pursue the good life for ourselves and each other.

Manthia Diawara teaches comparative literature and is the Director of the Africana Studies Program at New York University. He is the author of *African Cinema: Politics and Culture* (Bloomington: Indiana University Press, 1992), and editor of *Black American Cinema* (New York: Routledge, 1993).

"After the Love Has Gone": bio-politics and etho-poetics in the black public sphere

Paul Gilroy

The biological, with the notion of inevitability it entails, becomes more than an object *of spiritual life. It becomes its heart. The mysterious urgings of the blood, the appeals of heredity and the past for which the body serves as an enigmatic vehicle, lose the character of being problems that are subject to a solution put forward by a sovereignly free Self. Not only does the Self bring in the unknown elements of these problems in order to resolve them; the Self is also constituted by these elements. Man's essence no longer lies in freedom, but in a kind of bondage. To be truly oneself does not mean taking flight once more above contingent events that always remain foreign to the Self's freedom; on the contrary, it means becoming aware of the ineluctable original chain that is unique to our bodies, and above all accepting this chaining.*

EMMANUEL LEVINAS

A crowd of men and women moiled like nightmare figures in the smoke-green haze. The juke box was dinning and it was like looking into the depths of a murky cave. And now someone moved aside and looking down along the curve of the bar past the bobbing heads and shoulders I saw the juke box, lit up like a bad dream of the Fiery Furnace, shouting
Jelly, Jelly,
Jelly,
All night long.

RALPH ELLISON

I would like to thank Vron Ware, Gloria Watkins, Vikki Bell, Cora Gilroy Ware and Daniel Miller for conversations that have shaped this ongoing work.

Public Culture 1994, 7: 49-76

In a preliminary discussion of some of the tropes of freedom that have occupied and been created by the black public sphere, I want to point to some of the key ethical and political questions that arise when critically inclined intellectuals discover the special potency of popular cultural styles. These are often outlaw forms which may demand an end to disinterested and contemplative criticism but which pose even greater problems for politically engaged critics whose work – irrespective of their noblest motives – is revealed to be inadequate where it moves too swiftly and too simplistically to either condemn or celebrate. Where the unseasonal fruits of counterculture become popular and the marginal moves into the mainstream, it would be absurd to expect to find politics programmatically constituted. It would also be mistaken and certainly immodest for hyper-privileged people to anticipate that these forms of consciousness are doomed by their unholy locations to remain forever merely prepolitical.

A special version of these issues can be reconstructed where black vernacular forms have recently appeared as objects of serious academic scrutiny. It features strongly in discussions of Hip hop and Rap because of the way that these expressions precipitate and dramatise intracommunal conflicts over the meanings and forms of freedom, and because the extraordinary global transformation triggered by Hip hop was wholly unanticipated. With this unforeseen planetary change on our side, black critics have displayed a special reluctance to give up the qualified axiological authority that we fought so hard to attain. However, I believe that we are still largely subject to a special condition of dependency upon the "ethnic" authenticity that vernacular forms manifest and which critical discourses suggest only they can confer upon a range of other less obviously authentic cultural activities. These problems of value, of judgment and of course, of politics have been compounded in a time of great uncertainty about the limits of racial particularity and racial solidarity. Though it has a wider currency, the special authority that authentic vernacular forms supposedly supply has been invoked by the critics who are most comfortable with absolutist definitions of culture. It specifies the elusive quality of racialised difference that they alone can claim to be able to comprehend and to paraphrase, if not exactly translate.

The desire to monopolise the practice of these transcultural skills and engage in the varieties of social regulation that they sanction, endows some critics with an extra investment in the uniqueness, purity and power of the vernacular.[1]

1. Recent work by African American academics, Tricia Rose and Michael Eric Dyson shares this quality in spite of their obvious political differences. See Tricia Rose *Black Noise: Rap Music and Black Culture in Contemporary America* (Middletown: Wesleyan University Press, 1994) and Michael Eric Dyson *Reflecting Black: African American Cultural Criticism* (Minneapolis: University of Minnesota Press, 1993).

However, that inflated uniqueness is punctured when underground phenomena appear amidst the brightness and glamour of the cultural industries and their insatiable machinery of commodification. It is understandable why commentators, especially academics, should desire to enlist the ruthless alterity of Hip hop as part of an argument for the legitimacy of our own interpretive activity. But what political and ethical issues arise when we do so? This question prompts a renewed engagement with questions of class and power that persistently disrupt the body-coded solidarities based on race and gender. Following on from this, in what sense might Hip hop be described as marginal today? Those who assert the marginality of Hip hop should be obliged to say where they imagine the centre might now be. Hip hop's marginality is as official, as routinised, as its overblown defiance; yet it is still represented as an outlaw form. This is a mystery that aches to be solved. Further clues may be furnished by delving into uncomfortable issues like Hip hop's corporate developmental association with the "subcultures" that grow up around television, advertising and cartoons or by interrogating the revolutionary conservatism that constitutes its routine political focus but which is oversimplified or more usually ignored by its academic celebrants.

Professor Henry Louis Gates, Jr.'s principled defence of Luther Campbell's 2 Live Crew is rightly remembered as an important historical moment in which these difficult issues were clarified. Four years later, the erasure of Campbell's Caribbean affiliations and his elective affinity for lily-white Luke Skywalker seem less problematic than his appetite for regionally based conflictual dialogue with west coast rappers, his enthusiastic involvement in the class-coded world of celebrity golf, his reported eagerness to become involved in publishing soft-core pornographic magazines, and most interesting of all, his recently disclosed enthusiasm for the work of the infamous English comedian Benny Hill. The contribution that Hill's gurning techniques or anglo-vernacular characters like Ernie the milkman may have made to the multiplicity, impurity and hybridity that is Hip hop surely provides the last nail in the coffin of ethnocentric accounts of its origins and development.

> "The way that I get updated on my thing is I get different girls, and I ask them what they like to do. *Playboy* been around for years, and *Penthouse*. Benny Hill been around a long time here . . . maybe I'll start going off and doing more of the Benny Hill type thing, and being more funny."[2]

2. Luther "Luke Skywalker" Campbell interview by Joseph Gallivan in *The Independent*, January 13, 1994, 26.

The Benny Hill effect dictates that syncretism is an unpredictable and surprising process. It also underlines the global reach of popular cultures as well as the complexity of their crossover dynamics. Crossing, like outer-national diaspora dispersal, is no longer something that can be conceptualised as a unidirectional or reversible process. The way back is barred. The very qualities in Hip hop that have led to it being identified not as one black culture among many but as the very *blackest* culture – one that provides the scale on which all the others can be evaluated – have a complex relationship to the signs of pleasure and danger that solicit identification from white affiliates and practitioners. Squeamish "insiderist" criticism cannot face either the extent to which white consumers currently support black culture[3] or the possible implications of transracial popularity for the political struggles against white supremacy that lie ahead. Neither can they accept the catholic tastes of the creators of the form whose loyalty to the phattest beats usually exceeds their commitment to imaginary racial purity and phenotypically coded musical production.[4]

The quest for better accounts of the processes of popular cultural syncretism and their changing political resonance demands several other urgent adjustments in the way that we approach the popular phenomena that are grouped together under the heading Hip hop. The first adjustment involves querying the hold that this outlaw form exerts on critical writers who see in it a quiet endorsement of their own desire that the world can be readily transformed into text – that nothing resists the power of language. This is a familiar problem that Michel Foucault has stated succinctly in his famous cautioning against reducing the bloody "open hazardous reality of conflict" to the "calm Platonic form of language and dialogue."[5] It bites sharply in this area especially when the phenomenology of musical forms is dismissed in favour of analysing lyrics, the video images that supplement them and the technology of Hip hop production. We also need far more patient and careful attention to the issues of gender and sexuality than critics have been inclined to engage in so far. These are the conduits of crossover potential as well as the unstable core of spuriously naturalised racial particularity. Finally, we

3. Tricia Rose's assertions that Hip hop is reducible to a core of invariant exclusively African American "black practices" that permanently resist both commodification and white appropriation typifies this mode of denial (ibid., 7 and 80–84 passim).

4. A good example of this is the use of Leiber and Stoller's "I Keep Forgettin'" as recorded by Michael MacDonald in the track "Regulate" by Nate Dogg and Warren G. This can also be found on the Deathrow/Atlantic records soundtrack album to *Above The Rim*.

5. Michel Foucault, "Truth and Power" in *Power/Knowledge*, ed. Colin Gordon (New York: 1980).

will have to produce a better understanding of the relationship between Hip hop and the other (sub)cultural styles with which it is in creative dialogue.

To address these issues I focus initially on the point where the eddies that Hip hop has produced destabilise and flow back into more recognisably traditional and predictable currents. I start by acknowledging the possibility that Hip hop has contributed to the reinvigoration of rhythm and blues, and address the slow jams and swing beat that – in Britain at least – have an altogether different potential for crossover appeal to white listeners whose support they do not actively seek. I shall begin and end with musical articulations of the apparently sex-obsessed culture that defines a privileged point of entry into the subaltern public sphere and affords a key to the notions of freedom that unexpectedly thrive there.

There is a significant moment in the old school re-mix of R. Kelly's number one hit, "Bump and Grind," currently sitting on top of the black music charts on both sides of the Atlantic. The singer recycles the famous hookline from the Five Stairsteps' 1969 hit "Ooh Child." Sticking closely to their melody and phrasing, he cautions or possibly promises the woman to whom his song of seduction is apparently addressed that "things are gonna get freakier." This transforms the relatively wholesome and optimistic spirit of the original which had comforted its listeners with the reassuring news that "things are gonna be easier." This is no longer plausible advice to the black listening public. R. Kelly remains more faithful to the profane muses of rhythm and blues than most of his fellow practitioners of Swing,[6] a hybrid offspring of Soul and Rap. However, his citation and adaptation of the earlier tune is not motivated by the desire to engage in the archaeology of living intertextual tradition. It works like a stolen sample or a borrowed instrumental riff to index the interperformative relationships that constitute a countercultural subculture. He makes the past audible in the here and now, but *subserviently*: history is conscripted into the service of the present.[7]

hermeneutic process

6. Check out "Sadie," the song dedicated to his mother on *12 play*, Jive Records, 1993.

7. This type of citation does not take the form of parody or pastiche. Its intentions are disciplinary and it is best understood as a creative ordering that does not always serve progressive impulses. It does not play with the gap between then and now but rather uses it to assert a spurious continuity that adds legitimacy and gravity to the contemporary. A second example of the shifting political resonance between these different periods in popular politics is provided by the way that the group Arrested Development borrowed parts of Sly and The Family Stone's "Everyday People" and changed it into "People Everyday." The earlier song was an affirmation of pluralism that pivoted on the chorus

There is a blue one who can't accept the green one

For living with a fat one trying to be a skinny one

And different strokes for different folks . . .

I am no better and neither are you

We are the same whatever we do

Kelly's subversive transformation of the older tune cut in the year that he was born, betrays oedipal impulses that are the cornerstone of this hidden modern tradition. In a small way, his gesture, which manages to be simultaneously insubordinate and reverent, expresses the contraction of the black public sphere. This process has developed closely in step with what might be termed the narrative shrinkage of the rhythm and blues idiom: one of the more pernicious effects of the preeminence of a Hip hop culture currently dominated by grim tales of sex, drugs and gun play. Kelly's cool pose is entirely complicit with what bell hooks has identified as the "life threatening choke hold (that) patriarchal masculinity imposes on black men."[8] It could be argued that the explicit repudiation of social amelioration Kelly's words contain, conveys something important about the imploded contemporary character of black political culture which finds it progressively more and more difficult to be political at all. However, I want to suggest something different and slightly more complex, namely that it is the association of repudiating progress with the assertive pursuit of sexual pleasure that provides a distinctive historical embodiment of the dismal moment in which public politics becomes unspeakable and bio-politics takes hold.[9]

R. Kelly's popularity is one of the many signs that the black body politic is now regularly represented internally and externally as an integral but "freaky" body. Racialised sex is an ephemeral residue of political rebellion. The androcentric and phallocratic presentation and representation of heterosexual coupling at which he excels is both the sign and the limit of a different charisma and a different utopia than those that Kenny Burke and his siblings had in mind in Chicago twenty-five years ago.[10] Their choice of the name "Stairsteps" for their pre-Jackson family quintet suggested upward momentum, racial elevation and communal movement towards something "brighter," something closer to the heavens if not to God. I want to explore the possibility that this goal, which was identifiable thanks to its illumination amidst the darkness of white supremacy that threatened

---

You love me—you hate me you know me and then
You can't figure out the bag I'm in
I am everyday people
The decisive line of antagonism between different "races" that the earlier song located and then erased is moved in the later one and is seen to operate within the racial group around the disrespectful drunken conduct of "brothers" towards the singer's "black queen."

8. bell hooks, *Black Looks* (Boston: South End Press, 1992), 113.
9. See Ferenc Fehér and Agnes Heller, *Biopolitics* (Aldershot: Avebury, 1994).
10. "I know this might sound funny coming out of my mouth but I do try to be different, I try to hit on a romantic sexual level, leaving just a touch to the imagination," R. Kelly interviewed in *Pride*, May/June 1994, 35.

to engulf it, was named Freedom—a word that has been steadily disappearing from the political language of blacks in the west and which will be even more remote from their consciousness now that the liberation of South Africa has been formally accomplished. I also want to mourn the disappearance of the pursuit of Freedom as an element in black vernacular culture, and to ask why it seems no longer appropriate or even plausible to speculate about the freedom of the subject of black politics in overdeveloped countries. Furthermore, I would like to examine the effects on the public political world of transposing that yearning for freedom into a different mode. This is signalled by the growing centrality of what might be called a racialised biopolitics of fucking: a means of bonding freedom and life. This move towards bio-politics is best understood as an outgrowth of the pattern identified as "identity politics" in earlier periods by a number of writers.[11] It is a mood in which the person is defined as the body and in which certain exemplary bodies for example, those of Mike Tyson and Michael Jordan, Naomi Campbell and Veronica Webb become instantiations of community.

This situation necessitates a different conception of freedom than those hitherto channelled into modern citizenship or developed in post-slave cultures where bodily and spiritual freedoms were sharply differentiated and freedom was more likely to be associated with death than life. Organic intellectuals on this historic frequency from Frederick Douglass to George Clinton suggested that the most valuable forms of freedom resided in the liberation of the mind. Dr. Funkenstein's prescription was "Free your mind and your ass will follow." Racialised bio-politics operates from an altogether different premise that refuses this distinction. It uses a reversal of these historic priorities to establish the limits of the authentic racial community exclusively through the visual representation of racial bodies—engaged in characteristic activities—usually sexual or sporting that ground and solicit identification if not solidarity. This development is problematic for several reasons. For one, it marks that racial community exclusively as a space of heterosexual activity and confirms the abandonment of any politics aside from the ongoing oppositional creativity of gendered self-cultivation: an activity that is endowed with almost sacred significance but undertaken in something of the same resolute spirit as working out with weights. If it survives, politics becomes an exclusively aesthetic concern with all the perils that implies, and the racial body, arranged suggestively with a precision that will be familiar to readers of de Sade, supplies its critical evaluative principle. Affiliates of the racialised collectivity

11. An insightful version of this is outlined by June Jordan in "Waiting For a Taxi" in *Technical Difficulties* (New York: Pantheon, 1992).

are thereby led "to focus the attention on themselves, to decipher, recognise and acknowledge themselves as subjects of desire, bringing into play between themselves and themselves a certain relationship that allows them to discover, in desire, the truth of their being . . ."[12]

The termination of talk about freedom and the proliferation of signs and talk about sexuality as racialised recreation have coincided. Together they point to a novel form of artistic production that goes beyond therapeutic cultures of compensation, where simple sameness supplied the premise and the entry ticket into an aesthetic sense of racial difference for which the sculpted male bodies that adorn albums by bands like Jodeci and crooners like RAab, are a notable popular signifier.[13] These silences and embodied signs yield insights into the changing and embattled character of the black public sphere. They represent the end of older notions of public interaction that helped to create and were themselves created by the forms of densely coded, verbally mediated intersubjective dialogue that nurtured racial solidarity and made the idea of an exclusive racialised identity a credible, operable one. The time-worn model of black publicity derived from sacred rituals and musical utility survives but in a vestigial and profane form. Its precious dialogical attributes retain a dwindling ethical significance even as this drains away and is replaced by morbid phenomena like the Americo-centric image of the black public sphere as the inner-city basketball court. This is an exclusively male stage for the theatre of power and kinship in which sound is displaced by vision and words are generally second to gestures. The natural aristocracy defined by means of bodily power and grace can announce its heroic godly presence there.[14] A hint of the significance of this location emerged in a recent interview with R. Kelly in *Vibe* magazine:

> Robert Kelly grew up all over the South Side of Chicago. He and his boys are into basketball, and three or four mornings a week they show up at one of their favorite courts (18th, 47th, 63rd, 67th or 115th street). "When I hit the court and people know me, it's 'Hell, naw, that's that guy that be singin'.' They don't realize I'm just a regular guy. I'm

12. Michel Foucault, *The Use of Pleasure* (Harmondsworth: Viking, 1986), 5.

13. See also Michael Jordan, *rare Air Michael on Michael*, ed. Mark Vancil (New York: Harper Collins, 1993).

14. George L. Mosse, *Nationalism and Sexuality* (Madison: University of Wisconsin Press, 1985), esp. chapter 3; Michael Jordan, *rare Air Michael on Michael*.

anxious to prove myself. I can ball just like you do. I'll take it to the
hole just like you, if not better."[15]

At present, the poetic topography of race and place centred on the basketball
court has no equivalent in Britain's black cultures. However, some of these points
about the relationship of identity, publicity and masculinity can be illustrated by
the popular reception of the black basketball action movie, *Above The Rim*. The
soundtrack from this movie features material from eighteen different artists and
it has been a powerful initial marketing tool for a film that promises to complete
and extend the narrative of "White Men Can't Jump" in a more gritty mode that
takes it reality effects from Hip hop's masculinist lexicon. The soundtrack has
displaced R. Kelly from the top of the album charts since I first sat down to write
this piece.

The popularity of film-associated anthologies like the "Above The Rim" album
offers important evidence that the independent power of music is waning while
the authority of the image culture on which music has become increasingly para-
sitic grows steadily. It was, after all a similar soundtrack album from the Bill
Duke film *Deep Cover* that first unleashed the talent of Snoop Doggy Dogg, the
young rapper from Long Beach who is the most successful artist in the history
of the style and who is now the centre of the moral and political panics about
gansta rap. One track from the "Above The Rim" set features D.J. Rogers, the
greatest male gospel singer of his generation, who has been induced by producer
Dr. Dre to sing "Doggie Style," a song that endorses and amplifies Snoop's historic
call to cultivate a set of distinctive sexual habits that can bring certainty, confidence
and resoluteness back to racialised being:

> Let's do it doggie style
> I really like to ride it doggie style . . .
> baby come closer I want to undress you
> I'm gonna give it to you baby until you can take no more . . .
> you and I on the floor let's get freaky . . .
> baby don't you move you'll disturb my groove . . .

15. *Vibe*, 2, 4 (May 1994): 72. The same article offers these interesting observations about
Kelly's living space: "He lives downtown on the Loop, in a sparsely decorated one-bedroom apartment.
'Where I live it's like Batman in Gotham City. No one knows where I live. If you come to my crib,
you have to be blindfolded . . . It's not just an apartment to me. I hear my music in there. I never
have any company because that's my solitude. My being silent about my personal life allows me to
express it in the studio.'"

turnover lay your head down so I can get freaky
please let me lick you in my favourite way
turnover baby and back up into me so let me love you down
there's no need to worry I'm your doggy style man.

A chorus of singers interposes appropriate exhortations. This is more than the pursuit of sexual pleasure as compensation for the wrongs wrought in the name of white supremacy. We shall discover below that it is more even than a dionysian alternative to the asceticism of figures like Ice Cube, who have responded to contemporary uncertainties about racial identity and solidarity with an austerity program that articulates some ancient priestly notions about the association of sexual abstention with the acquisition of knowledge and the forms of self-love necessitated by communal reconstruction.[16]

The changed composition and signification of the black body politic has been associated with a number of other social and technological shifts that cannot be explored in detail here though they must be noted in passing. This transformation cannot be separated from the privatisation of both cultural production and use — a long-term trend that has important implications for attempts to defend the political significance of black popular culture. The basketball court configuration of the public sphere is suggestive here. It indicates that the vernacular forms that were once called street culture have largely left the public world of the streets, a world no longer seen primarily as a privileged space for the elaboration of cultural authenticity but rather as the location of violence, crime and social pathology. The vital unfolding of racialised culture is now projected as taking place in discrete private, semi-private and private public settings that can be found, like the ball court, between the axes established by the bedroom and the car. The family supplies the sole institutional site for bio-politics and, as I have pointed out elsewhere, a radical localism operating under the sign "hood" projects community as a simple accumulation of symmetrical family units.[17] The family remains

16. See his discussion with Angela Davis in *Transition* 58 (1992): 192. It includes the following exchange:

Ice Cube [I.C.]: Did anyone in the Black Panther organization smoke?
Angela Davis [A.D.]: I'm sure they did.
I.C.: Did anybody drink?
A.D.: I'm sure they did.
I.C.: That ain't loving yourself. . . . To me the best organisation for black people is the Nation of Islam. It is the best organisation: brothers don't drink, don't smoke, ain't chasin' women. They have one job. . . .

17. Paul Gilroy, "It's a family affair: black culture and the trope of kinship" in *Small Acts* (London and New York: Serpent's Tail, 1994).

important because it narrows the horizons of any lingering aspiration towards social change. But as Jodeci makes clear, the sanctity and integrity of the family can be readily sacrificed when more important hedonistic objectives come into view. The duty of parental care exists in opposition to the space of sexual intimacy where the most intense meanings of being black are established:

> girl where is our child?
> send it to your mother's for a while
> all my friends are gone you know I send them home
> girl I live for you so I don't give a fuck about the news
> so please turn off the T.V.
> and if you give a damn about me I wanna hear you moan
> lets be alone
> what's better than you and me? you're better than a damn movie
> our love is so much fun
> let's do some freaky shit and then I'll make you come . . .

The gender-neutrality of the child in the torrid narrative suggests extreme paternal indifference rather than political correctness. It is clearly significant that on this scale of excitement it is cinema that provides the bench mark. The fact that RAab's agenda for an evening at home is similar to that proposed by Devanté Swing and the boys can be gleaned from something as simple as the list of song titles on his album: "Try My Love," "Foreplay," "Where She At?" "Feel Me," "Give In To Me," "Give It A Try," "You're The One," "Close The Door," "Can't Let Go," "Good Lovin'," and "It's Just Like That." His album jacket warns prospective purchasers that his bass-heavy music will destroy their audio systems unless they make technical adjustments. He then supplies what amounts to a moral health warning in case his paean to the joys of recreational sex is misunderstood.

> This album is dedicated to all the brothers and sisters who believe mo-
> nogamous relationships still work. The songs on this album are about
> one brother's involvement with one sister. We brothers have got to stop
> treatin' and callin' our sisters bitches and whores. They are true exten-
> sions of our existence. Sisters have got to wake up also—Stop compet-
> ing with each other and respect your fellow sister and their situations,
> no matter what it is. We have got to turn this shit around and stop hurt-
> ing one another. We are only destroying one another. Can't you see

what's goin on? Can't you see it's wrong? Our ancestors are very disappointed. Peace.[18]

The patterned use of black music reveals much about the changing quality of the subaltern public culture. The dominant place of radio in fixing the limits of the black sphere as an interpretive community has been ceded to video in ways that compromise the power of sound and the dialogic principles on which the black vernacular was built in times past. Interestingly Snoop Doggy Dogg has dramatised each medium's different claims for the right to represent the culture as a whole in the snippets of humour and drama inserted between his rapped contributions on his album, also entitled *Doggy Style*. The proliferation of jokes, sketches and other humorous material on recent black popular music recordings does more than fill up the enhanced playing time made possible by the CD format. This tactic is common to recent offerings by Snoop, DRS, 7669 and Xscape. It seems to be a bid to simulate and thus recover a variety of dialogical interaction that has been inhibited by the technology of production but is sought by underground users nonetheless. This tactic may also provide carefully constructed cues to the crossover listenership that can attune them to the signs of pleasure and danger that they desire. The proliferation of these dramatic inserts is yet another indication that the foundational authority of the performance event has been undermined by the emergence of musical forms that cannot be faithfully or readily translated into concert settings as a result of their technological base. The impact of problems arising from the political economy of clubs and other venues should also be noted. Faced with these changes, street culture has become many things, most notably "jeep culture" as cars have become larger scale equivalents of the walkman—a piece of technology named by a word which, by lacking a plural signifies its association with the same sad process of social privatisation.

While everyone else was following N.W.A. into naming their bands with mysterious sequences of initials or numbers that only initiates could decode with U.N.V., P.O.V., S.W.V., D.R.S., 7669 as the most obvious examples, R. Kelly called his musical backup team Public Announcement, a name that bypassed the voguish urge to encrypt. It openly acknowledged a different historic obligation to service the alternative, subaltern public spheres that have hosted the processes of vernacular identity formation through a variety of different communicative

18. RAab, *You're The One* (Rip It Records, 1002-2, 1993). Available from the Independent Label Coalition.

technologies: print, radio, audio, video, and in a wide range of settings at various distances from the core event of cultural performance.

These successive communicative technologies organise space and time in different ways and have solicited and fostered different kinds of identification. They create and manipulate memory in dissimilar ways and stage the corporeal and physical enigmas of cultural identity in contrasting processes. Their political effects are various and contradictory but the long-term tendency for music, sound and text to give way to image cannot be dismissed. We must ask whether scopic identification and desire differ from what might be called the alternative "orphic" configurations organised around music and hearing. Do the latter privilege the imaginary over the symbolic? The growing dominance of specularity over aurality contributes a special force to representations of the exemplary racial body arrested in the gaze of desiring and identifying subjects. Misrecognised, objectified and verified, these images have become the storehouses of racial alterity now that the production of subjectivity operates through different sensory and technological mechanisms. We must be clear about what is gained and what may be lost in the contemporary displacement of sound from the epicentre of black cultural production:

> In sound, and in the consciousness termed hearing, there is in fact a break with the self-complete world of vision and art. In its entirety, sound is a ringing, clanging scandal. Whereas in vision, form is wedded to content in such a way as to appease it, in sound the perceptible quality overflows so that form can no longer contain its content. A real rent is produced in the world, through which the world that is *here* prolongs a dimension that cannot be converted into vision.[19]

The Trials of Freedom

Knowledge is freedom and ignorance is slavery . . .

MILES DAVIS

Contemporary studies of black vernacular culture are just as silent as Hip hop about the concept of freedom and its political and metaphysical significance. This is puzzling given the complex historical connections between slavery and freedom that are evident in the forms black culture assumes and the ways it is engaged

19. Emmanuel Levinas, "The Transcendence of Words" in *The Levinas Reader*, ed. Sean Hand. (Oxford: Blackwell, 1989), 147.

by its producers and its users. Freedom has sometimes emerged as a theme in the writing of black history, and the dialectical interrelation of freedom and slavery has been addressed. Where this has happened, however, freedom has usually been presented as a solitary event: a break-point or rupture. It is seen as a threshold that was irrevocably crossed once slavery was formally declared to be over and populations of ex-slaves moved uneasily into the new spaces of enhanced autonomy—intimate, private, civic, economic—that the concept helped to define. The desire to acquire civic and economic freedoms and the pursuit of personal freedoms had been closely aligned during the period of struggles against slavery. Considerable tension between these different dynamics developed in the post-emancipation period. The fundamental shift represented by the Jubilee was felt to require the opening of a new chapter in the narrative of black history, even where the forms of civil society in which the newly freed found themselves instituted novel unfreedoms that compounded powerlessness, immiseration and poverty or retained and modified patterns of racialised domination from the slave period.[20] Freedom was seen to be relevant primarily because it represented the termination of slavery rather than the beginning of a different sequence of struggles in which its own meanings would be established and its future limits identified. Once formal free status was gained it could appear that there was no further need to elaborate the distinctive meanings that freedom acquired among people radically estranged from the promise and practice of freedom by generations of servitude enforced by terror. The end of slavery produced several new "technical" solutions to the problems of discovering and regulating free black selves.

> After the coming of freedom there were two points upon which practi-
> cally all the people on our place were agreed, and I feel that this was
> generally true throughout the South: that they must change their names,
> and that they must leave the old plantation for at least a few days or
> weeks in order that they might feel really sure that they were free.[21]

It was only among blacks in the United States that ready access to political institutions defined freedom's post-slavery boundaries. Even in that exceptional situation, the limits of freedom had to be first found and then tested. Leon Litwack

20. Eric Foner, *Nothing But Freedom* (Baton Rouge and London: Louisiana State University Press, 1983).

21. Booker T. Washington, *Up From Slavery* (New York: Airmont Books, 1967), 27.

has pointed to the significant role of marriage in symbolising and demonstrating the free status of the freed slaves.[22] The place of the family, the significance of domesticity and the need to acquire clearly demarcated spaces for intimate and private activity are all important issues in the technologies of the free self that have left lingering imprints upon today's libidinal economies and erotic allegories of political desire. The relatively limited role of obviously political institutions in establishing the history of those incomplete emancipations, which did not straightforwardly deliver substantive freedom in the form of political rights, is therefore something that needs to be explored carefully. If bell hooks is right, the compensatory taking up of patriarchal masculinity by ex-slaves and their descendants might be fruitfully linked to critical analysis of the development of democracy compromised by the imperatives of white supremacy. The coercive regimes that followed modern racial slavery under the banners of freedom were, just as slavery had been, internal to western civilisation. Their histories complicate the history of democracy and the assumption of social and moral progress towards which that heroic tale is often directed.

Under the guidance of ideologues who were self-consciously developing the arts of governing, disciplining and educating the post-slave self, the former slaves and their descendants gradually and unevenly acquired the freedoms to vote, associate, organise and communicate. They became bearers of rights and practitioners of skills that confirmed their equal value as free people in circumstances that made liberty and equality impracticable though not unthinkable. Their descendants continue to stretch the bounds of the civility that enclosed and promoted these rights. It would be mistaken to assume that the gap between formal, rhetorical declarations of black emancipation and the practical realisation of democratic hopes defines and exhausts the politics of being free. I suggest that, however important the relatively narrow understanding of freedom centred on political rights has been, it leaves vast areas of thinking about freedom and the desire to be seen to be free, untouched. A politics of freedom (and indeed of being free) needs to be addressed today with a special sensitivity because the meanings of freedom and the idioms through which it is apprehended have become extremely

22. "No sooner had emancipation been acknowledged that thousands of 'married' couples, with the encouragement of black preachers and northern white missionaries, hastened to secure their marital vows, both legally and spiritually. . . . The insistence of teachers, missionaries and Freedman's Bureau officers that blacks formalize their marriages stemmed from the notion that legal sanction was necessary for sexual and moral restraint and that ex-slaves had to be incubated with 'the obligations of the married state in civilized life.'" Leon F. Litwack, *Been In the Storm So Long: The Aftermath of Slavery* (London: Athlone Press, 1988), 240. See also chapter 5, "How Free IS Free?"

significant for interpretations of contemporary popular culture. Important work has already been undertaken in this area by anthropologist Daniel Miller,[23] by historians of African American religion such as Mechal Sobel[24] and Charles H. Long,[25] and in particular by Lawrence Levine whose invaluable study *Black Culture and Black Consciousness*[26] points to important historical connections between the subcultural reproduction of gender and mythic and heroic representations of freedom. Freedom has been less of an issue in broadly sociological studies of the utility and practice of black vernacular forms both sacred and profane.[27]

Rather than delve into the forms assumed and promoted by the protean consciousness of freedom, analysts have usually investigated the impact of becoming free on the slaves and on their patterns of cultural production. Exploring the transformations wrought by Jubilee and the effects of its ritual commemoration can however proceed without confronting either the value of freedom itself as an element in the lives of ex-slaves or the distinctive idiomatic practices through which they strove to represent the psychological, social and economic differences freedom made: to themselves, to their descendants and to the slave masters and mistresses who were themselves embarking on a journey out of slavery and ceasing to be oppressors and becoming exploiters. The memory of slavery is seldom addressed though the silences and evasions around slavery revealed by popular culture make this more understandable. I have suggested that the dominance of love and loss stories in black popular musical forms embraces the condition of being in pain, transcodes and interweaves the different yearnings for personal and civic freedoms and preserves the memories of suffering and loss in a usable—irreducibly ethical—form.[28] The incorporated memories of unfreedom and terror are cultivated in co-memorative practices.[29] Song and the social rituals that surround it became a valuable means to cultivate a rapport with

23. D. Miller, "Absolute Freedom in Trinidad," *Man* 26 (1991): 323–41.

24. Mechal Sobel, *Trabelin' On: The Slave Journey To An Afro-Baptist Faith* (Princeton: Princeton University Press, 1988).

25. Charles H. Long, *Significations* (Philadelphia: Fortress Press, 1986).

26. Oxford: Oxford University Press, 1977.

27. Michael Eric Dyson is again typical of these problems. He notes that in the black vernacular "personal freedom often is envisioned through tropes of sexual release" but takes this observation no further (ibid., 279). It is not solely a matter of "release," though this choice of words has the virtue of making a connection with slavery explicit.

28. Paul Gilroy, *The Black Atlantic* (Cambridge: Harvard University Press, 1993), chapter 6.

29. On this concept see Paul Connerton's useful book, *How Societies Remember* (Cambridge, Cambridge University Press, 1989), section 3, "Bodily Practices."

the presence of suffering and with death. Amidst the terror of slavery, where bodily and spiritual freedoms were readily distinguished along lines suggested by christianity — if not African cosmology — death was itself often understood as an escape. It offered the opportunity to acquire a higher, heteronymous freedom in which the mortal body, unshackled at last, would be cast aside as the newly liberated soul soared heavenward or took its place in the ancestral pantheon. Many practices that were forged in the habitus of slavery have lingered on. But today the social memory of slavery has itself been repressed or set aside and the tradition of dynamic remembrance it founded is being assaulted from all sides. The memory of slavery is seen as an encumbrance or an old skin that has to be shed before an authentic life of racialised self-love can be attained.[30]

The contemporary popular music of R. Kelly, Snoop Doggy Dogg, S.W.V. and the rest registers these changes. The sharpest break between the older patterns and bio-politics is evident where love stories mutate into sex stories. Even when they were systematically profane, the modes of intersubjectivity described and sometimes practised in earlier stages in the unfolding of rhythm and blues were informed by the proximity of the sacred and the definitions of spiritual love that were cultivated there. Spirituality cast long shadows over emergent forms of secular and profane creativity in which songs of passion were often simultaneously songs of protest. Today, song is being relegated to the role of soundtrack for the expansion of the image world and the game of truth is updated. The new rules are fixed via a different, I am tempted to say post-modern, conception of mortality. The traditional cultivation of a rapport with the presence of death is recast because death is no longer a transition or release.[31] Doctor Dre, the producer of Snoop's records calls his label Death Row Records. The changed value and understanding of death that has developed amidst the AIDS crisis, the drug economy and the militarisation of inner-city life is thus another factor reshaping the black public sphere and its historicity:

Daily life becomes a perpetual dress rehearsal for death. What is being rehearsed . . . is *ephemerality* and *evanescence* of things that humans may acquire and bonds that humans may weave. The impact of such daily rehearsal seems to be similar to one achieved by some preventive

30. Shahrazad Ali, *Are You Still A Slave?* (Philadelphia: Civilized Publications, n.d.).

31. This is powerfully transmitted and its relationship to the problematics of freedom illuminated by several tracks by Ice Cube's crew Da Lench Mob. See for example, "Capital Punishment in America" and "Freedom Got an A.K." both from their album *Guerrillas In The Mist* (Street Knowledge 7-92206-2).

inoculations: if taken in daily, in partly detoxicated and thus non-deadly doses, the awesome poison seems to lose its venom. Instead, it prompts immunity and indifference to the toxin in the inoculated organism.[32]

It bears repetition that bio-politics specifies that the person is identified only in terms of their body. The very best that this change precipitates is a principled anti-christian confrontation with the idea that life continues after death. It is the refusal of these religious antidotes to death that is often described as nihilism.[33] In these circumstances, the desire to be free is closely linked with the desire to be seen to be free and with the pursuit of an individual and embodied intensity of experience that contrasts sharply with the collective and spiritual forms of immortality esteemed in times gone by. Jean Luc Nancy has emphasised how freedom is linked to a politics of representation.[34] This relationship accumulates special significance where race becomes the rationality for denying and withholding liberty and where studied indifference to the death and suffering of others provides a shortcut to the enduring notoriety and celebrity associated with gangsterdom. This is now a social phenomenon by virtue of its antisociality.

As old certainties about the fixed limits of racial identity have lost their power to convince, ontological security capable of answering a radically reduced sense of the value of life has been sought in the naturalising power of gender difference and sex as well as in the ability to cheat death and take life. Sex and gender are experienced – lived conflictually – at a heightened pitch that somehow connotes race. Gender difference and racialised gender codes provide a special cipher for a mode of racial authenticity that is as evasive as it is desirable. In these circumstances, the iterative re-presentation of gender, gender conflicts and sexualities contributes a supple confidence and stability to essentialist absolute notions of racial particularity. These may, like Onyx and other homophobic Ragga stars such as Buju Banton, demand the death of all "batty bwoy" as the price of their reproduction over time. They may, like Jodeci, perform highly stylised ritual celebrations of heterosexual intimacy that suspend and transcend the everyday incoherence and asymmetry of gender, turning them into an ordered narrative of racial being and becoming. With these specific examples in mind, it is necessary to acknowledge that the centrality of gender to black popular cultures can also

32. Zygmunt Bauman, *Mortality, Immortality and Other Life Strategies* (Oxford: Polity, 1993), 187–8. See also Ernst Bloch and Theodor W. Adorno, "Something's Missing" in *The Utopian Function of Art And Literature*, ed. Ernst Bloch (Cambridge: MIT Press, 1988), pp. 5–8.

33. Nas, "Life's A Bitch" from the CD *Illmatic* (Columbia, CK 57684, 1994).

34. Jean Luc Nancy, *The Experience of Freedom* (Stanford: Stanford University Press, 1993).

be analysed as an alternative articulation of freedom that associates autonomous agency with sexual desire and promotes the symbolic exercise of power in the special domain that sexuality provides. In this crepuscular space, Bell Biv Devoe, a group who have taken the basketball tropes considerably further than anyone else, uses them to provide a coy invitation to practice anal intercourse; D.R.S. (Dirty Rotten Scoundrels) issue their female associates the simple command to "strip" and S.W.V. (Sisters With Voices) urge their partners to go "Downtown" and discover a way to their heart between their thighs.

> You've been wondering how you can make it better
> baby its easy to turn my world inside out
> your discovery will take us to another place
> baby of that there is no doubt
> I've been waiting for the special moment, anticipating all the things
>   you'll do to me
> make the first step to release my emotions and take the road to ecstasy
> you've got to go downtown . . . to taste the sweetness will be enough
> keep on doing doing what you're doing
> 'til you feel the passion burning up inside of me
> if you do me right we'll be making love all through the night
> when you uncover the mystery
> take it nice and slow baby don't rush the feeling.[35]

This is the context in which the allure and the etho-poetics of doing it doggy style should be situated. These are far from novel themes in black popular culture. Their significance, however, has been transformed by the silencing of other racialised discourses that would qualify and therefore contest their representative status, by their increasing distance from sacred and spiritual concerns and by the bio-political focus that terminates the vernacular conception of the mind/body dualism as well as the modernist aspirations towards racial uplift that were once figured through the language of public-political citizenship.

Nihilism and Pseudo-Freedom

> an AK talks and bullshit runs
> I wish I had time to count all my guns . . .

35. S.W.V., *It's About Time* (RCA 07863 66074-2, 1992). See also S.W.V., *The Remixes* (RCA, 07863-66401-2, 1994).

so get the fuck out of the way when I spray
freedom got an AK . . .
don't come to me with no petition
come to me with ammunition . . .

DA LENCH MOB

The theme of freedom remains important because it relates directly to contemporary debates about the antisocial consequences of black nihilism.[36] Influential interpretations of contemporary black politics have stressed the meaninglessness, lovelessness and hopelessness of black metropolitan life and argued that the chronic ethical crisis from which they apparently stem generates further symptoms of black misery in the homophobia, misogyny, antisemitism and fundamentalist nationalisms currently being affirmed in black political cultures. The corrosive power of this vernacular nihilism is traced to a variety of different causal mechanisms. Sometimes it is seen as a capitulation to the market values — individualism, ruthlessness and indifference to others — that dominate the mainstream corporate world and its popular cultural commodities. Alternatively, it has been interpreted as a set of ethnic habits peculiar to blacks. Whether it is a mechanistic response to racism and material privation or a more creative ethnic trait, it has been readily linked to the patterns of household organisation, kinship and community that supposedly distinguish black social life. Lastly, it is viewed as a structural feature of deindustrialized capitalism, which no longer has need for the living labour of terminally broken black communities that are marginal to the ongoing practice of flexible accumulation, and that may be contemptuous of the limited economic opportunities offered to them by neo-slave employment in what is termed the service sector.

The concept of the underclass mediates these different accounts of black nihilism. Each explanation offers a tiny rational kernel in a large mystical shell, but even when taken together, they do not satisfy. The nexus of consciousness and behaviour that is reduced to the pejorative term nihilism is associated with idiomatic representations of freedom. Its main contemporary genres and styles are property, sex and the means of violence. From this perspective, nihilism ceases to be antisocial and becomes social in the obvious sense of the term: it generates community and specifies the fortified boundaries of racial particularity.

36. Cornel West, "Nihilism in Black America" in *Race Matters* (Boston: Beacon Press, 1993). See also Ishmael Reed, *Airing Dirty Laundry* (Reading, MA: Addison Wesley, 1993).

Once again, the mediated, sedimented memory of slavery provides a valuable starting point in understanding the development of this vernacular pattern. For example, it directs attention towards the complex symbolism of wealth in black popular culture. The visual culture of Hip hop pivoted briefly on the alchemical transformation of iron shackles into gold chains.[37] Racialised by Mr. T whose bold exploits live on in the lost valley of cable television, gold chains externalised the changing price of the (wage) slave's labour power – calculated on the basis of exchange value. The gold in the chains expressed the limits of the money economy in which they circulated but which they were also able to transcend, especially in times of crisis. The free humanity formerly bestowed by God could now be conveyed in displays of wealth that far exceeded the value of a person – of a body. The same sort of ostentation can be detected in some contemporary Hip hoppers' appetite for cars as symbols of status, wealth and masculine power.

Dre boasts of a collection of cars: a white Chevy Blazer, a convertible
300 sec Benz, a 735 BMW, two 64s and a Nissan Pathfinder (My
mom's jacked my Pathfinder, she's like my sister, she looks young.
She's flossing in my shit so I guess I only have five cars.)[38]

Moving towards a consideration of the forms that the relationship between civic and personal freedoms might take in the post-liberal age, we must cultivate the ability to disentangle the ludic from the programmatic and find any threads of politics that run between them. One may appreciate that the problems displayed in these attempts to reckon with freedom were born from slavery, but the civic freedoms of the modern west which constitute the privileged object of these enquiries were not antithetical to slavery and other forms of legal and legitimate

37. The actor Mr. T anticipated the views of a generation of old school Hip hoppers when in 1985 he gave this explanation of his flashy taste in jewellery:

The gold chains are a symbol that reminds me of my great African ancestors, who were brought over here as slaves with iron chains on their ankles, on their wrists, their necks and sometimes around their waists. I turned my chains into gold, so my statement is this: the fact that I wear gold chains instead of iron chains is because I am still a slave, only my price tag is higher now. I am still bought and sold by the powers that be in this society, white people, but this time they pay me on demand, millions and millions of dollars for my services. I demand it and they pay it . . . Yes, I am still a slave in this society, but I am still free by God. "How are you still a slave Mr T.?" You see the only thing that interests this society is money. And the only thing that it fears and respects is more money. *An Autobiography by Mr T* (London: W. H. Allen, 1985), 4.

This account of the connection between slavery and identity links personal autonomy with the signs of wealth and the memory of terror. The condition of slavery persists but is changed by divine grace and the very worldly capacity to hire oneself out to others.

38. dream hampton, "G down," *The Source*, September, 1993, 68.

bondage. The enduring effects of slavery are most evident in the oft stated desires for freedom from the servitude of work and freedom from oppressive, unjust law. They can also be felt in the identification of freedom with death that marks some versions of black christianity very deeply and defers emancipation and the possibility of redemption to a better, future world. Equipped, among other things, with the living traces of an African onto-theology, slaves in the western hemisphere neither sought nor anticipated that mode of dominating the external world which provided Europeans with an essential precondition for development of a consciousness of freedom. This process has been well described by Murray Bookchin:

> Domination and freedom become interchangeable terms in a common project of subjugating nature *and* humanity — each of which is used as the excuse to validate control of one by the other. The reasoning involved is strictly circular. The machine has not only run away without the driver, but the driver has become a mere part of the machine.[39]

Because it was so reliant on the institutionalisation of their unfree labour, the slaves viewed the civilising process with scepticism and its ethical claims with extreme suspicion.[40] Their hermeneutic agency grounded a vernacular culture premised on the possibility that freedom should be pursued outside of the rules, codes and expectations of colour-coded civilisation. The transgression of those codes was itself a sign that freedom was being claimed. It presented the possibility of an (anti)politics animated by the desire to violate — a negation of unjust, oppressive and therefore illegitimate authority. By breaking these rules in small, though ritualised ways it was possible to deface the clean edifice of white supremacy that fortified tainted and therefore inauthentic freedoms. Cultures of insubordination located more substantive and worthwhile freedoms in the capacity to follow moral imperatives in restricted circumstances. They were elaborated through the media of music and dance as well as through writing. Music expressed and confirmed unfreedom while evolving in complex patterns that pointed beyond misery towards reciprocity and prefigured the democracy yet to come in their antiphonic forms. Dance refined the exercise of autonomous power in the body by claiming it back from the absolute sovereignty of work. It produced the alternative "natural"

---

39. Murray Bookchin, *The Ecology of Freedom* (Palo Alto: Cheshire Books, 1982), 272.

40. Frederick Douglass, *My Bondage My Freedom* (New York: Miller, Orton and Mulligan, 1855), 50.

hierarchy wholly antithetical to the order required by the institutions of white supremacy which today forms the basis of black sports cultures.

The Return of the Moral Agent. . . in Canine Form?

> One cannot entirely refuse the face of an animal. It is via the face that one understands, for example a dog. Yet the priority here is not found in the animal but in the human face. . . . The phenomenon of the face is not in its purest form in the dog. In the dog, in the animal there are other phenomena. For example, the force of nature is pure vitality. It is more this which characterizes the dog. But it also has a face.
>
> EMMANUEL LEVINAS

Before I can conclude, I must raise, even if only to set aside, the question of whether Snoop Doggy Dogg's best known oral trademark: "1–8–7 on an undercover cop" might simply be an idiomatic restatement of some very well-known modernist anxieties over the limits of existential agency, autonomy and subjectivity in particular, about the relationship between self-making and deliberately taking the life of the other.[41] Snoop's music and rapping remains doggedly faithful to the antiphonic forms that link new world black styles to their African antecedents. The fading public sphere is configured negatively but it is still just about recognisable as a profane transcoding of the black christian congregation. Snoop's instructions to his audience, "If you don't give a shit like I don't give a shit wave your mother-fuckin' fingers in the air," aren't very far from the cry of the old school rappers whose crossover ambitions required that they curse less, or even from preachers who sought similar gestures of solidarity from their audiences.[42] In any form, these are gestures that enforce the priority of the saying over the said. We must remember that in this vernacular, dog is a verb as well as a noun.

41. See June Jordan, "Beyond Apocalypse Now" in *Civil Wars* (Boston: Beacon Press, 1981), esp. 171; and Robert C. Solomon, *From Rationalism To Existentialism* (Hassocks: Harvester, 1972), chapter 7. See also the discussion of Albert Camus's *L'Etranger* in Edward Said, *Culture and Imperialism* (London: Chatto and Windus, 1993).

42. Reporting his recent performances in London, *Hip Hop Connection* noted this dynamic in operation. "At times this gig resembled a game of Snoop Says. . . 'Throw ya hands in the air,' he'd yell and the audience dutifully obeyed. They were strangely content. It didn't occur to them that Doggystyle's instrumental backing is ideally suited to a live concert. Dre's tuneful production means Snoop's performance should entail musicians, not a cheap impersonal DAT. Unperturbed by this glaring omission, fans avidly sang along to Snoop's casual patter," 62 (April 1994): 114. See also Walter F. Pitts, Jr., *Old Ship of Zion The Afro-Baptist Ritual in the African Diaspora* (New York: Oxford University Press, 1993).

The sleeve of Snoop's Album, "Doggy Style" is printed on recycled paper. He uses it to send out extra special thanks to—among other people—Golgatha Community Baptist Church (presumably the place where his career as a performer started as a chorister and pianist). The G side of Snoop's album begins with his best known track. Its title is formed by two foundational questions. They arise like siblings at the heart of the historic dialogue that demands completion of the special ontological inquires in which newly-freed slaves engaged as they strove to define and clarify the boundaries of their new status as free modern individuals: "WHO AM I (WHAT'S MY NAME)?" Understandably Snoop asserts that his work has no political significance whatsoever. When pressed to operate in that restricted mode his rather conventional opinions seem to be a long way from anything that could reasonably be called nihilist.

> As far as me being political, the only thing I can say is the mutha-fuckin' U.S. can start giving money to the 'hood, giving opportunity and starting businesses, something to make niggas not want to kill each another. Give them some kind of job and finances 'cos the killin ain't over love nor money. They are killin and jackin one another 'cos there ain't no opportunity. As long as its black-on-black or black-on-brown it's cool—they don't like black-on-white. They send national guards like when we took off on their ass in 4.29.92, armed forces and army mutha-fuckas with big ass machine guns—on account of niggas stealing. . . .[43]

Is the cartoon on the cover presenting Snoop as a dog a more reliable guide to the nihilism and antisocial qualities of his work? Why would a young African American choose, at this point, to present himself to the world with the features, with the identity, of a dog?[44] How does Snoop's manipulation of the dog mask that he did not invent, but which he has used so creatively, facilitate his crossover celebrity? Is he locating and testing out the limits of a plausible humanity or creating a new and sustainable relationship with nature within and without? Does the cat-chasing, dog-catcher-outwitting-dog persona simply seek to make a virtue out of immiseration and insult in the familiar process of semiotic inversion capable of changing curse words into words of praise, of revalorising the word Nigger?

43. *Hip Hop Connection* 62 (April 1994): 31.
44. Edmund Leach, "Anthropological aspects of language: animal categories and verbal abuse" in *New Directions in The Study of Language*, ed. E. H. Lenneberg (Cambridge: MIT Press, 1964), 23–63. See also Yi Fu Tuan, *Dominance and Affection: The Making of Pets* (New Haven: Yale University Press, 1984).

Is there a sense in which calling himself a dog expresses an accurate evaluation of the social status of young black men? What comment on the meaning of humanity does Snoop's movement between bodies — between identities — express? A dog is not a fox, a lion, a rabbit or a signifyin' monkey. Snoop is not a dog. His filling the mask of undifferentiated racialised otherness with quizzical canine features reveals something about the operation of white supremacy and the cultures of compensation that answer it. It is a political and, I believe a moral gesture. Choosing to be a low-down dirty dog values the subhuman rather than the hyper-humanity promoted through bio-politics and its visible signatures. It would be missing the main point to overemphasize that the dog is a sign for Snoop's victim status as well as his sexual habits or that the dog sometimes requires the techno-scientific resources of a firearm before it can interact with humans on equal terms. In opting to be seen as a dog he refuses identification with the perfected, invulnerable male body that has become the standard currency of black popular culture cementing the dangerous link between bodily health and racial purity, dissolving the boundary line between singers and athletes and producing strange phenomena like R. Kelly's eroticised appropriation of Michael Jordan's divine masculinity and Shaquille O'Neal's career as a singer and rapper. Snoop's "morphing" between the human and the canine displays those elements of identity that are not reducible to the six-foot-four-inch body of his sometimes owner, "Calvin Broadus." Something is left over when this operation is performed. The metamorphosis requires that we confront Snoop's reflexive capacities. His stylised portrayal of the gangsta self as protean, shape-shifting and multiple is probably less significant than the full, vulgar, antibourgeois force of the black vernacular that crouches behind it.[45] His low-down dirty self directs public attention to the difficult zones where people become less than human. In a capitalist society things regularly take on the social characteristics of people. Emmanuel Levinas has reminded us that the fate and the role of animals can be quite different.[46]

The other side of Doggy Style commences with a bathroom scenario that gives the proceedings a "private" framing moment. It is a throwback to a previous era in the odyssey of rhythm and blues when the discourse of racial authenticity called for the removal of clothing rather than the exchange of human skin for

---

45. Peter Stallybrass and Allon White, *The Politics and Poetics of Transgression* (London: Methuen, 1986).

46. Emmanuel Levinas, "The Name of a Dog, or Natural Rights" in *Difficult Freedom Essays on Judaism* (London: Athlone, 1990).

canine fur. This little drama presents Snoop in conversation with a girlfriend. He is resenting the intrusion of the public world into their space of intimacy. Their conversation makes no mention of soul, but it is the bond between them. They stick closely to a script refined on hundreds of "turn out the lights and light a candle" soul records. However, their moves are not legitimated by references to any notion of love. The dog and the bitch belong together. They are a couple but their association does not bring about sexual healing. There is no healing in their encounter for the power of sex is not at work here as a means of naturalising racial difference. Nor is the unhappy union of bodily health and racial purity being celebrated. In this bathtub, cleanliness is not next to godliness though funkiness may be. Their funky, bestial sex is not about authenticity and offers no moment of communal redemption nor any private means to stabilise the reconstructed racial self—male or female. Snoop's work exceeds the masculinist erasure of the sexual agency of black women that it does undoubtedly contain.[47]

We have seen that doggy style *style* is part of a public conversation about sex and intimacy, power, powerlessness and bodily pleasure that can be reconstructed even from the fragments of antiphonal communication that have been captured in commodity form and circulated multi-nationally on that basis. I want to end by suggesting that the ethical and political significance of Snoop's affirmation of blackness in dog-face has one more important layer. Its simultaneous questioning of humanity and proximity can be used not only to reinterpret what passes as nihilism, but also to construct an argument about the positive value of intersubjectivity in black political cultures which are now subject-centred to the point of solipsism. Snoop's dog may also point to an escape route out of the current impasse in thinking about racialised identity. Arguing against those who would deny black popular culture any philosophical and metaphysical currency, we can bring the etho-poetical qualities in his call to do it doggy style into focus by inquiring why individuals should recognise themselves as subjects of freaky sexuality and by asking about the premium that this talk about sex places on touch and the moral proximity of the other. Without wanting to supply a couple of esoteric "ethnic" footnotes in the history of the desiring subject, it seems worthwhile to try and situate Snoop's dog and the chain of equivalences in which it appears somewhere in the genealogy of techniques of the black self.

The radically alienated eroticism towards which he and his canine-identified peers direct our attention might perversely contribute some desirable ethical

---

47. It is useful to compare "Doggy Style" with the out and out misogyny of DRS and other spokesmen for gangsterdom.

grounding to the debased black public sphere. We need to talk more, not less, about sex. The "dual solitude" transmitted and celebrated in the popular trope of doing it doggy style is not about a naive or pastoral mutuality. It breaks with the monadological structure that has been instituted under the stern discipline of racial authenticity and proposes another mode of intimacy that might help to recreate a link between moral stances and vernacular metaphors of erotic, worldly love. A periodisation of the subaltern modernity which encompasses this possibility is established in the movement from "domestic allegories of political desire"[48] towards political allegories of private desire. Perhaps this conservation about sex can also rehabilitate the untimely issues of intersubjective responsibility and accountability that have been expelled from the interpretative community during the reign of ethnic absolutism and its bodily signs.

The sociality established by talk about sex culminates in an invitation to acknowledge what Zygmunt Bauman, again citing Levinas, describes as the preontological space of ethics.[49] In this setting we can call it a being *for* the other or non-being that exists prior to the racial metaphysics that currently dominates Hip hop's revolutionary conservatism. This ethical core was central to the musical cultures of the new world as they adapted sacred patterns to secular exigencies. It was undervalued and then sacrificed. Snoop, R. Kelly, S.W.V. and the rest are already playing their parts in its revitalisation. My anxiety is that the revolutionary conservatism which dominates Hip hop is likely to have limited patience with them. Revolutionary conservatism's enthusiasm for the market means that commercial achievements will be respected. However, impurity and profanity cannot be tolerated in the long run because they contribute nothing to the heroics of racial reconstruction. Authoritarians and censors can play the authenticity card too. Revolutionary conservatism. This formulation takes us immediately to the limits of our available political vocabulary. There is something explicitly revolutionary in the presentation of violence as the key principle of social and political interaction, and perhaps also in the hatreds of democracy, academicism, decadence, tepidity, weakness and softness in general that are regularly rehearsed. Conservatism is signalled loud and clear in the joyless rigidity of the gender roles that are specified in an absolutist approach to both ethics and racial particularity and, above all, in a gloomy presentation of black humanity composed of limited creatures who require tradition, pedagogy and organisation. This seems

48. Claudia Tate, *Domestic Allegories of Political Desire* (Oxford: Oxford, 1992), esp. chapters 3 and 7.

49. Zygmunt Bauman, *Postmodern Ethics* (Oxford: Blackwell, 1993), 92–98.

to go hand-in-hand with a fear and contempt of the masses. Ice Cube has reported this revealing conversation with Minister Farakhan: "Mentally, he told me, the people are babies. They are addicted to sex and violence. So if you've got medicine to give them, then put the medicine inside some soda so they get both and it won't be hard for them to digest."[50]

It is important to remember that the dangers deriving from the fusion of bio-politics and revolutionary conservatism are not to be found in Hip hop alone. Yet the conflict between them and other more democratic and emancipatory possibilities is readily visible there. Market-driven black popular culture is making politics aesthetic usually as a precondition for marketing hollow defiance. It is no longer communism that responds immodestly to this grave danger by imagining that it can politicise art but rather an insurgent intellectual practice that reacts to these fascistic perils by revealing the extent to which popular art has already been politicised in unforeseen ways.

Paul Gilroy teaches in the Sociology Department at Goldsmiths' College, University of London. He is the author of *The Black Atlantic Modernity and Double Consciousness* (Cambridge: Harvard University Press, 1993) and is currently writing a book about revolutionary conservatism and "bio-politics" in popular culture.

50. Interviewed by Ekow Eshun, *The Face* 65 (February 1994): 91.

"Can you be BLACK and Look at This?": Reading the Rodney King Video(s)

Elizabeth Alexander

> *I still carry it with me all the time. I prayed for years for it
> to be taken away, not to be able to remember it.*
>
> BETTY SHABAZZ
> on seeing Malcolm X's murder[1]
>
> *Memory resides nowhere, and in every cell.*
>
> SAUL SCHANBERG[2]

At the heart of this essay is a desire to find a language to talk about "my people." My people is, of course, romantic language, but I keep returning to it as I think about the videotaped police beating of Rodney King, wanting the term to reflect the understanding that race is a complex fiction but one that is perfectly real in significant aspects of all of our day-to-day lives.

No satisfactory terminology in current use adequately represents how I am describing a knowledge and sense of African American group identification which

The author would like to thank the group of scholars convened by Lindon Barrett at the University of California-Irvine in May, 1993, for the conference, "Contesting Boundaries in African-American Cultural Study," for their rigorous, generous commentary on an earlier version of this paper; Jonathan Stockdale for his fine research assistance; Paul Rogers, for extensive bibliographic suggestions; and *Public Culture's* editors and outside readers—especially Lauren Berlant—for their patient assistance in bringing this work to its present form.

1. Marshall Frady, "The Children of Malcolm," *The New Yorker*, October 12, 1992, 78.
2. *Natural Health*, March/April, 1993, 42.

Public Culture 1994, 7: 77–94

is more expansive than the inevitable biological reductions of race and the artifactual constraints of culture. What do black people say to each other to describe their relationship to their racial group, when that relationship is crucially forged by incidents of physical and psychic violence which boil down to the "fact" of abject blackness? Put another way, how does an incident like King's beating consolidate group affiliations by making blackness an unavoidable, irreducible sign which despite its abjection leaves creative space for group self-definition and self-knowledge?

The colloquial adoption of *tribe* seemed for a time to speak to a history and group identification that is claimed rather than merely received, and theorized by the people in that group. It seemed to speak to the group recognition and knowledge that arose as a functional aspect of the originary rupture of the Middle Passage which gave birth to the African-American in all the violent and blank possibility of the hyphen, the slash. It seemed to suggest how a group organizes memory in a way that was useful to the project here of naming the ghostly or ancestral aspect of memory that vitalizes everyday life. But tribe carries with it a history of usage which erases difference and erects limiting, patronizing ethnic constructs, and this history eclipsed my attempt to reclaim derogatory usage.[3]

The stories of violence and the subsequent responsive group knowledges and strategies are compelling even in light of the profound differences between African Americans. This essay considers the inchoate way that black people might understand themselves to be part of a larger group. I mean this more than I mean political, ethnic, subcultural or diasporic. I am talking about what it is to think of oneself, in this day and age, as having *a people*.

Black bodies in pain for public consumption have been an American national spectacle for centuries.[4] This history moves from public rapes, beatings and

---

3. I am grateful to Carol A. Breckenridge and Saidiya Hartman for helping me think about this term.

4. I say "bodies" with an understanding informed by and indebted to Hortense Spiller's provocative meditation on "body" and "flesh": "But I would make a distinction in this case between 'body' and 'flesh' and impose that distinction as the central one between captive and liberated subject-positions. In that sense, before the 'body' there is the 'flesh,' that zero degree of social conceptualization that does not escape concealment under the brush of discourse, or the reflexes of iconography. Even though the European hegemonies stole bodies — some of them female — out of West African communities in concert with the African 'middleman,' we regard this human and social irreparability as high crimes against the *flesh*, as the person of African females and African males registered the wounding. If we think of the flesh as a primary narrative, then we mean its seared, divided, ripped-apartness, riveted to the ship's hole, fallen, or 'escaped' overboard." ("Mama's Baby, Papa's Maybe: An American Grammar Book," *diacritics* Summer 1987, 67).

lynchings to the gladiatorial arenas of basketball and boxing. In the 1990s African American bodies on videotape have been the site on which national trauma — sexual harassment, date rape, drug abuse, AIDS, racial and economic urban conflict — has been dramatized. The cases I refer to here are, of course, former Washington, D. C. mayor Marion Barry's videotaped crack-smoking and subsequent arrest; the Clarence Thomas Senate hearings; Mike Tyson's rape trial; Magic Johnson and Arthur Ashe's televised press conferences about their HIV and AIDS status; and, of course, the Rodney King beating. The cycle continues as the nation today sits transfixed before the O. J. Simpson case. In each of these traumatic instances, black bodies and their attendant dramas are publicly consumed by the larger populace. White men have been the primary stagers and consumers of the historical spectacles I have mentioned, but in one way or another, black people also have been looking, forging a traumatized collective historical memory which is reinvoked at contemporary sites of conflict.[5]

What collective versions of African American male bodily history do different groups of viewers, then, bring to George Holliday's eighty-one second videotape of Rodney King being beaten by four white Los Angeles police officers while a crowd of other officers watched? When these officers were first put on trial in Simi Valley, and when the jury came back with its not guilty verdicts, what metaphorization of the black male body had to have been already in place that invoked a national historical memory (constructed by whites), a code in which African Americans are nonetheless perfectly literate?

By presenting an archive of a series of cases I articulate the ways in which a practical memory exists and crucially informs African Americans about the lived realities of how violence and its potential informs our understanding of our individual selves as a larger group. The videotaped condensation produced by Court TV of the first, Simi Valley trial[6] reveals the ways in which freeze-framing

5. Here Homi K. Bhabha's observations on rumour and panic are useful, even as he veers from my own conception of how transmission—"pass[ing] it on"—takes place: "The indeterminacy of rumour constitutes its importance as a social discourse. Its intersubjective, communal adhesiveness lies in its enunciative aspect. Its performative power of circulation results in the contagious spreading, 'an almost uncontrollable impulse to pass it on to another person'. The iterative action of rumour, its *circulation* and *contagion*, links it with panic—as one of the *affects* of insurgency. Rumour and panic are, in moments of social crises, double sites of enunciation that weave their stories around the disjunctive 'present' or the 'not-there' of discourse. . . . The indeterminate circulation of meaning as rumour or conspiracy, with its perverse, psychic affects of panic, constitutes the intersubjective realm of revolt and resistance." *The Location of Culture* (London: Routledge, 1994), 200.

6. "The 'Rodney King' Case: What the Jury Saw in *California v. Powell*," 1992, Courtroom Television Network. Courtroom proceedings cited are from this videotape.

distorted and dehistoricized the beating. It also displays how a language of black male bestiality and hyper-virility, along with myths of drug abuse and superhuman strength, were deployed during the trial. King was described as a "buffed-out" "probable ex-con," "bear-like," "like a wounded animal," "aggressive," "combative," and "equate[d] . . . with a monster." Closing defense statements continually named a "we," referring to the non-black racial composition of the Simi Valley jury. Attorney Michael Stone, speaking of Los Angeles police officers, concluded with "they don't get paid to roll around in the dirt with the likes of Rodney King." These sensationalist codes erased both Rodney King's individual bodily history within the event and a collective African American male bodily history, and supplanted it with a myth of white male victimization: hence, the statement by Sergeant Stacy Koon's laywer that "there's only one person who's in charge of this situation and that's Rodney Glenn King."

The narrative space between the nationally televised videotape and the Court TV version opens an avenue to think about what various national imaginations—primarily racially determined but also marked by region, class, gender—bring to the viewing of this episode. This space also raises questions concerning how bodily experience, both individually experienced bodily trauma as well as collective cultural trauma, comes to reside in the flesh as forms of memory reactivated and articulated at moments of collective spectatorship.

Despite the prevalence of anti-essentialist, post-identity discourses, I still believe there is a place for a bottom line. The bottom line here is that different groups possess sometimes-subconscious collective memories which are frequently forged and maintained through a storytelling tradition, however difficult that may be to pin down, as well as through individual experience. When a black man can be set on fire amidst racial epithets in the street because he inhabits a black body, as recently occurred in Florida, there must be a place for theorizing black bodily experience within the larger discourse of identity politics.

If any one aphorism can characterize the experience of black people in this country, it might be that the white-authored national narrative deliberately contradicts the histories our bodies know. There have always been narratives to justify the barbaric practices of slavery and lynching. African Americans have always existed in a countercitizen relationship to the law; how else to contend with knowing oneself as a whole human being when the Constitution defined one as three-fifths? The American way with regard to the actual lived experience of African Americans has been to write a counternarrative which erased bodily information as we knew it and substituted a countertext which in many cases has become a version of national memory.

Some sympathetic white colleagues discussing the King beating anxiously exempt themselves from the category of oppressor, even when they have not been placed there, by saying that they too were nauseated and traumatized by watching the beating. This is no doubt true, but it is not my interest here. The far more potent terrain is the one that allows us to explore the ways in which traumatized African American viewers have been taught a sorry lesson of their continual physical vulnerability in the United States that concurrently helps shape how to understand ourselves as a "we," even when that we is differentiated. The King beating, and the anguished court cases and insurrections which followed, reminded us that there is such a thing as *bottom line blackness* with regard to the violence which erases other differentiations and highlights race.

Two other cases help describe the way the Rodney King videotape was experienced as an aftershock, an event in an open series of national events: nineteenth-century slave accounts of witnessed violence and the 1955 lynching of Emmett Till. These cases help us understand how, to use the Biblical phrase James Baldwin has already deployed, "the evidence of things not seen" is crucial to understanding what African American spectators bring to the all-too-visible texts at hand of spectacular slave violence and the story of a brutalized Emmett Till.

A Witness and a Participant

What do the scenes of communally witnessed violence in slave narratives tell us about the way that text is inscribed in African American flesh? Witnessing can be aural as well as ocular. Furthermore, those who receive stories become witnesses once removed, but witnesses nonetheless. Frederick Douglass, in his 1845 narrative, recalls watching a beating at the hands of his first master, Captain Anthony:

> He would at times seem to take great pleasure in whipping a slave. I
> have often been awakened at the dawn of day by the most heart-rending
> of shrieks of an own aunt of mine, whom he used to tie up to a joist,
> and whip upon her naked back till she was literally covered with blood.
> No words, no tears, no prayers, from his gory victim, seemed to move
> his iron heart from its bloody purpose. The louder she screamed, the
> harder he whipped; and where the blood ran fastest, there he whipped
> longest. He would whip her to make her scream, and whip her to make
> her hush; and not until overcome by fatigue, would he cease to swing
> the blood-clotted cowskin. I remember the first time I ever witnessed

this horrible exhibition. I was quite a child, but I well remember it. I shall never forget it whilst I remember any thing. It was the first of a long series of such outrages, of which I was doomed to be a witness and a participant. It struck me with awful force. It was the blood-stained gate, the entrance to the hell of slavery, through which I was about to pass. It was a most terrible spectacle. I wish I could commit to paper the feelings with which I beheld it.[7]

Douglass's repetition of "he whipped" and its variations replicates the falling of the awful blows. The staccato, structurally unvaried, repetitive sentences toward the end of the passage, in contrast to the liquid syntax of other parts of the book, reveal Douglass increasingly at a loss for words to describe what he has witnessed. More specifically, he can scarcely articulate what it means for that visual narrative to become forever a part of his consciousness. Yet, what linguistically knits this passage together at its close is the phrase, "I remember," repeated three times. Douglass feels "doomed to be both a witness and a participant." The tableau "struck" him with the same "awful force" of the blows. At the passage's close, he experiences a birthing of sorts as he travels through the "blood-stained gate," his body brought into the realization of itself as vulnerable and black.

On the next page, Douglass describes his Aunt Hester being whipped:

[A]fter rolling up his sleeves, he commenced to lay on the heavy cow-skin, and soon the warm, red blood (amid heart-rending shrieks from her, and horrid oaths from him) came dripping to the floor. I was so terrified and horror-stricken at the sight, that I hid myself in a closet, and dared not venture out till long after the bloody transaction was over. I expected it would be my turn next. It was all new to me. I had never seen anything like it before. (52)

One of course can not *see* that blood runs "warm"; Douglass's synesthetic response is instantly empathetic, and the memory is recorded in a vocabulary of known bodily sensation. He imbibes the experience, which is metaphorically imprinted upon his now traumatized flesh in the shrieks experienced as "heart-rending" and which left him "horror-stricken." The mere sound of the voice of the overseer, who in the previous sentence Douglass has described as "whip[ping] a woman, causing the blood to run a half hour at a time," is "enough to chill the blood and

7. Frederick Douglass, *Narrative of the Life of Frederick Douglass, An American Slave* (1845), edited with an introduction by Houston A. Baker, Jr. (New York: Penguin Books, 1982), 51.

stiffen the hair of an ordinary man" (55). Once again, these corporeal images of terror suggest that "experience" can be taken into the body via witnessing and recorded in memory as knowledge. This knowledge is necessary to one who believes "it would be my turn next." The knowledge of that violence and his vulnerability to it is, paradoxically, the armor which can take him out of the closet in which he has hidden but which he must inevitably leave. For if nothing else, the horrors of slavery were no longer "new" to him; from this point in the text forward, he would figure his way out of that institution.

In Harriet Jacobs' *Incidents in the Life of a Slave Girl*, protagonist Linda Brent's response to witnessed violence contrasts sharply with the response of white spectators.[8] Mrs. Flint, for example, "could sit in her easy chair, and see a woman whipped, till the blood trickled from every stroke of the lash" (12). But when Brent watches a fellow slave tied to a joist and whipped, "I shall never forget that night. Never before, in my life, had I heard hundreds of blows fall, in succession, on a human being. His piteous groans, and his 'O, pray don't massa,' rang in my ear for months afterwards" (13). Hearing, too, is central to witnessing. Sounds here haunt the mind as much as visual images. In this regard, the freeze-framed Simi Valley videotape, stripped of a soundtrack in which falling blows and bystanders' screams are audible, disallows the possibility that the sounds of terror could imprint themselves on the jury's mind. When Brent sees someone sold away from his mother—not physical violence, precisely, but emotional torture—she writes, "could you have seen that mother clinging to her child, when they fastened the irons upon his wrist; could you have heard the heart-rending groans, and seen her bloodshot eyes wander wildly from face to face, vainly pleading for mercy; could you have witnessed that scene as I saw it, you would exclaim, *Slavery is damnable!*" (23) As in Douglass, "heart-rending" and "bloodshot" work both literally and metaphorically to show the ways the body has a language which "speaks" what it has witnessed. Brent speaks here to white women readers, exhorting them to reject Mrs. Flint's perspective and assume instead her own, the perspective of a witness rather than a spectator.

In *The History of Mary Prince*, violence which is witnessed is quickly followed in the narrative by violence to Prince herself.[9] She understands that what happens to another threatens *her*:

[handwritten margin note: this conflates the witness and the juror — what matters here is the conflation of "experience" with "evidence"]

8. Harriett A. Jacobs, *Incidents in the Life of a Slave Girl* (1861), L. Maria Child, edited with an introduction by Jean Fagan Yellin (Cambridge: Harvard University Press, 1987).
9. *The History of Mary Prince, A West Indian Slave. Related by Herself* (1831), edited by Moira Ferguson, with a preface by Ziggi Alexander (London: Pandora, 1987). Further citations will be made parenthetically.

Both my master and mistress seemed to think that they had a right to
ill-use [the slave boys] at their pleasure; and very often accompanied
their commands with blows, whether the children were behaving well
or ill. I have seen their flesh ragged and raw with licks. Lick-lick—they
were never secure one moment from a blow, and their lives were
passed in continual fear. My mistress was not content with using the
whip, but often pinched their cheeks and arms in the most cruel manner. My pity for these poor boys was soon transferred to myself; for I
was licked, and flogged, and pinched by her pitiless fingers in the neck
and arms, exactly as they were. To strip me naked—to hang me up by
the wrists and lay my flesh open with the cow-skin, was an ordinary
punishment for even a slight offence. (56)

To have "pity" for the boys is transferred to Prince herself; she understands her
safety is as threatened as theirs. The repetition here of variations on "lick" again
recalls the mimetic effect seen in the Douglass passage, but more so, it emphasizes
Prince's artifice in constructing the violent spectacle. The narrative time of the
event is slowed down, knit together with homophonic words like "ill," "pinched,"
"pity," "pitiless," "fingers," "strip," and "wrist," and framed. Prince artfully makes
a stylized tableau that her readers can more empathically experience.

Prince then watches a pregnant woman, Hetty, whipped over and over again:

The consequence was that poor Hetty was brought to bed before her
time, and was delivered after severe labor of a dead child. She appeared to recover after her confinement, so far that she was repeatedly
flogged by both master and mistress afterwards; but her former strength
never returned to her. Ere long her body and limbs swelled to a great
size; and she lay on a mat in the kitchen, till the water burst out of her
and she died. All the slaves said that death was a good thing for poor
Hetty; but I cried very much for her death. The manner of it filled me
with horror. I could not bear to think about it; yet it was always present
to my mind for many a day. (57)

After this litany, you might say, of course these scenes of horror would stay
forever with those who saw them, knowing as they did that their fate was bound
up in a system of domination and violence to bodies and to memory. But I am
building here a case for a collective memory that rests in the present moment,
which was activated by watching the King videotape, but which has been constructed as much by storytelling in multiple media as by personal, actual experi-

ence. The conundrum of being unable to "bear to think about" something which is "always present to my mind" is precisely the legacy wrought by state-sanctioned violence against African Americans such as the Rodney King beating. To see is unbearable, both unto itself as well as for what is means about one's own likely fate. But knowledge of this pervasive violence provides necessary information of the very real forces threatening African Americans. In the absence of first-person witnessing, the stories are passed along so that everyone knows the parameters in which their bodies move.

Responses of poor and working-class Angelenos of color to the Rodney King videotape augment this point. Rodney King was beaten by officers of the Los Angeles Police Department who specifically embody the state as experienced in the day-to-day lives of the people who made the following three statements reported in the newspaper, *Revolutionary Worker*:

> You know where I was when I first heard about the verdict? I was lay-ing down in my bed asleep and when I heard the words not guilty on my TV I instantly woke up. It was a pain that went from the top of my head to the tip of my toes. It was an empty, hollow feeling. It was a rage inside of me, burning. I wanted to kill. I wanted to kill.

> By the time they was done I needed 28 stitches in my head. When I saw the Rodney King video I thought of myself laying on the ground and getting beat. I felt the same way all our people felt when we blew up.

> Somebody brought a video to school—the video of Rodney King—and then somebody put it on the television and then everybody just started to break windows and everything—then some people got so mad they broke the television.[10]

Again, the violence that is watched, this time on the television, is experienced, as it were, in the bodies of the spectators who feel themselves implicated in Rodney King's fate. The language employed by the first person is a corporeal one, "heard" and then experienced in his nervous system as "a pain that went from the top of my head to the tip of my toes." The entire body responds. More dramatically, the second speaker abandons simile; he himself "needed 28 stitches" and felt himself "laying on the ground and getting beat." The third speaker makes

10. Michael Slate, *Shockwaves: Report from the L.A. Rebellion* (Chicago: Revolutionary Worker, 1993).

the explicit connection between a sense of collective violation and consequent physical response. The video is seen in school, a community. This community acts without hesitation and, according to this account, in tandem and agreement that a violation has taken place in which the entire community is implicated, and which demands a physical response.

Hortense Spillers writes: "These undecipherable markings on the captive body render a kind of hieroglyphics of the flesh whose severe disjunctures come to be hidden to the cultural seeing by skin color. We might well ask if this phenomenon of marking and branding actually 'transfers' from one generation to another, finding its various *symbolic substitutions* in an efficacy of meanings that repeat the initiating moments?"[11] Haile Gerima's film *Sankofa* asks audiences to regard the connections between an African American present, an African past, and the space of slavery between. A persistent motif of the film's plantation scenes is eyes which watch black comrades being beaten, raped, terrorized, killed. Little is said in these scenes in which the violent legacy is passed along, but Gerima's camera sees eyes everywhere, eyes watching in eloquent, legible witness.

Emmett Till

> the avid insistence of detail
> pretending insight or information
> the length of gash across the dead boy's loins
> his grieving mother's lamentation
> the severed lips, how many burns
> his gouged out eyes
> sewed shut upon the screaming covers
> louder than life
> all over
> the veiled warning, the secret relish
> of a black child's mutilated body.
>
> AUDRE LORDE[12]

Here is the story in summary: In August 1955, in Money, Mississippi, a fourteen-year old Chicago black boy named Emmett Till, nicknamed Bobo, was visiting

11. Spillers, "Mama's Baby," 67.
12. Audre Lorde, "Afterimages," in *Chosen Poems Old and New* (New York: W. W. Norton and Company, 1982), 104.

relatives and was shot in the head and thrown in the river with a mammoth cotton gin fan tied around his neck, for allegedly whistling at a white woman.[13] In some versions of the story, he was found with his cut-off penis stuffed in his mouth. His body was shipped to Chicago and his mother decided he should have an open casket funeral; the whole world would see what had been done to her son. According to the Chicago-based, black news weekly *Jet*, "more than 600,000, in an unending procession, later viewed the body" at the funeral home.[14] A photograph of Till in the casket—his head mottled and swollen many times its normal size—ran in *Jet*, and largely through that medium, both the picture and Till's story became legendary. The caption of the close-up photograph of Till's face read: "Mutilated face of victim was left unretouched by mortician at the mother's request. She said she wanted 'all the world' to witness the atrocity" (*Jet*, 8).

Emmett Till's story has inspired entire works such as Bebe Moore Campbell's *Your Blues Ain't Like Mine*, Toni Morrison's play, *Dreaming Emmett* and Gwendolyn Brooks's famous pair of poems, "A Bronzeville Mother Loiters in Mississippi. Meanwhile, a Mississippi Mother Burns Bacon" and "The Last Quatrain of the Ballad of Emmett Till" and Audre Lorde's poem, "Afterimages" (quoted above). The lasting impact of the photograph and the story is also illustrated in several autobiographical accounts.[15] In Anne Moody's memoir, *Coming of Age in Mississippi*, she writes:

Up until his death I had heard of Negroes found floating in a river or dead somewhere with their bodies riddled with bullets. But I didn't know the mystery behind these killings then. I remember once when I was only seven I heard Mama and one of my aunts talking about some Negro who had been beaten to death. "Just like them low-down skunks killed him they will do the same to us."[16]

Charlayne Hunter-Gault remembers the killing in her autobiography, *In My Place*:

13. Accounts of the fan's weight vary between seventy-five and 150 pounds.
14. *Jet*, 8, 19 (1955): 8.
15. James Baldwin astutely places the attention on Till's murder in context: "The *only* reason, after all, that we have heard of Emmett Till is that he happened to come whistling down the road—an obscure country road—at the very moment the road found itself most threatened: at the very beginning of the segration-desegregation—not yet integration—crisis, under the knell of the Supreme Court's *all deliberate speed*, when various "moderate" Southern governors were asking Black people to segregate themselves, *for the good of both races*, and when the President of the United States was, on this subject, so eloquently silent that one *knew* that, in his heart, he did not approve of a mongrelization of the races." *The Evidence of Things Not Seen* (New York: Holt, Rinehart, and Winston, 1985), 40–41.
16. Anne Moody, *Coming of Age in Mississippi* (New York: The Dial Press, 1968), 104.

From time to time, things happened that intruded on our protected reality. The murder of Emmett Till was one such instance. It happened in August, 1955, and maybe because he was more or less our age, it gripped us in a way that perhaps even the lynching of an older Black man might not have. "It was the first time we'd known a young person to die," recalled Wilma, who, like me, was then entering eighth grade. For both of us, pictures of his limp, watersoaked body in the newspapers and in *Jet*, Black America's weekly news bible, were worse than any image we had ever seen outside of a horror movie. . . . None of us could ever forget the haunting gray image of the dead and waterlogged young boy; we just put it on hold."[17]

Shelby Steele writes of the murder in an autobiographical essay:

The single story that sat atop the pinnacle of racial victimization for us was that of Emmett Till, the Northern black teenager who, on a visit to the South in 1955, was killed and grotesquely mutilated for supposedly looking at or whistling at (we were never sure which, though we argued the point endlessly) a white woman. Oh, how we probed his story, finding in his youth and Northern upbringing the quintessential embodiment of black innocence, brought down by a white evil so portentous and apocalyptical, so gnarled and hideous, that it left us with a feeling not far from awe. By telling his story and others like it, we came to *feel* the immutability of our victimization, its utter indigenousness, as a thing on this earth like dirt or sand or water.[18]

For black writers of a certain age, and perhaps of a certain region, a certain proximity to Southern roots, Emmett Till's story is a touchstone. It was the basis for a rite of passage that indoctrinated these young people into understanding the vulnerability of their own black bodies, coming of age, and the way in which their fate was interchangeable with Till's. It also was a step in the consolidation of their understanding of themselves as black in America. It is in this regard that black women have taken the story to be emblematic, though Till's fate was carried out in the name of stereotypical black male sexuality. These passages show how storytelling works to create collective countermemory of trauma as those stories also terrorize.

17. Charlayne Hunter-Gault, *In My Place* (New York: Farrar Straus Giroux, 1992), 116–117.
18. Shelby Steele, "On Being Black and Middle-Class," *Commentary*, January 1988, 43.

In Muhammad Ali's autobiography, *The Greatest*, Till's murder is a formative touchstone of young Cassius Clay's adolescence:

93

**Reading the Rodney
King Video(s)**

> Emmett Till and I were about the same age. A week after he was mur-
> dered in Sunflower County, Mississippi, I stood on the corner with a
> gang of boys, looking at pictures of him in the black newspapers and
> magazines. In one he was laughing and happy. In the other, his head
> was swollen and bashed in, his eyes bulging out of their sockets and his
> mouth twisted and broken. His mother had done a bold thing. She re-
> fused to let him be buried until hundreds and thousands marched past
> his open casket in Chicago and looked down at his mutilated body. I
> felt a deep kinship to him when I learned he was born the same year
> and day that I was. My father and I talked about it at night and drama-
> tized the crime. I couldn't get Emmett out of my mind until one evening
> I thought of a way to get back at white people for his death. That night
> I sneaked out of my house and walked down to Ronnie King's and told
> him my plan. It was late at night when we reached the old railroad sta-
> tion on Louisville's East Side. I remember a poster of a thin white man
> in striped pants and a top hat who pointed at us above the words Uncle
> Sam wants you. We stopped and hurled stones at it, and then broke into
> the shoeshine boy's shed and stole two iron shoe rests and took them to
> the railroad tracks. We planted them deep on the tracks and waited.
> When a big blue diesel engine came around the bend, it hit the shoe
> rests and pushed them nearly thirty feet before one of the wheels locked
> and sprang from the track. I remember the loud sound of the ties rip-
> ping up. I broke out running, Ronnie behind me, and then I looked
> back. I'll never forget the eyes of the man in the poster, staring at us:
> Uncle Sam wants you. It took two days to get up enough nerve to go
> back there. A work crew was still cleaning up the debris. And the man
> in the poster was still pointing. I always knew that sooner or later he
> would confront me, and I would confront him.[19]

Seeing the picture of the dead boy's ruined body makes young Cassius feel "a
deep kinship." He and his father "dramatize the crime," which, like the young
people quoted in the *Revolutionary Worker* who saw the King tape in school
and smashed the television, became a catalyst for action. The train symbolizes

19. Muhammad Ali, *The Greatest* (New York: Random House, 1975), 34–35.

commerce and technology, the unrealized dreams of black migration north as well as the reverse migration south which got Till killed. Clay responds not with the legendary pulchritude of his bare, magnificent body, but rather with stone — a tool from nature — and the iron shoe rests. In destroying the shoeshine rests he destroys an enduring symbol of black servitude. The iron shoe rest of the black shoeshine "boy" and all it stands for is both a tool for destruction and is symbolically destroyed. Clay undercuts his physical might, the mythology of Douglass whipping Covey, acknowledging that no black male body alone can triumph over consolidated white male might. The looming Uncle Sam Wants You poster allows Clay to articulate in the incident a relationship between himself and state power.

We remember Till because of all that his story embodies, and because of the horror burned into our nightmares and imaginations with the photograph. Till's body was disfigured but still a body that can be imagined as kin to, but nonetheless distinct, from our own. The focus in American narratives of violence against blacks in the popular imagination is usually male. The whipped male slave, the lynched man, Emmett Till, Rodney King: all of these are familiar and explicit in the popular imagination. Black boys and men present a particular kind of physical threat in the white American imagination, a threat that must be contained. Countless stories of violence are made spectacular in order to let black people know who is in control, such as when Louisiana Ku Klux Klansmen in the 1940s tied bodies of lynched black men to the fronts of their cars and drove them through crowds of black children.[20] Thus, while black men are contained when these images are made public, black viewers are taking in evidence that provides ground for collective identification with trauma. The Emmett Till narratives illustrate how, in order to survive, black people have paradoxically had to witness their own murder and defilement and then pass along the epic tale of violation.

Rodney King

> Outside the door of no return, our arms linked
> from habit, a vendor spies the pain. Don't
> cry, he says. It wasn't you or me. It's just
>
> history. It's all over.
>
> EISA DAVIS[21]

20. This is an anecdote that was told to me by a teacher at Dunbar High School in Chicago in April of 1993, but there are many, many such stories which circulate in black communities and discourse.

21. Eisa Davis, "Maison Des Esclaves, Goree Island, Senegal" (Unpublished poem).

An article in the February 2, 1993 *New York Times* described life for the four Los Angeles police officers as they awaited their second trial, after being acquitted in the Simi Valley trial of violating Rodney King.[22] Sergeant Stacy Koon, who was "in charge" on the night of the beating, says he has just been declared "psychologically disabled" for work and lists the physical disorders he says have plagued him since the incident: trouble sleeping, "stomach problems," "high blood pressure," and teeth grinding. His days are now spent poring over some 17,000 pages of trial testimony and watching, over and over and over again, the tape of the beating on a big-screen television in his living room. He takes the tape on speaking tours, he projects it on different walls at home, he demands that visitors watch it and listen to his narrative:

> There's 82 seconds of use of force on this tape, and there's thirty frames per second. There's like 2,500 frames on this tape and I've looked at every single one of them not once but a buzillion times, and the more I look at the tape the more I see in it. . . . When I started playing this tape, and I started blowing it up to ten inches, like I'd blow it up on the wall right behind you here, fill up the whole wall over the stairwell, and all of a sudden, this thing came to life! You blow it up to full size for people, or even half size, if you see Rodney King four feet tall in that picture as opposed to three inches, boy, you see a whole bunch of stuff. . . . He's like a bobo doll. Ever hit one? Comes back and forth, back and forth. That's exactly what he's doing. Get him down on the ground. Prone is safe. Up is not. That is what we're trying to do is keep him on the ground, because if he gets up it's going to be a deadly force situation. . . . This [new trial] is going to be fun. This is high comedy.

Koon creates a narrative to justify his authority, and the more he sees it, the more he believes it. He watches it over and over, larger and larger, yet he does not see himself physically magnified as he does King. For different reasons, in these moments of collective trauma, to use the words of the visual artist Adrian Piper, white and black spectators "pretend not to know what you know,"[23] both for self-justification and psychic survival. Many narratives were created to de-

22. Seth Mydans, "Their Lives Consumed, Officers Await 2d Trail," *New York Times*, February 2, 1993, A9.

23. Adrian Piper, *Pretend* (New York: John Weber Gallery, 1990).

scribe the same eighty-one seconds of videotape, and vast amounts of energy and cultural memory were expended to preserve these versions of the truth.

The concept of videotaped national memory was crucial to the Rodney King beating and subsequent Los Angeles riot/insurrection. Videotaped footage of the black teenager Latasha Harlins being shot to death by a Korean shopkeeper preceded King; white motorist Reginald Denny being pulled from his truck and beaten by several African American men during the disturbances formed the other video bookend. The videotape of Desiree Washington dancing in her beauty pageant the day after she was raped by Mike Tyson was used to attempt to prove that she could not possibly have been violated. Videotape imprints constructed bodily histories on a jury's consciousness, and, in a national arena amplifies or denies the story an African American body appears to be telling.

The defense in the Simi Valley trial employed familiar language of black bestiality to construct Rodney King as a threat to the officers. The lawyers also slowed down the famous videotape so that it no longer existed in "real time" but rather in a slow dance of stylized movement that could as easily be read as self-defense or as a threat. The slowed-down tape recorded neither the sound of falling blows nor the screams from King and the witnesses. The movement existed frame by frame rather than in real time.[24] The rabidly conservative Rush Limbaugh utilized the same technique on his television show, when he played a snippet of the tape over and over and over again until it *did* look like Rodney King was advancing on the police officers, and there was no context for the movement. There is something compulsive, manipulative and dishonest about Limbaugh and Koon watching over and over and over again the same piece of film and using it to consolidate a self-justifying narrative.

Black artists have invoked Rodney King's beating in different ways. Spike Lee opens *Malcolm X* with the videotape; Portia Cobb's own videotape invokes the beating with repeated tapping noises juxtaposed with young people of color discussing the case and police brutality; Branford Marsalis's saxophone wails as many times as police batons landed on King's body.[25] These artists each responded to King's beating in different ways, but all resisted the documentary form that dehistoricizes both the body and the event. These artistic examples mitigate against

24. Others have discussed the phenomenon. See especially "The Rules of the Game," Patricia J. Williams in *Reading Rodney King*, ed. Robert Gooding-Williams (New York: Routledge, 1993), 51–55 and "Picture Imperfect," Patricia Greenfield and Paul Kibbey, *New York Times*, April 1, 1993, A-15.

25. Portia Cobb, "No Justice, No Peace," 1993.

a history of narratives of dominion which attempt to talk black people out of what their bodies know.

Pat Ward Williams, while not responding to King, nonetheless questions the ways in which documentary photography has inadequately represented black life. She also questions the role of the photographer and his failure to *act* as witness. In "Accused/Blowtorch/Padlock," she reinscribes an African-American narrative onto a photograph of a man being lynched, which she found in *The Best of Life Magazine*.[26] Her handwritten narrative–crammed within and practically spilling over the frame–begins with her sense of trouble, "something is going on here," "I didn't see it right away." It also expresses her sense of wanting not to believe that the picture tells the story it does, not simply the overt story of a lynching but the far more troubling story of the complicity of the photographer, who watches but does not witness, who perpetuates, who is then in effect part of the lynch mob.

Williams invokes collective memory in three ways. She says that "*Life* magazine published this picture," and then, "Who took this picture?" "*Life* answers– Page 141–no credit." *Life* magazine has become life itself, and the irony of a refusal to attribute agency or take responsibility for the crime committed. She says, "could Hitler show pictures of the Holocaust to keep the Jews in line?" And then, with the line, "Can you be BLACK and look at this?" she forces viewers to confront the idea of memory that would indelibly affect the very way that someone sees what is before them. Williams's reframing of the picture, the slowing down of the narrative action and blowing up of individual parts, is the same technique with a remarkably different purpose than the reconstructions by Court TV or Rush Limbaugh of the King video. The close-up of the image emphasizes the chains biting at the flesh, pulling the arms practically out of the socket, pulling against the chains away from the tree. She writes, "he doesn't look lynched yet . . .WHO took this picture? Couldn't he just as easily let the man go? Did he take his camera and then come back with a blowtorch?" Then the narrative breaks into anguished grammatical fragments reminiscent of passages cited above from slave narratives. "Where do you torture someone BURN off an ear? Melt an eye? A screaming mouth How can this photograph exist?"

26. Pat Ward Williams,"Accused/Blowtorch/Padlock," 1986, mixed media, photograph, silkscreen, 60x100," in *The Decade Show: Frameworks of Identity in the 1980s* (New York: Museum of Contemporary Hispanic Art, The New Museum of Contemporary Art, The Studio Museum in Harlem, 1990), plate XC.

Williams's final plea, "Somebody do something," is a call to action. Both Williams and the lawyers for the police officers felt the need, for drastically different reasons, to overlay and articulate their version of the collective narrative on the public text. Williams's work asks the questions: What do people do with their history of horror? What does it mean to bear witness in the act of watching a retelling? What does it mean to carry cultural memory in the flesh? She shows how to work with images that many would rather forget, and she shows why such images need to be remembered.

Elizabeth Alexander teaches in the English Department at the University of Chicago. She is the author of *The Venus Hottentot* (University Press of Virginia, 1990) and is working on a book about black masculinity and a second collection of poems, *Body of Life*.

PHOTO ESSAYS

Hope Reclaimed:
South African Elections, May 1994

Refuge Refused:
Haitians, Borders and Democracy

The Sun shall never set on so glorious a

human achievement.

Never, never, and never again shall it be that this beautiful

land will again experience the oppression of one by another

and suffer the indignity of being the skunk of the world.

Nelson Mandela, Inaugural Speech, Pretoria, May 10, 1994

At Cape Town's Grand Parade, the day before the inauguration in

Pretoria, Nelson Mandela addressed a crowd from a balcony of City

Hall. His speech followed reconciliatory scenes in the Houses of

Parliament, when for the first time Black South Africans took their seats

as members of Parliament to elect a president. Unless otherwise noted,

these photographs were taken at this pre-inaugural celebration in the

heart of Cape Town.

© Carol A. Breckenridge

Hope Reclaimed:

South African Elections May 1994

© Fernando Coronil

Democracy is based on the majority

principle . . . at the same time democracy also

requires that the rights of political and other

minorities be safeguarded.

Nelson Mandela, Cape Town Address, May 9, 1994

Perhaps it was history that ordained that it be here, the Cape of Good

Hope, that we should lay the foundation stone of our new nation. For it

was here at this Cape, over three centuries ago, that there began the

fateful convergence of the peoples of Africa, Europe and Asia on

these shores.

Nelson Mandela, Cape Town Address, May 9, 1994

"You see, when you are improvising, you are free. But I'm telling you, you've got to learn to be free. You've got to struggle hard for that freedom."

From Njabulo Ndebele's short story "Uncle" in *Fools* (1983).

Children in the Chris
Hani squatter camp,
Frauschhock, outside
Cape Town, May 1994.

© Carol A. Breckenridge

So here we were at last: thirty years before, we had left as South

Africans, and we were now returning as "foreigners."

Lewis Nkosi, *TLS*, April 1, 1994, p. 5.

Public Culture 1994, 7: 96–101

© Len Kaminsky

Refuge Refused:

Haitians,

Borders

and

Democracy

New York City, Spring 1993.
Haitians and their supporters
protest at Immigration and
Naturalization Headquarters
against Clinton's interdiction
policy.

Left: Krome Detention Center, Miami, 1985. Right: Miami, 1985.

Opposite: Krome Detention Center, Miami, 1985/6. A woman waits with a friend hoping to see her husband, who had been detained for eighteen months. Then and until August 1994, Cuban boat people have been released within forty-eight hours, while Haitians are commonly detained or interdicted at sea and returned to Haiti.

Photograph © Len Kaminsky

Len Kaminsky was Assistant Director of the Haitian Refugee Center in Miami (1984–1988) and is now involved in organizing the New York-based Haitian American Legal Defense and Educational Fund to protect the civil rights of Haitians in the United States.

Public Culture 1994, 7: 102–104

Washington, D.C., 1993. Haitians demonstrate to
support Aristide and demand the release of HIV-positive
Haitians interned at Guantanamo Naval Base.

Krome Detention Center,
Miami, 1985/6. Citizens of
Dade United protest "illegal"
refugees and the Rodino Bill
which allowed for the
adjustment of Haitian refugees
from illegal to legal status.
(SALAD: Spanish American
League Against Discrimination)

Negotiating and Transforming the Public Sphere: African American Political Life in the Transition from Slavery to Freedom

Elsa Barkley Brown

On April 15, 1880, Margaret Osborne, Jane Green, Susan Washington, Molly Branch, Susan Gray, Mary A. Soach and "over two hundred other prominent sisters of the church" petitioned the Richmond, Virginia, First African Baptist Church's business meeting to allow women to vote on the pastor:

> We the sisters of the church feeling that we are interested in the welfare
> of the same and also working hard to finish the house and have been
> working by night and day . . . We know you have adopted a law in the
> church that the business must be done by the male members. We don't
> desire to alter that law, nor do we desire to have anything to do with
> the business of the church, we only ask to have a vote in electing or dis-

An earlier version of this paper was presented at "The Black Public Sphere in the Reagan-Bush Era Conference," Chicago Humanities Institute, University of Chicago in October 1993, where I benefitted from the comments of Kenneth Warren and the discussion of the conference participants. Thanks also to Carol A. Breckenridge and to two anonymous reviewers for their comments, and to Nataki H Goodall for her critical eye and unflagging support. The writing of this essay was facilitated by a research leave from the University of Michigan and research fellowships at the W.E.B. Du Bois Institute for Afro-American Research, Harvard University; and the Virginia Center for the Humanities.

Public Culture 1994, 7: 107–146

missing him. We whose names are attached to this petition ask you to grant us this privilege.[1]

The circumstances surrounding these women's petition suggest the kinds of changes taking place internally in late-nineteenth and early-twentieth century black Richmond and other southern black communities. In the immediate post-Civil War era women had voted in mass meetings and Republican Party conventions held at First African, thus contradicting gender-based assumptions within the larger society about politics, political engagement and appropriate forms of political behavior. Now, women sitting in the same church were petitioning for the right to vote in an internal community institution, couching the petition in terms designed to minimize the request and avoid a challenge to men's authority and position.

Scholars' assumptions of an unbroken line of exclusion of African American women from formal political associations in the late-nineteenth century has obscured fundamental changes in the political understandings within African American communities in the transition from slavery to freedom. Women in First African and in other arenas were seeking in the late-nineteenth century not a new authority but rather a lost authority, one they now often sought to justify on a distinctively female basis. As these women petitioned for their rights within the church and as other women formed voluntary associations in turn-of-the-century Richmond they were not, as often depicted in the scholarly literature, emerging into the political arena through such actions. Rather these women were attempting to retain space they traditionally had held in the immediate post-emancipation period. This essay explores the processes of public discourse within Richmond and other southern black communities and the factors which led to increasingly more clearly gendered and class spaces within those communities to understand why women by the 1880s and 1890s needed to create their own pulpits from which to speak—to restore their voices to the community. This exploration suggests how the ideas, process, meanings and practice of freedom changed within late-nineteenth-century southern African American communities and what the implications of those changes may be for our visions of freedom and for the possibilities of African American community in the late-twentieth century.

1. Petition of Mrs. Margaret Osborne, et al. To the deacons and members of the First Baptist Church, April 15, 1880, recorded in First African Baptist Church, Richmond City, Minutes, Book II, June 27, 1880 (microfilm), Archives, Virginia State Library and Archives, Richmond, Virginia (hereafter cited as FABC).

After emancipation, African American men, women and children, as part of black communities throughout the South struggled to define on their own terms the meaning of freedom and in the process to construct communities of struggle. Much of the literature on Reconstruction portrays freed African Americans as rapidly and readily adopting a gendered private-public dichotomy.[2] Much of the literature on the nineteenth-century public sphere constructs a masculine liberal bourgeois public with a female counterpublic.[3] This essay, focusing on the civic geography of post-Civil War black Richmond suggests the problematic of applying such generalizations to African American life in the late-nineteenth century South. In the immediate post-emancipation era black Richmonders enacted their understandings of democratic political discourse through mass meetings attended and participated in (including voting) by men, women and children and through mass participation in Republican Party conventions. They carried these notions of political participation into the state Capitol engaging from the gallery in the debates on the constitutional convention floor.

2. The idea of the immediate adoption of a gendered public-private dichotomy pervades much of the historical literature on post-Civil War black communities. It is most directly argued by Jacqueline Jones: "the vitality of the political process, tainted though it was by virulent racial prejudice and violence, provided black men with a public forum distinct from the private sphere inhabited by their womenfolk. Black men predominated in this arena because, like other groups in nineteenth-century America, they believed that males alone were responsible for—and capable of—the serious business of politicking," *Labor of Love, Labor of Sorrow: Black Women, Work, and the Family from Slavery to the Present* (New York: Basic Books, 1985), 66. But it is also an accepted tenet of otherwise rigorous analyses such as Eric Foner, *Reconstruction: America's Unfinished Revolution 1863–1877* (New York: Harper and Row, 1988), esp. 87.

3. Many recent discussions of the public sphere among U.S. scholars have orbited around the work of Jürgen Habermas whose 1962 *Strukturwandel der Öffentlichkeit* was published in 1989 in English as *The Structural Transformation of the Public Sphere: An Inquiry into a Category of Bourgeois Society*, trans. Thomas Burger with assistance of Frederick Lawrence (Cambridge: MIT Press). See also, Jürgen Habermas, "The Public Sphere: An Encyclopedia Article (1964)," *New German Critique* 1 (Fall 1974): 49–55. Critics who have emphasized the masculine bias in the liberal bourgeois public sphere and posited a female counterpublic include Nancy Fraser, "Rethinking the Public Sphere: A Contribution to the Critique of Actually Existing Democracy" and Mary Ryan, "Gender and Public Access: Women's Politics in Nineteenth-Century America," both in *Habermas and the Public Sphere*, ed. Craig Calhoun (Cambridge: MIT Press, 1992), 109–142 and 259–289, respectively. See also, Nancy Fraser, "What's Critical About Critical Theory? The Case of Habermas and Gender," in Nancy Fraser, *Unruly Practices: Power, Discourse, and Gender in Contemporary Social Theory* (Minneapolis: University of Minnesota Press, 1989); Mary Ryan, *Women in Public: Between Banners and Ballots, 1825–1880* (Baltimore: John Hopkins University Press, 1990); Joan B. Landes, *Women and the Public Sphere in the Age of the French Revolution* (Ithaca: Cornell University Press, 1988); Rita Felski, *Beyond Feminist Aesthetics: Feminist Literature and Social Change* (Cambridge: Harvard University Press, 1989), 154–182. Focusing on contemporary politics, Iris Marion Young offers a critique of an ideal public sphere in which the universal citizen is not only masculine but also white and bourgeois, *Justice and the Politics of Difference* (Princeton: Princeton University Press, 1990).

Central to African Americans' construction of a fully democratic notion of political discourse was the church as a foundation of the black public sphere.[4] In the post-slavery era, church buildings also served as meeting halls and auditoriums as well as educational and recreational facilities, employment and social service bureaus and bulletin boards. First African, especially, with a seating capacity of nearly 4000, was the site of large political gatherings. Schools such as Richmond Theological Seminary and Richmond Colored High and Normal School held their annual commencement exercises at First African Baptist, allowing these events to become community celebrations. Other groups, such as the Temperance Union were regularly granted the church for their meetings or rallies. As a political space occupied by men, women and children, literate and nonliterate, ex-slave and formerly free, church members and nonmembers, the availability and use of First African for mass meetings enabled the construction of political concerns in democratic space. This is not to suggest that official versions and spokespersons were not produced, but these official versions were the product of a fairly egalitarian discourse and, therefore, represented the conditions of black Richmonders of differing classes, ages and genders. Within black Richmonders' construction of the public sphere, the forms of discourse varied from the prayer to the stump speech to the testimonies regarding outrages against freedpeople to shouted interventions from the galleries into the debates on the legislative floor. By the very nature of their participation—the inclusion of women and children, the engagement through prayer, the disregard of formal rules for speakers and audience, the engagement from the galleries in the formal legislative sessions—Afro-Richmonders challenged liberal bourgeois notions of rational discourse. Many white observers considered their unorthodox political engagements to be signs of their unfamiliarity and perhaps unreadiness for politics.[5]

4. For a study that conceptualizes the history of the black church in relation to Habermas's theory of the public sphere, see Evelyn Brooks Higginbotham, *Righteous Discontent: The Women's Movement in the Black Baptist Church 1880–1920* (Cambridge: Harvard University Press, 1993), esp. 7–13. Higginbotham describes "the black church not as the embodiment of ministerial authority or of any individual's private interests and pronouncements, but as a social space for discussion of public concerns" (1993:10).

5. Similar negotiations and pronouncements occurred in other post-emancipation societies. For a discussion of the ways in which British colonial officers sought to impose ideas of a liberal democratic moral and political order, with its attendant gender relations, on former slaves in the West Indies and then pronounced these ex-slaves incapable of responsible citizenship when they failed to wholly adopt such, see Thomas C. Holt, "'The Essence of the Contract': The Articulation of Race, Gender, and Political Economy in British Emancipation Policy, 1838–1866," paper presented at "The Black Public Sphere in the Reagan-Bush Era Conference," Chicago Humanities Institute, The University of Chicago, October 1993 (cited with permission of Holt).

In the decades following emancipation as black Richmonders struggled to achieve even a measured amount of freedom, the black public sphere emerged as more fractured and perhaps less democratic at the end of the nineteenth century, yet even then it retained strong elements of a democratic agenda. This essay examines the changing constructions of political space and community discourse in the post-emancipation era.

Envisioning Freedom

In April 1865, when Union troops marched into Richmond, jubilant African American men, women and children poured into the streets and crowded into their churches to dance, kiss, hug, pray, sing and shout. They assembled in First African, Third Street African Methodist, Ebenezer and Second African not merely because of the need to thank God for their deliverance but also because the churches were the only institutional spaces, and in the case of First African certainly the largest space, owned by African Americans themselves.[6] As the process of reconstruction unfolded, black Richmonders continued to meet regularly in their churches, now not merely to rejoice. If Afro-Richmonders had thought freedom would accompany emancipation, the events of the first few weeks and months of Union occupation quickly disabused them of such ideas. Throughout the summer and fall of 1865 black Richmonders reported numerous violations of their rights. Among them were pass and curfew regulations designed to curtail black mobility and force African American men and women out of the city to labor in the rural areas. Pass and curfew violators (800 in the first week of June) were detained in bullpens—one for women and children, a separate one for men—away from and often unknown to family members. Black Richmonders also detailed numerous incidents of disrespectful treatment, verbal abuse, physical assault and torture. "Many poor women" told "tales of their frights and robberies"; vendors told of goods destroyed by military police. Private homes were not immune to the intrusions of civilian and military white men. One couple was confronted by soldiers, one of whom stood over them in bed "threatening to blow

6. The question of ownership was one of the first issues Afro-Richmonders addressed, as antebellum law had required the titles be in the names of white male supervising committees although the black congregants had themselves bought and paid for the buildings. Through a series of struggles black churchgoers had by the end of 1866 obtained titles to all of their church buildings. See *New York Tribune*, June 17, 1865; Peter Randolph, *From Slave Cabin to Pulpit* (Boston: Earle, 1893), 94–95; John Thomas O'Brien, Jr., "From Bondage to Citizenship: The Richmond Black Community, 1865–1867" (Ph.D. diss., University of Rochester, 1974), 273–275.

out their brains if they moved" while others "pillage[d] the house of money, watches, underclothing, etc."[7] Many spoke of the sexual abuse of black women: "gobbling up of the most likely looking negro women, thrown into the cells, robbed and ravished at the will of the guard." Men and women in the vicinity of the jail testified "to hearing women scream frightfully almost every night."[8]

7. Statement of Jenny Scott, wife of Ned Scott, colored, June 8, 1865; Statement of Richard Adams, colored, June 8, 1865; Statement of Nelson E. Hamilton, June 9, 1865; Statement of Lewis Harris, June 9, 1865; Statement of Wm. Ferguson, June 9, 1865; Statement of Albert Brooks, colored, June 10, 1865; Statement of Thomas Lucas, colored, June 12, 1865; Statement of Washington Hutchinson, Summer 1865; Statement of Edward Davenport, n.d.; Statement of Bernard H. Roberts, n.d.; Statement of Albert Williams, n.d.; Statement of Thos. J. Wayer, n.d.; Statement of Harry R. Jones, n.d.; Statement of Wellington Booker, n.d.; Statement of Stephen Jones, n.d.; Statement of John Oliver of Mass., n.d.; Wm. M. Davis to Col. O. Brown, June 9, 1865, all in Records of the Assistant Commissioner for the State of Virginia, Bureau of Refugees, Freedmen and Abandoned Lands, 1865–1869, Record Group 105, M1048, reel 59, National Archives, Washington, D.C.; *New York Tribune*, June 12, 17, August 1, 8, 1865; *Richmond Times*, July 26, 1865; S.E.C. (Sarah Chase) to Mrs. May, May 25, 1865, in Henry L. Swint, ed., *Dear Ones at Home: Letters from Contraband Camps* (Nashville: Vanderbilt University Press, 1966), 159–160; Julia A. Wilbur in *The Pennsylvania Freedman's Bulletin*, I (August 1865), 52, quoted in John T. O'Brien, "Reconstruction in Richmond: White Restoration and Black Protest, April–June 1865," *Virginia Magazine of History and Biography*, 89, 3 (July 1981): 273, 275.

8. *New York Tribune*, August 1, 8, 1865. One of the most neglected areas of Reconstruction history and of African American history in general, is that of violence against women. This has led to the still prevalent assumption that black women were less likely to be victims of racial violence and the generalization that this reflects the fact that black women were less threatening than black men. Historian W. Fitzhugh Brundage, for example, concludes that black women had "greater leeway" to "voice their opinions and anger without suffering extralegal violence themselves," *Lynching in the New South: Georgia and Virginia, 1880–1930* (Urbana: University of Illinois Press, 1993), 80–81, 322–323n. This reflects both the emphasis on lynching as the major form of racial violence, and the limited historical attention to the black women who were lynched (at least fifteen between 1889 and 1898; at least seventy–six between 1882 and 1927). Even those ostensibly attuned to issues of gender and sexuality still assume that "the greatest violence was reserved for black men"; see, for example, Martha Hodes, "The Sexualization of Reconstruction Politics: White Women and Black Men in the South after the Civil War," *Journal of the History of Sexuality* 3 (January 1993): 404. Yet the evidence from Richmond and elsewhere suggests that the extent of violence against black women is greater than previously recognized, even greater than reported at the time. One North Carolina man, Essic Harris, giving testimony to the Senate committee investigating Ku Klux Klan terror, reported the rape of black women was so frequent as to be "an old saying by now." Essic Harris testimony, July 1, 1871, in U.S. Congress, *Testimony Taken by the Joint Select Committee to Inquire into the Condition of Affairs in the Late Insurrectionary States* Vol.: *North Carolina* (Washington: GPO, 1872), 100. Only recently have historians begun to uncover and analyze sexual violence against black women as an integral part of Reconstruction history. See for example, the dissertation-in-progress by Hannah Rosen, University of Chicago, which examines the rapes connected with the 1866 Memphis race riot. See also, Catherine Clinton, "Reconstructing Freedwomen," *Divided Houses: Gender and the Civil War*, eds. Catherine Clinton and Nina Silber (New York: Oxford University Press, 1992), chapter 17.

The regular meetings in the African churches, originally ones of jubilation, quickly became the basis for constructing a discourse about freedom and organizing large-scale mass protest. On June 10, 1865 over 3000 assembled at First African to hear the report of the investigating committee which had conducted hearings and gathered the evidence and depositions necessary to present black Richmonders' case directly to Governor Francis H. Pierpoint and to the "chief head of all authority," the President of the United States. The protest memorial drawn up during the meeting was ratified at meetings in each of the other churches and money was raised through church collections to send six representatives (one from each church in Richmond and one from First Baptist, Manchester) to Washington. On Friday, June 16, these delegates delivered the mass meeting's protest directly to President Andrew Johnson:[9] "Mr. President: We have been appointed a committee by a public meeting of the colored people of Richmond, Va., to make known . . . the wrongs, as we conceive them to be, by which we are sorely oppressed." In their memorial, as in their meetings, black Richmonders recounted not merely the abuses but they also used their individual stories to construct a collective history and to combat the idea of being "idle negroes" unprepared for freedom.[10]

We represent a population of more than 20,000 colored people, including Richmond and Manchester, . . . more than 6,000 of our people are members in good standing of Christian churches, and nearly our whole population constantly attend divine services. Among us there are at least 2,000 men who are worth $200 to $500; 200 who have property valued at from $1,000 to $5,000, and a number who are worth from $5,000 to $20,000 . . .

9. *New York Tribune* June 12, 17, 1865.

10. The *Richmond Times* (May 24, 1865), in refusing to publish black Richmonders' statements of protest, reasoned that they were mistaken in believing that they were all oppressed by the military and civilian officials; only the "idle negroes" were targets of military restrictions and inspections. Throughout the early months of emancipation both white southerners and white Unionists defined freedpeople's mobility in search of family or better jobs and in expression of their new found freedom as evidence of an unwillingness to work. Similarly, those who chose to vend goods on city streets rather than signing work contracts with white employers were seen as lazy or idle. See, O'Brien, "From Bondage to Citizenship," 117–131; see also various communications among the military command reprinted in U.S. War Department, *The War of the Rebellion: A Compilation of the Official Records of the Union and Confederate Armies*, Series I, Volume XLV, Part III-*Correspondence, Etc.* (Washington: GPO, 1894), 835, 932–933, 1005–1006, 1091, 1094–1095, 1107–1108, 1131–1132.

public sphere

collective

cf 129

The law of Slavery severely punished those who taught us to read and write, but, not withstanding this, 3,000 of us can read, and at least 2,000 can read and write, and a large number of us are engaged in useful and profitable employment on our own account.

The community they described was one based in a collective ethos; it was not merely their industry but also their responsibility which was the basis on which they claimed their rights.

None of our people are in the alms-house, and when we were slaves the aged and infirm who were turned away from the homes of hard masters, who had been enriched by their toil, our benevolent societies supported while they lived, and buried when they died, and comparatively few of us have found it necessary to ask for Government rations, which have been so bountifully bestowed upon the unrepentant Rebels of Richmond.

They reminded Johnson of the efforts black men and women in Richmond had taken to support the Union forces against the Confederacy.

During the whole of the Slaveholders' Rebellion we have been true and loyal to the United States Government; . . . We have given aid and comfort to the soldiers of Freedom (for which several of our people, of both sexes, have been severely punished by stripes and imprisonment). We have been their pilots and their scouts, and have safely conducted them through many perilous adventures.

They declared themselves the loyal citizens of the United States, those the federal government should be supporting. And finally they invoked the religious destiny that emancipation had reaffirmed, reminding the President of a "motto once inscribed over the portals of an Egyptian temple, '*Know all ye who exercise power, that God hates injustice!*'"[11]

Mindful of others' versions of their history, standing and entitlements, black Richmonders also moved to have their own story widely circulated. When local white newspapers refused to publish their account, they had it published in the

11. *New York Tribune*, June 17, 1865.

New York Tribune.[12] Throughout 1865 and 1866 black Richmonders continued to meet regularly in mass meetings where men, women and children collectively participated in constructing and announcing their own story of community and freedom.[13] The story told in those mass meetings, published in northern white newspapers, carried in protest to Union officials, was also carried into the streets as black Richmonders inserted themselves in the preexisting national political traditions and at the same time widened those traditions. John O'Brien has noted that in the immediate aftermath of emancipation, black Richmonders developed their own political calendar, celebrating four civic holidays: January 1; George Washington's birthday; April 3 (emancipation day); and July 4.[14] White Richmonders were horrified as they watched former slaves claim civic holidays and traditions they believed to be the historical possession of white Americans and occupy spaces, like Capitol Square, which had formerly been reserved for white residents.[15]

The underlying values and assumptions that would pervade much of black people's political struggles in the city were forged in slavery and war and in the weeks following emancipation. Military regulations which limited black mobility and made finding and reunifying family members even more difficult placed the economic interests of white men and women above the material and social interests of African Americans. The bullpens, which detained many away from their families, and the raids on black homes, which made all space public and subject to the interests of the state, obliterated any possible distinctions between public and private spheres. Demanding passes and evidence of employment denied black Richmonders the right to act and to be treated not as economic units and/or

12. Black Richmonders were countering the very different image of their community put forth not only by white southerners but also by Union officers. Major-General H. W. Halleck, for example, emphasized the goodwill between Rebel and Union soldiers, both "brave and honest men, although differing in opinion and action"; justified the military restrictions on African Americans; and reported a lack of marriage relationships among African Americans "and the consequent irresponsibility of the parents for the care and support of their offspring." He argued that "colored females," especially, needed legal restrictions, supervision and suitable punishments, because "being released from the restraints imposed by their former masters and mistresses, . . . naturally fall into dissolute habits." H. W. Halleck, Major-General, Commanding, Headquarters Military Division of the James, Richmond, Va. to Hon. E. M. Stanton, Secretary of War, June 26, 1865, in U.S. War Department, *The War of the Rebellion*, 1295–1297. Halleck was one of the Union officers who was reassigned to a different command as a result of the June protest.

13. O'Brien details these meetings in "From Bondage to Citizenship," chapters 6–9.

14. O'Brien, "From Bondage to Citizenship," 326.

15. See, for example, *Richmond Enquirer*, February 23, 1866; *Richmond Dispatch*, July 6, 1866; *Richmond Times*, July 6, 1866.

property but as social beings and family members. The difficulty of finding decent housing at affordable prices further impeded freedpeople's efforts to bring their families together. All of these obstacles to and expectations of family life were part of what Eric Foner speaks of as the "'politicization' of every day life."[16]

These political issues underpinned Afro-Richmonders' petition to Johnson and would continue to underpin their political struggles in late-nineteenth century Richmond. Even as they fashioned individual stories into a collective history, black Richmonders could and did differ on the means by which they might secure freedom—vigorously debating issues such as the necessity of confiscation.[17] But they also understood freedom as a collective struggle. When they entered the formal political arena through Republican party politics in 1867 this understanding was the foundation for their initial engagement with issues of suffrage and democracy. As Julie Saville has observed for South Carolina, freedpeople in Richmond "were not so much converted to the Republican party as they were prepared to convert the Republican party to themselves."[18] The post-Civil War southern black public sphere was forged in jubilation and struggle as African American men, women and children claimed their own history and set forth their own political ideals.

All the resources of black Richmonders became elements in their political struggles. The *Richmond Whig*, intending to ridicule the inappropriateness of freepeople's behaviors and assumptions, highlighted the politicized nature of all aspects of black life during Reconstruction; the freedpeople's "mass meetings, committee meetings, and meetings of the different societies all have political significance. The superstitions of the colored people are availed on, and religion and Radicalism are all jumbled together. Every night they have meetings and musterings, harangues and sermons, singing and praying—all looking to political results."[19] Similarly the *Richmond Dispatch* reported an 1867 Republican meeting which began with "Harris, colored" offering "the most remarkable" prayer "we have ever heard. It was frequently interrupted by laughter and manifestations of applause":

Oh, Lord God, bless our enemies—bless President Johnson. We would not even have him sent to hell. Come, oh come, good Lord, and touch

16. Foner, *Reconstruction*, 122.

17. *Richmond Dispatch*, April 19, 1867; *New York Times*, April 19, 1867.

18. Julie Saville, "A Measure of Freedom: From Slave to Wage Laborer in South Carolina, 1860–1868" (Ph.D diss., Yale University, 1986), 273.

19. *Richmond Whig*, April 1, 1867.

his heart even while I am talking with you here to-night. [Amen.] Show him the error of his ways. Have mercy upon our 'Moses,' [Sarcastic. Great laughter and amens.] who, like Esau, has sold his birthright for a morsel of pottage—took us in the wilderness and left us there. Come down upon him, oh Lord, with thy blessing. God bless us in our meeting to-night, and help us in what we do. God forbid that we should choose any Conservative that has the spirit of the devil in his heart, and whose feet take hold on hell. God bless our friend—true and tried—Mr. Hunnicut, who has stood a great many sorrows and I think he can stand a great many more. [Laughter.] Bless our judge, Mr. Underwood, who is down here among us, and don't let anything harm a hair of his head.[20]

What the *Whig* and the *Dispatch* captured was a political culture in which the wide range of institutional and noninstitutional resources of individuals and the community as a whole became the basis for defining, claiming and securing freedom in post-emancipation Richmond. The church provided more than physical space, financial resources and a communication network; it also provided a cultural base that validated emotion and experience as ways of knowing, and drew on a collective call and response, encouraging the active participation of all.[21]

Virginia's rejection of the Fourteenth Amendment brought the state under the Reconstruction Act of 1867; a constitutional convention became prerequisite for full restoration to the Union. Black men, enfranchised for the delegate selection and ratification ballots, were to have their first opportunity to engage in the

---

20. *Richmond Dispatch*, October 5, 1867.

21. Aldon Morris makes a similar argument regarding the church and the modern civil rights movement, emphasizing the ways in which the church served as a physical, financial and cultural resource, with its sermons, songs, testimonies and prayers becoming political resources in the mobilization of participants and in the construction and communication of political ideology. *The Origins of the Civil Rights Movement: Black Communities Organizing for Change* (New York: Free Press, 1984). See also, Robin D. G. Kelley, "'Comrades, Praise Gawd for Lenin and Them!': Ideology and Culture Among Black Communists in Alabama, 1930–1935," *Science and Society* 52, 1 (Spring 1988): 59–82; Brenda McCallum, "Songs of Work and Songs of Worship: Sanctifying Black Unionism in the Southern City of Steel," *New York Folklore* 14, 1 & 2 (1988): 9–33. For an argument that eliminating emotions and aesthetics from acceptable forms of public discourse becomes a means to eliminate particular groups of people from active participation in public life, see Iris Marion Young, "Impartiality and the Civic Public: Some Implications of Feminist Critiques of Moral and Political Theory," in *Feminism as Critique: On the Politics of Gender,* eds. Seyla Benhabib and Drucilla Cornell (Minneapolis: University of Minnesota, 1987), 56–76.

political parties and legislative chambers of the state. The struggles in which they had engaged in the two years since emancipation influenced the manner of black Richmonders' initial participation in the formal political arena of conventions and voting. On August 1, 1867, the day the Republican state convention opened in Richmond to adopt a platform for the upcoming state constitutional convention, thousands of African American men, women and children absented themselves from their employment and joined the delegates at the convention site, First African Baptist Church.[22] Tobacco factories, lacking a major portion of their workers, were forced to close for the day.

This pattern persisted whenever a major issue came before the state and city Republican conventions held during the summer and fall of 1867, or the state constitutional convention which convened in Richmond from December 1867 to March 1868. A *New York Times* reporter estimated that "the entire colored population of Richmond" attended the October 1867 local Republican convention where delegates to the state constitutional convention were nominated. Noting that female domestic servants were a large portion of those in attendance, the correspondent reported: "as is usual on such occasions, families which employ servants were forced to cook their own dinners, or content themselves with a cold lunch. Not only had Sambo gone to the Convention, but Dinah was there also."[23]

These men and women did not absent themselves from work just to be onlookers at the proceedings, but to be active participants. They assumed as equal a

22. The following discussion of collective enfranchisement as the basis for black women's political activism in the post-Civil War era is drawn from Elsa Barkley Brown, "To Catch the Vision of Freedom: Reconstructing Southern Black Women's Political History, 1865–1880," in *To Be a Citizen*, eds. Arlene Avakian, Joyce Berkman, John Bracey, Bettye Collier-Thomas, and Ann Gordon (Amherst: University of Massachusetts Press, forthcoming).

23. *Richmond Dispatch*, August 1, 2, September 30, October 9, 1867; *New York Times*, August 1, 2, 6, October 18, 1867. My discussion of these events follows closely Peter J. Rachleff, *Black Labor in the South: Richmond, Virginia, 1865–1890* (Philadelphia: Temple University Press, 1984), 45–46. See also Richard L. Morton, *The Negro in Virginia Politics, 1865–1902,* Publications of the University of Virginia Phelps-Stokes Fellowship Papers Number Four (Charlottesville: University of Virginia Press, 1919), 40–43. Similar reports issued from other areas throughout the South, causing one chronicler to report that "the Southern ballot-box" was as much "the vexation of housekeepers" as it was of farmers, businessmen, statesmen or others: "Elections were preceded by political meetings, often incendiary in character, which all one's servants must attend." Election day itself could also be a problem. As one Tennessean reported in 1867, "Negro women went [to the polls], too; my wife was her own cook and chambermaid," Myrta Lockett Avary, *Dixie After the War: An Exposition of Social Conditions Existing in the South, During the Twelve Years Succeeding the Fall of Richmond* (New York: Doubleday, Page and Co., 1906; reprint, New York: Negro Universities Press, 1969), 282–284. See also, Susan Bradford Eppes for similar occurrences in Florida, *Through Some Eventful Years* ([1926] reprint ed., Gainesville: University of Florida Press, 1968).

right to be present and participate as the delegates themselves, a fact they made abundantly clear at the August 1867 Republican state convention. Having begun to arrive four hours before the opening session, African American men and women had filled the meeting place long before the delegates arrived. Having showed up to speak for themselves, they did not assume delegates had priority — in discussion or in seating. Disgusted at the scene, as well as unable to find a seat, the conservative white Republican delegates removed to the Capitol Square to convene an outdoor session. That was quite acceptable to the several thousand additional African American men and women who, unable to squeeze into the church, were now still able to participate in the important discussions and to vote down the proposals of the conservative faction.[24]

Black men, women and children were also active participants throughout the state constitutional convention. A *New York Times* reporter commented on the tendency for the galleries to be crowded "with the 'unprivileged,' and altogether black." At issue was not just these men and women's presence but also their behavior. White women, for example, certainly on occasion sat in the convention's gallery as visitors silently observing the proceedings; these African Americans, however, participated from the gallery, loudly engaging in the debates. At points of heated controversy, black delegates turned to the crowds as they made their addresses on the convention floor, obviously soliciting and relying upon mass participation. Outside the convention hours, mass meetings were held to discuss and vote on the major issues. At these gatherings vote was either by voice or rising and men, women and children voted. These meetings were not mock assemblies; they were important gatherings at which the community made plans for freedom. The most radical black Republican faction argued that the major convention issues should actually be settled at these mass meetings with delegates merely casting the community's vote on the convention floor. Though this did not occur, black delegates were no doubt influenced by both the mass meetings and the African American presence in the galleries, both of which included women.[25]

24. *Richmond Dispatch*, August 1, 2, 1867; *New York Times*, August 2, 6, 1867; see also Rachleff, *Black Labor in the South*, 45; Morton, *Negro in Virginia Politics*, 40–43.

25. The October 1867 city Republican ward meetings and nominating convention adopted the practice common in the black community's mass meetings: a voice or standing vote which enfranchised men, women, and children. See, for example, the October eighth Second Ward meeting for delegate selection: "All who favored Mr. Washburne were first requested to rise, and forty were found on the floor, including women." *Richmond Dispatch*, September 20, October 9, 1867; January 2, 4, 14, 23, 24, February 15, 25, April 3, 8, 25, 1868; *New York Times*, August 6, October 15, 18, 1867; January 11, 1868; Rachleff, *Black Labor in the South*, 45–49; Avary, *Dixie After the War*, 229–231, 254.

Black Richmonders were operating in two separate political arenas: an internal one and an external one. While these arenas were related, they each proceeded from different assumptions, had different purposes, and therefore operated according to different rules. Within the internal political process women were enfranchised and participated in all public forums—the parades, rallies, mass meetings and the conventions themselves.[26] Richmond was not atypical in this regard.[27]

The issue of children's participation is an interesting one, suggestive of the means by which personal experience rather than societal norms shaped ex-slaves' vision of politics. A similarly telling example was in the initial proposal of the African National Congress that the new South African constitution set the voting age at fourteen, a testament to those young people, as those in Soweto, who experienced the ravages of apartheid and whose fight against it helped bring about the political negotiations to secure African political rights and self-determination.

26. Compare black women's active participation in Richmond's formal politics—internal and external—in the first decades after the Civil War to Michael McGerr's assessment that nineteenth-century "women were allowed into the male political realm only to play typical feminine roles—to cook, sew, and cheer for men and to symbolize virtue and beauty. Men denied women the central experiences of the popular style: not only the ballot but also the experience of mass mobilization." McGerr's analysis fails to acknowledge the racial basis of his study, i.e., it is an assessment of white women's political participation, Michael McGerr, "Political Style and Women's Power, 1830–1930," *Journal of American History* 77 (December 1990): 864–885, esp. 867. My analysis also differs substantially from Mary P. Ryan, *Women in Public*. Ryan gives only cursory attention to African Americans but finds black women's political expression in the Civil War and Reconstruction eras restricted "with particular severity" and "buried beneath the surface of the public sphere," see, 146–147, 156, *passim*.

27. For women's participation in political parades in Louisville, Kentucky, Mobile, Alabama, and Charleston, South Carolina, see Herbert G. Gutman, *The Black Family in Slavery and Freedom*, 380; *Liberator*, July 21, 1865 and *New York Daily Tribune*, April 4, 1865, both reprinted in *The Trouble They Seen: Black People Tell the Story of Reconstruction*, ed. Dorothy Sterling (Garden City, New York: Doubleday, 1976), 2–4. In other areas of Virginia besides Richmond and in South Carolina and Louisiana men and women participated in the political meetings. See, for example, Vincent Harding, *There Is A River: The Black Struggle for Freedom in America* (New York: Harcourt Brace Jovanovich, 1981), 294–297; Rupert Sargent Holland, ed., *Letters and Diary of Laura M. Towne Written from the Sea Islands of South Carolina 1862–1884* (Cambridge: Riverside Press, 1912; reprint ed., New York: Negro Universities Press, 1969), 183; Testimony of John H. Burch given before a Senate committee appointed to investigate the exodus of black men and women from Louisiana, Senate Report 693, 46th Congress, 2nd Session, part 2, 232–233 reprinted in *A Documentary History of the Negro People in the United States*, 2 vols., ed. Herbert Aptheker (New York: Citadel Press, 1951), 2: 721–722; Thomas Holt, *Black Over White: Negro Political Leadership in South Carolina during Reconstruction* (Urbana: University of Illinois Press, 1977), 34–35. Graphic artists recognized the participation of women as a regular feature of parades, mass meetings, and conventions as evidenced by their illustrations. See "The Celebration of Emancipation Day in Charleston" from *Leslie's Illustrated Newspaper* reprinted in Francis Butler Simkins and Robert Hilliard Woody, *South Carolina During Reconstruction* (Chapel Hill: University of North Carolina Press, 1932; reprint ed., Gloucester, Mass.: Peter Smith, 1966), facing 364; "Electioneering at the South," *Harper's Weekly*, July 25, 1868 reprinted in Foner, *Reconstruction*, fol. 386; "Colored People's Convention in Session" reprinted in Sterling, *The Trouble They Seen*, 65.

It was the state constitutional convention, however, which would decide African American women's and men's status in the political process external to the African American community. When the Virginia convention began its deliberation regarding the franchise, Thomas Bayne, a black delegate from Norfolk, argued the inherent link between freedom and suffrage, and contended that those who opposed universal suffrage were actually opposing the freedom of African American people. In rejoinder, E. L. Gibson, a Conservative white delegate, enunciated several principles of republican representative government. Contending that "a man might be free and still not have the right to vote," Gibson explained the fallacy of assuming that this civil right was an inherent corollary to freedom: if the right were inherent then it would belong to both sexes and to all from "the first moment of existence" and to foreigners immediately. This was "an absurdity too egregious to be contemplated."[28] And yet, this "absurd" notion of political rights was what was in practice in the Richmond black community— males and females voted without regard to age, the thousands of rural migrants who came into Richmond suffered no waiting period but immediately possessed the full rights of the community. What was absurd to Gibson and most white men—Republican or Democrat—was obviously quite rational to many black Richmonders. Two very different conceptions of freedom and public participation in the political process were in place.

In the end only men obtained the legal franchise. The impact of this decision is neither inconsequential nor fully definitive. African American women were by law excluded from the formal political arena external to their community. Yet this does not mean that they were not active in that arena; witness Richmond women's participation in the Republican and the constitutional conventions. Southern black men and women debated the issue of women's suffrage in both the external and internal political arenas. In Nansemond County, Virginia, for example, the mass meetings resolved that women should be granted the legal franchise; in Richmond, while a number of participants in a mass meeting supported female suffrage, the majority opinion swung against it.[29] But the meaning of that decision was not as straightforward as it may seem. The debate as to whether women should be given the vote in the external political arena occurred in internal political arena mass meetings where women participated and voted

28. *New York Times*, January 11, 22, 1868; *The Debates and Proceedings of the Constitutional Convention of the State of Virginia, Assembled at the City of Richmond* (Richmond, 1868), 505–507, 524–527.
29. *Richmond Dispatch*, June 18, 1867; Rachleff, *Black Labor in the South*, 48.

not just before and during, *but also after* the negative decision regarding legal enfranchisement. This maintained the status quo in the external community; ironically enough, the status quo in the internal community was maintained as well – women continued to have the vote. African American men and women clearly operated within two distinct political systems.

Focusing on formal disfranchisement obscures women's continued participation in the external political arena. In Richmond and throughout the South exclusion from legal enfranchisement did not prevent African American women from shaping the vote and the political decisions. Throughout the late 1860s and 1870s women continued to participate in political meetings in large numbers and to organize political societies. Some like the Rising Daughters of Liberty and the Daughters of the Union Victory in Richmond or the United Daughters of Liberty organized by coal miners' wives living outside Manchester had all-female memberships. Others, like the 2000 member National Political Aid Society, the Union League of Richmond and the Union Equal Rights League of Manchester had male and female members. Even though white Republicans made efforts to exclude them from further participation in political meetings by the late 1860s, African American women in Virginia, South Carolina, Louisiana and elsewhere were still attending these meetings in the 1870s.

Women's presence at these meetings was anything but passive. In the violent political atmosphere of the last years of Reconstruction, they had an especially important and dangerous role. In South Carolina, for example, while the men participated in the meeting, the women guarded the guns – thus serving in part as the protectors of the meeting. For those women and men who lived in outlying areas of Richmond and attended outdoor meetings, political participation was a particularly dangerous matter, a fact they clearly recognized. Meetings were guarded by posted sentinels with guns who questioned the intent of any suspicious people, usually white men, coming to the meeting. A reporter for the *Richmond Daily Dispatch* described one such encounter when he attempted to cover a political meeting of fifty women and twenty-five men.[30]

Women as well as men took election day off from work and went to the polls. Fraud, intimidation and violence became the order of election days. White newspapers and politicians threatened loss of jobs, homes and lives. Afro-Richmonders countered with a group presence. Often even those living within

30. Rachleff, *Black Labor in the South*, 31–32; *Richmond Daily Dispatch*, May 10, 1867; *New Nation*, November 22, 29, December 6, 1866; Holt, *Black Over White*, 35; Avary, *Dixie After the War*.

the city and short distances from the polling places went early, even the night before, and camped out at the polls, hoping that their early presence would require the acceptance of their vote and that the group presence would provide protection from violence and intimidation. In the highly charged political atmosphere of late-nineteenth century Richmond it was no small matter for these women and men to participate in political meetings and show up at the election sites. The reasons for the group presence at the polls were varied. African American women in Virginia, Mississippi, South Carolina and elsewhere understood themselves to have a vital stake in African American men's franchise. The fact that only men had been granted the vote did not at all mean that only men should exercise the vote. Women throughout the South initiated sanctions against men who voted Democratic; some went along to the polls to insure a properly cast ballot. As increasing white fraud made black men's voting more difficult, early arrival at the polls was partly intended to counter such efforts.

Although election days in Richmond were not as violent as they were elsewhere throughout Virginia and other parts of the South, guns were used to intimidate and defraud. It is also probable that in Richmond, as elsewhere throughout the South, when black men went to camp out overnight at the polls, households feared leaving women and children unprotected at home. Thus the women's presence, just as the group presence of the men, may have been a sign of the need for collective protection. If Richmond women were at all like their sisters in South Carolina and Danville, they may have carried weapons with them—to protect themselves and/or help protect the male voters.[31] Women and children's presence reflects their excitement about the franchise but also their understanding of the dangers involved in voting. The necessity for a group presence at the polls reinforced the sense of collective enfranchisement. Women's presence at the polls was both a negative sanction and a positive expression of the degree to which they understood the men's franchise to be a new political opportunity for themselves as well as their children.

In the dangerous political atmosphere of the late-nineteenth century, the vote took on a sacred and collective character. Black men and women in Richmond, as throughout the South, initiated sanctions against those black men perceived

31. Barkley Brown, "To Catch the Vision of Freedom"; *Richmond Enquirer*, October 22, 1867; *Richmond Whig*, October 19, 1867; Robert E. Martin, "Negro Disfranchisement in Virginia," *The Howard University Studies in the Social Sciences*, I (Washington, D. C., 1938): 65–79; *Richmond Afro-American*, December 2, 1962; Mrs. Violet Keeling's testimony before Senate investigating committee, February 18, 1884, Senate Report No. 579, 48th Congress, 1st Session, reprinted in Aptheker, *Documentary History*, 2: 739–741.

as violating the collective good by supporting the Conservative forces. Black Democrats were subject to the severest exclusion: disciplined within or quite often expelled from their churches and mutual benefit societies; denied board and lodging with black families. Additionally, mobs jeered, jostled and sometimes beat black Democrats or rescued those who were arrested for such acts. Women were often reported to be in the forefront of this activity. Similarly, black women were said to have "exercised a positive influence upon some men who were inclined to hesitate or be indifferent" during the early 1880s Readjuster campaigns.[32]

All of this suggests that African American women and men understood the vote as a collective, not an individual possession; and furthermore, that African American women, unable to cast a separate vote, viewed African American men's vote as equally theirs. They believed that franchise should be cast in the best interest of both. This is not the nineteenth century patriarchal notion that men voted on behalf of their wives and children. By that assumption women had no individual wills; rather men operated in women's best interest because women were assumed to have no right of input. African American women assumed the political rights that came with being a member of the community even though they were denied the political rights they thought should come with being citizens of the state.

32. Barkley Brown, "To Catch the Vision of Freedom"; Howard N. Rabinowitz, *Race Relations in the Urban South, 1865-1880* (New York: Oxford University Press, 1978), 222; Alrutheus Ambush Taylor, *The Negro in the Reconstruction of Virginia* (Washington, D.C.: The Association for the Study of Negro Life and History, 1926), 181, 269; Michael B. Chesson, "Richmond's Black Councilmen, 1871-96," in *Southern Black Leaders of the Reconstruction Era*, ed. Howard N. Rabinowitz (Urbana: University of Illinois Press, 1982), 219n; Peter J. Rachleff, "Black, White and Gray: Working-Class Activism in Richmond, Virginia, 1865-1890" (Ph.D. diss., University of Pittsburgh, 1981), 473, 488n; *Richmond Dispatch*, October 25, 26, 1872; September 14, 1874; Avary, *Dixie After the War*, 285-286, 347; Thomas J. Evans, Alexander Sands, N. A. Sturdivant, et al., Richmond, to Major-General Schofield, October 31, 1867, reprinted in *Documents of the Constitutional Convention of the State of Virginia* (Richmond: Office of the *New Nation*, 1867), 22-23; John H. Gilmer to Gen. Schofield reprinted in *New York Times*, October 30, 1867; *New York Times*, November 3, 1867; Wendell P. Dabney, "Rough autobiographical sketch of his boyhood years," (typescript, n.d.), 98-99, microfilm copy in Wendell P. Dabney Papers, Cincinnati Historical Society, Cincinnati, Ohio; Proceedings before Military Commissioner, City of Richmond, 26 October 1867 in the case of Winston Jackson filed as G-423 1867 Letters Received, ser. 5068, 1st Reconstruction Military District, Records of the U.S. Army Continental Commands, Record Group 393, Pt. 1, National Archives [SS-1049] (bracketed numbers refer to files in the Freedmen and Southern Society Project, University of Maryland; I thank Leslie S. Rowland, project director, for facilitating my access to these files); George F. Bragg, Jr., Baltimore, Maryland, to Dr. Woodson, August 26, 1926, reprinted in "Communications," *Journal of Negro History* XI (1926), 677.

To justify their political participation Richmond and other southern black women in the immediate post-Civil War period did not need to rely on arguments of superior female morality or public motherhood. Their own cultural, economic and political traditions provided rationale enough. An understanding of collective autonomy was the basis on which African Americans reconstructed families, developed communal institutions, constructed schools and engaged in formal politics after emancipation. The participation of women and children in the external and internal political arenas was part of a larger political worldview of ex-slaves and free men and women, a worldview fundamentally shaped by an understanding that freedom, in reality, would accrue to each of them individually only when it was acquired by all of them collectively. Such a worldview contrasted sharply with the "possessive individualism" of liberal democracy.[33] This sense of suffrage as a collective, not an individual possession was the foundation for much of African American women's political activities in the post-Civil War era.[34] Within these understandings the boundary lines between men's and women's political behavior were less clearly drawn and active participation in the political arenas—internal or external—seldom required a retreat into womanhood or manhood as its justification.

Even in the organization of militia units, post-emancipation black Richmonders, at least for a time, rejected the liberal bourgeois ideal of a solely male civic domain. By 1886 black men had organized three militia companies. By the late 1870s black women had also organized a militia company, although apparently only for ceremonial purposes; it reportedly was active only before and during emancipation celebrations. Its members conducted preparatory drills on Broad Street, one of Richmond's main thoroughfares. Frank Anthony, the man who prepared and drilled the women's company, demanded military precision and observance of regular military commands.[35] Unlike the men participating in the

33. See Thomas C. Holt, "'An Empire over the Mind': Emancipation, Race, and Ideology in the British West Indies and the American South," in *Region, Race, and Reconstruction: Essays in Honor of C. Vann Woodward*, ed. J. Morgan Kousser and James M. McPherson (New York: Oxford University Press, 1982), 283–314; also David Montgomery, *The American Civil War and the Meanings of Freedom: An Inaugural Lecture delivered before the University of Oxford on 24 February 1987* (Oxford: Clarendon Press, 1987), 11–13.

34. This is not to suggest that African American women did not desire the vote nor that they did not often disagree with the actions taken by some black men. One should, however, be careful about imposing presentist notions of gender equality on these women. Clearly for them the question was not an abstract notion of individual gender equality but rather one of community. That such a vision might become over time a lead into a patriarchal conception of gender roles is not a reason to dismiss the equity of its inception.

35. Dabney, "Rough autobiographical sketch," 17–18.

militias, who came from working-class, artisan, business and professional backgrounds, the women were probably working-class. Although they served no self-defense role, their drilling in Richmond streets and marching in parades challenged ideas and assumptions about appropriate public behavior held by both white southerners and white Unionists. The women's unit not only challenged, as did the men's, the idea of black subservience, but also suggested wholly new forms and meanings of respectable female behavior. There is no evidence concerning how long this women's unit survived or the causes of its demise. We can speculate that, besides horrifying whites, such a unit may have also become unacceptable to a number of black Richmonders. Increasingly, concerns about respectable behavior were connected to the public behavior of the working class and of women. This black women's militia, however, suggests the fluidity of gender notions in the early years of emancipation. The brevity of its appearance suggests how questions of public behavior became integral within black Richmond, just as they had been within the larger society. Yet for a time the actions of these women declared that perhaps no area of political participation or public ceremony was strictly a male domain.

Renegotiating Public Life

The 1880 First African women's petition followed three contentious church meetings, some lasting until two or three o'clock in the morning, at which the congregants considered dismissing and/or excluding the pastor, the Reverend James H. Holmes. This discussion was initiated at an April fifth meeting where two women were charged with fighting about the pastor. The April sixth meeting considered charges of "unchristian conduct" on the part of Holmes; those men present voted to exclude Holmes. A meeting on April eleventh endorsed a protest signed by all but two of the deacons against the earlier proceedings. The protest charged the anti-Holmes faction with trying to "dispose of the deacons, take charge of prayer meetings, the Sunday school and revolutionize things generally." The discussions which ensued over the next two months split the congregation; the May and June church business meetings were "disorderly" and "boisterous." Holmes and the deacons called in the mayor, city court judge, and chief of police to support the pastor and the police to remove or arrest those members of the congregation designated as "rebellious." After the anti-Holmes faction was removed from the church, the June meeting expelled forty-six men for "rebelliously attempting to overthrow and seize upon the church government." It also excluded the two women initially charged, one for fighting and the other for tattling;

exonerated Holmes "from all false" accusations; and thanked the civil officers who attended the meeting and restored order. Only after these actions did the church consider the women's petition which had been presented in the midst of the controversy more than two months earlier.[36]

First African's records do not adequately reveal the nature of gender relations within the church in the late 1860s and 1870s. We do know that the pre-Civil War sex-segregated seating patterns were abandoned by Richmond black Baptist churches immediately after the Civil War and that by the late 1860s women "not only had a voice, but voted in the business meetings" of Ebenezer Baptist Church.[37] Women who voted in political meetings held in First African in the 1860s and 1870s may have carried this participation over to church business meetings. Often in the immediate post-Civil War period, business and political meetings were not clearly distinguishable.

The petition of the women of First African makes clear, however, that by the early 1880s, while women attended and apparently participated in church meetings, the men had "adopted a law in the church that the business must be done by the male members." Whether Margaret Osborne, Jane Green, and others thought that their voices and interests were being inadequately represented, even ignored by the deacons, or wanted to add their voices to those, including the deacons, who were struggling to retain Holmes and control of First African, these women understood that they would have to defend their own rights. The women argued their right to decide on the pastor, justifying their petition by both their work on behalf of the church and the importance of their economic support to the church's ongoing activities and to the pastor's salary. Not until after the matter of Holmes's exclusion was settled were the petitioners granted their request. Since they apparently remained within First African, the petitioners' organization probably indicates that they were not among those dissatisfied with Holmes. It does suggest, however, their dissatisfaction with church procedure and the place of women in church polity. Still, the petition was conservative and

36. FABC, II, April 5, 6, 11, May 3, June 27, 1880.

37. First African minutes for 1841–1859 and 1875–1930, are available at First African and on microfilm in Archives, Virginia State Library. The Civil War and immediate post-emancipation minutes apparently have not survived. Peter Randolph, who came to Richmond from Massachusetts within weeks of emancipation and became the first black man elected pastor of Ebenezer Baptist, attributed both the change in seating patterns and the formal inclusion of women as voters in church business meetings to his own progressivism. Whether or not he initiated such measures, it is unlikely either change would have been effected without wide acceptance within the congregation. Randolph, *From Slave Cabin to Pulpit*, 89.

the women denied any intention to demand full voting rights in church matters. The petition was not taken as a challenge to church authority, as were the actions of the anti-Holmes faction. When brought up for a vote in the June meeting, the women's petition was adopted by a vote of 413 to 16.[38]

The women's petition and the vote in favor of it suggest the tenuous and ambiguous position that women had come to occupy both within First African and within the internal political arena more generally. They participated actively in church meetings but the authority for that participation and the question of limiting women's role resurfaced throughout the late-nineteenth century. In the 1890s the women of First African would again have to demand their rights, this time against challenges to their very presence at church meetings, when a deacon sought to prohibit women from even attending First African business meetings. The women protested and the church responded quickly by requiring the deacon to apologize to the women and assure them that they were welcome at the meetings. The degree of women's participation and decision-making powers, however, remained ambiguous.

In 1901–1902 during another crisis period in First African, a number of men sought to blame the problems on women. John Mitchell, Jr., a member of First African and editor of the *Richmond Planet*, cited the active participation of women ("ladies who knew nothing of the machinery at work or the deep laid plans on foot") and children ("Sunday School scholars from 8 years of age upward") in church affairs, suggesting that they did not comprehend the proceedings and had been easily misled or manipulated by male factions. Deacon J. C. Farley cited women's active participation in church meetings as the problem, reminding the congregation that "it was the rule of the church" that women were only allowed to vote on the pastor but had extended their participation far past that. And the new minister, the Reverend W. T. Johnson, admonished the women, saying that "the brethren could almost fight in the church meeting and when they went out they would shake hands and laugh and talk. But the sisters would talk about it going up Broad St. and everybody would know what they had done." First African women rejected these assessments of their church's problems. A significant number walked out rather than have their participation censured; those who remained reportedly refused to be silent but continually "talked out in the meeting." Sister Margaret Hewlett later sought out the editor of the *Richmond Planet* to voice her opposition to the men's denunciation of women's roles and to make clear that

38. FABC, II, June 27, 1880.

the women thought the church's problems lay in the male leadership, saying specifically "the deacons were the cause of all the trouble anyway."[39]

In the early 1890s the *Virginia Baptist* publicized its belief that women, in exceeding their proper places in the church by attempting to preach, and in the community by their "deplorable" efforts to "exercise the right of suffrage," would lose their "womanliness."[40] The complexity of gender relations within the African American community was such that at the same time First African was debating women's attendance at church meetings and the *Virginia Baptist* was advocating a severely restricted women's role, other women such as Alice Kemp were known throughout the community as the authors of prominent male ministers' sermons and women such as the Reverend Mrs. Carter were establishing their reputations as "soul-stirring" preachers. The *Richmond Planet* reported these women's activities without fanfare, as if they were commonplace. The debate over women's roles also had become commonplace. The Reverend Anthony Binga, pastor of First Baptist (Manchester), noted the debate in his sermon on Church Polity; Binga supported women teaching Sunday School, participating in prayer-meetings and voting "on any subject pertaining to the interest of the church" including the pastor; but he interpreted the Bible as forbidding women "throwing off that modesty that should adorn her sex, and taking man's place in the pulpit." The subject received community-wide attention in June 1895 when Ebenezer Baptist Church staged a debate between the ministers of Second Baptist (Manchester) and Mount Carmel, judged by other ministers from Fourth Baptist, First African, First Baptist (Manchester) and others on the subject, "Resolved that a woman has every right and privilege that a man has in the christian church."[41]

[handwritten margin note: public writing debate over woman in church and politics (suffrage)]

39. FABC, III November 7, 20, 1899; *Richmond Planet*, July 6, 20, August 10, 31, 1901, March 8, 15, 1902. Similar debates must have occurred in Ebenezer Baptist Church as well. In approving the conduct of business at Ebenezer, Mitchell noted that "only the male members were permitted to vote" on the appointment of a new pastor, *Richmond Planet*, September 14, 1901. These debates over gender roles within black churches occurred on congregational and denominational levels. For studies which examine these debates at the state and/or national level, see, for example, Higginbotham, *Righteous Discontent*; Glenda Gilmore, "Gender and Jim Crow: Women and the Politics of White Supremacy in North Carolina, 1896–1920" (Ph.D. diss., University of North Carolina, Chapel Hill, 1992); Cheryl Townsend Gilkes, "'Together and in Harness': Women's Traditions in the Sanctified Church," *Signs: Journal of Women in Culture and Society* 10 (Summer 1985): 678–699.

40. *Virginia Baptist* cited in *Woman's Era*, 1 (September 1894), 8.

41. *Richmond Planet*, July 26, 1890; June 8, 1895; September 17, 24, November 19, 1898; September 9, 1899; Anthony Binga, Jr., *Sermons on Several Occasions*, I (Richmond, 1889), 97–99. Both Kemp and Carter were Baptist. A few women also conducted services in the Methodist church. Evangelist Annie E. Brown, for example, conducted two weeks of revival services at Leigh Street Methodist Episcopal Church in 1900, *Richmond Planet*, April 28, 1900. Even when one

The debates within First African and other churches over women's roles were part of a series of political struggles within black Richmond in the late-nineteenth and early-twentieth centuries. As formal political gains, initially secured, began to recede and economic promise became less certain and less surely tied to political advancement, the political struggles over relationships between the working-class and the newly emergent middle-class, between men and women, between literate and nonliterate, increasingly became issues among Afro-Richmonders. Briefly examining how the sites of public discourse changed and how discussions regarding qualifications for and nature of individual participation developed suggests the degree to which debates over space and relationships represented important changes in many black Richmonders' assumptions about freedom itself.

The authority of the church in personal and civil matters decreased over the late-nineteenth and early-twentieth centuries. The church quietly acknowledged these changes without directly confronting the issue of its changed authority. The use of civil authorities to resolve the church dispute, especially since individual members continued to face censure if they relied on civil rather than church sanctions in a dispute with another member, suggests the degree to which First African tried to maintain its traditional authority over its members while acknowledging the limitations of its powers. First African turned outside not only itself but also the black community by inviting the intervention of the mayor, police chief and judge.[42] The decreasing authority of the church, however, accompanied a shrinking sphere of influence and activity for the church and the development of secular institutions and structures to take over, compete for, or share functions traditionally connected to the church as institution and structure. The changing church axis suggests important developments in the structures, nature and understandings of community in black Richmond.

"female preacher . . . took up station" outside a Manchester barbershop and preached against the male members, claiming they were "leading the young down to perdition," the *Planet*'s Manchester correspondent did not denounce her right to preach but rather suggested that if she "is called to preach the gospel, and is sanctified, as some say, why not organize a church of sanctification," rather than stand on street corners issuing "broad and uncalled for" attacks upon other ministers, *Richmond Planet*, December 12, 1896.

42. In July 1880 a council representing nine Richmond black Baptist churches censured First African for having called the police. "The First African Baptist Church, Richmond, Virginia, to the Messengers & Churches in General Ecclesiastical Council Assembled," in FABC, II, following April 3, 1881 minutes. For late-nineteenth century disciplinary procedures with regard to members who got civil warrants against other members, see for example, FABC, II, January 7, October 6, 1884; February 3, 1890.

After the Reverend James Holmes and the deacons of First African survived the 1880 challenge to their leadership, one of their first actions was to establish a regulation that church business meetings be closed to all but members. They had argued that it was outside agitators who had instigated and sustained the disorder and opposition. While this reflects concerns about internal church business, the closing off of the church was reflected in other central ways which potentially had more far-reaching consequences, and suggests the particularization of interests, concerns and functions of internal community institutions, and the changed nature of internal community politics. Having completed, at considerable expense, their new edifice, First African worried about avoiding damage and excess wear and tear. In November 1882 the church adopted regulations designed to eliminate the crowds of people attending weddings in the church by requiring guest lists and tickets, and to deny entirely the use of the main auditorium with the largest capacity for "programmes, closing of public schools, political meetings or feasts." In February 1883 when the Acme Lyceum requested use of the main auditorium for a lecture by Frederick Douglass, the church, following its new regulations, refused to grant the request, although it did offer as substitute the use of its smaller lecture room. That same year it denied the use of the church for the Colored High and Normal closing. The paucity of facilities available to black Richmonders meant that these activities now had to be held in much smaller facilities and the possibilities for the large mass meetings which First African had previously hosted were now reduced. Political meetings and other activities moved to other, smaller church sites or to some of the new halls being erected by some of the societies and businessmen. The latter, however, were more expensive to obtain since their rental was a major source of revenue for the group or individual owner; it also often particularized the meeting or occasion to a specific segment of the community. Without the large facility of First African, graduations and school closings could no longer be the traditional community-wide mass celebrations. Denied the use of First African and barred from the Richmond Theatre where the white high school students had their graduation, the 1883 Colored High and Normal graduation class held their exercises in a small classroom where very few could attend.[43]

43. FABC, II, June 27, November 6, 1882; February 5, April 2, 1883. Wendell P. Dabney, a member of that 1883 graduating class, remembered the students as having met in early June and "determined not to go to any church. That we would go to the Richmond Theatre or no where." He calls this "the first school strike by Negro pupils on record in the Unites States!" First African had, however, already denied the use of its facilities because of its new regulation. There is some evidence that, subsequent to the students' action, other black churches may have supported the young people by denying their facilities as well. Dabney, "Rough autobiographical sketch of his boyhood years,"

First African restricting use of church lead to fragmentation of community rituals
cf. 136

First African did not initiate and was not singly responsible for the changing nature of Republican Party participation, but its actions reinforced the narrower sense of party politics that white Republicans had already tried to enforce. Disturbed at black influence over Republican meetings, beginning in 1870 white Republican officials had taken steps to limit popular participation and influence in party deliberations. First they moved the party conventions from First African to the United States courtroom, a facility which held many fewer people and was removed from the black community; then they closed the gallery, thus allowing none but official delegates to attend and participate. In such a setting they were able to adopt a more conservative platform. Black Republicans had continued, however, to hold mass meetings, often when dissatisfied with the official Republican deliberations. When they were dissatisfied with Republican nominees for municipal office that came from the 1870 closed party convention, for example, black Republicans agreed to convene their own sessions and make their own nominations.[44]

In increasingly delimiting the church's use, distinguishing more clearly between sacred and secular activities as when it began to disallow certain kinds of entertainments in its facilities or on its behalf, and attempting to reserve the church for what was now designated as the "sacred," First African contributed to the increasing segmentation of black Richmond.[45] With the loss of the largest capacity structure some black Richmonders recognized the need to reestablish a community space. Edward A. Randolph, founder and first editor of the *Richmond Planet*, used Acme Literary Association meetings to argue regularly throughout 1883 and 1884 for the construction of a hall, a public meeting place within the community. His call was reinforced when the Choral Association was denied use of the Richmond Theatre and had to have its production in a small mutual benefit society hall, an inadequate facility for such a production. The construction of a large auditorium on the top floor of the Grand Fountain, United Order of True Reformers' bank and office building when it opened in 1890 was an effort to provide that space. It could hold larger gatherings than the other halls and most churches but still had only a small percentage of the seating capacity of

107–109; Wendell P. Dabney, *Maggie L. Walker and the I. O. of Saint Luke: The Woman and Her Work* (Cincinnati: Dabney Publishing Co., 1927), 32–33. *New York Globe*, June 23, 1883.

44. Rachleff, "Black, White, and Gray," 307–309.

45. See, for example, the discussion of the reconfiguration of leisure space, including the barring of cakewalks and other dancing from the church, in Elsa Barkley Brown and Gregg D. Kimball, "Mapping the Terrain of Black Richmond," *Journal of Urban History* (forthcoming).

First African.[46] A mass meeting on the scale common in the 1860s and 1870s could be held only outside the community and the facilities for such were often closed to African Americans.

As political meetings moved to private halls rather than church buildings, they became less mass meetings not only in the numerical sense; they also became more gatherings of an exclusive group of party regulars. This signaled not only a change in the role of the church but also a change in the nature of politics in black Richmond. The emerging format gave business and professional men, especially, greater control over the formal political process. First African's prohibitions against mass meetings, school closings, and other programs did not last long; the need and desire of members and other Afro-Richmonders for a space which could truly contain a community-wide activity eventually led members to ignore their prohibition. But instituting the prohibition had not only significantly affected community activities in the early 1880s; it also meant that, even after strict enforcement was curtailed, decisions about using the church for graduation exercises, political meetings and other activities were now subjects of debate. Afro-Richmonders could no longer assume the church as a community meeting place; instead they had to argue such. The church remained an important community institution, but it increasingly shared power with both civil authorities and other community institutions such as mutual benefit and fraternal societies.

The efforts by white Republican officials to limit popular decision-making and the decreased accessibility of First African as a community-wide meeting place affected a politics which had been based in mass participation. Mass meetings were still held throughout the late-nineteenth century, but they were now less regular. These changes were exacerbated by the struggle to retain the vote and office-holding and the necessity, therefore, to counter various tactics of both white Republicans and Democrats. The fraudulent tactics employed to eliminate black voters, for example, led some black Republicans, like John Mitchell, who continued to argue against literacy qualifications for voting, in the 1890s to encourage nonliterate black men to abstain from voting. Difficulty with many of the election officials' questions and with the ballots could not only delay the line but also the nonliterate voter's rights and/or ballot would more likely be challenged.

46. *New York Globe*, October 1883–January 1884. Estimates of the True Reformers' auditorium's seating capacity range from 900 to 1500 to 2000. Nearly 4000 people had been able to attend the March 1867 mass meeting held in First African in support of the Federal Sherman Bill. With their new edifices erected in 1890, Sixth Mount Zion and Sharon Baptist Churches had seating capacity of 1400 and 1200 respectively; most churches seated far fewer, Rachleff, *Black Labor in the South*, 40; *Richmond Planet*, March 14, May 31, 1890.

Mitchell thought it important to get those least likely to be challenged or disqualified, and most capable of correctly marking the ballots, through the lines first before polls closed on them. While Mitchell argued for a temporary change in practice – not perspective – regarding the right of all to vote, his and other prominent black Republicans' prioritizing of the literate voter significantly changed the makeup of the presumed electorate.

As the divisions between black and white Republicans became deeper in the 1890s, Mitchell and other black Republicans began to hold small Republican caucuses in selected homes, in essence attempting to control ward conventions by predetermining nominees and issues. The ward conventions themselves were often held in halls rather than the larger churches. The organization in 1898 of a Central Republican League which would oversee black Republican activities through sub-Leagues in all the city's wards reinforced the narrowing party politics framework. Republican Party decision-making was now more clearly limited to Party regulars; the mass of black voters and other election activists were expected to support these channels of decision-making.[47] These changes, consistent with democratic politics and republican representative government as practiced in late-nineteenth century United States, served to limit the power and influence of most black Richmonders in the electoral arena. If many black men abandoned electoral politics even before formal disfranchisement, it was in large measure due to the effectiveness of the extra-legal disfranchisement efforts of white men. The exclusion from real decision-making power within the Republican Party and, in this respect within the community, was also decisive.

The increasingly limited notion of political decision-makers which these changes encouraged is also evident in other ways. In 1896 during a factional dispute among black Republicans, John Mitchell challenged the decisions made in one meeting by noting that a substantial portion of those attending and participating were not even "legal voters," that is they were women. Although he espoused feminine dress and comportment, Mitchell supported women's rights and championed Dr. Sarah G. Jones's success as a physician as evidence of women's equality. He also endorsed women's suffrage while advising black women to understand the racism of the white women's suffrage movement and not to align themselves with it. Despite these personal convictions, Mitchell could dismiss or minimize opposing factions by a reference to the participation of women, suggesting the ways in which the

47. For information on the Central Republican League, see *Richmond Planet*, August–September 1898; *Richmond Evening Leader*, August 6, 16, 24, 27, 30, September 1, 28, October 12, 1898; *Richmond Times*, August 3, September 3, 11, 1898; *Richmond Dispatch*, September 14, 1898.

meanings and understandings of politics, of appropriate political actors and even of the ownership of the franchise had changed in the late-nineteenth century.[48]

Questions of qualifications for participation in the external political arena and internal community institutions were now frequent. During the conflictual 1901 business meeting at First African, for example, John Mitchell, Jr., questioned his opponents' right to participate even though they were all church members by pointing out their unfamiliarity with parliamentary procedure or their inelegant ways of speaking. The women, who were the targets of much of Mitchell's challenge, refused to accept these as criteria for their participation and even denigrated what he put forth as his formal qualifications by talking out when he got up to speak, saying derisively, "Don't he look pretty."[49] Questions of formal education had already affected the congregation in fundamental ways, most obviously in the late-nineteenth century debate over song, a debate which represented a significant change in the basis of collective consciousness.

The antiphonal nature of the traditional church service at First African and many black churches reinforced a sense of community. The services included spontaneous verbal and nonverbal interaction between minister and prayer, speaker and congregation thus allowing for the active participation of everyone in the worship service. It was this cultural discourse that was carried over into the political meetings. One important element that bound the congregation together was song; as Lawrence Levine has noted, through their collective song churchgoers "meld[ed] individual consciousness into the group consciousness."[50] However, the practice of lining hymns which was basic to collective song was one which white visitors often referred to when they described what they perceived as the unrefined black church services. Some black churchgoers saw the elimination of this practice as part of the work of uplifting the religious style and uplifting the race. But with the elimination of this practice, those unable to read and follow the lyrics in a song book were now unable to participate, to be fully a part of the community, the collective. It was the equivalent of being deprived of a voice,

---

48. *Richmond Planet*, January 26, 1895; October 17, 1896. Similarly, when black Republican men formed the Negro Protective Association in 1898 to organize to retain their vote and political influence, one of the most controversial discussions concerned whether to allow a women's auxiliary, the main purpose of which would be to raise monies for electoral activities. Because of heated opposition the proposal was abandoned. *Proceedings of the Negro Protective Association of Virginia, Held Tuesday, May 18th, 1897, in the True Reformers' Hall, Richmond, Va.*.

49. *Richmond Planet*, July 6, 1901.

50. Lawrence Levine, *Black Culture and Black Consciousness: Afro-American Folk Thought from Slavery to Freedom* (New York: Oxford University Press, 1977).

all the more significant in an oral culture. Daniel Webster Davis, a member of First African and pastor of Second Baptist (Manchester) as well as public school teacher, suggested such in his poem, "De Linin' Ub De Hymns":

Dar's a mighty row in Zion, an' de debbil's gittin'
    high,

. . . .

'Twuz 'bout a berry leetle thing—de linin' ub a
    hymn.
De young folks say 'tain't stylish to lin' um out
    no mo';
Dat dey's got edikashun, an' dey wants us all to
    know
Dey likes to hab dar singin'-books a-holin' fore dar
    eyes,
An' sing de hymns right straight along 'to man-
    shuns in de skies.'

. . . .

An' ef de ol' folks will kumplain 'cause dey is ol'
    an' blin',
An' slabry's chain don' kep' dem back frum larnin'
    how to read—
Dat dey mus' take a corner seat, an' let de young
    folks lead.

. . . .

We don' edikate our boys an' gals, an' would do
    de same again;

. . . .

De sarmon's highfalutin', an' de church am mighty
    fin';

. . . .

De ol'-time groans an' shouts an' moans am passin'
    out ub sight—
Edikashun changed all dat, an' we belebe it right,
We should serb God wid 'telligence; fur dis one
    thing I plead:
Jes' lebe a leetle place in church fur dem ez kin not
    read.[51]

51. Daniel Webster Davis, "'De Linin' Ub De Hymns," 'Weh Down Souf and Other Poems (Cleveland: The Helman-Taylor Company, 1897), 54–56.

The debates about women's roles in the church and in the more formal political arenas, like the debate over lining the hymns, were part of widespread discussions about the nature of community, of participation and of freedom.

The proliferation of scholarly works centered on the flowering of black women's political activity in the late-nineteenth and early-twentieth centuries[52] has perhaps left the impression that this was the inaugural moment or even height of black women's participation in politics. Overt or not, the suggestion seems to be that black women came to political prominence as (because) black men lost political power.[53] In much of this scholarship the reasons for black women's "emergence" are usually tied to external factors. For example, the development of black women's clubs in the late-nineteenth century and their important roles in the political struggles of the twentieth century most often have been seen by historians as the result of the increasing development of such entities in the larger society and as reaction to vitriolic attacks on the morality of black women. Such a perspective explains this important political force solely in terms of external dynamics, but external factors alone cannot account for this development.[54] The

52. The scholarly emphasis on this latter period is not merely a reflection of available sources. It also reflects the conceptual paradigms that have guided the investigation of black women's politics: a focus on the national level, often with minimal attention to different patterns within the North and the South; the acceptance of what Suzanne Lebsock has called the "consensus . . . that for women the standard form of political participation" in the nineteenth century "was the voluntary association"; an emphasis on autonomous women's organizations; and a focus on excavating political (and feminist) texts. This scholarly emphasis has produced a number of insightful works about the period; among them are Higginbotham, *Righteous Discontent*; Gilmore, "Gender and Jim Crow"; Hazel V. Carby, *Reconstructing Womanhood: The Emergence of the Afro-American Woman Novelist* (New York: Oxford University Press, 1987); Claudia Tate, *Domestic Allegories of Political Desire: The Black Heroine's Text at the Turn of the Century* (New York: Oxford University Press, 1992). Quote is from Suzanne Lebsock, "Women and American Politics, 1880–1920," in *Women, Politics, and Change*, eds. Louise A. Tilly and Patricia Gurin (New York: Russell Sage Foundation, 1990), 36.

53. Seeing the 1880–1920 period as "the greatest political age for women (including black women)," Suzanne Lebsock raises the question "what does it signify" that such occurred at "the worst" age for black people; "an age of disfranchisement and increasing legal discrimination," "Women and American Politics," 59, 37. Glenda Gilmore, in an otherwise thoughtful and nuanced study, contends that black women in North Carolina gained political prominence at the turn-of-the-century as (because) black men vanished from politics—either leaving the state altogether or sequestering themselves in a nonpolitical world, "Gender and Jim Crow," chapter 5. It is an idea, however, that is often unstated but implicit in much literature which imagines black women's turn-of-the-century club movement as their initial emergence into politics. Such a narrative contributes to the fiction that black women were safer in the Jim Crow South than were black men.

54. I am indebted to Stephanie J. Shaw for making the point that it was internal community dynamics more so than external factors which gave rise to the black women's clubs in the late-nineteenth century. See, Stephanie J. Shaw, "Black Club Women and the Creation of the National Association of Colored Women," *Journal of Women's History* 3 (1991): 10–25. In the end, my analysis of what those internal factors were differs somewhat from Shaw's; she attributes their rise to migration and

internal political arena, which in the immediate post-Civil War era was grounded in the notion of a collective voice which gave men, women and children a platform and allowed them all participation, came increasingly in the late-nineteenth century to be shaped by a narrowing notion of politics and appropriate political behavior.

While mass meetings continued to be held, the more regular forums for political discussions were literary societies, ward meetings, mutual benefit society and fraternal society meetings, women's clubs, labor organizations, newspapers, streetcorners, kitchens, washtubs and saloons. In the development of literary societies as a primary venue for public discussion, one can see the class and gender assumptions that by the turn-of-the-century came to be central to the political organization of black Richmond. While some, as the Langston Literary Association, had male members only, most of the literary societies founded in the 1880s and 1890s had middle-class and working-class men and women members. Despite the inclusive nature of the membership and often of the officers, the form of discussion which developed privileged middle-class males. Unlike mass meetings where many people might take the floor in planned and unplanned expositions and attendees might freely interrupt or talk back to speakers, thus allowing and building mass participation, literary forums announced discussion topics in advance; charged individual members, apparently almost always male, to prepare a paper on the subject; and designated specific, also male, members to reply.

The discussions that then ensued were open to all present but the structure privileged those familiar with the conventions of formal debate. Women, who served as officers and attended in large numbers, may have joined in the discussion but their official roles were designated as the cultural arm of the forum—reading poetry, singing songs, often with political content appropriate to the occasion. The questions under consideration at the meetings often betrayed the class bias of the forum. Even when the discussions centered on some aspect of working-class life and behavior, the conversation was conducted by middle-class men. The purpose of the forums, as articulated by the Acme Literary Society, suggested the passive observer/learner position that most were expected to take: to hold "discussions, lectures, and to consider questions of vital importance to our people, so that the masses of them may be drawn out to be entertained, enlightened, and

the resultant presence of a newly migrated group within the community in the 1890s, who sought to recreate in these communities the associational life they had left in their home communities.

instructed thereby."[55] Given the exclusionary nature of the discussion in these literary forums, even though welcoming a wide audience, it is understandable that far more working-class black men and women saw the Knights of Labor as their principal political vehicle in the late 1880s.[56]

In the changing circumstances of the late-nineteenth century, working-class men and women and middle-class women were increasingly disfranchised within the black community, just as middle-class black men were increasingly disfranchised in the larger society. Men and women, working-class and middle-class, at the turn-of-the-century were struggling to move back to a political authority they once had—internally and externally. As they did so they each often justified such authority along distinctively gendered and class-based lines.

African American men countered the image of themselves as uncivilized, beastly rapists—an image white southerners used to justify disfranchisement, segregation and violence—with efforts to demonstrate their own manhood and to define white males as uncivilized and savage.[57] While white Richmonders told stories of black barbarity, John Mitchell, Jr., inverted the tale. The *Richmond Planet*, for example, repeatedly focused on the sexual perversions of white men with cases of rape and incest and spoke of white men in terms designed to suggest their barbarism: "Southern white folks have gone to roasting Negroes, we presume the next step will be to eat them."[58] In the process of unmanning white males, however, Mitchell and others developed a narrative of endangered black women. Urban areas, once sites of opportunity for women, became sexually dangerous places for the unprotected female, easy prey to deceitful and barbarous white

55. *New York Globe*, 1883 and 1884, *passim*; Acme quote is June 23, 1883; *Richmond Planet*, July 26, 1890; January 12, 1895; 1890–1895, *passim*.

56. For a discussion of black Richmonders' participation in the Knights of Labor, see Rachleff, *Black Labor in the South*, chapters 7–12.

57. Efforts to demonstrate manhood increasingly took on class and status dimensions. For an example of this, see the discussion of black militias and the military ritual taken on by black fraternal orders such as the Knights of Pythias, in Barkley Brown and Kimball, "Mapping the Terrain."

58. See for example, *Richmond Planet*, June 11, 1891; February 24, September 22, 1900; February 16, 1901; October 25, November 1, December 20, 1902. Ida Wells-Barnett, in her struggle against the violence aimed at black women and black men, also challenged the links between white supremacy and manliness. For a discussion of Wells-Barnett's writings in this regard, see Gail Bederman, "'Civilization,' the Decline of Middle-Class Manliness, and Ida B. Well's Antilynching Campaign (1892–94)," *Radical History Review* 52 (Winter 1992): 5–30. Similarly, Frances Ellen Watkins Harper and Anna Julia Cooper associated Anglo-Saxon "imperialism with unrestrained patriarchal power," depicting white males as bestial devourers "of lands and peoples." Hazel V. Carby, "'On the Threshold of Woman's Era': Lynching, Empire, and Sexuality in Black Feminist Theory," *Critical Inquiry* 12 (Autumn 1985): 265.

males.[59] Black men's political rights were essential so that they could do as men should—protect their communities, homes, families, women. The focus on manhood could, initially, be the venue for discussing domestic violence as well. For example, the Reverend Anthony Binga, sermonizing against physical abuse of one's wife drew on the discourse of manhood: "I have never seen a man whip his wife. I mean a *man*. Everyone who wears a hat or a coat is not a *man*. I mean a *man*." And the members of First African took as a serious issue of concern the case of a husband who had infected his wife with syphilis.[60] Concurrent with the narrative of sexual danger in the city and the larger society was an implied corollary narrative of protection within one's own community. Thus the discourse on manhood could keep the concern with violence against women in the public discussion while at the same time setting the stage for issues of domestic abuse and other forms of intraracial violence, which could be evidence of the uncivility of black men, to be silenced as politically dangerous.

In drawing on the new narrative of endangered women, middle-class black women, increasingly disfranchised by the connections between manhood and citizenship in the new political discourse, turned the focus from themselves and on to the working class, enabling middle-class women to project themselves as the protectors of their less fortunate sisters. In this manner they reinserted themselves into a public political role.[61] Autonomous women's organizations, such

59. The idea of sexual danger had been a part of the Reconstruction era discourse, as evidenced in the mass indignation meetings and testimonies. Then, however, it was constructed as a matter of general interest, part of the general discussion of repression of African Americans. Now a more clearly gendered discourse developed where violence against men was linked to state repression and the struggle against it to freedom and violence against women became a matter of specific interest, increasingly eliminated from the general discussions.

60. First African also excluded men found to have physically abused their wives. Binga, "Duty of Husband to Wife," in Binga, *Sermons on Several Occasions*, I, 304–305 (emphasis in original); FABC, II, August 6, September 3, November 5, 1883, April 7, 1884. Ultimately the members of First African were at a loss as to how to deal with the sexually transmitted disease but the persistence of the church's efforts to take it up suggests the degree to which some members considered this a serious issue.

61. It is important to note the constructed nature of this narrative. Suzanne Lebsock has taken the development of women's clubs with these concerns as possible evidence of the increased instances of exploitation of women, "Women and American Politics," 45. I suggest that the exploitation is not increased or even of greater concern, but that the venues for expressing and acting on that concern and the ideology through which this happens—both the narrative of endangerment and the narrative of protection—are the new, changed phenomenon. While the emphasis on motherhood and womanly virtues which undergirded the ideology of middle-class women as protectors may resonate with much of the work on middle-class white women's political activism in this period, it is important to bear in mind two distinctions: African American women's prior history of inclusion, not exclusion, shaped their discourse of womanhood and their construction of gender roles; they did so not in concert with

as the Richmond Women's League (later the Richmond Mothers' Club) or women's divisions within other organizations such as the Standing Committee on Domestic Economy of the Hampton Negro Conference, developed to serve these functions. These associations promulgated class-specific ideas of respectability, in part justifying their public role through the need to impart such protective measures to working-class women. Specific constructions of womanhood, as manhood, thus became central to the arguments for political rights. Through discussions of manhood and womanhood, middle-class men and women constructed themselves as respectable and entitled, and sought to use such constructions to throw a mantle of protection over their working-class brothers and sisters. By increasingly claiming sexual violence as a women's issue, middle-class black women claimed a political/public space for themselves but they also contributed to an emerging tendency to divert issues of sexual violence to a lesser plane and to see them as the specific interest of women, not bound up in the general concerns and struggle for freedom. This set the stage for the masculine conception of liberation struggle which would emerge in the twentieth century.[62]

Collective History/Collective Memory

In July 1895 three black women — Mary Abernathy, Pokey Barnes and her mother, Mary Barnes — were convicted in Lunenberg County, Virginia, of murdering a white woman. When the women were moved to the state penitentiary in Richmond their case became a cause célèbre in the black community there. For over a year black men and women in Richmond struggled to keep the Lunenberg women from being hung or returned to Lunenberg County for a retrial, fearing that a return to Lunenberg would mean death, the women lynched at the hands of an angry white mob. The community succeeded and the three women were eventually released.

The organization of black Richmonders in defense of these women partly illustrates the increasingly gendered nature of internal community politics. Men

ideas in the larger society but in opposition as white Americans continued to deny African Americans the privileges of manhood or the protections of womanhood, reinforcing the commonality rather than the separateness of men's and women's roles.

62. James Oliver Horton and Lois E. Horton suggest that a masculine conception of liberation, based on violence as an emancipatory tool available principally to men, developed within African American political rhetoric in the North in the antebellum period. "Violence, Protest, and Identity: Black Manhood in Antebellum America," in James Oliver Horton, *Free People of Color: Inside the African American Community* (Washington, D.C.: Smithsonian Institution Press, 1993), chapter 4.

[handwritten margin notes: "Women as victims (i.e.) mothers"]

and women were portrayed as having decidedly different roles in the defense; one avenue of defense was to draw on ideas of motherhood in defending these three women; and the Lunenberg women's release called forth very particular discussions of respectability and womanhood. John Mitchell, Jr., portrayed himself as the militant defender of the women. Women, led by schoolteacher Rosa Dixon Bowser, organized the Richmond Women's League for the purposes of raising funds for the women's defense, visiting them in jail and supporting their husbands and families. Through her column in the *Woman's Era* and her participation in the National Federation of Afro-American Women, Bowser, as did Mitchell, brought the case to national attention. The front page stories in Mitchell's *Planet* emphasized the Lunenberg women as mothers, especially reporting on Mary Abernathy's pregnancy and the birth of her child in her jail cell. While the pictures and stories during the fourteen-month struggle for their release portrayed the women as simply clad, barefoot, farm women the announcement of Pokey Barnes's final victory was accompanied by a photograph of her now transformed into a true Victorian woman with elegant balloon-sleeved dress, a symbol of respectable womanhood. Later descriptions of Barnes, on speaking engagements, emphasized her dress: "a neat fitting, changeable silk gown and . . . a black felt hat, trimmed with black velvet and ostrich plumes." Mitchell emphasized the importance of this transformation: "The picture showing what Pokey Barnes looked like when brought to Richmond the first time and what she appears to-day will be a startling revelation to the public and will fill with amazement the conservative people everywhere when they realize what a terrible blunder the execution of this young woman would have been." He thus suggested that it was her ability to be a respectable woman (signified superficially by a class-based standard of dress) which was the justification for his and others' protection of her.[63]

63. Abernathy's and the Barnes' trials, incarceration, retrials, and eventual releases can be followed in the *Richmond Planet*, July 1895–October 1896; *Richmond Times*, July 23, 1895; *Richmond Dispatch*, September 13–19, October 2, 23, November 8, 9, 12, 14, 16, 21, 23, 24, 27, 28, 1895; July 5, 1896. For Bowser's discussion of the formation of the Women's League to protect the Lunenberg women, see *Woman's Era*, October and November 1895; Charles Wesley, *History of the National Association of Colored Women*. The first photographs of the women in the *Planet* appear August 3, 1895. The first picture of "Mary Abernathy and Her Babe" was published February 15, 1896. The post-release photograph of Pokey Barnes and Mitchell's comment regarding it appeared June 27, 1896. For a description of Barnes' attire, see March 6, 1897. Discussions of the case can be found in Brundage, *Lynching in the New South*; and Samuel N. Pincus, *The Virginia Supreme Court, Blacks and the Law 1870–1902* (New York: Garland Publishing, 1990), chapter 11. Brundage emphasizes the role of Governor O'Ferrall, and Samuel Pincus emphasizes the legal maneuverings which prevented the women's certain lynching. While emphasizing the importance of Mitchell's stands against lynching, Ann Alexander dismisses the prolonged front page coverage of the Lunenberg case in the *Richmond Planet* as mere sensationalism. "Black Protest in the New South: John Mitchell,

But the year-long discussion of these women's fates (the front page of nearly every issue of the *Richmond Planet* from July 1895 through early fall 1896 was devoted to these cases and included pictures of the women and sketches of their cabins) occurred alongside stories about lynchings or near lynchings of black men. Importantly, therefore, when black Richmonders spoke of lynching in the late-nineteenth century, they had no reason to assume the victim as male. When a freed Pokey Barnes rode as "mascot" in the 1896 Jackson Ward election rally parade, the idea of Mitchell and other black men as defenders was reinforced. But also affirmed was the underlying understanding that violence, including state repression, was a real threat to African American women as much as men. This meant that the reconstruction of clearly delineated notions of womanhood and manhood as the basis for political activism remained relatively ambiguous in late-nineteenth century black Richmond. But issues of class and gender were increasingly evident, as when Pokey Barnes and Mitchell accepted public speaking engagements—ones in which she was clearly expected to be the silent symbol of oppression and he the vocal proponent of resistance. Barnes, countering that assumption, set forth her own understandings of her role and qualifications, contradicting the class and gender assumptions of Mitchell and of those who invited them: "she said that she was not an educated lecturer and did not have any D.D.'s or M.D.'s to her name, but she was simply Pokey Barnes, c.s. (common sense)." Her two-hour lecture on her ordeal, while giving credit to Mitchell, established herself as not only victim but also heroine.[64]

The rescue of the Lunenberg women by black Richmonders brought women's struggles to the fore of black rights and reaffirmed violence against women as

---

Jr., (1863–1929) and the *Richmond Planet*" (Ph.D. diss., Duke University, 1973), 152–153. Yet it is certain that it was the continuous efforts of black men and women in Richmond which created the climate of protection for Pokey Barnes, Mary Abernathy and Mary Barnes, keeping their cases in the public eye, encouraging government and judicial officials to intervene, and providing the financial resources necessary to acquire a team of prominent white men as defense attorneys and advocates for the Lunenberg women. Pamela Henry has pointed to the focus on motherhood as a central point of the *Planet*'s defensive strategy and suggested the futility of such a strategy in an era when black women were denied the protections of Victorian womanhood. Pamela J. Henry, "Crime, Punishment and African American Women in the South, 1880–1940," paper for Research Seminar in African American Women's History, University of Michigan, Fall 1992 (cited by permission of Henry). I am uncomfortably cognizant of the fact that my narrative also, for the most part, silences Mary Abernathy and Pokey and Mary Barnes. This reflects my primary interest in understanding what this case illuminates about black Richmond. Abernathy and the Barneses, their lives and their cases, are certainly worthy of investigation in their own right; Suzanne Lebsock is currently undertaking such a study.

64. *Richmond Planet*, March 6, 1897.

part of their collective history and struggle. At the same time black Richmonders struggled to create a new category of womanhood that would be respected and protected, and of middle-class womanhood and manhood that could protect.[65] The plight of the Lunenberg women reaffirmed the collective history of black men and women at the same time as it invigorated increasingly distinct political vehicles for middle-class black men and women.

Just as disfranchisement, segregation, lynching and other violence denied the privileges of masculinity to African American men; segregation, lynching, sexual violence and accusations of immorality denied the protections of womanhood to African American women. Increasingly black women relied on constructing not only a respectable womanhood but, in large measure, an invisible womanhood. Hoping that a desexualized persona might provide the protection to themselves and their communities that seemed otherwise unobtainable, many black women carefully covered up all public suggestions of sexuality, even of sexual abuse. In the process issues specific to black women were increasingly eliminated from public discussion and collective memory.[66] In the late-twentieth century therefore

65. The narrative of class and gender, protectors and protected, was not uncontested. For example, the women of the Independent Order of Saint Luke offered a counternarrative which emphasized the possibilities of urban life not only for the middle-class but importantly the possibilities of urban life for single, working-class black women who, through their collective efforts, could be their own protectors. Still further, they suggested that women—working-class and middle-class—through their political and economic resources, could become men's protectors. Reinterpreting the standards for "race men" to require support for women's rights, they thus reinserted women's condition and rights as a barometer of freedom and progress. Some aspects of the Saint Lukes' ideas regarding the relationship between the well-being of women and the well-being of men and of the community as a whole are traced in Elsa Barkley Brown, "Womanist Consciousness: Maggie Lena Walker and the Independent Order of Saint Luke," *Signs: Journal of Women in Culture and Society* 14, 3 (Spring 1989): 610–633.

66. It is important to understand this desexualization of black women as not merely a middle-class phenomenon imposed on working-class women. Many working-class women resisted and forged their own notions of sexuality and respectability. But many working-class women also, independent of the middle-class and from their own experiences, embraced a desexualized image. Who better than a domestic worker faced with the sexual exploitation of her employer might hope that invisibility would provide protection? Histories which deal with respectability, sexuality, and politics in all its complexity in black women's lives have yet to be written. For beginning discussions see Darlene Clark Hine, "Rape and the Culture of Dissemblance: Preliminary Thoughts on the Inner Lives of Black Midwestern Women," *Signs: Journal of Women in Culture and Society* 14 (Summer 1989): 919–920; Elsa Barkley Brown, "'What Has Happened Here': The Politics of Difference in Women's History and Feminist Politics," *Feminist Studies* 18 (Summer 1992): 295–312; Paula Giddings, "The Last Taboo," in *Race-ing Justice, En-gendering Power: Essays on Anita Hill, Clarence Thomas, and the Construction of Social Reality*, ed. Toni Morrison (New York: Pantheon Books, 1992), 441–463.

many African Americans have come to link a history of repression and racial violence exclusively to challenges to black masculinity and thus to establish a notion of freedom and black liberation which bifurcates public discussion and privileges men's history and experiences. In 1991 when Supreme Court justice nominee Clarence Thomas challenged his questioners by calling the Senate Judiciary Committee hearings a "high-tech lynching," black Americans were divided in their response. Some men and women supported his analysis; others opposed either Thomas's analogy or his right to, in using such, assume the mantle of black manhood that he had so often rejected. Few people, however, questioned the assumption basic to Thomas's analogy that lynching and other forms of violence had historically been a masculine experience. Similarly, when black people across the country responded to the video of Los Angeles policemen's brutal beating of Rodney King, a narrative of state repression against black men followed.[67] The masculine focus is most evident in the widespread public discussion of "endangered" black men. While, appropriately focusing attention on the physical, economic and social violence which surrounds and engulfs many black men in the late-twentieth century United States, much of this discussion trivializes, or ignores the violence of many black women's lives—as victims of rape and other forms of sexual abuse, murder, drugs and alcohol, poverty and the devastation of AIDS. Seldom are discussions of rape and domestic violence included in summits on black-on-black crime. The masculinization of race progress which this implies often has some black leaders, looking to ways to improve the lot of men, not only omitting women from the picture but often even accepting the violence against women. What else can explain how Mike Tyson, even before he was charged with the rape of an eighteen-year-old black woman, would have been projected by ministers of the National Baptist Convention as a role model for young black men? By what standards would a man who had already publically acknowledged that he enjoyed brutalizing women have been put forward as a role model—unless rescuing black men from poverty and inner-city death at any price, including violence against women, was the standard by which the good of the race was being defined?

Such is the long term consequence of political strategies developed in the late-nineteenth century to empower black men and black women. Understandable

67. Bytches With Problems, "Wanted," is one effort by young black women to democratize the discussion of repressive violence; focusing on the often sexualized nature of police brutality against black women, they remind us that such is often less likely to be included in statistics or acknowledged in the public discussion. *The Bytches* (Noface Records, 1991).

and necessary in their day, they served to maintain a democratic agenda even as black political life became more divided. Eventually, however, the experiences of men were remembered as central to African American's struggles but the experiences of women, including the physical violence—lynchings, rapes, sexual and other forms of physical abuse as employees in white homes, domestic abuse— as well as the economic and social violence which has so permeated the history of black women in the United States, were not as vividly and importantly retained in our memory. We give life and validity to our constructions of race, community and politics by giving those constructions a history. Those who construct masculine notions of blackness and race progress and who claim only some forms of violence as central to African American liberation struggles are claiming/ remembering a particular history. African American collective memory in the late-twentieth century often appears partial, distorted and dismembered. The definitions and issues of political struggle which can come from that partial memory are limited. Before we can construct truly participatory discussions around a fully democratic agenda where the history and struggles of women and men are raised as issues of general interest necessary to the liberation of all, we have some powerful lot of rerembering to do.[68]

Elsa Barkley Brown teaches in the History Department and the Center for Afroamerican and African Studies at the University of Michigan. She is an associate editor of the two volume work, *Black Women in America: An Historical Encyclopedia* (Brooklyn: Carlson Publishing, 1993). Her articles have appeared in *Signs*, *Sage*, *History Workshop* and *Feminist Studies*. Her current research concerns African Americans in post-emancipation Richmond, Virginia.

68. Elsa Barkley Brown, "Imaging Lynching: African American Women, Communities of Struggle, and Collective Memory," in *African American Women Speak Out: Responses to Anita Hill-Clarence Thomas*, ed. Geneva Smitherman (Detroit: Wayne State University, forthcoming).

Race, Identity and Political Activism: The Shifting Contours of the African American Public Sphere

Steven Gregory

We in Corona-East Elmhurst are people who live with blacks but in a white community. We think outside of our community.

AN AFRICAN AMERICAN COMMUNITY ACTIVIST

In 1988 a multi-ethnic committee of neighborhood activists met in the basement of an African American church in Corona, Queens in New York City to discuss ways of improving intergroup relations. The committee, calling itself the Cultural Awareness Council, had been formed two years earlier in the wake of the racial attack on three black men by whites in Howard Beach. Most of the members of the Council, which included Jews, Asians and Latinos, were from the neighboring community of Jackson Heights and had been invited to the church by its newly appointed pastor. For the five church members who attended, all well over sixty, the sparsely furnished church basement was steeped in local political history. During the 1960s, voter registration drives, school desegregation battles and political campaigns had been discussed and planned here. The basement had also housed the church's Head Start Program. Square wooden cupboards that once held the preschoolers' lunch boxes still lined one of the walls. Most of the black church members present that evening had participated in those activities. For example, John Booker, a retired real estate agent in his eighties, had served on the Board of Trustees of the Congregational Church during the 1960s and played a key role in organizing church-based antipoverty programs. When the former pastor of the church ran for City Council in 1963, challenging Corona's white Democratic party machine, Booker worked to forge alliances with reform Democrats in predominantly white Jackson Heights.

Public Culture 1994, 7: 147–164

The memory of this coalition-building during the 1960s framed the opening of discussion. Judy Grubin, the Jewish founder of the Council, began the meeting by recalling the long-standing relationship that activists in Jackson Heights have had with African Americans in Corona and East Elmhurst. With the assembly seated in a wide circle, she recounted the struggle twenty years before to desegregate the community's schools. Grubin went on to describe the Council's purpose; "We were formed to discuss the cultures and traditions of different groups, and to open up a dialogue. Sharing diverse ethnic backgrounds is just the first step towards promoting harmony among people." Glancing at her clipboard, Grubin explained the format of the Council's meetings, held monthly at various locations in Queens, "Each person in the circle talks personally about their particular ethnic background and the experiences that they've had in the neighborhood."

Mrs. Blanche Hubbert, a church member and part-time caterer in her seventies, frowned and peered over her glasses at John Booker. "What do I want to be talkin' about my ethnic background for?" she asked him. Booker shrugged his shoulders and then focused his attention on the first speaker, Zakallah Prasada, a slender man from Pakistan. Prasada described how during the Iranian hostage crisis he and his wife had been harassed by people because they are Muslims. "Two times they burned our mosque in Corona," he reported. "For me, religious freedom is the most important issue." Yanghee Hahn, a woman from Korea, described cultural misunderstandings between Korean merchants and African Americans, and emphasized the importance of good communication. When Blanche Hubbert's turn came, she hesitated and fidgeted with her notepad. After an awkward silence, she spoke about food stereotypes, suggesting that this too was a form of prejudice. "I'm a caterer," she said, "and people always assume that I'm going to serve collard greens."

John Bell, who was next, appeared annoyed. Just turning seventy, Bell had been a labor organizer in the furriers union and active in Harlem politics during the 1930s. Looking youthful and debonair, Bell stood, striking a pose that betrayed decades of political speaking. "John Booker and I are the only ones here who have been active in both communities," he began, motioning to Mr. Booker at his side. "It seems like history is repeating itself! All that you have experienced here," he continued, gesturing to the group from Jackson Heights, "we already experienced. We have to become a political force, not a social one."

For John Bell, as for many African Americans in Corona, the post-civil rights period represents less a political victory than a rupture with politics. The sense that "history is repeating itself" registers not merely the awareness that the struggle for racial equality is not yet over, but more profoundly, the perception that its conditions of possibility, both political and discursive, have been weakened, if not undermined. Blanche Hubbert's choice of a story about catering and collard greens was neither intended to be humorous, nor to trivialize the question of racism. Rather, it was a strained attempt to convey the complex politics of race in the United States through the reductive logic of cultural misunderstanding. The Awareness Council's strategy for addressing the problem of intergroup relations captures in microcosm important changes in how many Americans have come to think—and not think—about issues of race, politics and social justice in the post-civil rights era. The (re)construction of racial and other systemic inequalities as problems of individual awareness, communication and sensitivity characterizes how a host of social issues, ranging from racially motivated violence to multicultural education, are framed in contemporary discussions, debates and scholarly research.

The case of Corona not only affirms the persistence of racial inequalities, it also reveals the power relations and practices that obscure and mask inequality. Put another way, in the post-civil rights period why have issues of racial inequality receded from public debate and contestation in the political life of African Americans in Corona? The answer lies in changes in institutional power arrangements that disarticulate questions of race from important arenas of political activism and discourse in Corona, thereby shielding practices of racial subordination from public debate and contestation.

This depoliticizing of race in local activism can be viewed in part as the result of a harnessing of the public sphere of African American neighborhood life to state-sponsored mechanisms of political participation, established in the wake of civil rights era activism and urban unrest. By directing attention to this restructuring of the public sphere of black community life—that is, to the multiple social arenas where people deliberate about neighborhood needs and formulate strategies for political action—I want to challenge a view that is prominent in discussions about the inner city. This view holds that the increasing intensity of the effects of racial inequalities or inner-city poverty is tied to a decay of black civil society, promoted by an exodus of the middle classes.[1] This view offers a reductive and decontextualized perspective on class identities, narrowly conceptualizing African American class formation as a function of occupational mobility. Equally important, this exodus model deflects attention from the institutional power rela-

1. See, for example, William J. Wilson, *The Truly Disadvantaged* (Chicago: University of Chicago, 1987) and Elijah Anderson, *Streetwise: Race, Class and Change in an Urban Community* (Chicago: University of Chicago, 1990).

tions and practices through which racial inequalities and class asymmetries are secured, negotiated and contested in the everyday lives of urban African Americans.

The state's role in shaping and reshaping the socio-political terrain on which African Americans in Corona interpret their needs, construct their identities and formulate their political commitments needs to be stressed. The heterogeneity and plasticity of African American identities can be seen in the social processes through which black class identities are formulated and reworked, "subject to the continuous play of history, culture and power."[2]

Inner-City Exodus and the Politics of the Public Sphere

The debate about the degree to which class stratification has occurred among African Americans has tended to gravitate around the work William Julius Wilson. Wilson has proposed that since 1940 the black occupational structure has shown a "consistent pattern of job upgrading," leading to growth in the ranks of the black working and middle classes.[3] However, this job mobility has not benefited all sectors of the black population equally: structural changes in the economy decreased the number of entry-level jobs for poorly educated, low-skilled blacks at the very time that their more educated and skilled counterparts were experiencing upward job mobility. Thus, despite gains made by the black work force, Wilson argues that there has been "an uneven development of economic resources in the black community" and the "income gap between the black poor and higher-income groups has widened."[4] Wilson also points to what he sees as the rise of an intense form of poverty concentrated in inner cities and linked to an array of social problems unprecedented in black community life. The emergence of this persistent form of ghetto poverty presents a paradox for Wilson, and he presents this paradox as a challenge to those who stress the importance of contemporary discrimination in producing black poverty. Backers of this "discrimination thesis," Wilson writes,

> find it difficult to explain why the economic position of poor urban
> blacks actually deteriorated during the very period in which the most

2. Stuart Hall, "Cultural Identity and Diaspora," in *Identity: Community, Culture, Difference,* ed. Jonathan Rutherford (London: Lawrence and Wishart, 1990), xx.

3. William J. Wilson, *The Declining Significance of Race* (Chicago: University of Chicago, 1978), 129.

4. Ibid., 134.

sweeping anti-discrimination legislation and programs were enacted and implemented. Their emphasis on discrimination is even more problematic, in view of the economic progress of the black middle class during the same period.[5]

Wilson's solution to this paradox rests partly on his analysis of changes in the economy, which undermined the period's gains for the black poor. To this macroeconomic argument Wilson adds a sociological one that relates changes in black occupational structure to the concentration of the black poor in inner cities. In Wilson's view, changes in occupational structure widened the income gap between the poor and non-poor, provoking an outmigration of the working and middle classes from inner-city areas. The exodus of the non-poor, Wilson contends, weakened community institutions and divested the inner cities of "mainstream role models that help keep alive the perception that education is meaningful, that steady employment is a viable alternative to welfare, and that family stability is the norm, not the exception."[6]

The case of Corona contrasts with the exodus hypothesis proposed by Wilson and variously challenged by others.[7] Corona did *not* experience a wholesale exodus of the black middle classes and a weakening of its civic infrastructure. Rather, deepening class divisions interacted with state interventions to harness the social institutions of black civil society to arenas of political activism where race was shielded from contestation, and where community needs and demands were increasingly refracted through the property-based interests and ideologies of middle-class homeowners. By directing attention to these changes in institutional power arrangements *within* African American communities, the role of the state can be seen both in shaping the process of black class formation, and in articulating its specific political, economic and ideological effects. From this perspective, the isolation of the inner-city poor becomes less the result of the flight of middle

5. Wilson 1987, 30.
6. Ibid., 56.
7. See Douglas Massey and Mitchell Eggers, "The Ecology of Inequality: Minorities and the Concentration of Poverty, 1970–1980," *American Journal of Sociology* 95 (1990): 1175-77; Douglas Massey and Nancy A. Denton, *American Apartheid: Segregation and the Making of the Underclass* (Cambridge: Harvard University, 1993); Robin D. G. Kelly, "The Black Poor and the Politics of Opposition in a New South City, 1929–1970," in *The Underclass Debate*, ed. Michael B. Katz (Princeton: Princeton University, 1993), 293–333; Thomas F. Jackson, "The State, the Movement, and the Urban Poor: The War on Poverty and Political Mobilization in the 1960s," in *The Underclass Debate*, ed. Michael B. Katz (Princeton: Princeton University, 1993), 403–439; and Adolph Reed, "The Underclass Myth," *The Progressive* 55 (August 1991): 18–20.

class social, cultural and institutional capital than it is an effect of a restructuring of political life in ways that shield racial inequalities from civic activism. This can be readily seen by examining activism in the context of the public sphere.

Jürgen Habermas's book, *The Structural Transformation of the Public Sphere* investigates the development of the "liberal model of the bourgeois public sphere," which emerges along with the widening of political participation and the consolidation of citizenship rights in early modern Europe.[8] As a counterweight to the absolutist state, the bourgeois public acted as a mediator between society and the state, holding the state accountable to "publicity" and to the critical scrutiny of an organized body of public opinion. In its mature form, this mediating role meant transmitting the interests of the bourgeoisie to the state through "forms of legally guaranteed free speech, free press, and free assembly, and eventually through the parliamentary institutions of representative government."[9] Habermas contends that the utopian potential of the bourgeois public sphere was never realized. The contradictions of capitalist development giving rise to monopoly capitalism, state intervention in social conflicts, and the fragmentation of the public into competing interest groups undermined the liberal ideal of an autonomous public sphere, where citizens could engage in rational-critical deliberation, unfettered by state power and the market economy.[10]

Habermas's account of the rise and transformation of the public sphere has been repeatedly critiqued.[11] The criticism most relevant here is that Habermas largely ignores "plebeian" and other competing, often oppositional public spheres. "From the beginning," writes Nancy Fraser, "counterpublics contested the exclusionary norms of the 'official' bourgeois public sphere, elaborating alternative styles of political behavior and alternative norms of public speech."[12] Pointing to contemporary social movements, Fraser notes that members of subordinated groups, such as women, people of color, lesbians and gays have found it politically important to constitute alternative, or "subaltern counterpublics"; that is, "parallel discursive arenas where those excluded from dominant discourses, invent and

8. Cambridge: MIT Press, 1991, xviii.

9. Nancy Fraser, "Rethinking the Public Sphere," in *The Phantom Public Sphere*," ed. Bruce Robbins (Minneapolis: University of Minnesota, 1993), 4.

10. Geoff Eley, "Nations, Publics, and Political Cultures: Placing Habermas in the Nineteenth Century," in *Habermas and the Public Sphere*, ed. Craig Calhoun (Cambridge: MIT Press, 1992), 289–339.

11. See for example, Dana R. Villa, "Postmodernism and the Public Sphere," *American Political Science Review* 86:3 (1992), 712–721.

12. Fraser 1993, 8.

circulate *counter*discourses, so as to formulate oppositional interpretations of their identities, interests, and needs."[13] The proliferation of such counterpublics allows issues that were previously shielded from contestation to be publicly argued. Through public deliberation and contestation across a range of discursive arenas and publics, Fraser suggests, issues and concerns become *politicized* and therefore, subject to political struggle.[14]

The idea of a subaltern public sphere highlights the problem of understanding how specific power arrangements shape and reshape the discursive spaces within which social groups interpret their needs, invent their identities and collectively formulate their political commitments. Put another way, the presence of a counterpublic can direct attention to the public arenas where micro-level discursive interactions are shaped by wider institutional power arrangements and discourses, and it locates the process of politicization and the formation of oppositional identities in social relations and practices that engender, or incite public deliberation and debate. In the case of Corona, the shift in the focus of political activism in the post-civil rights era is a shift from issues of racial inequality to the quality of life concerns of middle-class homeowners. This shift can be read, in part, as the effect of a restructuring of the public sphere of black neighborhood life as seen from the perspective of the face-to-face associational settings of neighborhood activism.[15]

Black Resistance and State Reform

Corona and the adjoining neighborhood of East Elmhurst today form the second largest concentration of African Americans in Queens County, New York. The two communities have a common history and common institutions, and are considered by residents and nonresidents alike to be a single black community. African American families began settling in Corona at the turn of the century. Many early arrivals were skilled workers, household workers, and professionals who

---

13. Ibid., 14.

14. Nancy Fraser, *Unruly Practices* (Minneapolis: University of Minnesota, 1989).

15. In this essay I say less about structures of mass-mediated public communication which play an increasingly important role in the production, circulation and consumption of meaning in the imagining of publics. For accounts of these structures, see Craig Calhoun, "Tiananmen, Television, and the Public Sphere," *Public Culture* 2:1 (1989), 54–71; Bruce Robbins, "Introduction," *The Phantom Public Sphere* (Minneapolis: University of Minnesota, 1992), vi–xxvi; Miriam Hansen, "Unstable Mixtures, Dilated Spheres: Negt and Kluge's *The Public Sphere and Experience*, Twenty Years Later," *Public Culture* 5:2 (1993), 179–212.

left congested areas of black settlement in Manhattan in search of homeownership and better living conditions in Queens. In 1910 black settlement in Corona was boosted when the Pennsylvania Railroad completed construction of the Sunnyside Yards in Long Island City, just west of Corona. African Americans, employed as Pullman porters, maids, cooks and in other railroad-related jobs moved to Corona to be closer to the Sunnyside Yards. Many Corona women found employment with commercial laundries and other local industries servicing the railroad. Prior to the Second World War, African Americans lived throughout Corona alongside European, working-class immigrants.

As their numbers grew during the 1920s and 1930s, black Corona residents organized an infrastructure of churches and voluntary associations, such as the Elks, Prince Hall Masons and Urban Big Sisters, while maintaining important social, cultural and political ties to Harlem. Black social clubs proliferated, carving up Corona society into overlapping, and often competing social sets, along age, gender and class lines.[16] Older residents often speak of the period between the world wars as a Golden Age, a time when the area boasted a "better class of people" and "good society." A weekly feature of the *New York Age*, New York's leading black newspaper of the period, was called Corona Chatter, which regularly reported on Corona society and community events during the 1930s. Written by We Seven, seven anonymous residents, Corona Chatter was a gossip column that provided an important forum where claims to status and class identity were publicly aired and contested, often along the axis of gender. In a caustic response to the announcement of a cocktail party hosted by the Glamour Girl Social Club, We Seven wrote: "There are several chippies in Corona who claim to be sub-debutantes. Where did they get this? A point of reality [sic], they are just a bunch of plain Corona chicks. The meaning of sub-debs is to be found in the dictionary and you will find that they are far from that so-called society class."[17]

During the 1930s Corona's black population increased fifty percent and the community began to exert its political muscle. Black political clubs established patron-client relations with white political kingpins, exchanging patronage for Corona's growing black vote. One prominent realtor and "race politician" organized boycotts of local businesses that refused to hire blacks and, together with local ministers, picketed the 1939 World's Fair for its discriminatory hiring prac-

16. See St. Clair Drake and Horace Cayton, *Black Metropolis* (New York: Harcourt, Brace and Company, 1945) and E. Franklin Frazier, *Black Bourgeoisie* (New York: Collier, 1962).

17. *New York Age*, 11 March 1939, 7.

tices. Black voluntary associations, such as the Negro Youth Association, the Phyllis Wheatly Sewing Circle and Corona's social clubs provided resources and labor for these actions, as well as important public forums for cultivating oppositional views and styles of political behavior. For example, in a 1941 Corona Chatter column, the Musketeer Social Club appealed to the "Negro people of Corona" to mobilize for a boycott of a segregated local theater. Far from merely providing "status without substance," as Franklin Frazier wrote of black bourgeois society, Corona's voluntary associations formed a fluid, heterogeneous and, from the vantage point of white society, largely invisible network of constituencies or publics, which could be, and often were mobilized for political activities.

By 1950 the black population of Corona had reached nearly 10,000. Those who arrived during the 1940s and 1950s were more diverse economically than had been their working and middle-class predecessors. Many had arrived directly from the South in search of jobs during the war. Other were displaced from nearby Flushing, when a slum area was cleared through the federal Urban Renewal, or, as James Baldwin put it, "Negro removal program." Housing in black sections of Corona deteriorated as single family homes were converted into apartments and rooming houses. "Whatever happened to the Corona of old?" asked the editors of Corona Chatter. "It is getting so that desirable and respectable families, migrating from other parts, venture further out on Long Island to avoid Corona."[18]

Rapid population growth, coupled with overcrowded housing and poor city services, promoted a differentiation of the area along the lines of race and class. Whites fled black areas of Corona for other sections of Long Island while many middle-class black families left declining areas of Corona and bought homes in the adjoining, more affluent community of East Elmhurst. Although the socioeconomic differences between the two areas remained fluid and contested, moving out of Corona became increasingly meaningful as a marker of status and economic stability for middle-class homeowners in East Elmhurst. To enhance and emphasize their distinction, residents of East Elmhurst pressured the postal service to have their area assigned a separate zip code. One woman, who had moved with her family to East Elmhurst from Corona in 1952, told me: "If you didn't have a college degree, the neighbors would walk all over you." She added: "I was surrounded by people who owned their own businesses, and they got to putting on airs. So I told them, 'I pay the same taxes as you all, I throw out *just* as much garbage as you do, and I do just as much for my children.' *That* stopped them!"

18. *New York Age*, 7 November 1941, 8.

Neighborhood deterioration, fueled by post-war suburbanization, black in-migration and structural weaknesses in the urban economy, sharpened the perception of class and status differences between the two areas. But it also heightened awareness among activists that Corona's growing problems of poverty, housing deterioration and poor city services were tied to its lack of political power as a *black* community. Real and imagined class differences remained important in articulating black identities and in shaping the specific effects of racial exclusion. But the impact of neighborhood decline, underscored for many the vulnerability of African American residents across class lines to wider structures and processes of racial exclusion.

During the 1960s and 1970s, African Americans in Corona pursued a range of strategies to address the interrelated goals of political empowerment and neighborhood preservation. Given its constricted playing field of the patronage system, politics was for many synonymous with corruption and narrow, sectarian interests; yet politics came to be seen as vital to the preservation of black neighborhood life. Indeed, civil rights era activism is distinguished from earlier periods of mobilization by the widespread politicization of the social networks and institutions of black civil society. This process of politicization involved both an expansion of the range of power relations contested by activists in Corona, as well as a proliferation of the public arenas within which such contests took place.

A broad spectrum of issues—ranging from school segregation and political exclusion, to unemployment and racist mortgage lending practices—became targets for social activism, and were publicized as *interrelated* effects of structural economic and political inequalities.[19] A campaign flyer circulated during the unsuccessful campaign of a Corona minister for the City Council in 1963, illustrates the close interweaving of neighborhood concerns with structural economic issues and the national agenda of the Civil Rights Movement. Reverend Robert D. Sherard, the flyer reads, "will lead the community's fight for civil rights for all and an end to discrimination, a full employment economy, improved and integrated education, better housing for low- and middle income families, consumer protection against increased fares, rates and prices, and honest, efficient and responsible government." In addition to this proliferation of contested issues, the public arenas, where these inequalities were defined and acted upon, expanded to embrace a heterogeneous array of social networks and institutions. For example, although Corona's churches had played a minor role at best in earlier political

19. See Ira Katznelson, *City Trenches* (Chicago: University of Chicago, 1981).

contests, they provided an important political base for much of the activism in Corona during the 1960s and 1970s.

This rapid politicization of black civil society had multiple causes, linked to national and local political and economic conditions. The Civil Rights Movement provided both a new political vocabulary and model of social mobilization which rearticulated the meaning, terrain and borders of politics. Corona activists formed ad hoc, direct action committees, which drew support from an assortment of social networks and institutions. One committee, the Independent Citizens for Good Government, adopted strategies used by the Southern Christian Leadership Conference (SCLS) in its Crusade for Citizenship, and convened activists from an unprecedented array of political clubs, voluntary associations and churches to address political empowerment, school desegregation and other issues. The federally sponsored Urban Renewal and War on Poverty programs created new, although short-lived political spaces where activists could deliberate about community interests and needs. Federal regulations intended to promote the "maximum feasible participation" of residents in poverty areas led to the creation of citizens' advisory bodies such as Corona's Community Action Council (1961) and the Urban Action Task Force (1968). These citizens' councils convened diverse groups of activists, whose political skills and identities had been honed within a range of political arenas, including the trade union movement, school-based parents associations, and in emerging sectors of the Black Power and Black Nationalist movements.

Although offering only limited participation in decision-making, these government-sponsored citizens' advisory councils provided important public arenas where activists learned the mechanics, as well as structural weaknesses of urban governing regimes.[20] For example, in Corona as elsewhere, activists often appropriated the federal rhetoric of citizen participation, and the institutional resources provided by the government's War on Poverty to press demands against local governing agencies and political elites. In so doing, they extended the concept of "maximum feasible participation" to goals and arenas of activism that reached beyond the service-coordination focus on the War on Poverty. In Corona, activists working through antipoverty agencies mobilized voters against local politicians, and organized parents in struggles over the control of schools.

20. On this issue see Susan S. Fainstein and Norman I. Fainstein, *Urban Political Movements* (Englewood Cliffs, NJ: Prentice Hall, 1974) and "Economic Change, National Policy and the System of Cities," in *Restructuring the City*, eds. Susan S. Fainstein, Norman I. Fainstein, et al. (New York: Longman, 1983), 1–26.

To briefly summarize, the civil rights period witnessed an expansion of the public sphere of black political activism. This involved the politicization of existing public arenas, such as the churches, block clubs and other civic institutions, as well as the creation of new political spaces, in part through federal and local attempts to manage civil rights era activism through strategies of bureaucratic enfranchisement. The proliferation and coordination of these insurgent groups or counterpublics was evidenced in neighborhood struggles. Activism in Corona was characterized by intense coalition-building, often cross-cutting class, ideological and racial lines. For example, in 1964, the Independent Citizens for Good Government joined with the NAACP, black Republican and Democratic political clubs, block associations and an interdenominational coalition of churches to establish the Ad Hoc Committee for Voter Registration. "We have pledged to put aside all individual differences," wrote the Committee's chair in a letter to community residents, "and work as one to achieve our objective."

Similarly, when the 1968 New York City teachers' strike threatened to close local schools, the Corona branch of the Black Panther Party, many of whose members had been recruited from the Enforcers, a Corona street gang, joined in demonstrations with a multiracial coalition of parents and members of the largely middle-class East Elmhurst Civic Association. In the early 1970s block and civic associations worked closely with clergy, parents' groups and members of the Black Panther Party and Nation of Islam to pressure the city to fund a community library specializing in black history and culture.

These struggles produced important results. Through the War on Poverty, community action agencies were established to provide job training, day-care and other social services. Political decentralization in New York led to the creation of government-sponsored, citizens' advisory boards intended to bridge the gap between local communities and city government. Black community activists were appointed and elected to newly formed institutions such as the Community Board, the Police Precinct Council and the Local Community School Board. Finally, voter registration drives of the 1960s mobilized black voters, making them a force to be reckoned with by local white politicians. In 1974, following a power-sharing agreement with the Queens County Democratic Party, Corona-East Elmhurst elected Helen Marshall, a parents' association activist, to be a State Assembly District Leader and later a member of the State Assembly.

These civil rights era gains increased African American representation in electoral politics, in the administration of social welfare programs and on newly formed citizens' advisory boards. However, as I proposed below, the state's response to the insurgent politics of the 1960s was to restructure political space in ways that shielded racial inequalities from contestation, while empowering class-specific forms of civic activism and consciousness.

Contested Publics

The opening of opportunities for political participation in government bureaucracies and mainstream political parties served to funnel activists in Corona into specialized public arenas, where community needs were interpreted and framed in narrow, enclaved contexts. The antipoverty program in Corona led to the creation of highly specialized neighborhood service corporations, bureaucratically tied to a tangled assortment of city, state and federal agencies. In 1970 these community action agencies were consolidated under the aegis of Elmcor Youth and Adult Services, a multiservice agency providing job training, housing assistance and other services. Poverty, once interpreted as an effect of an interrelated set of racially constructed inequalities, was reframed as an administrative problem, which would be managed, as Thomas Jackson puts it, in a "segregated 'arena' of poverty politics."[21]

Elmcor was not only dependent on government agencies for funding, but was also constrained to interpret and respond to community needs in ways that complied with the bureaucratic, client-driven service strategies of its funding sources. Moreover, the viability of Elmcor depended less on the political mobilization of residents than on the tactical support of local political elites. Elwanda Young, the executive director of Elmcor and a former Black Panther Party activist, spoke to how this client-based service strategy restricted social interaction across class lines:

> I'm thinking about the clients we serve and how they might even begin
> to interact with upper class blacks and there's no type of connection.
> Their paths never cross anymore. The only possible connection might
> be in the church where you might have this grassroots person still at-
> tending this church. But other than that there's little opportunity for
> them to meet.

An equally important effect of this process was to remove the issue of poverty from the purview of institutions, such as the church, the NAACP and other civic

21. Thomas Jackson, "The State, the Movement, and the Urban Poor: The War on Poverty and Political Mobilization in the 1960s," in *The Underclass Debate*, ed. Michael B. Katz (Princeton: Princeton University Press, 1993).

groups, which had earlier played important roles in defining and publicizing the *political* significance of black poverty. It was not that the membership and leaders of these groups had lost interest in the "plight of the poor"; rather, their roles in both defining and mobilizing residents to *act* on the issue of poverty were superseded through the bureaucratic institutionalization of the War on Poverty. As one former pastor of the Corona Congregational Church put it, "The loyalty of the people went to Borough Hall, rather than to the church and what it was doing."

This separation of the issue of black poverty from the public arenas of neighborhood activism was exacerbated by state actions limiting citizens' involvement in community development. As early as 1965 the United States Conference of Mayors, alarmed by African American and Latino political mobilization in cities, pressured the federal government to prohibit voter registration activities by federally funded community action agencies. In 1974, under the Nixon administration's new federalism policy, the Community Development Block Grant (CDBG) program was established, which weakened federal requirements for citizen participation by relegating decisions concerning community participation to local officials.[22]

Similarly, the funneling of activists into mainstream channels of political participation fragmented interrelated community issues and restricted their deliberation to highly specialized governing elites. Problems in the schools, for example, today fall under the jurisdiction of the Local Community School Board. Housing, zoning and other issues pertaining to the performance of city agencies are managed by a politically appointed Community Board. Each of these governing bodies has its own electoral or appointment process, meeting schedule and decision-making protocol, rendering the mechanics or political participation confounding, if not inaccessible to most community residents.

Bureaucratic enfranchisement also narrowed the range of neighborhood concerns deliberated and contested in public through Corona's voluntary associations. Problems of run-down housing and police misconduct, for example, were once focal points for community mobilization and coalition-building, and are now routinely channeled through the formal complaint mechanisms of government-sponsored institutions. Once relatively autonomous, even oppositional civic groups, such as the NAACP, block clubs and civic associations, today work in tandem with local politicians and city officials, translating neighborhood needs and demands into the narrow service categories and power-evasive worldviews

22. Fainstein and Fainstein, 1983.

of city officials. For example, at a meeting of the East Elmhurst-Corona Civic Association, which I attended in 1989, an official from the Department of Sanitation was invited to respond to complaints about services, which residents felt were inferior to those provided in neighboring white communities. The Sanitation Department's community liaison gave a presentation on his agency's efforts to better serve the neighborhood. The official's presentation provides an example not only of how expert knowledge is bureaucratically deployed to fragment and depoliticize community issues, but also of how officially sanctioned ideologies penetrate local contexts, in this case to redefine a problem of political weakness as one of moral crisis. In response to complaints about erratic garbage collection, the Sanitation Department official cited statistics on the number of summonses that had been issued in the area for "behavioral incidents"; that is, for the failure of residents to sweep the fronts of their homes and businesses. Continuing in a more philosophical vein, he observed, "Garbage is no longer out of sight, out of mind. There is a moral breakdown in our society that includes crime, drugs, garbage and everything. It is the young *kids* who don't care about your houses and don't have values and morals."

This example suggests how bureaucratic incorporation depoliticizes racial inequalities, disarticulating related community needs, while directing demands into enclaved arenas of political participation. Bureaucratic incorporation has also shaped the political effects of deepening black class divisions. The arenas of activism that opened in the post-civil rights period have proven to be disproportionately responsive to middle-class homeowners who are organized into tightly knit networks of block and civic associations.

Block associations, once referred to by the area's state assemblywoman as the "building blocks" of the community, criss-cross East Elmhurst and to a lesser extent Corona. These block clubs have proven to be important resources for government, for gauging, and whenever possible, regulating public reaction to controversial policies. Through them problems of poor services, housing decline and inadequate police protection can be micro-managed and contained by city officials at the local, block-focused level. For this and other reasons, block clubs and their umbrella organization, the East Elmhurst-Corona Civic Association, are important venues for state and private sector intervention in neighborhood politics. Accordingly, these block and civic clubs enjoy privileged access to power.

This concentration of political power is refracted through the prism of class. As David Harvey has pointed out, a strong correlation exists between homeownership and community activism through block and civic clubs.[23] In fact today there are more than twice as many block associations active in middle-class East Elmhurst as there are in Corona, a relation which reflects East Elmhurst's higher rate of homeownership. In short, the mechanisms of political participation that emerged in the post-civil rights era served to disproportionately empower middle-class homeowners by responding vigorously both to their class-specific forms of civic activism and their property-based interpretations of community needs.

The complex restructuring of Corona's political landscape has given rise to forms of political discourse, subjectivity and activism that emphasize the defense of household equity and residential privilege, not unlike the "slow growth" movements that Mike Davis has associated with homeowner politics and its ideology of "responsible environmentalism."[24] The ascendancy of homeowner politics in Corona registers wider political transformations that have occurred in many cities within the context of global economic restructuring. Economic restructuring in the United States, driven by the crisis of the Fordist regime of accumulation in the 1970s, accelerated the deindustrialization of central cities and incited important changes in the pattern of state intervention. Specifically, as Manuel Castells points out, the emphasis in state intervention shifted from strategies of social redistribution to policies aggressively facilitating capital accumulation.[25] In New York City this economic and political restructuring provided a context for reorienting policy priorities away from community-based development initiatives and toward fiscal austerity and economic development strategies promoting capital accumulation in post-industrial growth areas, such as finance and real estate.[26] As a result, in Corona and other communities, land-use politics has come to dominate the local political agenda, as governing alliances of city officials, bureaucrats and private land development interests appeal to, and attempt to marshal tightly knit networks of homeowners to support elite-driven land-use strategies.

Thus the arenas of political participation that have proven the most accessible and responsive to African Americans in Corona are precisely those within which the land-use strategies of governing elites resonate with, or better, interpellate property-based constructions of black middle-class identity. Here I stress how

23. "Labor, Capital and Class Struggle around the Built Environment in Advanced Capitalist Societies," in *Urbanization and Conflicts in Market Societies*, ed. K. R. Cox (New York: Methuen, 1978), 9–37.

24. Mike Davis, *City of Quartz* (London: Verso, 1990), 156–160.

25. *The Informational City* (Cambridge, MA: Blackwell, 1989).

26. Ibid. See also Robert Fitch, *The Assassination of New York* (London: Verso, 1993) and Susan S. Fainstein, *The City Builders* (Cambridge, MA: Blackwell, 1994).

institutional power arrangements and practices both engender and hinder particular constructions of political needs, identity and interests.

Finally, the ideological contours and contradictions of this quality of life politics can be seen in a 1989 meeting of the East Elmhurst-Corona Civic Association. The association met at the La Guardia Airport Holiday Inn to consider a New York State-funded proposal to establish a group home for mentally retarded adolescents in East Elmhurst. The plan had already been rejected by the 99th Street Block Association, where the state had purchased a building for the group home. State Assemblywoman Helen Marshall invited representatives of the not-for-profit agency sponsoring the home to present its plan to the community. After the presentation, Civic Association members were invited to question the home's sponsors. One resident asked, "Shouldn't you come to the community *first* before you contract to buy a house?" The representative responded with a question: "Do you ask permission from neighbors when you move into a new neighborhood? We see our home as one big family." This response provoked an angry outburst from the audience, since it seemed to conflate the establishment of the group home with the experience of black families moving into segregated white neighborhoods. Assemblywoman Marshall tried to restore calm, assuring the audience that the area's Community Board would hold a public hearing later in the month.

"Will there be drug testing?" a young woman asked. "The residents will be mentally retarded adolescents and not drug addicts," came the response. The audience again erupted in anger. "No way! We have enough problems with our own families," one man stated. A second shouted: "I don't want them; I live two doors away. I'm a pretty good shotgun artist," he added, menacingly. A woman asked: "How can you force this on us when we don't want it? Our property values will go down. This is basically a business and a quality of life decision for us." Assemblywoman Marshall, again trying to calm the audience, stood and addressed the representative. "You see, Mr. Farnum, this is a *black* community and everyone has put their life savings into this community. We care *so* much about the disadvantaged that we already have 481 beds for special populations. We did our share, but the city didn't do its share."

The Civic Association's response to the proposal for the group home suggests that these public spheres of black middle-class activism can also be sites for contesting governing practices and for rearticulating class identities. Association members challenged the sponsor's compliance with both the procedures of bureaucratic service provision ("Will there be drug testing?") and the legitimating conventions of urban regime politics ("Shouldn't you come to the community *first* before you go into contract?"). Although these critical responses were narrowly framed as a defense of property and family values, they did question the right of the state and its allies to dictate patterns of urban land-use.

But more importantly, Assemblywoman Marshall's assertion that Corona "is a black community" and that the "city didn't do its share" disrupted the construction of black middle-class identity as raceless and overdetermined by property values. By naming Corona a black community, Marshall recovered the specificity of race, reframing the community's refusal to accommodate special populations as a wider issue of environmental justice. For like other communities of color, Corona has born a disproportionate share of quality of life threats within the increasingly polarized postindustrial city.[27] However, we need to be careful not to exaggerate the oppositional possibilities of this, or similar recoveries of wider relations of social injustice. The middle-class identities called into being within the public arenas of black homeowner activism are at once enabling and limiting, offering residents a specific perspective of elite power, as well as of the possibilities for resisting it.

What needs to be emphasized is the heterogeneity and plasticity of African American social identities and the multiplicity of public spaces where they are crafted. The ascendancy of homeowner politics is not a simple reflection or realization of an essential and monolithic black middle-class identity. Rather, it is a complex and often contradictory result of the interplay of resistance and state power—"a war of position," as Gramsci put it, in which the stakes are the very surfaces (what I have been calling the public sphere) on which people imagine their political needs, identities and projects. If we are to change this society, we must learn much more about the church basements, hotel meeting rooms and other public arenas where we do politics, and indeed, where politics does us.

Steven Gregory teaches anthropology and Africana Studies at New York University. His recent work has appeared in *Cultural Anthropology, Diaspora* and *Po-LAR*. He is co-editor with Roger Sanjek of the forthcoming volume *Race* (Rutgers University Press) and is currently writing *Race and the Politics of Subjugation in the Post-Civil Rights Era*.

27. See Robert D. Bullard, ed., *Confronting Environmental Racism* (Boston: South End Press, 1993).

Black Cinderella?: Race and the Public Sphere in Brazil

Michael Hanchard

On June 26, 1993 an incident in Vitória, capital city of Espírito Santo, Brazil, drove another nail into the coffin of the ideology of Brazilian racial democracy. Ana Flávia Peçanha de Azeredo, a nineteen-year-old college student, was accosted and punched in the face by a forty-year-old woman and her eighteen-year-old son in the service elevator of an apartment building where Ms. Peçanha was visiting a friend. The physical assault was the result of an argument between the three over Ana Flávia's use of the elevator. The mother and son did not like the fact that this young black woman not only had entered their building and held up the social elevator to talk to a friend, forcing them to use the service elevator, but also that she had dared tell them to respect her after they informed her that "black and poor don't have a place here" in the building where they lived.[1]

This incident, like so many other acts of racist violence in Brazil, would have gone unnoticed if Ana Flávia's father, Albuino Azeredo was not the governor of the state of Espírito Santo. With the resources available to him, Governor Azeredo employed lawyers and physicians to examine his daughter's situation, and filed suit against Teresina and Rodrigo Stange, the alleged assailants. If convicted of racial discrimination under Article Five of the federal Constitution,

I would like to thank Kit Belgum, Claudia Briones, Richard Graham and Hendrick Kraay for their helpful comments on an earlier version of this paper.

1. See "Cinderela Negra" in *Veja*, 7 de Julho, 1993, p. 66–71.

Public Culture 1994, 7: 165–185

both mother and son could be sent to prison for one to five years. Ironically, the Brazilian press referred to Ana Flávia as the black Cinderella, with her father the Governor playing the role of prince. One may wonder, however, which Cinderella were they referring to? The one who is fitted with the errant glass slipper and who lives with the prince happily ever after, or the one who wears worn-out clothing and spends her days performing domestic labor? In fact, as a woman of African descent, Ana Flávia is neither. She is closer to a composite of status-filled and status-less roles in Brazilian society; considered a member of Brazil's elite when identified by birth, treated as a lowly, powerless member of society when identified by race.

The tale of black Cinderella is resonant with many of the constitutional, legal, cultural and societal issues of Afro-Brazilians within the Brazilian public sphere. It encapsulates the intersection of race, citizenship and modernity in a society that in theory is committed to liberal-democratic principles, but in practice still struggles with the legacies of patron-clientelism, racial slavery and oppression. The above incident might seem commonsensical enough from a comparative perspective, but within the context of Brazilian racial politics it further confirms the denial of full citizenship to people of African descent in Brazil during this most recent period of democratization. Comparatively, it also attests to the pervasiveness of black subjectivity in societies under the template of modernity, both inside and outside the West. The public sphere, far from being simply the location of bourgeois culture's prized subject—the individual—has also been the place where the West's others have been displaced and marginalized, inside and outside its borders. Indeed, as I will argue in this explication and critique of notions of the public sphere put forth by several social and political theorists, it has been upheld as the benchmark of modernity, the principal indicator of political and socio-economic development.

People of African descent, however, have been granted contingent and partial citizenship within these spheres, and only as a consequence of their own political struggles that have gone beyond the boundaries of liberal discourse. What I would like to demonstrate in this essay is the symbolic function of Afro-Brazilians within Brazilian society as bearers of noncitizenship, in accordance with racist ideologies and practices by the Brazilian state and in civil society during the nineteenth and twentieth centuries. In short Afro-Brazilians—like many other Afro-diasporic populations—have been depicted as embodying the antithesis of modernity.

This depiction, however, has two specific implications for scholarly intervention. First, it highlights modernity's limitations in terms of racial politics, and the manner in which its ideals have been intrinsically racialized. Second, it highlights the abstractness of theorizing on citizenship and the public sphere by theorists like Charles Taylor and Jürgen Habermas, as well as the radical disjuncture between ideals of the public sphere and their historical embodiments.

While many theorists have considered racism within the public sphere as a mere aberration along the road to modernity, I suggest that the distinctly oppressive conditions under which people of African descent have lived partially constitute modernity and the public sphere. Racial difference is but one of modernity's internal contradictions and disjunctures; it has been a criteria of both citizenship and noncitizenship.

Through a brief analysis of the Afro-Brazilian public sphere I examine how the dialectics of race and modernity are embodied in Brazilian racial politics. This in turn suggests first that Afro-Brazilians have been accorded partial and contingent access to the public sphere, a domain which has been defined explicitly and implicitly as white. While this in itself is no innovative conclusion, it can be utilized to interrogate the notion of the bourgeois public sphere as the sole arena or possibility for cultural articulation. This then leads to my second point: through segregation and other forms of racial alienation, alternative public spheres operate within a broadly defined public sphere. Marginalized groups create territorial and epistemological communities for themselves as a consequence of their subordinate location within the bourgeois public sphere. Along these lines, Afro-Brazilians have constructed public spheres of their own which critique Brazil's societal and political norms.

Race and the Public Sphere

In his pathbreaking work, *The Structural Transformation of the Public Sphere*, Jürgen Habermas defines the bourgeois public sphere as "the sphere of private people come together as a public; they soon claimed the public sphere regulated from above against the public authorities themselves, to engage them in a debate over the general rules governing relations in the basically privatized but publicly relevant sphere of commodity exchange and social labor."[2] The important historical precedent, within Habermas's interpretation, lies in the confrontation between "public authority," namely, depersonalized state power, and individual, propertied subjects over the "private sphere of society that has become publicly rele-

2. Jürgen Habermas, *The Structural Transformation of the Public Sphere* (Cambridge: MIT Press, 1991), 27.

vant."[3] With the advent of capitalism, commerce and the related growth of mass news and information, propertied subjects came to use reason in ways formerly reserved for private concerns such as the domestic economy and household management and private business interests. This interface would radically shift the locus of power from feudal landlords to state institutions and socially engaged, private citizens who had become public.

Rather than engage in an extended discussion of Habermas's explication of the public sphere, for which there is already an extensive literature,[4] I shall point out several contradictions that emerged from this historical precedent and have been commented upon by public sphere specialists and social theorists more generally. While the creation of this new public sphere did supplant the old, becoming the dominant, most logical social forum and institution in countries like France, Germany (Brubaker, 1992), Britain and Denmark, it did not automatically sever the formerly dominant modes of economic and political relations (Robinson 1983). Unpropertied social groups, who were never *private* citizens under the previous socio-economic order, still remained outside the category of citizen within the new public sphere. The mark of difference—education, religious affiliations, dress, habits, speech, language, an entire way of life—haunted these unpropertied social groups as they were reinscribed into newly subordinate social relationships.

Thus the bourgeois public sphere was simultaneously expansive and exclusive. It burgeoned with new forms of social inequality to parallel new forms of public authority and financial organization. Yet the working classes were neither entirely nor permanently outside the new social order, since universal suffrage, freedom of assembly and association, provided certain sectors of working-class groups the opportunity to contest the inequalities of the new order, and in the process, construct what I shall call micro-public spheres, that is spheres of public articulation that were not limited to, but dominated by the idioms, norms and desires of working-class women and men.[5]

3. Habermas, *Structural Transformation*, 19.

4. For critiques of the exclusionary character of Habermas's public sphere, or rather, considerations of the evolution of micro-public spheres for groups and subjects excluded from participatory roles within the bourgeois version see Nancy Fraser, "Rethinking the Public Sphere: A Contribution to the Critique of Actually Existing Democracy," in Craig Calhoun, ed. *Jürgen Habermas and the Public Sphere* (Cambridge, MA: MIT Press, 1991), 109–142 and in the same volume Mary Ryan, "Gender and Public Access: Women and Politics in 19th Century America," 259–288.

5. The work of E. P. Thompson, *The Making of the English Working Class* (New York: Vintage Books, 1966), Paul Willis, *Learning to Labor* (New York: Columbia University Press, 1981), Raymond Williams, *The Country and the City* (New York: Oxford University Press, 1975), and George

The bourgeois public sphere's ability to be perceived not as one space among several, but as the only forum for all social groups to engage in normative debate – either amongst themselves or between two or more groups – was the crowning ideological achievement of bourgeois culture. Another way to view this (mis)perception relates to the evolving presumption that the bourgeois public sphere superseded private/public relations of the feudal order and, all previously subordinate subjects and groups henceforth operated as social and political equals. The reality, however, was that "the oligarchy of capital was replacing the oligarchy of birth" (Viotti 1985: 55). Habermas clearly recognized this contradiction within the remaking of civil society. Yet other social theorists, particularly liberal ones and architects of modernity in the New World did not, and in some cases ignored it completely. This misconception has led *the* public sphere to become reified by most analysts of it and of its virtues and problems. The most serious consequence of this reification is the equation of an ideal type public sphere with Western polities, thus ignoring the internal contradictions within Western polities themselves concerning the realities of racial and ethnic difference.

Race, Modernity and the Public Sphere in the New World

Habermas has suggested that the philosophical discourses of modernity are distinguished by their orientation towards the future, their need to negate previous conceptions of time and history. In *The Philosophical Discourses of Modernity*, Habermas applies Hegel's understanding of modernity: "Modernity can and will no longer borrow the criteria by which it takes its orientation from the models supplied by another epoch; *it has to create its normativity out of itself*. Modernity sees itself cast back upon itself without any possibility of escape."[6]

Yet modernity cannot efface history entirely. It needs history for points of reference from which to distinguish itself. A much greater impediment to complete historical denial was the discovery of the New World and the slave trade. This discovery led to the presence of New World and African people and/or their artifacts and other forms of production in the West, as well as in emergent New World nations. By the end of the nineteenth century, elites in most American nations decided to appropriate French or U.S. models of republicanism and liberal

---

Orwell, *The Road to Wigan Pier* (San Diego: Harcourt Brace Jovanovich, 1958) provides evidence of a public sphere of working classes that is quite distinct from more affluent counterparts.

6. Jürgen Habermas, *The Philosophical Discourses of Modernity*, (Cambridge: MIT Press, 1987), 7.

democracy in the transition from colony to free nation-state (Davis 1961). The fundamental contradiction in cultural terms that emerged from this was the presence of non-Western peoples amidst projects of modernity and the public sphere in the New World. Latin American elites and intellectuals had less difficulty reconciling European modernity's break with the past in nation-states with no previous *national*-state history (Cuba, Brazil, Colombia and Argentina, for example), than in accounting for the presence of sizable populations of "premodern people." Such populations were regarded as being without reason and rationality; they were treated as the ant colonies of Latin American modernity — excavating mines, constructing cities, harvesting crops, tending to children. They enabled those very same elites to become modern like their Western models.

In Brazil and many other Latin American countries, the shift from slave to wage labor was not as momentous an event as the shift from feudalism to capitalism in Europe. However the repercussions of this shift profoundly affected the dynamics of social interaction between landed and landless groups, as well as among white, indigenous and African-derived populations. This shift signalled the inauguration of *the modern moment* in Latin America, in which various nations in this region of the world attempted to pattern themselves after the nation-states and civilizations of Western Europe. Yet the modern moment in Latin America differed from its Western European model due to the relatively late growth of industry, mass communications networks and centralized state power. Furthermore, the landowning classes were not rendered obsolete but rather transformed their mode of social dominance. These historical differences complicated the evolution of an ideal type public sphere, for the slaveowners and landowners occupied the sociological location of the bourgeoisie without actually constituting a bourgeoisie themselves. Thus, the collision between feudal and slave labor on the one hand, and capitalist wage labor on the other, was not as radical as it may have appeared. The dominant ideological amalgam in Brazil came to be known as conservative liberalism. Viotti characterizes conservative liberalism as a contradiction between liberal discourse and liberal practice, the expressed interest in the bourgeoisie's economic project without its attendant political and "valuative" responsibilities, like respect for the rights of individuals (Viotti 1985: 55). Thus slavery and patron-clientelism fused with liberal rhetoric to create a much more ambiguous setting for civil society than in European nation-states.

The specific consequences for the various African slave populations in Brazil was first, that they were the last slave population in the New World to be granted emancipation (Conrad, 1983). Elites justified the long delay in unchaining the enslaved on the grounds that Brazilian slavery was actually less harsh than the working conditions of peasants and wage laborers in Southern Europe, and that slaves were actually spared the horrors of savage Africa by being transported to the more civilized and enlightened Brazil. This justification, buttressed by purported cultural differences between Portuguese and other European civilizations underpinned the now well known myth of racial democracy (Freyre 1946). The realities of Afro-Brazilian life by 1888, when slavery was abolished, were quite different. In 1871 slavery was clearly on the wane, and planters in the province of São Paulo decided to subsidize Southern European immigration to Brazil in order to develop a European proletariat, even though there were more free Afro-Brazilians than slaves in the province of São Paulo (Andrews 1991). It was a simultaneous expression of racial and economic interests through state implementation of racially and economically specific policies.

These policies basically disqualified freedpersons from objective market competition in the emergent capitalist marketplace, thus limiting their prospects regardless of occupational differentiation within Afro-Brazilian communities. Large landowners in most cases refused to hire former slaves, in part on the grounds that they were recalcitrant and demanded specific conditions under which they would labor, but largely due to their desire to engage in economic relationships with those whom they most resembled, even in subordinate roles. European immigrant labor was preferred despite the fact that many Afro-Brazilians were skilled laborers at the time of abolition, and already had the skills which Italian and other immigrants were just developing (Dean 1976). Previously freed Afro-Brazilians did not fare much better even though by 1872, seventy-four percent of all Afro-Brazilians were free (as compared to six percent in the South of the United States on the eve of emancipation).[7]

The employment practices were consistent with the marginalization of enslaved and free blacks during the period of national formation that culminated in Brazil's independence from Portugal. The first national elections of 1821 for a centralized government – one year before independence – created the electoral conditions for the Brazilian elite to participate in public debate about Brazil's transformation into an independent monarchy, but excluded those who remained enslaved until 1888 (Bastos 1994). Bastos suggests that the 1821 election was a defining moment in Brazilian political culture, for the new constitutional order helped integrate previously marginalized groups such as small merchants, artisans, salespeople

7. See Herbert S. Klein, "Nineteenth Century Brazil," in David Cohen and Jack P. Greene, eds. *Neither Slave nor Free: The Freedman of African Descent in the Slave Societies of the New World* (Baltimore: Johns Hopkins University Press, 1972); 309–334, 319.

and others by elevating them to the status of citizens. These groups were similar to those who constituted the petit bourgeoisie in revolutionary France by the late-eighteenth century. The Constitution of 1824 defined Brazil as a constitutional monarchy; it gave black freedmen the right to vote, but they could not be chosen as electors.[8]

The slave population was well aware of the struggles between monarchial nationalists and loyalists to the Portuguese Crown. In fact, slaves and mulattos were key participants on both sides. Moreover, Africans in Bahia, like their counterparts in other slave societies in the New World, used moments of elite crisis in Brazil to their own advantage, fomenting revolts and rebellions at critical moments of disunity among these elites who were largely rural landholders that had maintained their power after independence in 1822 (Kraay 1993). Revolts in 1835 and 1837 in Bahia led to waves of repression not only against blacks, but also against the poor and other urban elements who remained politically excluded after independence. In Salvador, Bahia, local officials responded to the 1835 revolt by African-Brazilians by imposing stringent laws that monitored the movement of freed and enslaved blacks. Porters and stevedores, who were predominantly black, had to be registered on a single list and were required to wear a copper bracelet engraved with their registry number (Reis 1993).

These and other acts suggest that by the 1830s in Brazil, the status of African and Afro-Brazilian slaves and *libertos* (freed slaves) held marginal distinctions, even though there were considerable social tensions between Brazilian and African-born slaves (Graham 1994). The free and the enslaved often worked side by side (Flory 1977). By this time, the Brazilian empire relied on the discourse of the social problem to refer to free and nonfree blacks as vagrants and idlers (*vadios e ociosos*) to avoid the complexities of distinguishing the *escravo* from the *liberto*.[9] As in the United States, blackness overrode the constitutional or legal mandate of citizenship for Afro-Brazilians. Republican institutions, despite their status as impartial purveyors of law and merit, actually institutionalized racist discourses and practices, and empowered many individuals who believed that African presences in Brazil doomed their nation to second-class status. Immigration laws and policies specifically prohibited nonwhite immigration to Brazil (Mitchell 1977), and there were congressional debates over the alleged racial

8. Brazil, *Constituição politica do Imperio do Brasil*, Art. 94 in combination with Articles 6 and 91, quoted in Graham.

9. Thomas Flory, "Race and Social Control in Independent Bahia," *Latin American Studies*, vol. 9, no. 2 (1977): 199–224, esp. 203.

inferiority of Africans, Chinese and Southern Europeans (Mitchell 1977). When coupled with the powerful albeit contradictory ideology of whitening which asserted that miscegenation would eventually eliminate people of African descent, Afro-Brazilians were remarginalized in the shift from slave to wage-labor in a manner which suggested far more than a desire to exclude these people from choice labor markets.

The politics of racial exclusion was even more comprehensive. The uneven but continuous oppression and marginalization of Afro-Brazilians in the late-nineteenth and early-twentieth centuries was an effort by Brazilian elites to expunge Afro-Brazilians and their cultural practices from their portrait of modernity. Modernity, in short, did not include Afro-Brazilians. They were the antithesis of a modern nation. This effort contrasted with the efforts of Brazilian Modernists such as Mário and Oswaldo de Andrade, the anthropologist Gilberto Freyre and even some politicians, who sought to refute the Positivist legacy in Brazil by suggesting that African and indigenous elements in their nation were uniquely Brazilian. It also contrasted with Afro-Brazilian modernism in dance, religious practice, drama and the plastic arts. Yet the landholding elites, the Catholic Church and culturally conservative politicians carried the day, setting the tone for any future discussion of Afro-Brazilian and national identity.

The irony of such maneuvers, which took place well into the 1930s, was the proliferation and expansion of African cultural presences within modern Brazil, presences that were stronger than in any other nation-state in the New World. These presences, at once residual and dominant in the sense that Raymond Williams uses these terms, are evidenced by national, transracial participation in Afro-Brazilian religions like Candomblé and Umbanda; and the importance of an African-derived corporal esthetics for a national standard of beauty.[10] In popular

10. See Williams's essay "Dominant, Residual and Emergent Cultures" in *Marxism and Literature*, (London: Oxford University Press, 1977). It may seem contradictory to suggest that the presence of Afro-Brazilian cultural practices and productions is at once residual and dominant, but it is the closest I can come at the present time in characterizing the pervasiveness of the "Africanisms" in Brazilian daily life and the relative powerlessness of Afro-Brazilian religious, cultural and political institutions relative to both state and civic institutions of the Brazilian polity. They are residual in a more explicitly political sense. Afro-Brazilian cultural practices are considered *national* practices, and are manipulated for their symbolic resonance by Brazilian elites to display the heterogenic cohesiveness of Brazilians; they are dominant in the sense that they are suffused in an almost transracial way throughout the norms and values of civil society. An example of this in Brazil, and found in Latin nations like Cuba and Venezuela, is a corporeal aesthetic of the female body which emphasizes distinctly African considerations of physical attractiveness—large hips, buttocks and narrow waist, with little attention to breast size—as opposed to the more Western standards of feminine beauty which in the twentieth century favor narrow hips and waist, large breasts and thin thighs. For a U.S. audience, or more broadly, those familiar with contemporary U.S. popular culture and rap

culture Samba was appropriated by the emergent middle classes in the 1940s. They were seeking a popular form of recreation, and selected Samba despite the disdain it evoked among elites who detected an expression of sensuality not found in the fox-trot or other European imports. By the 1940s, African elements of Brazilian culture were selectively integrated into the discourses of national identity. With the ascendance of the ideologies of racial democracy and whitening, Afro-Brazilians came to be considered part of the cultural economy, in which their women and men embodied sexual desire and lascivious pleasure. At the same time, Afro-Brazilians were denied access to virtually all institutions of civil society that would have given them equal footing with the middle classes of modernizing Brazil. Prestigious schools, neighborhoods, clubs and professions were closed off to Afro-Brazilians much in the way that they were to African-Americans in the United States, Afro-Cubans and other New World blacks during this period, only in more ambiguous, coded ways (Fernandes 1969; Andrews 1991). Thus in both eighteenth-century Europe and twentieth-century Latin America, the bourgeois public sphere was a contradictory, politically bifurcated domain, open to some groups and closed to others. The extent of marginality was, and is, determined by the degree and conditions of otherness on each continent.

Claims to citizenship and equality of opportunity in labor and ancillary markets could not be the hallmarks of Afro-Brazilians' modern identities. Instead the denial of participatory citizenship in the bourgeois public sphere for Afro-Brazilians marked their existence as subaltern elements of modern life. Yet they lived within this sphere nonetheless, so that any characterization of their lives as premodern or archaic (Fernandes 1969) ignores the discontinuity of modern time and the multiplicity of spheres within bourgeois civil society.

A common characteristic that Afro-Brazilians shared with their counterparts of the African diaspora in the New World was the constant attacks on their dignity. Charles Taylor identifies dignity as a key element in the constitution of the modern, individual self. It reflects "our power, our sense of dominating public space; or our invulnerability to power; or our self-sufficiency, our life having its own centre, or our being like and looked to by others, a centre of attention."[11]

music in particular, one would have to imagine Sir Mix-A-Lot's hit "Baby's Got Back" not merely as a popular song, but as an expression of a *national* disposition towards a particular standard of beauty, to appreciate the extent to which the fetishization of the *bunda* (buttocks) in Brazil is as much evidence of African presence as it is a specifically national cultural norm. The "Africanization" of the female bodily aesthetic (male gaze) is one of Brazil's distinctive features as a nation with the largest population of people of African descent outside of Nigeria.

11. Charles Taylor, *Sources of the Self: The Making of Modern Identity* (Cambridge: Harvard University Press, 1989), 15.

The keywords and phrases relevant to my critique of Taylor's passage are "public space," "invulnerability to power," "self-sufficiency" and "centre." Taylor appears to use the phrase "public space" in a manner indistinguishable from contemporary usage of "public sphere." This usage has come to be equated with civil society itself, in which a diverse array of interests, institutions and individuals are intertwined to constitute the modern moment. An important, if subtle, distinction could be made here that relates to a point I raised earlier about the totalizing quality implicit in the notion of the public sphere. This particular sphere could be a dimension of public space but not its totality, despite its representation as such. Yet, for Taylor, this form of dignity is seemingly universal and not limited to a particular sphere.

What happens to this notion of dignity when the role of racial or gendered inequality in Taylor's public space is viewed from theoretical and historical perspectives? In theoretical terms, is it possible for people who are denied the constitutional and normative rudiments of modern citizenship to operate in public space with such a *general* sense of dignity, a presumption of citizenship? Considering the previous discussion of Afro-Brazilians and the emergent public sphere in Brazil, would it not have been impossible for those porters and stevedores in Salvador, Bahia to have imagined that they could "dominate public space" even in the mild form that Taylor suggests? For Ana Flávia, the Governor's daughter, her inability to dominate public space as an individual stemmed from the lowly status accorded those who resemble her, regardless of their differences as individual, private citizens. Thus, the public and private distinctions so neatly laid out by Taylor collapse at the intersection of reason and coercion, power and powerlessness. Considering the legacy of the civil rights movement in the United States, the anti-apartheid movement in South Africa and other social movements engineered by people of African descent in distinct parts of the world, there clearly has not been "invulnerability to power" in public space for them in modern times.[12] The sense of self-sufficiency, which Taylor defines as the ability to provide for oneself, one's family, and to command respect, is structurally inaccessible for African-American communities of the New World.

12. Unless of course, one considers Gandhi's or King's nonviolent resistances as movements which, given their appeals to a higher moral order, projected a sense of invulnerability to the power of the state, colonial authority or dominant ethnic group. Yet one is still struck by the reality of their respective struggles; they made appeals based upon the moral authority of reason, and were answered with coercion, the highest form of unreason.

Despite Taylor's lofty standards and claims, his universalizing principles for the moral sources of dignity presuppose a subject who is male, property-owning, Western and white. His characterization is informed by what feminist psychoanalytic critics call the male gaze, a projection of his particular "subject position" onto the rest of the world, with the desire that others conform to the image he has of himself, and of others as a wished-for extension of himself (Mulvey 1989). In racial and gendered terms, being a "centre of attention" has distinct connotations for different racialized and gendered subjects.

As a communitarian Taylor could respond to this critique on theoretical and historical grounds. The claim might be made that the Brazilian polity is not the West that Taylor had in mind; this is a legitimate point since Brazilian society is pervaded by the confluence of feudalism and dependent capitalist culture. It could be further argued that both Habermas and Taylor have laid the economic, administrative and normative foundations for the public sphere/space and cannot be critiqued for the less-than-ideal functioning of these domains in the real world. After all, the histories of racial oppression shared among peoples of African descent in the West, which Habermas and Taylor briefly note and deplore, also disclose the malfunctioning of the public sphere according to its own principles. The eventual, if uneasy, inclusion of previously disenfranchised groups could be perceived as another triumph of reason and rationalization, a pit stop along the tortuous track toward liberal pluralism (Taylor) or democratic socialism (Habermas).

Such neat distinctions between Western and non-Western, ideal and practical public spheres have a flimsy ontological basis. They ignore the fact that the geographic distinctions of West and non-West are not only arbitrary but also neglectful of the role of Western *influences* globally, in hundreds of societies built upon variations of parliamentary, republican models. Moreover, such distinctions ignore the reaction within Western polities to the others, and the chasm between liberal theory and liberal history (Mehta 1990). Recent events in both Western and Eastern Europe demonstrate the intensity of reactions to otherness—anti-immigration violence, Neo-Nazism and other fascist movements—and how intensely the public sphere is *racialized*. This refutes positions supporting notions of abstract, individual propriety in the public sphere, and emphasizes the ways that citizenship is differentially embodied by race and gender. Modernity requires some sense of the past in order to distinguish itself, and it uses people of African descent in predominantly white nation-states as contrasting symbols of noncitizenship in the public sphere, just as colonial rulers have used "Third World"

peoples in the same manner (Chatterjee 1986). Afro-Brazilians, like so many
other people of African descent in the New World, are used for the same purpose.

181
Race and the Public
Sphere in Brazil

Blackness Then and Now

It is not really race in a narrow, phenotypical sense that links Ana Flávia, the
Governor's daughter, to the seemingly disparate incidents of the slave revolt in
1835 or the marginalization of Afro-Brazilians in the shift from slave to wage
labor between 1880 and 1920. More precisely, the *meanings* attached to purported
racial groups are markers that convey the alleged disparities in intellect, industri-
ousness, wealth, beauty and aesthetics – as well as the capacity to alter them.
As long as Brazilian society in general, whites and nonwhites alike, share a
commonsense basis for negative stereotypes of blacks and positive stereotypes
of whites, then the apparent fluidity historically associated with racial categorization in Brazil needs to be qualified. The preoccupation with color categories
belies the other dimension of racial "common sense" in Brazil: the widespread
belief held by many whites and nonwhites that Brazil is a racial democracy.

The equation of blackness with sloth, deceit, hypersexuality and waste of all
kinds is confirmed by the relative infrequency in which the terms *preto* or *negro*
(black) are used in daily life. Brazilians reluctantly use these terms in describing
others; they rarely describe friends this way, for fear of insulting them (Maggie
1988). This underscores the paradox of racial politics in Brazil and in much of
the hemisphere. While racial identification is more contextual in Brazil than in
other multi-racial polities certain limits also obtain. One person's mulatto is another's negro; yet negro remains a racial category many people do not want ascribed
to them. If preto or negro only meant dark skin color, then why would the usage
of these terms be any different from say, referring to someone as white? Part
of the reason for a multiplicity of descriptions for nonwhite Brazilians, particularly
for those whose African descent is visible in the texture of their hair, the shape
of their nose or buttocks, is because such categorizations attempt to avoid the mark
of blackness. Why is it more likely that a "colored" person would be described as
"brown" or "mulatto" than as half-white, nearly or quasi-white? Focus on the
numerous color categories in Brazilian racial politics can obscure the broader
racialized social totality in which these categories operate and the racial meanings
which *structure* social interactions and limit individuals' ability to simply choose
their own racial category.

When considered comparatively these examples illustrate limits of blackness
over historical/racial time. In the case of the 1835 revolt in Bahia, African-

Brazilians responded to their mistreatment through revolt, regardless of occupational distinctions among them. The animosity between Brazilian-born slaves, mulattos and whites on the one hand, and African-Brazilians on the other suggests at the least that blackness, laden with negative connotations, pertained to African-Brazilians and not necessarily to those who looked black. Ana Flávia, the daughter of a black man and a white woman, could easily be considered a mulatta in both contemporary and historical Brazil. Her blackness in the eyes of her assailants implies a broadening of the category of negro/a in Brazil and more importantly, an increasing polarization of racial categories. Her beating may signal that the mark of blackness has come to include Brazilians who are perceived as people of African descent, whether from Brazil or not. Unlike the distinctions between African- and Brazilian-born slaves in the previous century, Africanness—the parent symbol for blackness—no longer marks a place; it now marks a people.

The seemingly arbitrary manner in which Ana Flávia the mulatta could become Ana Flávia the negra affirms the greater importance of the interpretive, as opposed to the phenotypical, criterion of racial differentiation. Like McCarthyism in the United States and the military dictatorship from 1964 to 1985 in Brazil, the enemy is continually invented. Thus in the absence of "real" blacks, Ana Flávia becomes black, much in the same way that liberals and other moderates were transformed into communists during the era of anti-communist hysteria. Once identified as the enemy, the actual ideological or racial position of the signified has secondary importance. The meaning of racial or ideological difference attached to the individual or group is paramount for understanding the politics of polarization, of distancing the marginal or soon-to-be marginal subject from the center of the body politic.

This gives credence to Thomas Skidmore's assertion that Brazil's racial politics are becoming more and more like the relatively dichotomous patterns of racial interaction in the United States (Skidmore 1993). With the emergence of groups calling themselves Skinheads and Black Muslims in São Paulo, the existence of organizations that reflect the most obvious forms of and responses to racial animus affirms racially discriminatory practices in Brazil that are long-standing and embedded in the ideology of racial democracy. As far as I know such organizations are new to Brazil, yet such sentiments must have been in place for some time in order for them to assume organizational, collective form.

The meanings attached to blackness, whiteness and positions in between constitute the public aspect of the racial dimension of public spheres: these meanings are located in specific social contexts. Habermas's etymological and genealogical considerations of the terms publicity and public opinion are relevant here. Tracing the meaning and conceptualization of these terms in philosophers as diverse as Locke, Rousseau, Kant and Hegel, Habermas notes how public opinion was often meant to infer a normative matrix of the good, right and just in emergent civil societies of the West. Though Hegel would disparage public opinion as unmediated mass knowledge, each aforementioned philosopher acknowledged public opinion's power to convey a popular authority, what Foucault refers to as a regime of truth. Racist ideologies are facets of publicity and public opinion, insofar as they mark bodies to inform others of the meanings of those bodies in racial terms.

It is not, therefore, only discursive formations, processes of reason and rationalization, that shape publicity and public opinion about race. *Nondiscursive* formations also define people's location and degrees of participation in public realms. In short, it is the *structures* of race, racial difference and racism, which often go unsaid that provide the parameters of racial dynamics and the range of possibilities of discourse itself. This is why the Brazilian historian João Reis suggests that the Bahia slave revolt of 1835 was not, as previous historical accounts imply, merely a Muslim revolt of a certain category of slaves. Both slaves and *libertos* participated in the revolt, along with a high percentage of non-Muslim Africans. Reis regards the revolt as principally the result of an "embryonic Pan-African identity," an emergent ethnic consciousness among liberto and escravo participants that was forged by the similarity of racial and economic exploitation.[13] Religious affiliation was the vehicle through which the revolt's leadership emerged, but was certainly not the sole reason for the revolt itself.[14]

Moreover, the distinctions between escravo and liberto were principally *occupational* distinctions, which by themselves tell us little about the respective treatment accorded individuals from either category in the public sphere. As noted earlier, libertos were not given the same status or rights of whites, and could only vote in primary elections. Therefore, while the degree of racial/civic exclusion might have been less for the liberto, the nature and kind of exclusion was more similar than dissimilar to that of the escravo. Reis and Silva describe the broader context in which these occupational distinctions operated:

> If the freed black stopped being a slave, he did not exactly become a free man. He did not possess any political right and, even though con-

13. João Reis and Eduardo Silva, *Negociação e Conflitó: A Resisténcia Negra No Brasil Escravista* (São Paulo: Editora Schwarz, 1989), 109.

14. Reis notes that the *malês* decided upon Ramadan as the moment for revolt because it is a time when Allah is said to "control malignant spirits and reorder the affairs of the world." See Reis and Silva 1989, 122.

sidered a foreigner, was not granted the privileges of a citizen from another country. The stigma of slavery was irreducibly associated with the
color of his skin and above all, his origin. The free Africans were
treated by whites, blacks, browns and even by creoles as slaves. They
were not second or third class citizens. They were simply not citizens.[15]

At the level of resistance, however, the 1835 revolt is an historical example of
an activity which emerged from a micro-public sphere, one which operated outside
the purview of the liberal-minded but ultimately oligarchic elite within the dominant public sphere. The participants in the revolt were mindful of the activities
and crises of their masters and employers, and fashioned modes of racial and
ethnic consciousness in response to them. The simultaneity of these two spheres
suggests that an elite public sphere, such as in the case of nineteenth-century
Brazil or eighteenth-century Europe, is also an essentially *privatized* domain.
This privatization is also apparent in twentieth-century Brazil, as Ana Flávia was
rudely reminded that public space is not necessarily a democratic space. It is not
democratic precisely because of the manner in which it is privatized for members
of a certain race and/or class. Thus, while the old Brazilian adage that "money
whitens" is true in certain cases, it is equally true that blackness taints.

This leads us to another understanding of how the public sphere and public
space is privatized by the manner in which its privileged subjects or citizens
publicly discriminate against the less privileged. Even in circumstances where
citizenship is a given, as in contemporary Brazil, some people are considered
lesser citizens than others. Racial prejudice is not only privately held but invariably, publicly articulated and at some level sanctioned. Thus the liberal presumption of reason in Habermas's formulation is often rebuffed at the lived conjunctures
of white and black, as in the case of Ana Flávia. It was precisely at this moment
that ideology and coercive power outstripped reason as the bordering, structuring
parameters of the elite public sphere. Moreover, contrary to the liberal – and
often communitarian – notion that citizens are abstract bearers of rights, black
Cinderella highlights the need to conceive of citizenship as that which should
inhere in concrete persons. Along with property, gender, age and reason, race
and racial difference imbue individuals with their concreteness, a material and
symbolic grounding of their existence.

15. Reis and Silva 1989: 106. The translation is mine.

As Wade (1993) has noted in his study of Afro-Colombians, one of the comparative peculiarities of Latin American racial politics has been its rhetorical collapse of racial difference under the banner of national identity. In Brazil, Mexico, Cuba, Venezuela, Colombia and other nations of the region, Afro-Latino Americans are supposedly without a racially specific identity, unlike their Afro-North American, Afro-European or English-speaking counterparts in the Caribbean. Some allege that this has been due to the absence of legislated racial discrimination and segregation. Such forms of racial apartheid have led to the development of parallel institutions in other multi-racial polities such as the United States. Thus, music, cuisine, dress and artifacts that would be representative of a particular racial, or more accurately, cultural group elsewhere appears as a national commodity in Latin American polities (Fry 1983).

Afro-Brazilian cultural production fit this model until the 1970s, when Afro-Brazilian cultural and political activists affiliated with the *movimento negro* began to explore symbolic linkages with other communities of the African diaspora. These explorations led to the formation of organizations and cultural expressions that were neither Brazilian nor national but Afro-diasporic. Ironically, racially specific Afro-Brazilian cultural practices, namely forms of expression produced and directed toward Afro-Brazilians, emerged during the height of the military dictatorship in Brazil. Black Soul, the dance hall phenomena of the 1970s that first emerged in Rio de Janeiro but later spread to other cities in the country, was the precursor to the African blocs (*blocos Afros*) such as Olodum and Illê-Aiyê. Such organizations have a specifically Afro-Brazilian leadership and constituency; they produce lyrics and musics that utilize Afro-Brazilian identity and racial discrimination as a principal theme.[16] These organizations are quite distinct from Samba schools, Candomblé, Umbanda and other Brazilian cultural artifacts that are perceived and manipulated as national symbols. In the realm of cultural and religious practice, *terreiros de candomblé*, samba schools, ethnic brotherhoods and the emergent *blocos Afros* like Agbara Dudu, Olodum and Ilê-Aiyê represent the increasing racialization of Afro-Brazilian cultural practice. Afro-Brazilians increasingly recognize the need to use cultural practice and production as an organizing principle against racial oppression, and as tools for constructing

16. For more information on Afro-Brazilian cultural practices, especially Black Soul, see *Orpheus and Power* (Hanchard 1994), "Religion, Class and Context: Continuities and Discontinuities in Brazilian Umbanda" (Brown and Bick 1987), and "Black Soul: Aglutinação espontanea ou identidade etnica" (Rodrigues da Silva 1983).

and enacting Afro-Brazilian identities. In many instances these organizations are successful attempts at creating both spaces and values of Afro-Brazilian identity and community which are related to but distinct from the Catholic Church, mass culture and markets. The emphasis on space within the *terreiro* provides the articulation of an alternative public sphere (Braga 1992; Elbein dos Santos and dos Santos 1984).

Organizations such as Olodum and Illê-Aiyê do not necessarily affirm an increasing polarization along clearly demarcated racial lines, but rather an increasing awareness among Afro-Brazilians and white Brazilians that Afro-Brazilians *can* use racial identity as a principle to organize collective action. It is not a sign of increasing racism among Afro-Brazilians, though at some level it is surely a response to racism in the land of racial democracy. The Afro-Brazilian public sphere shares a paradox with its white, more dominant counterpart: it is at once public and private.[17] Brazilian national culture has always translated and transformed Afro-Brazilian cultural practices into national cultural practices, thereby rendering them as commodities in popular culture to be consumed by all (Hanchard 1993, 1994). Thus, the question, just what is Afro-Brazilian culture? is much more complicated than in the United States, South Africa or Britain, where residential and other forms of racial segregation make distinct histories more obvious. It appears, however, that with the increasing racial polarization in Brazilian society, African blocs and other organizations are using music, dance and religion as explicit organizing principles to create schools, child care facilities, political and other organizations specifically for Afro-Brazilians. In turn, this increases tensions between a Brazilian elite that has historically claimed Afro-Brazilian cultural practices as simply Brazilian cultural practices, and Afro-Brazilian activists and intellectuals who seek to claim some form of autonomy within their own public sphere.

The struggles between dominant and subordinate racial groups, the politics of race, help constitute modernity and modernizing projects across the globe. It

17. The diaphanous nature of the barrier between black private and public spheres is also evident in other national contexts. Consider the following autobiographical observations of Wahneema Lubiano, a U.S. African-American theorist, on her childhood experiences as a preacher's daughter whose father's church was next door to a brothel. "Our church and our apartment were both private and public: the two constituted a space that described both the destitution and constellation of the neighborhood, and what black people in that neighborhood and town meant to themselves and to the larger social, economic and political space of the town. It marked us, we marked it." See Wahneema Lubiano, "If I Could Talk about It, This Is Not What I Would Say," *Assemblage* 20 (April 1993), 56.

uses racial phenotypes to assess, categorize and judge persons as citizens and noncitizens. Racial politics operate not only in a polity's defining moments but in the ongoing process of its re-creation. It permeates the minutiae of daily life: nervous, furtive glances are exchanged in elevators, men and women are rendered suspects without ever having committed a crime; not yet socialized by racist practices, white children run gleefully into the arms of their parents' racial others as their parents watch nervously. This is racial politics between whites and blacks in the late-twentieth century, and Brazil is no exception. For Ana Flávia – the black Cinderella – the clock struck midnight the moment she was born.

Michael Hanchard teaches political science in the Department of Political Science at Northwestern University. His recent publications include, *Orpheus and Power: Afro-Brazilian Social Movements in Rio de Janeiro and São Paulo, Brazil, 1945–1988* (Princeton University Press, 1994). His current research interests include political movements of the African diaspora, racial theory and Afro-modernism.

Literature Cited

"A Cinderela Negra," *Veja*, 7 de Julho, 1993, 66–73.

Andrews, George Reid. 1991. *Blacks and Whites in São Paulo, Brazil. 1888–1988.* Madison: University of Wisconsin.

Bastos P. Neves, Lùcia Maria. "As eleiçoes na construção do emperio Brasileiro: Os limites de uma nova practica da cultura politica Luso-Brasileira (1820–1823)." Paper presented at the workshop on Political Representation and Nation Building in Nineteenth-Century Latin America, University of Texas, Austin, March 7–9, 1994.

Braga, Julio. 1992. "Candomblé: Força e Resistência." *Afro-Asia* 15: 13–17.

Brown, Diana De G. and Mario Bick. 1987. "Religion, Class and Context: Continuities and Discontinuities in Brazilian Umbanda." *American Ethnologist* 14 (1): 73–93.

Brubaker, Rogers. 1992. *Citizenship and Nationhood in France and Germany.* Cambridge: Harvard University Press.

Calhoun, Craig, ed. 1991. *Jürgen Habermas and the Public Sphere.* Cambridge: MIT Press.

Chatterjee, Partha. 1986. *Nationalist Thought and the Colonial World.* London: Zed.

Conrad, Robert. 1983. *Children of God's Fire*. Princeton: Princeton University Press.

Davis, Harold. 1961. *Latin American Social Thought*. Washington, D.C.: The University Press of Washington, D.C.

Dean, Warren. 1976. *Rio Claro: A Brazilian Plantation System, 1820–1920*. Palo Alto: Stanford University Press.

Dirks, Nicholas B. 1991. "History as a Sign of the Modern." *Public Culture* 2 (2): 25–31.

Elbein dos Santos, Juana and Deoscoredes M. Dos Santos. 1984. "Religion and Black Culture." In *Africa in Latin America*, ed. Manuel Moreno Fraginals. New York: Holmes and Meir.

Fernandes, Florestan. 1969. *The Negro in Brazilian Society*. New York: Columbia University Press.

Flory, Thomas. 1977. "Race and Social Control in Independent Bahia." *Latin American Studies* (2): 199–224.

Freyre, Gilbert. 1946. *The Masters and the Slaves*. New York: Alfred A. Knopf.

Gilroy, Paul. 1987. *There Ain't No Black in the Union Jack*. London: Hutchinson.

Graham, Richard. "Free African Brazilians and the State in Slavery Times." Paper presented at the conference, Racial Politics in Contemporary Brazil, University of Texas, Austin, April 8–10, 1993.

Habermas, Jürgen. 1987. *The Philosophical Discourses of Modernity*. Cambridge: MIT Press.

———. 1991. *The Structural Transformation of the Public Sphere*. Cambridge: MIT Press.

Hanchard, Michael. 1993. "Culturalism versus Cultural Politics: Movimento Negro in Rio de Janeiro and São Paulo, Brazil." In *The Violence Within*, edited by Kay B. Warren, 57–86. Boulder, Colorado: Westview Press.

———. 1994. *Orpheus and Power: The Movimento Negro of Rio de Janeiro and São Paulo, Brazil, 1945–1988*. Princeton: Princeton University Press.

Klein, Herbert. 1972. "Nineteenth Century Brazil." In *Neither Slave nor Free: The Freedmen of African Descent in the New World*, edited by David Cohen and Jack Green, 309–334. Baltimore: The Johns Hopkins University Press.

Kraay, Hendrik. 1992. "As Terrifying as Expected: The Bahian Sabinada, 1837–1838." *Hispanic American Historical Review* 72(4): 501–521.

Lubiano, Wahneema. 1993. "If I Could Talk about It, This Is Not What I Would Say." *Assemblage* 20(April): 56–57.

Maggie, Yvonne. "O que se cala quando se fala do negro no Brazil" (Photocopy, 1988).

Mehta, Uday S. 1990. "Liberal Strategies of Exclusion." *Politics and Society.* 18 (4): 427–454.

Mitchell, Michael. 1977. "Racial Consciousness and the Political Attitudes and Behavior of Blacks in São Paulo, Brazil." Ph.D. diss. University of Michigan.

Mulvey, Laura. 1989. *Visual and Other Pleasures.* Bloomington: Indiana University Press.

Nishida, Mieko. 1993. "Manumission and Ethnicity in Brazil, 1808–1888." *Hispanic American Historical Review* 73: (3):361–391.

Orwell, George. 1958. *The Road to Wigan Pier.* San Diego: Harcourt Brace Jovanovich.

Prandi, Reginaldo. 1991. *Os Candombles de São Paulo.* São Paulo: Editora USP.

Reis, João. 1993. *Muslim Uprising of 1835 in Bahia.* Baltimore: Johns Hopkins University Press.

———. 1993. *Slave Rebellion in Brazil.* Baltimore: Johns Hopkins University Press.

Reis, João and Eduardo Silva. 1989. *Negociação e Conflito: A Resisténcia Negra No Brasil Escravista.* São Paulo: Editora Schwarz Ltda.

Robinson, Cedric. 1983. *Black Marxism.* London: Zed.

Rodrigues da Silva, Carlos Benedito. 1983. "Black Soul: Aglutinação Espontanea ou Identidade Etnica." In *Movimentos Sociais, Urbanos, Minorias Etnicas e Outros Estudos*, edited by L.A. Silva, et al., 245–62. Brasilia: ANPOCS.

Romero, Jose Luis. 1963. *A History of Argentine Political Thought.* Palo Alto: Stanford University Press.

Skidmore, Thomas. 1993. "Race Relations in Brazil." *Camões Center Quarterly* 4 (3–4): 49–61.

Taylor, Charles. 1989. *Sources of the Self: The Making of Modern Identity.* Cambridge: Harvard University Press.

Thompson, E.P. 1966. *The Making of the English Working Class.* New York: Vintage Books.

Viotti da Costa, Emilia. 1985. *The Brazilian Empire: Myths and Histories.* Chicago: University of Chicago Press.

Williams, Raymond. 1975. *The Country and the City.* New York: Oxford University Press.

Willis, Paul. 1981. *Learning to Labor: How Working Class Kids Get Working Class Jobs.* New York: Columbia University Press.

Bullet holes inside the
deserted Audobon
Ballroom, where
Malcolm X was
assassinated. Harlem,
New York.

Marilyn Nance

otesters demonstrating against the demolition of the Audobon Ballroom and demanding
 preservation as a memorial to Malcolm X. New York, 1990. The Economic
velopment Corporation of New York City is now renovating the Audubon, which will
:lude a Malcolm X memorial.

Black Global

Public Spheres

Buy Black.
Brooklyn, 1987.

We do not sell any
South African goods.
Brooklyn, 1985.

Kings and Queens Livery. Brooklyn.

Faded Beauties.
Fort Green, Brooklyn,
1990.

© Charles Martin

Mink.
New York, 1990.

© Charles Martin

Cosmetics shop.
Accra, Ghana,
1988.

Above: Alderwoman Dorothy
Tillman (left) at a party.
Checkerboard Blues Lounge,
Chicago, 1994.
Left: Carl Weatherby with student in
Blues in Schools Program. Chicago.

Home concert.
Brixton, England.

One Way?
Paris.

© Charles Martin

James Baldwin, after
the Richard Wright
Lecture. Yale
University.

© Charles Martin

Delecia Bey is a photographer based in Chicago. *Charles Martin* teaches in the Comparative Literature Department at Queens College, City University of New York. *Stephen Marc* teaches in the Photography Department at Columbia College Chicago; the photographs here are from his book, *The Black Transatlantic Experience* (Chicago: Columbia College Chicago, 1992). *Marilyn Nance* is a photographer and photojournalist based in New York City. *David Solzman* is a photographer and teaches in the Geography Department at the University of Illinois, Chicago.

Public Culture 1994, 7: 186–194

A Black Counterpublic?:
Economic Earthquakes, Racial
Agenda(s), and Black Politics

Michael C. Dawson

The dissension today within the Black community regarding its strategic direction is as widespread as it was a century ago with the final suppression of
democratic forces in the South. The contention and outright confusion within
the Black community over the future direction of political and social action have
their roots in several long-term structural changes in the American political economy and an ideological shift consolidated during the Reagan-Bush regime. The
combination of upheavals in the political economy, shifts that can be viewed as
earthquakes in terms of their implications for American society, and a consolidation of the right's stranglehold over political discourse have had grave consequences for Blacks specifically, and the disadvantaged more generally. One result
has been that the meaning of being Black, who is "allowed" to be Black, and the
content of a Black agenda(s), is now more fiercely contested within the Black
community than before. Essentialist notions of Blackness are themselves de-
servedly under attack both by those who point to the social construction of Black
identity and by materialists who argue that there has been sufficient diversion in
interests, not only along lines of class but also along gender lines, to make the
concept of a unified set of Black interests minimally a historical anachronism

I wish to thank Carol A. Breckenridge, Manthia Diawara, Alice Furumoto, Michael Hanchard,
Barbara Ransby, Lynn Sanders, Jackie Stevens, the participants and organizers of the "Black Public
Sphere in the Reagan-Bush Era Conference" at the University of Chicago (October 1993), and anony-
mous reviewers for insightful and constructive comments.

Public Culture 1994, 7: 195–223

and at worst nonsensical. Toni Morrison eloquently captures this sentiment when she states: "It is clear to the most reductionist intellect that black people think differently from one another; it is also clear that the time for undiscriminating racial unity has passed" (1992: xxx). Many disagree. Charles Henry argues for the need to rebuild Black unity and identity: "Is the loss of a national black identity a bad thing? I think it is, unless we believe that this country as a whole currently embodies those values and goals we seek to be identified with. If it does not, then we must seek to present alternative values and goals as forcefully as possible. This struggle is not new" (1992:40–41).

Both Morrison's and Henry's sentiments are based on the view that there has existed at some time in the recent past a Black identity that was sufficiently shared by people of African descent to forge a potent political unity based on shared goals, values and ideas. In Morrison's opinion such a unity is not only unrecoverable but also, to the degree that it is undiscriminating, it is undesirable. Henry believes that it is imperative to recover such a unity since the goals and values of African Americans are sufficiently different from that of the nation as a whole to require a separate political agenda and sufficient political unity to achieve this agenda. Various forms of empirical research can determine part of the bases of the tension produced by Morrison's and Henry's views. Questions such as the degree to which fundamental social cleavages exist within the Black community, and how African Americans perceive shared interests versus intra-group conflict can be meaningfully analyzed and answered. I will return to some of these empirical questions later in this essay. However, the tension between Morrison's and Henry's views raises important normative questions about the nature of debate among African Americans, the capacity of institutions within the Black community to facilitate democratic debate, and the relationship between debate within the Black community and debate between African Americans and other communities about race and American democracy. Further, the tension between the views of Morrison and Henry has as its roots conflicting conceptualizations of Black identity and whether such an identity is sufficiently present to forge a single Black agenda.[1]

African Americans and Habermas's Conception of Public Sphere

Habermas's conception of the public sphere as a setting and set of political institutions which facilitate the ability of citizens to discuss questions of common concern

1. Debate over the strategic direction(s) for Black politics has occupied the attention of many activists and scholars. For a sampling of very different approaches to the question of how social cleavages among African Americans affect the present and future of both racial identities and Black politics see Cohen 1994, Hill 1994, Morrison 1992, and Reed 1994.

provides a useful starting point to consider the types of political institutions needed in the Black community; such institutions might either restore coherence to Black politics or concur that a unified Black politics can be relegated to the dustbin of history. Indeed, it would be difficult to imagine a more propitious time than now to have a fully functioning Black public sphere of the Habermasian type, or more precisely a subaltern counterpublic of the type described by Nancy Fraser. In recent years bitter differences among African Americans have been provoked by issues such as: the relative importance of race and class; the relative efficacy (or inadequacies) of political versus economic strategies for Black advancement; how Black feminist groups help or harm Black efforts to improve conditions within the Black community; whether the special problems of Black women deserve more, less or the same amount of attention as those of Black men; and how to respond to the critical lack of state responsiveness to Black concerns and interests during this period.

A Black public sphere does not exist in contemporary America, if by that we mean a set of institutions, communication networks and practices which facilitate debate of causes and remedies to the current combination of political setbacks and economic devastation facing major segments of the Black community, and which facilitate the creation of oppositional formations and sites. I argue that such a public sphere did exist within the Black community as recently as the early 1970s. More precisely what no longer exists is a Black counterpublic of the type described by Fraser (1989). While I will later describe in some detail the features of such a counterpublic, two points should be considered at this juncture. First, the Black counterpublic is not a bourgeois sphere in the sense that Habermas describes; Black institutions and publics have been largely multi-class, at least up to 1970, due to the long regime of enforced segregation. Secondly, I assert that while the counterpublic has been multi-class, its leadership has been male and patriarchal, due in no small part to the importance of male religious leaders in the Black community. It is the challenges to patriarchal norms and the need for silenced voices to be heard that Morrison identifies as part of the reason that a single unified Black counterpublic is unlikely now and in the future. However, the combination of structural shifts in the international and American political economy, the consolidation of the political right's domination of public discourse and policy under Presidents Reagan and Bush, and conflict and diverging interests within the Black community have also contributed to the disintegration of the Black public sphere.

In this essay I consider the possibility of reconstituting a Black counterpublic. Public opinion research, I argue, can help us better understand some of the bases and barriers to forming such a sphere of debate and practice, assuming such a goal is desirable or that the historical conditions exist. However, for public opinion research to assist in determining the empirical grounds for such a project, a research agenda of Black *public* opinion must be forged out of the current developing research on African American *mass* opinion.[2] We start with a brief review of the concept of public sphere, counterpublic sphere, and their applicability to modern Black politics.

A Black Public Sphere?

Just as feminist critics have demonstrated that Habermas's concept of the bourgeois public sphere is both exclusionary and hegemonic, several aspects of his formulation from 1962 render it an inappropriate model for Black politics (Fraser 1989; Ryan 1989). Habermas consistently presented a romanticized version of Western European history (Eley 1989; Fraser 1989). Scholars have demonstrated that historically existing bourgeois public spheres were always exclusionary. Gender was a primary basis for education, and in some circumstances spheres were formed as a patriarchal alternative to existing spheres in which women's voices were prominent (Fraser 1989; Ryan 1989).[3] What emerged in these and other western polities was a variety of alternatives to the bourgeois and post-bourgeois public spheres that facilitated women's and other excluded groups access to public life. Several scholars explicitly make the connection between the

2. The distinction between mass opinion (formed by the state and other authorities through the media) versus public opinion (formed as part of critical debate and practice in the public sphere) is discussed at greater length in the conclusion. However, to foreshadow that discussion somewhat, I argue the following. The degree to which surveys can be used to *facilitate* critical public discussion as opposed to serving the private needs of corporate interests and the hegemonic needs of state and party actors depends on three factors: the methodological construction of the survey project; the use made of the survey results; and the political intentions of the survey researcher. The degree to which public opinion data and analyses are designed to foster debate within or between publics or are designed for private use and/or impose opinion on mass publics determines in part whether such research can be justly considered part of the institutional tools for building and maintaining public discourse. For a discussion of the dialogic aspects of survey research in research on racial politics, see Sanders 1994.

3. According to Fraser, Habermas makes four incorrect assumptions in his discussion of the European bourgeois public sphere. She argues that it was not (is not) possible to "bracket" differences within the sphere in such a way that citizens can "deliberate as if they were social equals." Furthermore, Habermas is wrong to the degree that he suggests that the creation of multiple spheres represents a move "away from . . . greater democracy" and his emphasis on the common good privileges the goals of the most advantaged sectors of a society. Finally, she argues that a functioning democratic public does not require a "sharp" demarcation between the borders of civil society and the state.

stratification of a society and the creation of alternative subaltern counterpublics (Fraser 1989; Ryan 1989). We can restate the thesis of Fraser and others as follows: Alternative public spheres have developed in western democracies at least in keeping with the fundamental constitutive stratification lines of a given society.

Fundamental constitutive stratification lines refer to how societies have been systematically organized to provide favorable outcomes for privileged groups. Favorable outcomes include: material goods; life chances, including the ability to capture resources; status; individual autonomy (consider the roles of women or slaves in many societies); and ideological privileging and degradation of a *group's* place in the social order. Most societies which reach a certain level of complexity have at least two such principles – gender and how economic activity, including the distribution of resources, is organized.[4] These systems of stratification systematically exclude specific social groups from the *bourgeois* public sphere. However, I agree with Fraser (1989) that the claim that these groups are excluded from *the* public sphere is an *ideological* claim since it privileges the bourgeois sphere as being *the sphere*. According to Fraser, the bourgeois public sphere becomes an instrument for a "historical transformation in the nature of political domination" which helps to establish new hegemonic "modes of domination" (1989:117).

The capital accumulation generated by European colonialism and the slave trade, created conditions for race to become an organizing principle. Race, gender and class, are socially constructed and historically contingent, and there is nothing deterministic about race becoming a constitutive organizing principle. The leap from race and racism as being part of the ideological structures of capitalism to being a constitutive organizing principle was not automatic. Yet, it did become such a principle for the United States, where white supremacy is not an ideology, but a system of power relations that structures society. Racism is an ideology based on the power and social relations which are organized by white supremacy. The system of stratification in the United States based on race and its ideological components served to exclude African Americans both formally and informally from participation within the American bourgeois public sphere. This system also encouraged exclusion of African Americans from subaltern counterpublics

4. I am undecided about "which came first," or if they came at the same time as de Beauvoir and many others argue. However, the anthropological research of Christine Ward Gailey supports the view that "gender hierarchy emerges in association with class relations and state structures" (Ward Gailey 1987: xv).

such as those associated with the labor, populist and women's movements of the late-nineteenth century. Indeed, part of the defeat of democratic forces alluded to in the opening relates to how these movements were captured by forces that excluded African Americans not only institutionally, but also as valid participants in the movements' discourses.

Re constrict

Thus, the formal expulsion of African Americans at the end of the nineteenth century from official spheres of public discourse and decision-making and the informal exclusion of African Americans from the mainstream of most oppositional movements, led to a dual strategy that was followed by African Americans until the 1960s. On the one hand, through the political agitation of those such as antilynching leader Ida B. Wells and the protests of organizations such as the NAACP, African Americans used a variety of tactics and approaches in the struggle to reinsert themselves into the channels of public discourse. Simultaneously, an active counterpublic was continued through organizations such as the Negro Women's Club Movement, the journals, meetings and activities of the fledgling civil rights organizations, the small but active literary cycles among Black women and men, the activities and debates of Black academics and through the Black church. The blossoming of Black organizational forms in political, economic and social arenas combined with the Harlem renaissance both strengthened the Black counterpublic and increased pressure for African American inclusion in official discourses and oppositional publics. These twin processes are part of a larger dialectical process. The activities of most of the major Black leaders and many of the Black organizations in the first half of the twentieth century — with the notable exception of Marcus Garvey — played major roles in both arenas. Ida B. Wells, who helped to shape national and international debate about lynching was also a key figure in the debates within the early Negro Women's Club Movement (Giddings 1984; Wells 1970). Similar dual roles were played by activists ranging from Du Bois and Randolph to the early Black cadre in the Communist Party of the United States (Naison 1983).

Tensions grew within the Black counterpublic as bourgeois masculinist norms were argued to be appropriate for regulating Black discourse and participation by some Black and mainly male leaders. The adoption of the norms from the dominant society shifted Black politics from the type of inclusionary participatory debate described by Brown during the early stages of Reconstruction, to the consistent attempts described by Wells and others to limit the participation of women in Black public discourse (Brown 1989; Wells 1970). However, while some powerful forces within the Black counterpublic were attempting to impose nonracially based dominant norms, other currents in the debates within the Black counterpublic provided the basis for both a devastating critique of American political institutions and values as well as suggestions about theoretical and institutional alternatives. During this period of the late-nineteenth and early-twentieth centuries many features of the Black counterpublic's role developed. Through the work of the Negro Women's Club Movement, Black women's activism became a crucial link between the women's suffrage and Black rights movements—a link that African American feminist groups continue to maintain. Radical critiques of American society also flourished within the Black community and were disseminated through the writings of those such as Du Bois. Throughout this period, which also witnessed the emergence and suppression of a radical trade union movement, African American activists within and outside of the trade union movement argued that an understanding of racial subordination and white supremacy had to be a central feature of any nonreductionist critique of American society. All of these trends influenced the interaction of racialized counterpublics throughout most of the twentieth century.

The African American Counterpublic and American Liberalism

This view of the Black counterpublic serving not only as a site for the criticism of existing American democratic institutions and practices, but also as the locus for a severe interrogation of American liberalism runs counter to the claims of some recent theorists. These theorists argue that African Americans have embraced and utilized American liberalism as a powerful source of opposition to slavery and white supremacy. Foner argues that nineteenth-century Black political thought, and indeed modern Black political thought and activism are grounded in "the republican traditions of the eighteenth century, particularly as expressed in the Declaration of Independence and the Constitution" (Foner 1984:60). Greenstone places Frederick Douglass in the same liberal reform tradition as John Adams and Daniel Webster (1993). Oakes explicitly makes the connection between Black political thought and liberalism:

> If any group of Americans might have been expected to repudiate liberalism for its complicity in the defense of slavery, racism and economic inequality—African-Americans are that group. The fact that black political leaders consistently claimed the liberal tradition as their own therefore constitutes a major problem in the history of American political culture. . . . black political thought . . . has never been divorced from the liberal tradition. From the late eighteenth century to the late twentieth,

blacks have successfully harnessed the themes of liberalism to the struggles against various forms of inequality. (1992:24, 27)

There are several fundamental problems with the uncomplicated if comforting, celebration of the location of Black political thought solidly within the mainstream of American liberalism. First, it does not fully appreciate the range of discourse during any given period within the Black counterpublic and overemphasizes a few prominent historical figures.[5] In particular, the importance of Black nationalism, the main challenger to the dominant trend of radical liberalism throughout most of the history of Black political thought, is systematically underrepresented. Except during the period of Reconstruction, Black nationalist intellectuals and activists played an active role in the Black counterpublic. It should not be surprising that in a society stratified by race—where African Americans have been systematically excluded from both the bourgeois public sphere and many oppositional counterpublics, where even in the twentieth century the idea that African Americans could freely choose their roles and associations in good liberal fashion seems ludicrously naive—nonliberal theoretical perspectives which emphasize the primacy of community should play a prominent role in the Black counterpublic. Both a lack of appreciation for the autonomy of the Black counterpublic and the ideological blinders of many scholars which lead them to miss the significance of major nationalist movements—Marcus Garvey, organizations such as the Nation of Islam, and intellectuals such as Martin Delaney—contribute to the lack of theorizing about the relationship of Black nationalist thought in the Black counterpublic and American liberalism.

Even during periods when the political rhetoric of African American activists was consistent with the liberal tradition, the actual political practice within Black communities has had decidedly nonliberal elements. Perhaps the most obvious example of a nonliberal (some would say antiliberal) political tradition within Black politics has been the consistent demand that *individual* African Americans take political stands that are perceived by the *community* as not harming the Black community. This norm is often systematically backed by community sanctioning

5. This is less true of Foner, who in a variety of short papers and his massive work on Reconstruction (1988) does consider a wide range of discourse within post-emancipation Black society. However, Foner's ability to make sweeping generalizations about Black political thought is hindered by the fact that the period he knows by far the best is the one period in American history when African Americans were both most optimistic and most prone to accept, albeit critically, American liberalism. His judgments on liberalism and Black political thought for other historical periods do not show the same appreciation for the nuances of Black political discourse as those of his work on Reconstruction.

and censoring of those perceived as transgressors. Brown and Foner detail how during Reconstruction Black Democrats were considered traitors, stripped of community-derived benefits and publicly condemned and humiliated (Brown 1989; Dawson in press; Foner 1988). This tradition remains strong even today when, due to the growing social and economic divisions within the Black community, there is now considerably less consensus on the Black tradition. Black supporters of the Republican Party are as intensely disdained by most African Americans as the Republican Party itself. Black conservatives such as Glenn Loury have complained throughout the recent period that they are ostracized and treated as traitors by other African Americans because of their conservatism. In the academy, liberals are periodically appalled, as the most recent darling of the conservative establishment becomes pilloried by a chorus of Black academics. Many African American academics regard the situation in very different terms. Perceived attacks on the Black community are not seen as the result of a courageous and creative talent, but as rank opportunism that imperils a community already under siege. While the empirical validity of either view can be assessed in any given case, the tradition of a public community censoring and sanctioning those seen as attacking the community represents a decidedly nonliberal tendency within Black political practice.

Virtually all of the major tendencies within Black political thought, except the historically weak trend of Black conservatism, have strongly deemphasized the privileged nature of private property. Former slaves such as Douglass would have found foul the idea of compensating former slave owners for their former property. By the 1930s, Du Bois who foreshadowed many of the transitions that African American intellectuals would make in the 1960s, had abandoned much of the liberal tradition in which earlier he had put so much faith. Fairly typical is this passage from *Dusk of Dawn*:

It was clear to me that agitation against race prejudice and a planned economy for bettering the economic condition of the American Negro were not antagonistic ideals but part of one ideal; that did not increase segregation; the segregation that was there and would remain for many years. But now I proposed that in economic lines, just as in lines of literature and religion, segregation should be planned and organized and carefully thought through. This plan did not establish a new segregation; it did not advocate segregation as the final solution of the race problem; exactly the contrary; but it did face the facts and faced them with thoughtfully mapped effort. (Du Bois 1986:777)

Du Bois's work in his later years provides an example of the need to better understand the autonomy of the Black counterpublic and the ways Black discourse cannot be confined within the boundaries of American liberalism. Du Bois and many other Black intellectuals and activists before and after him became members of an active Black left. The Black left had strong ties with White leftists, particularly during the heyday of the Communist Party, but still represented an indigenous force within the Black community that was fully engaged with other intellectuals, activists and members of the Black counterpublic (Kelley 1990; Naison 1983; Robinson 1983; Stuckey 1987).

While the Black left had both its doctrinaire wing as well as a more social-democratic element, even the beliefs of those who comprised the latter ran seriously counter to the tenets of White American liberalism. As the following passage from King's last presidential speech to the SCLC demonstrates, even relatively moderate Black leaders have tended to place demands on the state and limits on property that stretched the boundaries of liberalism:

> We [must] honestly face the fact that the movement must address itself to the question of restructuring the whole of American society. There are forty million poor people here. And one day we must ask the question, 'Why are there forty million poor people in America?' And when you begin to ask that question, you are raising questions about the economic system, about a broader distribution of wealth. When you ask that question, you begin to question the capitalistic economy. And I'm simply saying that more and more, we've got to begin to ask questions about the whole society. We are called upon to help the discouraged beggars in life's marketplace. But one day we must come to see that an edifice which produces beggars needs restructuring. . . . What I'm saying to you this morning is that communism forgets that life is individual. Capitalism forgets that life is social, and the kingdom of brotherhood is found neither in the thesis of communism nor the antithesis of capitalism but in a higher synthesis. It is found in a higher synthesis that combines the truths of both. Now, when I say question the whole society, it means ultimately coming to see that the problem of racism, the problem of economic exploitation, and the problem of war are all tied together. These are the triple evils that are interrelated. (1986:260)

These criticisms do not deny the presence of a strong liberal theme within Black political thought. The last statement by King, made at the height of his radicalism, still contains strong liberal elements. However, American liberalism is usually defined in such a way as to privilege the autonomy and liberty of the individual, skepticism of central state power and the sanctity of private property (Greenstone 1993; Oakes 1992; Waldron 1993). However, any sustained examination of the history of discourse within the Black counterpublic quickly reveals two important features of critical theory in the American context. First, there are strong historical traditions within Black political thought and practice that have elements which are at variance with the major tenets of American liberalism. Second, even the very strong liberal elements within Black political thought have explicit critiques of the consensual version of American liberalism as foundational components.

These two factors of the discourse within the Black counterpublic imply that Black political thought cannot be fully situated within American liberalism.[6] Deciding on what stance to take toward discourse within the Black counterpublic has been problematic for politicians, political activists and scholars who work within the liberal tradition, due to the nonliberal and radically transformed liberal currents found within the historical Black counterpublic. Two strategies prevail: to ignore the discourse entirely—forests of work on American political thought totally ignore political discourse among African Americans and Reed (1993) provides a good review of works in this genre; and, to announce that Black political thought is within the mainstream, and ignore or dismiss the tendencies within Black political thought at variance with the liberal tradition.[7] The formal and informal exclusion of African Americans from the polity provided a political basis for ignoring, except for purposes of surveillance, the Black counterpublic by the official public sphere well into the mid-twentieth century. However, interest in the Black counterpublic rapidly increased in the 1960s. This increase followed the combined pressures of the collapse of the legalistic mechanisms for exclusion

6. An additional consequence of not fully recognizing the diversity and autonomy of discourse within the Black counterpublic has been the tendency to view Black political discourse through the lenses of binary oppositions such as "black nationalism vs. assimilation" (Oakes 1992). As Pinder-hughes (1987) and Reed (1993) both argue, such an approach to Black political thought provides inadequate analytical power and impoverishes the task of attempting to understand the dialectic between a relatively autonomous indigenous discourse within the Black counterpublic and discourse between those within the subaltern counterpublic, and the dominant public about the nature and future course of the American polity.

7. This is often not the case with American conservatives. They quickly recognize and often exaggerate the radical and nonliberal elements of Black political thought and practice. The conservative critiques of King during the civil rights era, of Jesse Jackson's campaigns during the 1980s, and more recently of the failed nomination of Lani Guinier as Assistant Attorney General for Civil Rights provide three modern examples of this phenomenon.

of Blacks from formal participation within the polity, the exponential growth of the Black social movement which was responsible not only for the collapse of Jim Crow but also for a general increase in militancy in U.S. society, and the widening of the base and an increase in activity within the Black counterpublic. Throughout American history there has been a continual exchange between the Black counterpublic and other publics. The careers of Douglass, Wells, Du Bois and King were marked by their wide-ranging contacts and debates with Whites in their capacity as both individuals and representatives of major Black organizations (in Wells, Du Bois and King's case). The 1960s is the only period since the Reconstruction era that was marked both by the level of political debate and practice within the Black community, and by meaningful political exchanges and pragmatic cooperation between Blacks and Whites.[8] However, during the 1970s a set of transformations within the Black community, the American economy and the American political system once again reduced the level of interracial exchange and cooperation, and seriously undermined the Black counterpublic.

The Transformation of the African American Counterpublic

An often overlooked but critical feature of Habermas's formulation is the importance of the institutional bases for the bourgeois public sphere. Fraser's description of the feminist counterpublic also has at its base a wide variety of institutional forms including media and artistic outlets, bookstores, academic centers, and community service and organizational sites (Fraser 1989). Similarly, throughout Black history a multiplicity of Black institutions have formed the material basis for a subaltern counterpublic. An independent Black press, the production and circulation of socially and politically sharp popular Black music and the Black church have provided institutional bases for the Black counterpublic since the Civil War. The Black church was an essential part of the Black subaltern counterpublic

---

8. It is not a coincidence that more attention began to be paid to Black public opinion during this period by academics and private pollsters. The increased activity had an inherent regulatory function as the study of Black public opinion was seen within the framework of "race relations." Pollsters were less concerned about the historical development of Black thought and discourse and more concerned with how Blacks viewed American society and groups within American society and with trends within Black public opinion—were Blacks becoming more radical and dangerous?—and which sectors of the Black community were most disruptive. It is not surprising that the spurt of attention given to Black public opinion by organizations such as the University of Michigan-based American National Election Studies (1972) and the Harris organization's major studies in the late 1960s and early 1970s, died down once African Americans were once again no longer viewed as a threat to domestic tranquillity.

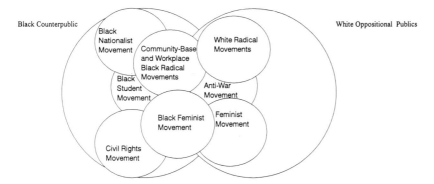

during each period. However, each period's subaltern counterpublic has also had a variety of secular organizational bases. Examples include the Negro Conventional Movement of the ante-bellum period, the Union Leagues of Reconstruction, the Negro Women's Club Movement of the late-nineteenth century, the organizations and debate that surrounded the Garvey movement and the civil rights organizations of the early 1960s. Both church and secular organizations within the Black community that were engaged both in intense political debate and practice proliferated during the 1960s and early 1970s. Church-based organizations such as the SCLC, student organizations such as the Black student unions, Black workers caucuses that spread like wildfire in settings as diverse as universities and auto plants, and community-based civil rights and Black power organizations all provided forums for debate over the direction of Black liberation, the relation of the Black political action to political activity occurring throughout the polity, and created an environment that closely linked political debate to political action. These overlapping sets of discourse communities provided the foundation for many of the social movements of Blacks and Whites during the height of the activism a generation ago (Fig. 1).

Unfortunately, a number of developments both within American society and the Black community severely undermined the institutional foundation for the Black counterpublic as well as Black access to White-dominated publics. The combination of state repression and internal dissension destroyed or severely harmed many civil rights and Black power organizations. The state, mainly but not exclusively, through the FBI's Counter Intelligence Program systematically

Figure 1. Intersections between Black and White Discourse and Activist Communities, 1966–1972.

targeted civil rights, Black student and Black militant organizations. State activities included harassing Dr. King, instigating intragroup violence, filing numerous charges against Black activists tying them and their organizational resources up in court often for years, and in the case of Chicago Black Panther leader Fred Hampton: assassination (Carson 1981, 1991; Garrow 1981; McAdam 1982).

The disintegration of the progressive and nationalist organizational bases of the Black counterpublic was aided in the middle 1970s by the near-fanatical attention that leftist forces dominated by people of color and Black nationalist forces devoted to the twin themes of theory building and even more specifically party building. The cadrification of groups as diverse as the New York based predominantly Puerto Rican, Young Lords Organization, the groups that came out of the radical Black labor organizing of Detroit's DRUM movement, the Chicano-based August 29th Movement and the originally nationalist Congress of African Peoples meant that experienced Black and other organizers of color were pulled out of the student movement, labor movement, cultural activities and community organizations to form small study groups and fight—often violently—in the name of building a myriad of vanguard political parties. This process destroyed formations such as the African Liberation Support Committee of the early and middle 1970s, which were able to mobilize tens of thousands of African Americans across the United States in the name of both African and Black liberation at home while facilitating debate about the future strategic orientation of Black movements, as group after group degenerated into small sects.[9]

A structural shift in the U.S. economy away from manufacturing and toward low-wage service industries also eroded the institutional base of the Black counterpublic, and, in particular, its points of contact with other oppositional forces. One of the critical aspects of the shift in the American economy, a shift that much of the industrialized world experienced throughout the 1970s and 1980s, was the shift from Fordist economic arrangements to a capitalist regime that emphasized flexible accumulation (Harvey 1989). This shift from a Fordist regime to one of flexible accumulation entailed dismantling large-scale industries in the West, destroying arrangements between labor, the state and corporations based on a small share of expanding profits being transferred to privileged sectors of

9. Reed (1994) provides an excellent analysis of this dismal history. Two differences I have with Reed's analysis are that I believe it is somewhat too attentive to East coast developments at the expense of the development of the radical wings of the Black movement in other parts of the country, and that it does not sufficiently estimate the state's role in aiding the disruption and disintegration of Black radical movements.

labor, and the forced dismembering of the welfare state (Harvey 1989). In the United States increased competition from Western Europe, Japan and the newly industrialized countries accelerated this process. Similarly, the move by producer countries such as the oil producers who tried to increasingly control the flow and price of raw materials had devastating effects on income and wages as evidenced by the decline of the real standard of living in the United States after the oil shocks of the early 1970s.

While the economic processes are well known, what is not as well understood, indeed it is usually totally missed, is how the Fordist regime in the United States integrated the racial and economic orders. For Blacks, the Fordist regime meant that Black economic gains were concentrated in the state and manufacturing sectors (see Dawson in press). These two sectors constituted the economic bases for the Black middle and working classes, the heart of most twentieth-century Black protest movements. This was a racialized economic order because Blacks were incorporated into the industrial order on a racially subordinate basis. A trenchant example is provided by Whatley and Wright (1994) where they describe how foundry workers' wages went from high to low as the work force shifted from White to Black. The system of White supremacy socially constructed labor markets and wages, as well as shaped the human capital endowments that Black workers could bring with them into increasingly competitive and high-skill labor markets (Whatley and Wright 1994). However, the shift to a system of flexible accumulation, which led to smaller workplaces, more homogenous work forces and the weakening of labor unions, meant that the moderate-waged bases of the Black working and middle classes were eviscerated. Moreover, under the new regimes Blacks were more likely to suffer from racial discrimination in the labor market (Kirschenman and Neckerman 1991; Johnson and Oliver 1990). Further, the spatial aspects of this transformation left inner-cities economically devastated as their economic base was removed and large sectors of urban minority residents lived in increasingly impoverished neighborhoods.

This transformation in the political economy had several major consequences. The impoverishing of the black working class, as both its manufacturing base and base in public employment disappeared, sharpened class divisions, as much of the stable Black working class now found its financial existence seriously imperiled (Dawson in press). From the fourth quarter of 1974 through the fourth quarter of 1992 there were exactly *five* quarters where Black unemployment was below ten percent (data compiled by author from Citibase electronic database). In all five sub-ten percent quarters the Black unemployment rate was over nine percent. States with previously high levels of Black industrial workers such as

Illinois and Michigan were hit particularly hard. Conditions of near permanent economic depression in many Black communities harmed their organizational bases as black organizations shrunk and disappeared when their financial status worsened and their programs were seen as less relevant to solving the problems of a devastated economy. The devastation of the economic base was accompanied by a significant decline in the political and economic strength of American trade unions. While the trade union movement from the 1930s through the 1960s never provided a panacea or the basis for multiracial mass organizing the left had hoped for, it did provide one of the few settings within which nonelite Blacks and Whites interacted and occasionally cooperated politically. It also provided a training ground for many of the Black leftist forces for the 1960s as well as for many future Black elected officials, e.g., Detroit's previous multiterm mayor, Coleman Young. After the 1970s, the trade union movement's ability to serve either as a site for interracial political discourse or as a valuable training ground for a wide range of Black activists was severely attenuated.

The transformation of the American political economy, combined with the dismantling of the formal mechanisms of segregation stimulated the growth in various segments of the Black middle class (Dawson, in press). Formal segregation and the entire White supremacist system of Jim Crow provided a monumental common target for African Americans and for many liberal and progressive Whites. As King (1967) and others argued, White support declined as the civil rights movement shifted to the North, and became increasingly perceived as a movement focused on economic demands. Black and White interracial cooperation plummeted, and more often than not, in political arenas ranging from local contests for mayor to national presidential politics, Blacks and Whites found themselves on opposite sides. The political gap between Blacks and Whites continued to grow through the early 1990s as different events such as the subway shootings by Bernard Goetz, the election and reign of Ronald Reagan, and the presidential campaigns of Jesse Jackson were assigned radically different meanings by Blacks and Whites (Dawson in press). By the early 1990s dialogue between White and Black communities had largely disappeared with the partial exception of the continued discourse between feminist women of Color and White feminists.

The dismantling of the formal barriers of segregation combined with the sharpening of economic divisions within the Black community also served to problematize Black political discourse. The lack of a single common goal unmasked the political relevance of already existing social cleavages. Sharpening economic divisions led to a divergence in Black mass opinion on questions such as whether policies of economic redistribution were desirable (Dawson in press). Perhaps even more important for considering the various purposes of subaltern publics as described by Fraser (1989), is that economic divisions are strongly associated within African American mass opinion with division over the degree to which race is seen as the driving force creating Black disadvantage, and what strategies African Americans should adopt at this time. Specifically, economic disadvantage facing both individuals and communities is strongly associated with a racialized view of the world and with a greater probability to support Black nationalist policies and organizational forms (Cohen and Dawson 1993; Dawson in press).

While the economic divisions in the Black community are politically important, Morrison's and Henry's analyses of the death of Black political unity based on some common Black identity had as their immediate spark the turmoil that erupted among African Americans when first confronted with the nomination of Clarence Thomas and the subsequent charges of sexual abuse brought against him by law professor Anita Hill. Throughout African American history Black women have played a leading role in the struggle against White supremacy. They have struggled with patriarchal attitudes within the Black community held by many Black men and some Black women that relegate Black women to a subordinate role in the struggle against oppression. They have also struggled to place issues of particular concern to Black women on the Black agenda (Cohen 1994; Davis 1981; Giddings 1984; Wells 1970). Black feminists became increasingly dissatisfied with the lack of political attention devoted to issues that had particular significance for them and with patriarchal ideologies being used as a weapon to justify their subordination in Black nationalist and church-based formations, as well as in some Black left organizations. The vulgar and brutal misogyny of Black leaders such as Elridge Cleaver and Stokely Carmichael further fuelled the explosion of Black feminist and womanist organizations, literatures, presses and debate. The increasingly vocal position advanced by some African Americans that the surest way to understand the Black condition was by understanding the intersection of race, gender and class with White supremacist, patriarchal and classist systems of stratification that mapped the terrain of American society (Crenshaw 1990) clashed with openly patriarchal analyses of the Black condition by many Black activists and intellectuals. Further, like Justice Thomas's supporters, many Blacks claimed that all Black men in a position to achieve power should never be publicly criticized even when their politics widely diverge from that of eighty-five percent of Blacks or when they had previously used power to abuse less powerful members of the Black community. The demand for uncritical support of Blacks in positions of power and the relegation of the specific concerns of Black women to a secondary status became increasingly intolerable. As Morrison states, "In matters of race and gender, it is now possible and necessary, as it seemed never to have been before, to speak about these matters without the barriers, the silences, the embarrassing gaps in discourse" (1992:xxx).

The new economic regime further intensified divisions within the Black community and disintegration of the Black counterpublic as a new wave of Black elected officials provided a buffer class that helped to delegitimate protest and circumscribe acceptable political discourse within the Black community. Three parallel processes were at work as many Black elected officials cooperated in narrowing the Black agenda through the 1970s and the 1980s. Black elected officials at the local level inherited cities that were devastated by the economic upheavals described above. They were severely limited in their ability to meet the demands of their disadvantaged constituents. Second, as Black elected officials began to have aspirations that necessitated attracting votes outside of the Black community (with the moderate exceptions of those such as Jesse Jackson and Harold Washington) they de-emphasized both their explicit racial appeals as well as political agendas that included economic redistribution—historically a fundamental political demand of the Black community (Dawson 1994; Persons 1993). Finally, many Black elected officials became incorporated into the new ruling regime of race relations management which entailed acting as a regulatory buffer dedicated to incremental changes in race relations and even smaller improvements in the economic plight of the poor (Hill 1994; Reed 1994).

The combined weight of the disintegration of the institutional bases of the Black counterpublic from the early 1970s and increasing Black skepticism that there is a bundle of issues and strategies that define a Black agenda leads us to ask if a subaltern counterpublic exists. If it does, how healthy is it now? The racial system of stratification which helped provide the material basis for the historical counterpublic still exists. American society is nowhere near the idea described by Charles Taylor when he asserted:

> From the democratic point of view, a person's ethnic identity is not his or her primary identity, and important as respect for diversity is in multicultural democratic societies, ethnic identity is not the foundation of recognition of equal values and the related idea of equal rights. . . . In other words, from the liberal democratic point of view a person has a right to claim equal recognition first and foremost on the basis of his or her universal human identity and potential not primarily on the basis of an ethnic identity. (1992:88).

And I argue that Baker exaggerates when he claims: "Any of us might encounter simply in our daily travels a black, Vietnamese-American, potential-MBA, Ivy-League, basketball-playing woman who is fully at ease with the transnational, material, and indisputably hybrid spaces in which she dwells" (1993:70).

Baker misses the point. Certainly, it is past the time to reject essentialist definitions of race, gender and other socially constructed categories. As Reed states:

> Of course race is real, but it is real only in the way that all social con-
> structs are real. Its reality is always contingent on historically circum-
> scribed contexts of meaning and patterns of social stratification. The suc-
> cess of civil rights activism in defeating the regime of official racial
> segregation, for example, . . . has helped to give rise to recent efforts
> to nail down a new, historically appropriate summary construction of
> black identity. (1992:138–139)

Some identities remain more salient than others in the political, economic and social realms. A new wave of empirical research conclusively demonstrates that in the 1990s race continues to structure where one can live, who one is likely to vote for, whether one is likely to encounter discrimination based on stereotypes when entering the labor market, and whether one's culture and intelligence are considered inferior (Dawson 1993c, in press; Jencks 1992). However, the disman-tling of the formal structures of segregation combined with the increasing impor-tance of identities based on other structures of stratification require that a Black subaltern counterpublic be reconstituted based on a new understanding of the issues, including patriarchy and economic oppression. This broadening of what is understood to be on the Black agenda must precede the formulation of a unifying set of discourses and political agenda. However, before we can consider the reconstitution of a Black counterpublic, a task that may no longer be possible, we have to consider one more major set of historic events. The terrain has become even more complex, and oppositional publics have come under increased external siege with the rosy dawning of the Reagan revolution in 1981.

Is There a Black Counterpublic in the 1990s in the Aftermath of the Reagan-Bush Regime?

While the economic earthquake described in the last section had its origins in the middle 1960s and accelerated in the 1970s, the ideological and political restructuring that accompanied this transformation was decisively accomplished in the 1980s by a number of extraordinarily conservative regimes including those of Margaret Thatcher, Helmut Kohl and Ronald Reagan. The advent of the Reagan-Bush regime redefined the acceptable in American political discourse. Civil rights leaders and organizations, feminists and other advocates of women rights, labor unions, gay rights activists, and those who opposed American militaristic intervention in the developing world were all pictured as outside of the bounds of acceptable, patriotic American discourse. They were portrayed by the Reagan administration as wild radicals and/or despicable opportunists who threatened the republic, American culture and the family. Further, Reagan's advisors as well as Bush's during 1984 were masters of invoking racist symbols in the guise of treasured American values in order to further politically divide the citizenry and isolate African Americans (Dawson 1993c; Kinder, et al. 1989).

A critical aspect of the Reagan administration's assault on African Americans was a massive ideological attack on the fruits of the Civil Rights movement. The Reagan administration refused to talk with the established leadership of the Black community, and through executive orders, supreme court appointments and congressional action it attempted to systematically overturn African American victories in the areas of voting rights, anti segregation legislation, education and economic advancement. The state's attack was reinforced by intellectual justification. Moving from the position held in the 1980s that all programs which favored Blacks should be repealed, some rightists in the academy during the 1990s argue that discrimination in the labor market was not only morally permissible due to the efficiency gained through employment discrimination, but that antidiscrimination law was a form of coercion unjustifiable in a liberal democracy based on Lockean principles (Murray 1984; Epstein 1992).

The attack on the unions, the social safety net and the ideological and institutional bases of all potential opposition was intended to further isolate African Americans. Initially, this strategy worked well. The transformation of Black politics from an activist and protest-oriented politics to one that was almost completely conducted through electoral politics encouraged political passivity among many African Americans. Black protest music and other potentially political art forms, which in an earlier era had become important because of their relation to mass social movements for justice and power, were now commodified instantly. This commodification of nearly all forms of Black artistic endeavor led to the grimly ironic sight of Bobby Seale and Al Sharpton playing caricatures of themselves. Once speakers' corners and other components of the Black counterpublic had actively engaged the Black community in debate about future strategic directions. The 1990s brings an incomprehensible sixty-second movie soundbite of activists and former activists speaking in tongues as audiences passively sit in either a movie theatre or at home cheering on activists of a previous generation. The ideological attacks on the unions and on the ideal that the state should play a central role in guaranteeing economic security for a nation's citizens also further isolated African Americans and justified the dismantling of the economic apparatus that had provided African Americans with modest gains from the early part of the century through the middle 1970s. Very few African American political leaders, let alone White politicians, were willing to advocate broad-based economic redistribution after the Reagan ideological onslaught. A partial but ultimately unsatisfactory exception can be found in the political platform of the second Jackson campaign (Jackson 1989). However, the lack of follow-through between elections meant that this agenda was largely left undiscussed and was never a centerpiece for political mobilization (Reed 1994). Although the rhetoric of Jackson during the campaigns was critical of American society, it was much more celebratory than that of King during the last years of his life or the pessimism found among African Americans in the 1990s (Dawson 1994).[10]

The question before us becomes, what is the basis in the 1990s for restructuring an oppositional subaltern public in the aftermath of a rightist backlash of historic proportions, an aftermath which has the so-called progressive party adopting much of the logic of its rightist predecessor (Dawson 1993). Some scholars argue that the beginnings of the renewal of the African American social movement can be seen in the innovative fusion of protest and electoral politics found in New York City and other urban areas (Jennings 1992). Clearly there is an increase in interesting combinations of movements, for example, the growing number of protests occurring at the intersection of movements of people of color and the environmental movement. Growing local protests centered on health care issues ranging from AIDS to the distribution of urban public health facilities also provide significant potential. Increasing cutbacks on college campuses could reinvigorate the student movement. In the late 1980s Black student organizing increased in response to racist incidents on campuses such as the University of Michigan and the University of Pennsylvania.

Scholars have also argued that rap music presents an oppositional urban artistic form that provides a medium which is to some degree controlled by indigenous cultural forms and that can savagely critique the terrain of urban conflict, and

10. Nearly two-thirds of African Americans believe that racial equality will either never be achieved or will not be achieved during their lifetime (Dawson 1994).

open up the bases for discourses on a range of subjects in the Black community, including sexism (Baker 1993; Kelley 1990; Rose 1989, 1990). Kelley argues:

> The cultural forms [African-American] youth invent and continually revise attempt to make meaning of their experiences as well as carve out free spaces for pleasure within those experiences. Though shaped unevenly by the demands of the marketplace, the more sophisticated lyricists not only offer complex descriptions of how racism continues to dominate day-to-day experiences with social institutions (i.e., police, prison, hospitals), but they also articulate an incipient critique of class-based oppression, the black bourgeoisie, and the one-dimensional nature of contemporary racial politics. (in press)

Clearly the rhymes of rappers such as Queen Latifah, Salt-N-Pepa, and MC Lyte challenge the misconception that rap is the exclusive domain of men. Their lyrics directly assert the rights and leadership capabilities of Black women as well as systematically attack Black men who would play or otherwise abuse Black women (Rose 1991). Further the increased distribution of Black fiction, the proliferation of politically oriented community-based cable TV shows and the increase in the number of Black movies with implicit or explicit political themes are regarded as positive elements in the increased circulation of ideas among African Americans.

However, significant barriers to revitalizing the Black counterpublic remain. Uncritical celebration by scholars such as Baker (1993) of some of the more viciously misogynist rappers such as NWA obscures the devastating harm that the misogyny of this popular and promoted commodity can do to attempts to revitalize democratic debate in the Black community. While rappers like Disposable Heroes of Hiphoprisy consistently criticize misogyny, homophobia and racist behaviors and institutions, they do not receive as much airtime—or sales—as vicious reactionary lyrics like "The Chronic" of Dr. Dre and Snoop Doggy Dogg. While public television audiences are enlightened by watching Michael Franti of the Disposable Heroes eloquently debate Bill Moyers, hundreds of thousands of youths are buying recordings like "The Chronic" which consistently depict Black women as less than human, not to be trusted, and to be objects deserving nothing except abuse. The more socially acute rap of their former colleague, Ice Cube, often promotes the same misogyny along with raps that acutely critique American racism. As Taylor (1992) and others argue, a prerequisite for democratic debate is the recognition of the humanity and dignity of all individuals within a community. There can be no mass-based Black counterpublic if Black women are continually denied the right to basic humanity and voice.

Both Chuck D of Public Enemy fame and Ice Cube have argued that the commodification of rap promotes the more destructive elements of gangsta rap. This is true as far as it goes. Yet progressive rap also needs critique, and listening to rap or watching progressive music does not substitute for critical debate. A significant part of the current problem in Black political discourse is the absence of critical social movements and political institutions capable of fostering debate of issues raised in socially critical rap and other artistic forms, political programs of activists and work of academics and intellectuals. A counterpublic can provide the institutional and political base to facilitate communication and criticism across these diverse elements. Several factors make rebuilding the institutional and political bases for a healthy Black counterpublic more difficult. Both mainstream political parties are engaged in a racial politics of distancing themselves from and attacking Black aspirations and Black-identified public policies, and consider this part of the formula for success. The trade union movement is at its weakest point since the middle of the century. The points of possible intersection between a Black counterpublic and other oppositional publics are still extremely limited. The traditional civil rights, progressive and nationalist organizations within the Black community are also in disarray. With these organizations collectively at their lowest ebb since the beginning of the century (with the possible exception of the decade of the Great Depression), no national and only weak local forces exist to provide the type of organizational base necessary for a flourishing counterpublic or multiple counterpublics.

Implications for the Study of Public Opinion

Public opinion researchers can play a role in the revitalization of a Black counterpublic. The study of African American mass opinion is in its infancy. This research has provided some valuable services such as modelling African American participation in the electoral system and describing Black policy preferences, and has begun to show the connections between economic and other cleavages within the Black community and political attitudes. However, this research has weaknesses shared by much American survey-based research on mass attitudes. Habermas's distinction between mass and public opinion helps highlight these weaknesses. How and to what extent the circulation of and participation in debates within social movements, indigenous organizations, and Black media and artistic outlets influence political attitudes of individuals is an empirical question. Empirical research can assess the differential impact of critical publicity and faddish, commodified, institutionally authorized opinion of the media, the state and powerful private interests. However, to transform mass opinion research into research on public opinion requires improvement on the current research.

One key aspect involves assessing the origins of opinion among the public. To what degree are these opinions shaped by institutions? What types of institutions, organizations, and political activity are associated with the political opinion of African Americans? The typical survey standpoint of individuals with preference isolated from societal influences would have to be abandoned as it has been in the better public opinion research. Historical and theoretical work to determine key political problems and questions facing a public would have to be undertaken to guide the construction of survey questionnaires. The practice of duplicating studies designed for largely White populations is inappropriate for a research agenda that is seeking to survey the terrain of public opinion in communities of Color. The concept of an opinion survey would itself have to be reevaluated. It is clear that survey research is about the only way to assess the configuration of public opinion in a large population. However, it is now necessary to introduce innovative research designs that would include components which would assess the communities and social and political networks of respondents as well as the political environments which shape their attitudes. More work that combines in-depth community studies with survey research would facilitate this task.

Such a research agenda would help provide information for assessing the degree of circulation of political debate among African Americans, its organizational and political base and which factors within contemporary Black politics have the best potential for revitalizing oppositional counterpublics. It would make public for critical debate the issues that different social forces among African Americans argue are central to social, economic and political progress. Further, such research can also crystallize and emphasize the smoldering issues that underlie the intense racial conflicts of this era. This research is not a substitute for practical political activity or hard theoretical work. Without becoming connected to institutionally grounded debate, it also risks becoming a relatively unproductive spectator sport. But such a research agenda could serve a valuable role in repairing the damage done to Black public opinion by the political, economic and social blows suffered during recent decades, and begin to reverse the reactionary counteroffensive that reached a modern peak under the recent right-wing administration.

Michael C. Dawson teaches in the Political Science Department at the University of Chicago. He has recently published "Neighborhood Poverty and African-

American Politics" with Cathy J. Cohen in *American Political Science Review* (June 1993) and his book, *Behind the Mule: Race, Class and African-American Politics* is forthcoming from Princeton University Press. He is currently principal investigator in the research project, National Black Politics Study; analyses of this survey of a national sample of African Americans will be contained in a series of papers and a book, *Freedom, Equality, and Self-Determination: The Historical Roots of Contemporary African-American Mass Political Thought.*

Literature Cited

Baker, Jr., Houston A. 1993. *Black Studies, Rap, and the Academy.* Chicago: The University of Chicago Press.

Brown, Elsa Barkley. 1989. "To Catch the Vision of Freedom: Reconstructing Southern Black Women's Political History, 1865–1885." Unpublished manuscript.

Carson, Clayborne. 1981. *In Struggle: SNCC and the Black Awakening of the 1960s.* Cambridge: Harvard University Press.

———. 1991. *Malcolm X: The FBI File.* New York: Carroll and Graf Publishers.

Cohen, Cathy J. 1994. "Contested Identities: Black Lesbian and Gay Identities and the Black Community's Response to AIDS." Unpublished manuscript.

Cohen, Cathy and Michael C. Dawson. 1993. "Neighborhood Poverty and African American Politics." *The American Political Science Review* 87:286–302.

Crenshaw, Kimberle. 1990. "A Black Feminist Critique of Antidiscrimination Law and Politics." In David Kairys, ed., *The Politics of Law: A Progressive Critique.* New York: Pantheon Books, 195–218.

Davis, Angela Y. 1981. *Women, Race, and Class.* New York: Vintage Books.

Dawson, Michael C. "Desperation and Hope: Du Bois, King, and American Citizenship." Unpublished manuscript.

———. "Some Preliminary Thoughts on Poverty, Space, and Political Beliefs." Unpublished manuscript.

———. *Behind the Mule: Race, Class, and African American Politics.* Princeton: Princeton University Press, in press.

———. 1993. "Demonization and Silence: Preliminary: Thoughts on the 1992 Presidential Election, the New Consensus on Race, and African-American Public Opinion." A paper presented at the Symposium on Race and American Political Culture, May 11, 1993, The University of Chicago.

_____. 1994. "Black Discontent: The Preliminary Report of the 1993–1994 National Black Politics Study." Report no. 1 from the 1993–1994 National Black Politics Working Paper Series, The University of Chicago.

Du Bois, William Edward Burghardt. 1986. *Dusk of Dawn*. In Nathan Huggins, ed., *Du Bois Writings*. New York: The Library of America, 549–802.

Eley, Geoff. 1989. "Nations, Publics, and Political Cultures: Placing Habermas in the Nineteenth Century." In Craig Calhoun, ed., *Habermas and the Public Sphere*, Cambridge: MIT Press, 289–339.

Epstein, Richard A. 1992. *Forbidden Grounds: The Case Against Employment Discrimination Laws*. Cambridge: Harvard University Press.

Foner, Eric. 1988. *Reconstruction: America's Unfinished Revolution, 1863–1877*. New York: Harper and Row.

_____. 1984. "Reconstruction and the Black Political Tradition." In Richard S. McCormick, ed., *Political Parties and and the Modern State*, New Brunswick: Rutgers University Press, 53–66.

Fraser, Nancy. 1989. "Rethinking the Public Sphere: A Contribution to the Critique of Actually Existing Democracy." In Craig Calhoun, ed., *Habermas and the Public Sphere*, Cambridge: MIT Press, 109–142.

Garrow, David J. 1981. *The FBI and Martin Luther King, Jr.* New York: Penguin Books.

Giddings, Paula. 1984. *When and Where I Enter: The Impact of Black Women on Race and Sex in America*. New York: William Morrow and Company.

Greenstone, J. David. 1993. *The Lincoln Persuasion: Remaking American Liberalism*. Princeton: Princeton University Press.

Habermas, Jürgen. 1989. [1962]. *The Structural Transformation of the Public Sphere: An Inquiry into a Category of Bourgeois Society*. Translated by Thomas Burger. Cambridge: MIT Press.

Harvey, David. 1989. *The Condition of Postmodernity*. Cambridge: Blackwell Publishers.

Henry, Charles P. 1992. "Clarence Thomas and the National Black Identity." *The Black Scholar* 22:40–41.

Hill, Rickey. 1994. "From a Culture of Struggle and Resistance to a Culture of Acquiescence and Displacement: Sketches on the Problematics of Contemporary Black Political Discourse." A paper presented at the 17th Annual Black Studies Conference at Olive-Harvey College. Chicago, Illinois. April 20–23, 1994.

Jackson, Jesse. 1989. "The Revival of Hope: The Platform of the 1988 Jesse Jackson for President Campaign." In Frank Clemente, ed., *Keep Hope Alive:*

Jesse Jackson's 1988 Presidential Campaign. Boston: South End Press, 41–54.

Jencks, Christopher. 1992. *Rethinking Social Policy: Race, Poverty, and the Underclass*. New York: HarperCollins.

Jennings, James. 1992. *The Politics of Black Empowerment: The Transformation of Black Activism in Urban America*. Detroit: Wayne State University Press.

Johnson, James H., Jr., and Melvin L. Oliver. 1990. "Economic Restructuring and Black Male Joblessness in U.S. Metropolitan Areas." Unpublished manuscript.

Kelley, Robin. 1990. *Hammer and Hoe: Alabama Communists During the Depression*. Chapel Hill: University of North Carolina Press.

———. "Kickin' Reality, Kickin' Ballistics: The Cultural Politics of Gangsta Rap in Postindustrial Los Angeles." In William Eric Perkins, ed., *Droppin' Science*. Philadelphia: Temple University Press, in press.

Kinder, Donald R., Tali Mendelberg, Michael C. Dawson, Lynn M. Sanders, Steven J. Rosenstone, Jocelyn Sargent and Cathy Cohen. 1989. "Race and the 1988 American Presidential Election." Paper prepared for the Annual Meeting of the American Political Science Association, Atlanta Georgia, August 30–September 3, 1989.

King, Martin Luther, Jr. 1967. *Where Do We Go From Here: Chaos or Community?* Boston: Beacon Hill Press.

———. 1986. "Where Do We Go From Here?" (speech). In James M. Washington, ed., *A Testament of Hope: The Essential Writings and Speeches of Martin Luther King, Jr.* San Francisco: Harper.

Kirschenman, Joleen and Kathryn M. Neckerman. 1991. "We'd Love to Hire Them, but . . .: The Meaning of Race for Employers." In Christopher Jencks and Paul E. Peterson, ed., *The Urban Underclass*, Washington, D.C.: The Brookings Institute, 203–232.

McAdam, Doug. 1982. *Political Process and the Development of Black Insurgency, 1930–1970*. Chicago: University of Chicago Press.

Morrison, Toni. 1992. Introduction. In Toni Morrison, ed. *Race-ing Justice, Engender-ing Power: Essays on Anita Hill, Clarence Thomas and the Construction of Social Reality*. New York: Pantheon Books, vii–xxx.

Murray, Charles. 1984. *Losing Ground: American Social Policy, 1950–1980*. New York: Basic Books.

Naison, Mark. 1983. *Communists in Harlem During the Depression*. New York: Grove Press.

Oakes, James. "The Liberal Dissensus." Unpublished manuscript.

Persons, Georgia, ed. 1993. Introduction. In *Dilemmas of Black Politics: Issues of Leadership and Strategy*. New York: HarperCollins College Publishers, 1–11.

Pinderhughes, Dianne. 1987. *Race and Ethnicity in Chicago Politics*. Urbana: University of Illinois Press.

Reed, Adolph, Jr. 1992. "Du Bois's 'Double Consciousness': Race and Gender in Progressive Era American Thought." *Studies in American Political Development* 6:93–139.

_____. "Fabianism and the Color Line: The Political Thought of W. E. B. Du Bois." Unpublished manuscript.

_____. "Sources of Demobilization in the New Black Political Regime: Incorporation, Ideological Capitulation and Radical Failure in the Post-Segregation Era." Unpublished manuscript.

Robinson, Cedric J. 1983. *Black Marxism: The Making of the Black Radical Tradition*. London: Zed Books.

Rose, Tricia. 1989. "Orality and Technology: Rap Music and Afro-American Cultural Resistance." *Popular Music and Society* 13:35–44.

_____. 1991. "Never Trust a Big Butt and a Smile." *Camera Obscura* 23:104–131.

Ryan, Mary P. 1989. "Gender and Public Access: Women's Politics in Nineteenth-Century America." In Craig Calhoun, ed., *Habermas and the Public Sphere*. Cambridge: MIT Press, 259–288.

Sanders, Lynn M. 1994. "What is Whiteness? Race of Interviewer Effects When All the Interviewers are Black." Unpublished manuscript.

Stuckey, Sterling. 1987. *Slave Culture: Nationalist Theory and the Foundations of Black America*. New York: Oxford University Press.

Taylor, Charles. 1992. *Multiculturism and "The Politics of Recognition."* Princeton: Princeton University Press.

Venkatesh, Sudhir A. 1993. "The Killing of Rail: Black Gangs and the Reconstitution of 'Community' in an Urban Ghetto." Paper prepared for The Politics of Race and the Reproduction of Racial Ideologies Workshop, The University of Chicago, November 12, 1993.

Waldron, Jeremy. 1993. "Theoretical Foundations of Liberalism." In *Liberal Rights: Collected Papers, 1981–1991*. Cambridge: Cambridge University Press, 35–62.

Ward Gailey, Christine. 1987. *Kinship to Kingship: Gender Hierarchy and State Formation in the Tongan Islands*. Austin: University of Texas Press.

Wells, Ida B. 1970. *Crusade for Justice: The Autobiography of Ida B. Wells*. Edited by Alfreda M. Duster. Chicago: University of Chicago Press.

Whatley, Warren and Gavin Wright. 1994. "Race, Human Capital, and Labour Markets in American History." Working Paper Number 7. Center for Afro-american and African Studies, The University of Michigan.

"A Nation of Thieves":
Consumption, Commerce, and
the Black Public Sphere

Regina Austin

I n so very many areas of public life, blacks are condemned and negatively stereotyped for engaging in activities that white people undertake without a second thought. Among the most significant of these is buying and selling goods and services. Despite the passage of state and federal antidiscrimination and public accommodations laws, blacks are still fighting for the right to shop and the right, if not the reason, to sell. Because blacks have not yet secured these rights, many of those who have the temerity to shop or to sell are treated like economic miscreants.

Shopping and selling by blacks, or more broadly consumption and commerce, are in essence considered deviant activities by many whites and by many blacks as well. It may be hard for some readers to accept the categorization of such mundane activities as deviance, but deviance is gauged, not by the intrinsic nature of an act, but by powerful peoples' responses to it.[1] Deviance is a social construct and a mechanism of social control. An activity may be labeled deviant even though it does not represent a threat to the social order.

For a more elaborately documented version of this work see Regina Austin, "'A Nation of Thieves': Securing Black People's Right to Shop and to Sell in White America," 1994 *Utah Law Review* 147. I thank Daniel Ecarius for his invaluable research assistance and Manthia Diawara for his support.

1. Howard S. Becker, *Outsiders: Studies in the Sociology of Deviance* (New York: Free Press, 1963), 9.

Public Culture 1994, 7: 225–248

Given the experiences of blacks' endeavoring to shop, there should be little doubt that black consumption is constructed as a form of deviance. Tales of the obstacles blacks encounter in trying to spend their money in white-owned shops and stores are legendary.[2] Blacks are treated as if they were all potential shoplifters, thieves or deadbeats.[3] There can hardly be a black person in urban America who has not been either denied entry to a store, closely watched, snubbed, questioned about her or his ability to pay for an item or stopped and detained for shoplifting. Salespeople are slow to wait on blacks and rude when they do, or too quick to wait on blacks whom they practically shove out the door. Although anecdotal evidence suggests that men are more likely to encounter such treatment, women are similarly victimized. Today, even the youngest black consumers are in for a good bit of distrust.

Any kind of ordinary face-to-face retail transaction can turn into a hassle for a black person. At the deli counter or the butcher shop blacks get cheated by short-weighting or being sold inferior products. Empirical research suggests that blacks pay more than whites for standardized products like cars where negotiation is required.[4] Blacks have problems obtaining credit to buy goods and must endure

2. Carl Husemoller Nightingale, *On the Edge: A History of Poor Black Children and Their American Dreams* (New York: Basic Books, 1993), 125–26 (describing the suspicion the white author witnessed when he went shopping with black kids from his inner-city Philadelphia neighborhood); Ze'ev Chafets, *Devil's Night: And Other Tales of Detroit* (New York: Random House, 1990), 33 (quoting a city neighborhood services official complaining that black children are required to walk with their hands at their sides or are allowed into stores one at a time); Joe R. Fagin, "The Continuing Significance of Race: Antiblack Discrimination in Public Places," *American Sociological Review* 56 (1991): 105–10 (describing blacks' responses to discrimination in places of public accommodations); Patricia Williams, "Spirit-Murdering the Messenger: The Discourse of Fingerpointing as the Law's Response to Racism," *University of Miami Law Review* 42 (1987): 128–29 (describing the author's reaction after being refused entry to a Benetton store); Diane, Negro Guinea Pig, "With Friends Like These . . .," *Sassy*, Sept. 1993, 84 (recounting the results of a experiment that sent a young black writer and her white friend as testers to an expensive jewelry store and an apartment for rent); Sara Rimer, "Shawn, 17: Running Past Many Obstacles," *New York Times*, 25 Apr. 1993, A1, L47 (describing how a shop owner, seeing a neatly dressed young black man admiring a shirt in the window, closes the door and locks it); Lena Williams, "When Blacks Shop, Bias Often Accompanies Sale," *New York Time*, 30 Apr. 1991, A1 (describing a range of discriminatory treatment blacks encounter in retail establishments).

3. I am black. When referring to black people, I use the third person plural throughout, rather than the first person, not to distance myself from other blacks, but for grammatical consistency (many of the experiences I describe are not my own) and to avoid the suggestion that there are no divisions among blacks based on class, age, gender, sexual orientation, religion, country of origin or ancestry and geographical location.

4. Ian Ayres, "Fair Driving: Gender and Race Discrimination in Retail Car Negotiations," *Harvard Law Review* 104 (1991): 817–73.

suspicious scrutiny if they pay by credit card or check.[5] They are also given a hard time when they want to return goods that are defective or unsatisfactory.

Shops and stores are not the only concerns where blacks receive poor service and inferior products.[6] Businesses that treat blacks badly run the gamut from airlines to health spas to movie theaters. Restaurants, for example, have many ways of letting black people know their business is not appreciated. Slow or no service is perhaps the most blatant form of discrimination, but I have experienced more subtle techniques like being escorted past empty tables in the front of a restaurant to a separate room at the back. On another occasion, I was served a crème brulée (a fancy French dessert) covered with salt, not sugar.

The harm that blacks suffer from disrespectful and disparate treatment goes beyond psychological pain or the sting of injustice in a legal regime supposedly dedicated to racial equality. The most disturbing aspect of the discriminatory service blacks experience in common ordinary commercial transactions is economic exploitation. When blacks pay the same prices as everyone else and get less in the way of service or merchandise, they are being cheated. Moreover, discriminatory service narrows blacks' choices regarding where to consume and impedes their ability to enter into efficient commercial transactions. Those merchants holding themselves out as being "willing" to deal with blacks can extract a premium for doing so. In addition, as is discussed more fully below, many of the maneuvers blacks employ to make consumption easier entail costs that add to the price of purchases. Finally, whites also are exploited by the disparate

5. Blacks are sometimes asked to supply additional identification when they pay by check and their race may be recorded on the back of the instrument. The stores maintain that they need information about race in order to prosecute check fraud claims. Rudolph A. Pyatt, Jr., "The Risks of Check-Coding by Race," *Washington Post*, 6 May 1991, F3; Derrick Z. Jackson, "Two Stores Record Race of Customers," *Boston Globe*, 6 June 1990, B1.

6. See, for example, Eugene Morris, "The Difference in Black and White," *American Demographics* 15 (Jan. 1993): 49 (reporting that flight attendants confront black travelers storing items in first-class bins because they do not assume that blacks fly first-class); Teresa Simons, "Health Spa Discrimination Suits Settled for $9.5 Million," *U.P.I.* 27 Feb. 1991 (citing claims that Holiday Spas both discouraged blacks from seeking membership through rushed tours of facilities and misstatement of the membership fees and treated black members in a discriminatory fashion, as in the case of a black female who was barred from wearing bare-midriff exercise outfits like those worn by whites); Lorraine Kidd, "African-American Moviegoers Complain About Segregation," *Gannett News Service*, 6 Sept. 1991 (reporting that the Wilmington, Delaware NAACP was investigating complaints that films about black life were being shown only in the worst theaters); Calvin Sims, "Restaurant Chain Settles Charges of Racial Bias," *New York Times*, 26 Mar. 1993, A14 (detailing claims of discrimination against the Denny's restaurant chain, including requirements that blacks pay a cover charge and refusals to honor requests for advertised special offers).

treatment blacks receive, although they hardly seem to notice. Whites who believe that concerns which discourage black patronage are more desirable than those that do not, pay a price for such exclusivity that has nothing to do with the quality of the goods or services otherwise provided. Blacks who scale the barriers these firms erect to bar them get similarly gypped for their effort. Of course, whites who shop for exclusivity may simply be responding to the reality that, when a concern begins to serve a disproportionate number of blacks, the quality of goods and services declines.

Service discrimination against blacks is facilitated by a complex ideology about blacks and their money that is compatible with the notion that black consumption is deviant behavior. Blacks are denied the treatment accorded whites because some merchants believe that black peoples' money isn't good enough for them. An equal or greater threat is posed by those merchants who believe that black money is too good, i.e., too good for blacks to be left with much of it. It is assumed that blacks do not earn their money honestly, work for it diligently, or spend it wisely. It is also assumed that when blacks have money—and most blacks do not ever have that much money—they squander it and cannot save it. If blacks are cheated in the course of commercial transactions, it is because they cheat themselves either by being unsophisticated and incompetent consumers or by making it difficult for a decent ethical person to make a profit from doing business with them. As a result, individual entrepreneurs feel perfectly justified in taking advantage of blacks as a means of privately policing or controlling blacks' monetary malefactions.

The perception that there is something wrong with blacks' pursuit of consumption impedes their ability to obtain legal redress for discriminatory treatment. Like the participants in widely acknowledged deviant subcultures, blacks have, as a practical matter, little recourse to law as they pursue their socially censured and discouraged commercial activities.

The absence of effective legal redress for indiscriminate scrutiny and disrespect is not, at least in the opinion of many shopkeepers and storeowners, the product of a regime that zealously favors merchants over shoppers. On the contrary, the proprietors of retail businesses maintain that they resort to tight security and extensive surveillance because the scheme of laws and provisions designed to deter and punish shoplifting are inefficient and ineffective.[7] Forced in their view

7. Merchant detention statutes privilege storeowners to search and detain in a reasonable manner shoppers reasonably suspected of shoplifting. However, a storeowner risks being sued for false imprisonment if the detention proves to have been unwarranted. See, for example, Clark v. K-Mart Corp., 495 N.W.2d 820 (Mich. Ct. App. 1992) (black woman erroneously detained for obtaining

to rely on security and surveillance, storeowners especially target blacks because blacks are supposedly overrepresented among lawbreakers; and storeowners cannot discern a law-abiding black from a potentially law-defying black. There is little in the law to prevent merchants from proceeding on these assumptions. Despite the ubiquity of blacks' experiences of discrimination, case law suggests that storeowners have rarely been charged with watching, detaining, or deterring shoppers in a racially-biased way.[8]

Furthermore, in a broad range of commercial settings where exclusionary or otherwise discriminatory service is against the law, enforcement is either slack or nonexistent. Violations of blacks' right to consume are dismissed as rudeness and incivility, or otherwise treated like social problems that are simply beyond the power of the law to control. Except in the most egregious circumstances, the discriminatory service blacks encounter as consumers is not amenable to the law's policing.[9]

---

free merchandise from a black salesperson allowed to proceed with a false imprisonment claim as well as one under the equal accommodations law). Criminal prosecution of shoplifters is expensive because it takes up the time of sales clerks and security officers and leaves valuable merchandise in police evidence lockers. Civil recovery laws entitle storeowners to recover damages and penalties from shoplifters, but the civil process does not generate as much deterrence as criminal prosecutions, and many shoplifters do not have the funds to pay a monetary judgment. Melissa G. Davis, Richard J. Lundman, & Ramiro Martinez Jr., "Private Corporate Justice: Store Police, Shoplifters, and Civil Recovery," *Social Problems* 38 (1991): 395–410; Angela Delli Santi, "A New Law in the War on Shoplifting," *New York Times*, 8 Aug. 1993, sec. 13NJ, 1; Stephanie Strom, "States Act to Combat Shoplifting," *New York Times*, 19 Sept. 1991, D1; Cynthia Mines, "Legislature Gives Retailers New Weapon in Battling Shoplifters," *Wichita Business Journal*, 16 July 1993, sec. 1, 9.

8. Washington v. Duty Free Shoppers, Ltd., 710 F. Supp. 1288 (N.D. Cal. 1988) (denying summary judgment to defendants accused of demanding passports and plane tickets of black customers when the store was not restricted to travellers, but was open to the general public); Ross v. Company Store, No. CV91 0115710-S, 1991 WL 204357 (Conn. Super. Ct. Oct. 1, 1991) (dismissing a claim brought under Unfair Trade Practices Act for discriminatory detention of blacks as potential shoplifters); K-Mart Corp. v. West Virginia Human Rights Comm'n, 383 S.E. 2d 277, 278 (W. Va. 1989) (store warned by the police about a band of shoplifting gypsies not liable for close scrutiny of a family of Syrian nationals, one of whom wore a loose-fitting Islamic dress). But see Lewis v. Doll, 765 P. 2d 1341 (Wash. Ct. App. 1989) (awarding judgment to a black man barred from entering a convenience store because the store had experienced a problem with blacks shoplifting).

9. Compare Stearnes v. Baur's Opera House, Inc., 788 F. Supp. 375 (C.D. Ill. 1992), *remanded and dismissed*, 3 F.3d 1142 (7th Cir. 1993) (awarding summary judgment to a dance bar which changed the type of music being played when it wanted to discourage black patrons); Perry v. Command Performance, 1991 WL 46475 (E.D. Pa. 1991) (ruling that a black patron whose hair a white beautician refused to fix had no action, *aff'd*), 945 F.2d 395 (3d Cir. 1991), *cert. denied*, 112 S. Ct. 1166 (1992); Totem Taxi, Inc. v. New York State Human Rights Appeal Bd., 480 N.E.2d 1075 (N.Y. 1985) (refusing to hold a cab company vicariously liable for a racial slur uttered by a driver because the company did not encourage, condone or approve of the conduct) with Harvey v. NYRAC, Inc., 813 F. Supp. 206 (E.D.N.Y. 1991) (denying defendant's motion for summary

As a result of the law's abdication, individual blacks resort to either compensatory moves or informal mechanisms of resistance to secure their right to shop. Most blacks try to prove themselves to be worthy shoppers, i.e., they sell themselves in order to be sold to. They dress up to go shopping in the hope that their appearance will convey the fact that they are both entitled to browse and capable of paying for any item they put their hands on. Some folks flash credit cards or engage the salesperson in conversations designed to reveal the shopper's class position or sophistication regarding the product. Others will buy expensive goods they do not really want just to prove that they have been misjudged by a salesclerk. Along the same lines, I sometimes give a waiter or cab driver a generous tip despite poor service in an effort to debunk the common complaint that blacks do not tip; I hope that the next black patron will reap the benefit of my generosity. These role-reversal techniques, which confuse the matter of who is selling what to whom, further facilitate the exploitation of black consumers by increasing the costs of going shopping, if not the amount actually spent on purchases.

Complaining about disrespectful treatment is an option, but it is often considered a waste of time.[10] Given the prevalence of poor service not motivated by racial animus, many blacks give the low-status, underpaid employee waiting on them the benefit of the doubt and proceed with caution when making a fuss. More defiant blacks purposefully make an obnoxious salesperson show them goods or otherwise waste her or his time and then leave the store without buying anything. Some blacks simply delight in being served by a subordinate white person and do not try to hide their relish. Still others operating in resistance mode dress any old way they want and dare store employees to mess with them.

Blacks have also mounted more formal, collective resistance to interference with their right to shop or consume. Boycotts have long been used by blacks to

---

judgment in an action where a car rental agency refused to rent luxury cars to blacks, including plaintiff who had reserved a car for her daughter's wedding); Zenon v. Restaurant Compostella, Inc., 790 F. Supp. 41 (D.P.R. 1992) (allowing an action by three black Puerto Ricans who waited for three hours to be served while whites were immediately seated); Jones v. City of Boston, 738 F. Supp. 604 (D. Mass. 1990) (denying summary judgment based on various laws guaranteeing access to places of public accommodation in a case brought by a black man whom a bartender referred to as a "nigger" in addressing white women with whom plaintiff had spoken); King v. Greyhound Lines, 656 P.2d 349 (Or. Ct. App. 1982) (holding racial slurs actionable under the Oregon public accommodations law in a case brought by a black man who attempted to return a bus ticket).

10. Rhonda Reynolds, "Facts & Figures: Courting Black Consumers," *Black Enterprise*, Sept. 1993, 43 (citing survey data indicating that, while sixty-five percent of blacks consult salespeople and fifty-nine percent feel disrespected by them, forty-eight percent viewed complaining about service as a waste of time).

protest their mistreatment as customers. The Montgomery bus boycott is probably the most notable example of blacks' using a refusal to deal as a weapon against discriminatory commercial behavior. The most well-publicized recent black grassroots consumer boycotts have targeted Korean merchants who responded to suspected shoplifters, often black females, with what some in the surrounding communities considered excessive force.[11]

Expanded political activity aimed largely at improving the terms and conditions on which blacks shop or consume is likely to encounter resistance from blacks on two grounds, both of which involve blacks' labeling their own commercial behavior deviant. First of all, many blacks consider various aspects of black consumption a vice of one sort or another and would do little or nothing to facilitate it. Secondly, protests against the conduct of nonblack vendors of goods and services often proceed on the assumption that a black clientele is better served by businesses owned by blacks. Many blacks consider this suggestion dubious. For them, commerce is little better than consumption in the ranking of worthwhile pursuits for black people. Both propositions warrant close analysis.

Consumption as Deviance in Black Cultural Criticism

Consumption as Alienation Roughly two sets of critical assessments of black consumption are generally found in black culture and reflected in scholarly literature. Both associate black consumption with deviance. The more prevalent stories

11. Boycotts have taken place throughout the nation. The two most notable boycotts occurred at opposite ends of the country. In Los Angeles, a female storekeeper got into a verbal altercation with Latasha Harlins, a black teenager, over a $1.78 bottle of orange juice and wound up shooting her in the back of the head. Protests and a boycott ensued. Seth Mydans, "Two Views of Protest at Korean Shop," *New York Times*, 24 Dec. 1991, A10; Wanda Coleman, "Blacks, Immigrants and America: Remembering Latasha," *Nation*, 15 Feb. 1993, 187. The shopkeeper received a suspended sentence and was placed on probation for the killing which was videotaped by an in-store surveillance camera. People v. Superior Court (Soon Ja Du), 7 Cal. Rptr.2d 177 (Cal. App. Ct. 1992). The killing of Ms. Harlins and the lenient sentence have been offered as explanations for the targeting of Korean-owned businesses during the rioting that followed the defense verdict in the state court trial of the police officers who beat motorist Rodney King. See generally Sumi K. Cho, "Korean Americans v. African Americans: Conflict and Construction," in *Reading Rodney King, Reading Urban Uprising*, ed. Robert Gooding-Williams (New York: Routledge, 1993), 196–214.

In New York City, the Family Red Apple grocery was boycotted after a black customer alleged that she was falsely accused of shoplifting and assaulted. Lisa W. Foderaro, "One Grocery Boycott Ends, But Earlier Siege Continues," *New York Times*, 17 May 1990, sec. 1, 38. See also Jang v. Brown, 560 N.Y.S.2d 307 (App. Div. 1990) (requiring that the police enforce an order enjoining picketing within 50 feet of store); People v. McLeod, 570 N.Y.S.2d 431 (Crim. Ct. 1991) (upholding a contempt action against a protestor who violated the injunction awarded to Jang).

associate black consumption with alienation. The second approach finds resistance in black consumption, particularly in the practices of black subcultures.

According to the alienation critiques, blacks consume conspicuously as a way of compensating for the humiliation and disappointments they incur by reason of being black, exploited, degraded and oppressed. Blacks use their dollars to buy what they cannot earn, namely status, which is the very thing advertising hype suggests pricey goods can supply. To a certain extent, everyone in the society is enticed by the possibility of creating an identity via consumption, but blacks, starving for rank and recognition because of racial discrimination, are thought to be more easily duped into parting with their hard-earned money and having little to show for it.

The alienation critics argue that the quest for status through consumption is hopeless because status, like style, is a moving target. Once the black consumer gets the latest thing, she or he will not be satisfied for long since the need for the thing grows out of a sense of inferiority and the possession of the thing is a constant reminder of that. Devalued, the thing possessed is put aside and the quest continues with another target, i.e., another thing.

The alienationists view the pursuit of status through the consumption of commodities as being detrimental to the black community. Unrestrained consumption diverts energy and resources that might be better used in the struggle against white supremacy. It generates, not cooperation, but competition which can be exhausting, when it is not deadly. Nothing illustrates this better than the shocking stories of black youths attacking and sometimes killing other young people in order to rob the victims of their earrings, sneakers and leather jackets. Poorer blacks who try to maintain an appearance of affluence they can ill afford are the primary targets of the alienationists. Poor adults are severely scolded for having perverse priorities, and their spending to buy status is treated like a form of thievery. Not only are they attempting to purloin a rank to which they are not entitled, they are doing so at the expense of their families and their people.

Ever mindful of the goal of advancing the race, the alienation critiques of black consumption do not totally dismiss the search for status via commodities as being contemptible and base. Rather, they distinguish between those statuses that are worth pursuing and those that are not. Consumption is acceptable if it is associated with the uplift of the race, as distinguished from consumption that is coarse and demeaning, or that affirms the worst black stereotypes. For instance, Cornel West, in an essay entitled "The Crisis of Black Leadership," maintains that "[t]he black dress suits with white shirts worn by Malcolm X and Martin Luther King signified the seriousness of their deep commitment to black freedom, whereas today the expensive tailored suits of black politicians symbolize their personal success and individual achievement."[12] By the same token:

> The Victorian three-piece suit—with a clock and chain in the vest— worn by W.E.B. Du Bois not only represented the age that shaped and molded him; it also dignified his sense of intellectual vocation, a sense of rendering service by means of critical intelligence and moral action. The shabby clothing worn by most black intellectuals these days may be seen as symbolizing their utter marginality behind the walls of academe and their sense of impotence in the wider world of American culture and politics.[13]

Pursuing the same line of analysis, the alienation critiques have traditionally urged poor blacks to adopt a simpler lifestyle, one unburdened by the quest for frivolous, showy things, one in which materialism is deemphasized and consumption is redirected into more refined, muted and dignified patterns. Poor blacks should be working hard to buy a house or to get their kids out of public school. The panacea is a nostalgic return to the quest for the American Dream exemplified by the way of life once known among black Americans as "striving." Strivers saved for the future, planned ahead, worked to overcome obstacles and helped themselves rather than rely on the government.[14]

A number of contemporary versions of the alienation critique take into account the disastrous impact contemporary conditions, like the crack trade and the hedonistic values of the Reagan era, have had on the lives of poor blacks. Cornel West, for example, argues that "[p]ost-modern culture is more and more a market culture dominated by gangster mentalities and self-destructive wantonness. This culture engulfs us all—yet its impact on the disadvantaged is devastating, resulting in extreme violence in everyday life."[15] Blacks have fallen into the clutches of "corporate market institutions . . . [that] have created a seductive way of life, a culture of consumption that capitalizes on every opportunity to make money."[16] These purveyors of pleasure have turned black life into one dictated by market forces and market moralities which threaten the very existence of black civil

---

12. Cornel West, *Race Matters* (Boston: Beacon Press, 1993), 37–38.

13. Ibid., 40.

14. Dwight Ernest Brooks, "Consumer Markets and Consumer Magazines: Black America and the Culture of Consumption, 1920–1960" (Ph.D. diss., University of Iowa, 1981), 139–40.

15. West, *Race Matters*, 5.

16. Ibid., 16.

society. The result is a form of nihilism, *"the lived experience of coping with a life of horrifying meaninglessness, hopelessness, and most important lovelessness."*[17] The cure is a politics of conversion with an ethic of love at its core.[18]

Historian Carl Husemoller Nightingale offers a similar analysis of alienation and the consumption practices of the black urban poor. However, his version concentrates on the very young and unstintingly indicts mainstream consumer culture for its abuse of poor black urban children.[19] According to Nightingale, poor blacks' current obsession with conspicuous consumption is more intense, and its effects more devastating than ever before because, via television, movies, billboards and other forms of advertising, black children have greater access to mainstream consumer culture than in the past.[20] Moreover, the mainstream has discovered black consumers and is pitching products directly to them. As a result, poor black kids are totally immersed in mainstream consumer culture, their "craving for things has gotten more persistent, and the demands for now outrageously expensive symbols of belonging and prestige have begun earlier in life."[21]

These are hard economic times for blacks on the lowest rungs of the economic ladder, and it is difficult for poor kids and their parents to buy the status symbols the kids feel they need in order to be accorded a measure of respect in this world.[22] The children who feel the greatest need for the commodities are the least likely to get them; they suffer disappointment, hurt, humiliation, anger and envy which lead to conflict and aggression.[23] By way of a remedy, Nightingale calls for a

national cultural renewal based around a series of core values that . . . include social responsibility to family, community, and the broader society and polity; opposition to violence and the search for alternative forms of expressing pain; and avoidance of the abuse of dominance across lines of gender, race, class, age, sexual preference, or physical or mental ability, and between humans and the environment.[24]

Consumption as Resistance While alienation critiques like those of West and Nightingale point to significant aspects of black consumption as evidence of defeat

17. Ibid., 14.
18. Ibid., 18–19.
19. Nightingale, *On the Edge*, 133–65, passim.
20. Ibid., 143.
21. Ibid., 153.
22. Ibid., 158.
23. Ibid., 158–62.
24. Ibid., 192.

and degradation, the alternatives find in many facets of black consumption signs of defiance, emancipation and victory over despair and self-destruction. This second set of approaches to black consumption is hipper and more fun. To those with an eye for resistance, consumption is about pleasure, performance and participation in prosperity.[25] Consumption is also the site of a struggle to exploit the transformative potential of commodities[26] by revealing the repressed or negated contradictions that underlie their production and distribution (as when young blacks wear an article of apparel with the price tag and labels in plain view) or by altering the image of, or "blackening," the most mass of mass/masked produced goods so as to subvert the generally received meaning of things (as when black women and men bleach their hair shades of blonde nowhere found in nature).

Resistant conspicuous consumption has been and remains an essential element of black deviant (in the mind of white society) subcultures. Today's B-boys with their baggy jeans, reversed baseball caps, fade haircuts, rap music and cool poses are the modern-day descendants of the zoot suiters of the 1940s about whom Malcolm X writes brilliantly in his autobiography.[27] The zoot suiters defiantly wore fluid, generously cut trousers when cloth was in short supply because of the war, and through dance and song created a time and space in which to escape the strictures of alienating wage labor.[28] One of the most sought-after look among contemporary B-boys consists of a classic hunting jacket layered over baggy khakis and Timberland boots.[29] Style watchers place this ensemble in the category of the survivalist look, which also includes camouflage fatigues and thermal half-face masks.[30] Females, for whom a tough exterior assures survival and acceptance in a male-dominated public life, may be dressed identically except for large gold earrings. According to cultural studies professor Trish Rose, this survivalist

25. See Mica Nava, *Changing Cultures: Feminism, Youth and Consumerism* (London: Sage Publications, 1991), 167 (arguing that consumption is "about dreams and consolation, communication and confrontation, image and identity"); Carl Gardner and Julie Sheppard, *Consuming Passion: The Rise of Retail Culture* (London: Unwin Hyman, 1989), 57 (contending that shopping is a form of recreation in which consumers enjoy the spectacle of stores and malls both as spectators and as participants).

26. Susan Willis, *A Primer for Daily Life* (London and New York: Routledge, 1991), 126–30.

27. Malcolm X and Alex Haley, *The Autobiography of Malcolm X* (New York: Grove Press, 1965), 39–55.

28. Robin D. G. Kelley, "The Riddle of the Zoot: Malcolm Little and Black Cultural Politics During World War II," in *Malcolm X: In Our Own Image*, ed. Joe Wood (New York: St. Martin's Press, 1992), 155–82.

29. Faye Penn and Chris Erikson, "The Youngest Thieves: High-Priced Fashions Have Teen Shoplifters Working Overtime," *Manhattan (New York) Spirit*, 26 Aug. 1993, 14.

30. Diane Cardwell, "Rapwear. Soulwear. Hipwear." *New York Times*, 14 Feb. 1993, sec. 9, 5.

look "taps into a post-Vietnam understanding of the urban terrain as a daily guerrilla war."[31] A more cynical explanation for the country estate aspect of the survivalist look, according to one Bronx teenager, is that "[t]hese clothes make people look white, rich and important."[32] Of course, the kids don't necessarily acquire their rugged outdoors togs the "old fashioned way." In some circles the preferred method of acquisition is shoplifting.

There are other examples of black deviance expressed in consumption. Gang members display their solidarity by wearing the gear of professional athletic teams with their distinctive color combinations and logos. In sartorial terms, the gang members are not unlike members of black Greek sororities and fraternities who dress in the hues, such as pink and green or crimson and cream, of their organizations.[33] The black and Hispanic gay men who partook of the ball scene depicted in the documentary *Paris is Burning* may have been foreclosed from the world of executives, pampered females and the military, but they were able to live out their fantasies through consumption conspicuously displayed on the ballroom floor.[34]

Those who make much of black cultural resistance recognize that the dominant white society simply does not tolerate challenges to the status quo such as those posed by various black consumption-oriented lifestyles. As a general matter, it responds to deviant subcultures in either or both of two ways. It may coopt the styles by turning them into commodities which are sold back to the originators and others, or it may label the styles deviant and attempt to repress them.[35] Either way the opportunity to use creative consumption to contradict the received meaning of things and to undermine the status quo is impaired.

Thus, drag has become a common feature of mass entertainment, and voguing — the gay ball dance form — was popularized by Madonna in a way that made it seem like she practically invented it: "Once mainstream America began to copy a subculture that was copying it, the subculture itself was no longer of interest to a wider audience, and whatever new opportunities existed for the principals [featured in *Paris Is Burning*] dried up."[36] While B-Boy attire has become main-

31. Ibid.

32. Penn and Erikson, "Youngest Thieves."

33. Lillian O. Holloman, "Black Sororities and Fraternities: A Case Study in Clothing Symbolism," in *Dress and Popular Culture*, ed. Patricia A. Cunningham and Susan Voso Lab (Bowling Green, Ohio: Bowling Green State University Popular Press, 1991), 46–60.

34. *Paris Is Burning* (Prestige Films, 1991).

35. Dick Hebdige, *Subculture: The Meaning of Style* (London: Methuen & Co., 1979; repr., London: Routledge, 1988), 94.

36. Jesse Green, "Paris Has Burned," *New York Times*, 18 Apr. 1993, sec. 9, 1.

stream adolescent garb, schools, amusement parks and malls have adopted dress codes that exclude young people wearing similar apparel (bandannas, athletic team gear, jogging suits, even pajamas with a billiard ball print) but said to be associated with gangs.[37]

Black consumption practices that hardly seem antisocial in that they are not associated with violent or aggressive behavior, may be regarded as deviance and dealt with accordingly. For example, more and more blacks are dressing in whole or in part in African garb to express their identity and racial solidarity or their adherence to the ideology of Afrocentricity. Yet such practices are under attack. A black lawyer in Washington, D.C. was ordered not to wear a kente cloth shawl to court.[38] Employers may forbid black female employees from wearing their hair braided, a practice common among African women.[39] White-owned producers of natural hair care products have appropriated terms associated with racial pride and black-ownership like African and kente and attempted to use trademark law to prohibit smaller black businesses from utilizing the words.[40]

Those who search for evidence of cultural resistance in black consumption are optimistic that cooptation of black subcultural styles will have some small positive effect, while repression will only fuel more defiance. They find comfort in the belief that blacks are constantly searching for opportunities to use commodities as weapons in the battle to turn the status quo upside down.

Beyond Alienation and Resistance: Commerce and Competition Both the alienation critiques and the resistance takes on black consumption have their strengths and weaknesses. The alienation critiques are on target when they decry conspicuous

37. Robert D. Davila, "Dress Code Racist?" *Sacramento Bee*, 5 May 1993, A1; Teresa Moore, "'Gang Attire' Ejections Prompt Suit Against Park," *San Francisco Chronicle*, 3 July 1991, A20; "Lawsuits Settled on Youths' Attire," *San Francisco Chronicle*, 13 Nov. 1992, A23; Pearl Stewart, "Dress Code Proposed for Oakland Schools," *San Francisco Chronicle*, 15 July 1991, A15.

38. Sabra Chartrand, "A Dispute Over Courtroom Attire, and Principles," *New York Times*, 19 June 1992, B8; Patrice Gaines-Carter, "D.C. Lawyer Told to Remove African Kente Cloth for Jury Trial," *Washington Post*, 23 May 1992, F1.

39. See Rogers v. American Airlines, 527 F. Supp. 229 (S.D.N.Y. 1981); Paulette M. Caldwell, "A Hair Piece: Perspectives on the Intersection of Race and Gender," *Duke Law Journal* 1991: 365–96.

40. Maitefa Angaza, "White Co. with 'African Pride' Sues Black Co. for Being 'African Natural'," *New York City Sun*, 22 Sept. 1993, 5; Lisa Jones, "Africa™," *Village Voice*, 24 Aug. 1993, 42. The litigation was terminated when the maker of African Pride products realized how sensitive the issue was for its consumers. Open Letter to the African American Community from Brian K. Marks, President of Shark Products, Inc., *New York Amsterdam News*, 15 Jan. 1994, 19.

consumption that is destructive of individuals, families and neighborhoods. Those who articulate the alienation critiques, however, too often fail to acknowledge the existence of class warfare among blacks, and the degree to which a bourgeois bias permeates the alienation perspectives. Because of this insensitivity to class concerns, their social censure of the buying behavior of poorer blacks often backfires by further entrapping poorer blacks in the cycle of conspicuous consumption. The very idea that a commodity is something poorer or less well-off folks are not supposed to have often makes them want it even more in order to teach the meddling black bourgeoisie a lesson.

The alienation critiques do not give blacks enough credit for struggling to combat the stifling effect of white supremacy. Blacks' tastes for expensive commodities are not solely attributable to the base reasons the critiques cite. The quest for quality is partly a response to a history of being cheated by inferior goods and inflated prices.[41] Furthermore, the notion advanced by the alienationists that blacks should buy certain things – and only certain things – as a way of gaining a station in life more nearly equal to that of whites leaves too little room for the operation of a black critical consciousness and alternative mechanisms for achieving status and recognition.

The alienation critiques do not say enough about the role consumption might play in blacks' pursuit of the good life. There has to be more to a black good life than simply countering what white people do to black people or doing tomorrow what white people will not let blacks do today. Good things and good times gauged by black folks' standards must figure somewhere in their liberation. If nothing else, consumption fuels production and production creates jobs. Commodities should be thought of as devices for packaging peoples' needs and desires in ways that create employment. The economic survival of black people depends upon creating markets or audiences for the products of their labor.

The consumption as resistance approaches avoid some of the criticism leveled against the alienation critiques by focusing on how black people change consumption, rather than on how consumption changes black people. Nonetheless, they are undermined by the fact that the resistance exponents tend to see rebellion everywhere, and rarely admit that when it comes to consuming things, it is difficult to distinguish transformation from cooptation. Exploiting contradictions is not quite the same as taking advantage of openings for reform.

41. Marcus Alexis, "Some Negro-White Differences in Consumption," in *The Black Consumer: Dimensions of Behavior and Strategy*, ed. George Joyce and A. P. Govoni (New York: Random House, 1971), 266.

[handwritten margin notes:] naive though there is some to evidence consumption not evident here so far (or it is not "resistance")

The consumption as resistance approaches overemphasize the significance of symbolic protest. Black subcultural lifestyles may indeed be a form of political expression or praxis, but they are seldom linked to an agenda for social, political or economic change.[42] For example, the tough exteriors displayed by B-boys and flygirls capitalize on their "power to discomfort," their power "to pose – to pose a threat."[43] Their appearance evidences their rejection of a subordinate status, but such symbolic defiance also confirms, it not compounds, their powerlessness, by leaving them vulnerable to the genuinely harsh repression meted out by police authorities who read their behavior literally.

Some of the more creative and venturesome participants in black youth culture, however, are successfully turning the products of their creativity into commodities produced and sold by them. The participants of other black subcultures would do well to exploit the unrealized potential for political mobilization and economic development inherent in their lifestyles too. But the efforts of young enterprising artists and media types of the Hip-Hop Generation to generate markets with their ingenuity have provoked an outcry against the commodification of black culture. In late capitalism all cultures are turned into commodities, not just black American culture. Black American culture is always already in the public domain where it is ripe to be ripped off by anyone paying attention. Adherence to black cultural modes and mores cannot be taken as a sign of solidarity or as a mark of economic authenticity or group origin; nor can it substitute for a political ideology. It is impossible to exclude whites from black cultural production; blacks simply have to be better at it than white people. Furthermore, there is nothing wrong with consciously connecting culture to consumption and production if the goal is to increase the availability of employment among blacks and the wealth controlled by black institutions and firms.

Both the consumption as resistance and the consumption as alienation approaches ignore the fact that consumption is an exercise of economic power.[44] Blacks have used various mechanisms, from marketing themselves[45] to holding "black dollar" days,[46] to impress white producers and sellers with the strength

42. Adolph Reed, Jr., "The Allure of Malcolm X and the Changing Character of Black Politics," in *Malcolm X: In Our Own Image*, 203 (arguing that cultural resistance which equates consumption and political action is a manifestation of the politics of evasion).

43. Dick Hebdige, *Hiding in the Light* (London and New York: Routledge, 1988), 18.

44. Nava, *Changing Cultures*, 197.

45. D. Parke Gibson, *The $30 Billion Negro* (New York: Macmillan Co., 1969) (explaining why white manufacturers and merchants should market to Negroes).

46. Under the NAACP's "Black Dollar Days" program, blacks were urged to make purchases with two-dollar bills and Susan B. Anthony dollars so that cash receipts at the end of the day would

of their buying power. Where there is respect for black consumers though, it can manifest itself in proposals to target them for rubbish like specialty brand cigarettes and high potency malt liquors that would not be marketed to anyone else. As long as blacks concentrate only on consumption and ignore the production and distribution of commodities, their buying power only sustains the status quo. Consumption is more disruptive, however, when its linkages to production and distribution are acknowledged, and consumption practices are altered in a way that attacks the discriminatory and oppressive manner in which goods are made and sold as well as bought.

The black consumer boycotts of the Great Depression and Civil Rights Era joined production and consumption as the subjects of protest.[47] The primary goal of these boycotts was not improved service, but positions for black employees at concerns where blacks spent their money. Blacks have sometimes moved beyond demanding jobs in white-owned firms to insisting upon black ownership of or participation in the businesses with which blacks deal. Grassroots boycotts have occasionally been used to challenge white ownership of businesses in black neighborhoods.[48] Increased utilization of minority contractors and the award of franchises to blacks are goals of the NAACP Fair-Share program which uses the threat of adverse publicity and boycotts to extract concessions from big companies that benefit from black consumption.[49] Actual sustained campaigns, however, must contend with the conviction held by many blacks that, if shopping is deviance, selling is outright depravity.

Get a Job!: Selling as Black Deviance

Blacks, especially the bourgeoisie, tend to be skeptical of selling as a means of employment. Selling is a form of hustling and hustling is hard, dirty, dishonest

---

reveal the extent of black buying power. Shelia M. Poole, "Black Consumers Make a Point About Buying Power," *Atlanta Constitution*, 31 Aug. 1991, C7; Edward J. Boyer, "Project to Demonstrate Buying Power of Blacks," *Los Angeles Times*, 27 Aug. 1985, sec. 1, 3; Sheila Rule, "Drive by N.A.A.C.P. Gets Mixed Results," *New York Times*, 7 Sept. 1983, A17.

47. Cheryl Lynn Greenberg, "*Or Does It Explode?: Black Harlem in the Great Depression* (New York: Oxford Press, 1991), 114–39.

48. Libby-Broadway Drive-in Inc. v. McDonald's, 391 N.E.2d 1 (Ill. App. Ct. 1979) (denying enforcement of an oral agreement for comparable properties made when a franchisee was persuaded to sell franchises to black owners following protest activity); Delano Village Cos. v. Orridge, 553 N.Y.S.2d 938 (Sup. Ct. 1990) (ruling that correspondence and a rent strike undertaken by tenants to prevent sale of a residential complex to a white developer are protected activities).

49. Calvin Simms, "The N.A.A.C.P. Means Business, " *New York Times*, 31 Aug. 1993, D1. See also Earl Picard, "The Corporate Intervention Strategy and Black Economic Development," *Black Scholar* 16, no. 5 (Sept./Oct. 1985): 14–22 (arguing that the strategy of negotiating with corporations

and demeaning work. It requires risk-taking. Unlike a good job, selling offers no guaranteed income and that is what many blacks want.[50]

In fact, many blacks find the idea of starting any kind of business and working for themselves unthinkable.[51] Commercial activity by blacks is discouraged *by blacks* relying on arguments from a number of sources ranging from black Christian theology to grassroots socialist critiques of the political economy to everyday jurisprudence. In his book *Black Folk's Guide to Business Success*, George Subira lists a score of attitudes that make black entrepreneurship seem like deviant behavior. Included are such notions as: Blacks are a poor people relegated to consuming as opposed to producing wealth; money and the love of it are the root of all evil; wealth is only made through the exploitation of others; one must have money to make money; white people are not going to let blacks make any real money; a lot of money weakens one's character; money is not the key to a happy, fulfilling life; and the government takes anything that one earns in taxes.[52] These sentiments are surely enough to shame some black people from trying to succeed in business.

I do not mean to overstate the pervasiveness or the effectiveness of these anticommercial sentiments in black culture. The cultural obstacles do not entirely deter blacks from going into businesses. Moreover, interest among blacks in running their own businesses and working for themselves is growing. Indeed, the minuscule participation of blacks in the business sector is hardly a matter of choice.

The negative assessment of commercial activity recounted here reflects the experiences of a law-abiding working class that has struggled mightily to hold on to low-paying, low-status jobs and a middle class that has achieved its position through government and professional service, and not through self-employment and business ownership. Their negative attitudes regarding entrepreneurship are the product of the notable lack of success of black businesses. The systematic destruction of black commerce and the repression of the development of a black commercial consciousness left blacks with little choice but to disparage entrepreneurship.

---

on behalf of black consumers who do not really form a cohesive bloc evades the increasing marginality of blacks in the sphere of production).

50. Jawanza Kunjufu, *Black Economics: Solutions for Economic and Community Empowerment* (Chicago: African American Images, 1991), 69.

51. George Subira, *Black Folks Guide to Business Success* (Newark, New Jersey: Very Serious Business Enterprises, 1986), *i*.

52. Subira, *Black Folks Guide*, 50–74 passim.

There have been and still are scores of systemic impediments to black entrepreneurship. Black business development has been impeded by the refusal of banks and other financial institutions to extend credit to black businesses on account of geographical redlining and the race of the borrower:[53] "[D]iscrimination in the labor market makes it difficult for blacks to generate the initial equity investments for business formulation."[54] Friends and family, possible sources of start-up capital, are no better situated than the would-be entrepreneur.[55] Moreover, blacks' foreclosure from the skilled labor trades has impeded the acquisition of the skills and experience required for self-employment.[56] Black businesses have been restricted to segregated markets offering little potential for growth.[57] The law has thrown its share of obstacles in the way of black economic development. The law has made it difficult for blacks to establish legitimate licensed businesses,[58] and failed to come to the aid of black businesspeople victimized by anticompetitive behavior, however violent and pernicious.[59] Given the difficulties blacks have encountered in running their own concerns legally or otherwise, blacks who could find some kind of job perhaps rightly concluded that the opportunity costs associated with forgoing employment and going into business for themselves were too high.

The attitudes keeping blacks from entering into business also affect their patronage of black concerns. As my earlier discussion of black consumption suggests,

53. Timothy Bates, *Banking on Black Enterprise: The Potential of Emerging Firms for Revitalizing Urban Economics* (Washington, D.C.: Joint Center for Political and Economic Studies, 1993), 74–85.

54. Timothy Bates, *Major Studies of Minority Business: A Bibliographic Review* (Washington, D.C.: Joint Center for Political and Economic Studies, 1993), 11.

55. Bates, *Banking on Black Enterprise*, 115.

56. Bates, *Major Studies of Minority Business*, 11.

57. John Sibley Butler, *Entrepreneurship and Self-Help Among Black Americans: A Reconstruction of Race and Economics* (Albany, N.Y.: State University of New York Press, 1991) 143–146.

58. Walter E. Williams, *The State Against Blacks* (New York: New Press, McGraw Hill, 1982), 67–123; Regina Austin, "'An Honest Living': Street Vendors, Municipal Regulation, and the Black Public Sphere, *Yale Law Journal* 103 (June 1994): 2119–2131. See also Bates, *Banking on Black Enterprise*, 20–21 (citing Southern Jim Crow licensing requirements that burdened black artisans and skilled tradesmen).

59. Ida B. Wells recounts the story of the 1892 lynching of three law-abiding Memphis blacks who ran a successful grocery store that competed with a white-owned store on the opposite corner. The businessmen were getting too independent and needed a lesson in subordination. See Ida B. Wells, *Southern Horrors: Lynch Law in All Its Phases* (New York: New York Age Print, 1892), 18–19. See also Butler, *Entrepreneurship and Self-Help*, 209 (attributing the 1921 destruction of the black Greenwood section of Tulsa, Oklahoma by rioting whites to the economic threat black prosperity posed).

blacks are exceptionally exploited consumers and as a result are suspicious of
entrepreneurs, black, white, brown or yellow, but most especially black.[60] Black
consumers simply do not believe that black concerns offer quality goods and
services at a reasonable price.[61] The sentiment extends to professionals as well;
many black people, if given a choice, prefer a white lawyer to a black one.[62]

Periodically blacks are urged to patronize black businesses in the name of
racial solidarity. The recent wave of Buy Black campaigns exhorts blacks to
patronize black businesses in order to maximize the recirculation of dollars among
blacks and thereby to strengthen the economy of black enclaves.[63] Yet it remains
unclear to many blacks why race should trump economic self-interest.[64] For them,
race, at best, tempers, but does not replace, efficiency as the top priority in
shopping.

If the appeals to racial solidarity work and blacks do direct their business to
black concerns, they want something in return: if not quality goods and services
or jobs, then contributions to the community that represent a payback by their
enterprising sisters and brothers. These expectations are disappointed when black
entrepreneurs either run their businesses to suit their own predilections or seek
to maximize profits and their own individual wealth. The disappointment provokes
charges, tinged with a certain amount of jealousy, that the successful entrepreneurs have forgotten where they came from. Maybe they have because they feel
they must. Economic self-interest cuts in both directions. If black merchants are
not good enough for black consumers, black consumers are not good enough for

60. Similar sentiments have been found among South African blacks. See Gillian Godsell, "Entrepreneurs Embattled: Barriers to Entrepreneurship in South Africa," in *The Culture of Entrepreneurship*, ed. Brigitte Berger (San Francisco: Institute for Contemporary Studies Press, 1991), 85.

61. Marc Bendick, Jr. and Mary Lou Egan, *Business Development in the Inner-City: Enterprise
with Community Links* (New York: New School for Social Research, 1991), 8–9.

62. Forty-seven percent of the respondents to an *Ebony* magazine readers' poll indicated that
they use the services of nonblack attorneys, while 35.6% consulted black lawyers. "Annual Readers
Poll," *Ebony*, Sept. 1993, 96. See also Shelly Branch and Caroline V. Clarke, "The Nation's Leading
Black Law Firms," *Black Enterprise*, Aug. 1993, 52 (reporting that "the nation's largest black businesses routinely shun the services of black firms").

63. Daryl Strickland, "'Buy Black'–Black Dollars Days Part of Effort to Fuel Community Business," *Seattle Times*, 27 Jan. 1992, B1.

64. For example, when told "that the store where she bought her granddaughter's clothes was
black-owned," Ethellen Richardson, a fifty-five-year-old office cleaner, said, "I think it's a great idea
and probably I'll shop here more often. . . . But I'll still look around for the best bargain." Sabra
Chartrand, "Urging Blacks to Help Themselves by Buying From Each Other," *New York Times*, 19
July 1992, sec. 1, 14. See also Kunjufu, *Black Economics*, 48–49 (illustrating the lack of consumer
loyalty for black businesses and calling upon consumers to be more considerate, patient, and understanding of the impact of black businesses).

black merchants. Black firms relegated to a black clientele generally have limited prospects for growth. Success requires branching out beyond the black enclave. This carries with it the charge, if not the actuality, of racial unaccountability.

The tension between black consumers and black businesses and the debate over the political significance of black patronage and black enterprise is nothing new. Changes in the global economy, however, may render the tension superfluous. No people should expect to survive in the new world economic order if it does not help itself.[65] Yet, blacks find it hard to do that. When combined with the strictures on black consumption and the material impediments to black enterprise, the anticommercial bias in black culture acts as a constraint on blacks' freedom to become more than marginally active participants in production and commerce.

Pursuing Consumption and Commerce, Cooperation and Competition Via the Black Public Sphere

In sum, then, black consumption and commerce are treated like deviance by the white-dominated mainstream. Moreover, there is no widespread contemporary black public analysis of black consumption or commerce that does not treat them as being deviant. As a result, blacks are condemned and exploited when they engage in consumption, and condemned and impeded when they engage in commerce. The construction of black consumption and commerce as forms of deviance reinforce one another, both culturally and materially. The cycle must be broken. Consumption and commerce are both essential to black liberation. Their significance must be reevaluated and legitimacy must be restored to each.

To accomplish this transformation and to generate beneficial productive activity, blacks need to pursue a rational self-interestedness that focuses upon building a universal, expansive, cooperative black public sphere.[66] The black public sphere contemplated here is not bounded by geography, but by the limits of the technology which facilitates social, political and economic interaction among people tied by

---

65. Joel Kotkin, *Tribes: How Race, Religion, and Identity Determine Success in the New Global Economy* (New York: Random House, 1993).

66. I use the term "public sphere" to encompass the realm of both markets and audiences. The public sphere to which I refer is more expansive than the realm of public debate and deliberation with which the term is associated in the work of Jürgen Habermas. On the multiplicity of public spheres, see generally Nancy Fraser, "Rethinking the Public Sphere: A Contribution to the Critique of Actually Existing Democracy," in *The Phantom Public Sphere*, ed. Bruce Robbins (Minneapolis: University of Minnesota Press, 1993), 1–32.

culture and affinity, not physical proximity. The black public sphere is the arena in which the mass of black people can pursue a good material and cultural existence through a strategy that is both practical and critical of the contemporary socioeconomic status quo.

Blacks must move beyond reactive resistance to higher levels of intragroup cooperation and intergroup competition. Through the conscious development of their own public sphere, blacks should be able to achieve a degree of autonomy from the values and institutions of the dominant white-supremacist mainstream. The black public sphere should put black people to work, working for themselves. The purpose of strengthening the black public sphere, however, is not to secure separatism or total self-sufficiency. Rather, the black public sphere should be where blacks are at the center of a universe of markets and audiences that integrate whites and other nonblacks into arenas controlled by blacks, rather than the other way around. The institutions of the black public sphere should not only assure a good life for blacks, but also be exemplary of the pursuit of the common good. To this end, the institutions of the black public sphere must strive for excellence and thereby challenge the white elites' conceit that only they are capable of building institutions worth preserving.

As a first step in creating this black public sphere, blacks need to realize that their consumption and commerce are more desirable than deviant. Generating collective pro-production, pro-distribution attitudes is one place to start. Black people talk about shopping all the time. The consumption as resistance analysis is correct: shopping is a form of performance and entertainment, and the occasion for black/white and black/nonblack interactions and confrontations. But so is selling. Blacks need a set of stories and practices that pertain to the production and distribution side of commercial transactions. They need narratives that debunk the lies about blacks and their money and about blacks and commerce that too many blacks believe. Blacks need to brag about their enterprising ancestors. Not every family can boast of having a Madam C. J. Walker (the hair products manufacturer who became America's first black female millionaire) somewhere on the tree, but a self-employed carpenter or a rooming house proprietor ought to be as significant as a teacher or a doctor. Blacks need to tell complex and nuanced stories about black businesses that could not be established, that are poorly run, or that perform beyond expectations. Those interested in civil rights should focus attention not only on denials of voting rights and employment discrimination, but also on commercial disputes that reveal the subordinate status to which black business has been relegated and the systematic exclusion of blacks from full participation in the sphere of commerce.

Blacks must be cognizant of the class divisions within their communities and create mechanisms to assure distributive justice among their own people. Given that many blacks distrust businesses organized along capitalist lines, it is important that the number and scope of alternative economic arrangements be expanded. Black churches run successful enterprises that are not operated on a for-profit basis; church-owned shopping areas, housing projects and credit unions represent the legacy of a black tradition of mutual aid and communal self-help. Blacks have not had as much experience with secular black cooperatives;[67] effort should be put into increasing their number. New forms of cooperative activity, like nonmarket moneyless service exchanges or cooperation circles which allow participants to swap time, labor and services, should also be explored.[68]

Since for-profit enterprises are an inescapable feature of a viable black public sphere, the issue of exploitation of blacks by blacks must be addressed in a frank and thorough way. The fear of being unfairly used and the lack of mutual trust makes collective endeavors, be they families or factories, difficult for many black people. Blacks cannot realistically expect to effect wholesale changes in the character of the American economy, but they can work to institutionalize mechanisms that insure greater economic cooperation among blacks of different classes, lessen the exploitation of black consumers by returning profits to the communities in which they are generated, and ameliorate the great disparities in access to capital between rich and poor. There must be means for guaranteeing the recirculation of money brought into the black community. The concept of the *black dollar* must have behind it established mechanisms of capital accumulation and capital venture.

If blacks are to prosper as a group, they will need a strong ethnic identity and sense of mutual dependence and trust. Blacks must create and articulate ethical ways of treating each other in commercial transactions. They need the cultural equivalent of a black commercial code which will create a climate in which the purveyors of goods and services have the discipline to make good on

67. Harold Cruse, *Plural But Equal: A Critical Study of Blacks and Minorities and America's Plural Society* (New York: William Morrow & Co., 1987), 111–14, 148–49, 177, 340–41 (criticizing the civil rights establishment for failing to pursue an economic agenda that should have included cooperatives as called for by several commentators including E. Franklin Frazier and George S. Schuyler); Harold Cruse, *The Crisis of the Negro Intellectual* (New York: William Morrow & Co, 1967), 137–39, 173 (recounting the failure of the Communists in the 1930s to pursue the cooperative model as a solution to black people's economic woes because of a fear of black nationalism).

68. See generally Claus Offe and Rolf G. Heinze, *Beyond Employment: Time, Work and the Informal Economy* (Philadelphia: Temple University Press, 1992).

their assurances of quality, and the purchasers, acting confidently in reliance, will look upon their patronage as a matter of commitment to a common, higher cause. Such would be the equivalent of a kosher standard of production.

The question of whether the class inequality created by certain kinds of entrepreneurial activity requiring collective support is sufficiently offset by gains in blacks' overall socioeconomic position should be debated in the black public sphere. For example, blacks have been urged to back enterprises that are in nontraditional areas like wholesaling, general construction and skill-intensive services, that do not serve a black clientele, and that are located outside of black enclaves, because they tend to employ black people wherever the firms are situated.[69] Though small businesses are hardly the cure for high rates of black unemployment, greater participation of blacks in the labor force may be linked to the welfare of black-owned enterprises that hire blacks. Increased employment and rising incomes for blacks will increase the viability of small black-owned retail establishments and the internal labor markets of black enclaves. Improvements in the overall economic position of blacks might be beneficial in ameliorating the troubles blacks incur in consuming. If blacks had greater economic clout, they might seem to be more worthy consumers and receive more courteous treatment. Of course, if blacks had greater economic clout, they might also care less.

Finally, there should be a structure of feeling, a sentiment that economic resistance is something every black can engage in every day. Blacks should easily take on the mantle of outlaws or bandits, for example, when it comes to passing dollars from one black hand to the next as many times as possible before the dollars fall into the grasp of someone else. That is not the way it is supposed to be. The white-dominated power structure has done such a good job of making blacks out to be thieves that it can steal from them with impunity. Furthermore, by making blacks suspicious of commerce by making commerce the equivalent of thievery, it has reduced the ability of blacks to turn their buying power into selling power, and their selling power into institutions and firms they control. Who's fooling whom here? *Blacks* are not the nation of thieves they are made out to be. The problems blacks encounter in the areas of shopping and selling, consumption and commerce are manifestations of a chronic race-class-gender

69. Bates, *Banking on Black Enterprise*, 11, 15, 62, 77. See also Arnold Schuchter, "Conjoining Black Revolution and Private Enterprise," in *Black Business Enterprise: Historical and Contemporary Perspectives*, ed. Ronald W. Bailey (New York: Basic Books, 1971), 219 (listing the benefits to minority communities of small suppliers of goods and services to major industries).

struggle being waged without effective institutional political organizations. This context is ripe for a modern-day variant of social banditry.[70]

Regina Austin teaches in the Law School at the University of Pennsylvania. Her recent publications include "An Honest Living": Street Vendors, Municipal Regulation, and the Black Public Sphere" (103 *Yale Law Journal* 2119, June 1994). Her current research concerns black mobility and taxicab regulation, and sexual vulnerability and night-shift work.

---

70. Eric Hobsbawm, *Bandits* 2d ed. (Harmondsworth, England: Penguin Books, 1985), 150–64.

X Marks the Spot: The Ambiguities of African Trading in the Commerce of the Black Public Sphere

Rosemary J. Coombe and Paul Stoller

The presence and practices of West African traders in the commercial vending spaces of Harlem raise provocative questions about the possible parameters of black politics and its publics. Such spaces pose complicated issues of authenticity and value, the real and the counterfeit, the commodity and its publicity, as well as the confrontation of the complicitous meanings of Africa and America that mark the nexus of the global and the local in the African American. The place where Songhay men from Niger sell goods marked with Malcolm's X in the centre of the African American cultural community marks an anxious intersection of global and local forces—a crossroads that compels us to attend to the transnational and intercultural relationships that characterize contemporary black public spheres.

This discussion opens with an overview of those global processes of capital restructuring that provide a context for understanding the presence of West Africans in African American communities. To comprehend the multiply mediated spaces where migrants congregate in the informal economies of global cities and to avoid a singularity of perspective, we assert a methodological and formal commitment to mobile positionings. To explore such spaces culturally and politically, we suggest a consideration of *place* in which surfaces are taken seriously to appraise the ways in which the postcolonial and the postmodern come into vexing relationship. The surfaces to be examined include commodified images and

Public Culture 1994, 7: 249–274

their polyvocality in intercultural commerce – T-shirts, baseball caps, billboards, videos, price tags, and advertisements – trademarks that signify ambiguously in transcultural exchange. We will explore a multiplicity of significances at one site: the relations of publicity and counterpublicity that constitute both the African and the American that define the People's Market in Harlem.

In 1992, the same year that Songhay vendors from Niger sold "counterfeit" Malcolm X goods to black youth on the streets in Harlem, Joe Wood issued an invitation to black activists and intellectuals "to critique Malcolm X and to make sense of Malcolm X's currency among us, and to make sense of *Blackness* itself – its meaning today and its usefulness as a concept to African Americans" (Wood 1992:3). The responses he received, collectively published as *Malcolm X: In Our Own Image*, embody a diversity of positions, but all share an attitude of ambivalence towards the commodification of black cultural politics in conditions of late capitalism. The perspectives of these writers (and their ambivalent positionings) frame our ethnographic observations, for in these juxtapositions heteroglossia is maintained and the complexities of cultural politics in the black public sphere are evoked.

Restructuring the Global

Yes, the turn to Malcolm in part reflects deepening frustration with material conditions . . . but more importantly, it reproduces the vicarious, or even apolitical, approach to politics that undergirded the earlier romanticizations of King and Jackson. . . . The result is a radicalism that gives away some of the most important conceptual ground to defenders of the status quo. This is a radicalism that cannot effectively challenge questionable reifications such as the manufacturing/service sector job dichotomy, the representation of deindustrialization as if it were natural law. . . . There is nothing that understanding the "real" Malcolm X – an impossibility in any event – could do to clarify or to help formulate positions regarding those phenomena, neither the internal nor the external forces shaping black political life. Invoking his image in these circumstances amounts to wishing away the complexities that face us.

ADOLPH REED (1992:224; 226)

Concerned with the political effects of iconicizing Malcolm X, Adolph Reed critically addresses the tendency to consider commodity consumption as a form of cultural politics. He berates those who fail to place forms of "signifyin(g)"

(Gates 1988; Wallace 1990) into relations of production and distribution or fail to address the increasing economic marginalization of black peoples in the face of global capital restructuring. One need not share Reed's dichotomous world view, which divorces the expressive from the instrumental and the symbolic from the practical, to share his sense of the need to forge wider webs of structural connection when addressing black politics and the commerce of the public sphere. We seek to illuminate a number of relationships between processes of capital restructuring, African migrations, informal economies, African American cultural forms, and those signifiers which simultaneously mask and reveal the politics appropriate to postcolonial contexts.

"Global capital restructuring" is a phrase that attempts to encompass multiple phenomena: the emergence of a global economy; the compression of the time-space aspects of social relations; the dispersion of manufacturing production to ever-shifting sites around the globe; the proliferation of export-processing zones in indebted areas facing World Bank and IMF pressure; the growth of international finance markets; the increasing feminization of the global manufacturing labour force; new migration patterns; the resurgence of informal economies; and new forms of economic polarization (Dickens 1992; Harvey 1989; Mitter 1987; Mittelman; Mollenkopf 1991; Portes et al., 1989; Sassen 1991a, 1991b, 1993, 1994a, 1994b). This international web of communications and investments, production and consumption, linked by telecommunications technologies, is not, in fact, global. It connects select parts of the globe while it simply spans others. In addition to increasing economic polarization within societies and regions, the so-called global economy has marginalized millions. According to World Bank projections, the number of the world's poor in Asia and Latin America will steadily drop, whereas in sub-Saharan Africa, "the number of poor will rise by 85 million to 265 million in the year 2000. . . . Sub-Saharan Africa's percentage of the world's poor will double from 16 to 32%" (Mittelman). African peoples obviously experience the economic repercussions of globalization for their opportunities are clearly circumscribed by the conditions of international debt restructuring and the vagaries of international currency markets (Callaghy and Ravenhill 1993). The experiences of some West Africans negotiating within spaces of opportunity and constraint forged by forces of globalization will later be addressed.

Geographers assert that globalization *takes place*; it is a process with multiple spatial coordinates. The spaces in which processes of globalization are perhaps most evident are the urban centres from which the global flows of capital, goods, and information that are commonly referred to as the economy are managed. The "flexible accumulation of capital" (Harvey 1989), however global a process, is realized locally in transformations of the social, demographic, economic, and political structures of particular areas. Saskia Sassen (1991b, 1994b) has shown that particular cities – "global cities" strategically positioned to coordinate and dominate global flows of capital, information, imagery, people, and things – have become nodal points linking a vast international web of communications that manages a worldwide network of factories, service outlets and financial markets. While the dispersion of production and plants speeds the decline of old manufacturing centers, the associated need for centralized management and control over these dispersed sites feeds the growth of global servicing centers, creating economic concentration in a limited number of cities (1991b:325).

An understanding of the social restructuring of global cities discloses how social dislocations such as the influx of West Africans into African American communities "takes place." New York City was one of the first global cities. In the last two decades it has been socially and spatially restructured by new forms of capital accumulation based upon finance and the globalization of manufacturing. Like other global cities, it has experienced a profound increase in income polarization, class realignments, influxes of migrants and new norms of consumption that contribute to the growth of an informal sector.

New elites are created as service industries begin to congregate in those cities that contain the managerial capacity to oversee the global dispersal of production, transportation and marketing. Advertising executives, accountants, investment dealers, real estate agents, bankers, foreign exchange dealers and lawyers form the core of a new informational elite. But concurrent with the growth of this elite is the emergence of a disenfranchised working class without benefits, health protection, or job security. Among them can be counted an army of female clerical workers, other workers who toil in "downgraded manufacturing" sectors, low-skill workers who provide the increasingly specialized consumer services that urban elites demand, and finally, a growing number of people, like street vendors and gypsy cab drivers, who work outside of the formal labour force in the informal economy (Sassen 1991a, 1991b, 1993, 1994b). Due to the increased social and economic polarization that defines it, the global city has also been deemed a "dual city" (Mollenkopf 1991). The duality is between a comparatively cohesive "core" group of professionals who are "hooked up" to the global corporate economy and an ethnically and culturally diverse "periphery" that is increasingly unable to organize politically in order to influence the "core" upon which its limited forms of security depend.[1]

1. New social cleavages emerge in these cities due to the same forces that attract capital and labour. As demands for ever more specialized services for those corporations engaged in the global economy draw more and more professionally educated people into these cities, new markets for

The massive increase in subcontracting to small informal enterprises and the growth of unregulated entrepreneurial activity is considered to be a by-product of the global restructuring of capital—the shift from Fordist to flexible regimes of capital accumulation (Portes et al., 1989). Although traditional theories of economic development predicted the decline of informal enterprise, that is, income-generating operations functioning outside of formal regulatory frameworks, there has been a vast increase in such operations in the last decade, especially in global cities. An informal economy presupposes a formal economy which entails that the same goods and services are being produced within the framework of the law. The term informal sector has come to replace more pejorative terms like the black market and the underground economy, for what makes an activity informal is not its substance, the validity of the goods or services produced, the character of the labour force or the site of production, but the fact that "it is unregulated by the institutions of society, in a legal and social environment in which similar activities are regulated" (Castells and Portes 1989:12). The parent who purchases day care service without filling out social security forms, the

---

goods and services are created, and new sources of supply emerge to meet these demands. Whereas economic growth in the post-World War II era sustained the growth of a middle class, through capital-intensive investment in manufacturing, mass production, and the consumption of standardized products, which in turn created conditions conducive to unionization and worker empowerment (Sassen 1991a: 83), today's new urban elites demand gentrified housing, specialized products, small, full-service retail shops close to home, catered and pre-prepared foods, restaurants, and dry cleaning outlets (86). These are labour intensive rather than capital-intensive enterprises in which small scale production and subcontracting are obvious means of increasing profits. Whereas middle-class suburban growth in the Fordist period depended upon capital investments in land, road construction, automobiles, large supermarkets, mass outlets, and nationally advertised goods (all things which require large workforces in large workplaces), today's professional elites create markets for goods and services produced in small scale enterprises—subcontractors, family enterprises, sweatshops and households (86). Such low-wage workers are paid minimum wages, have no job security, and by virtue of their working conditions, are often isolated and unable to organize. These workers in turn, also require goods and services, thus creating markets for lower priced goods than even the mass retail chains can provide. The needs of low-wage workers are met by lower-waged workers, often immigrants, and increasingly women and children subject to patriarchal family restrictions, and isolated by language barriers and fear of deportation. The management and servicing of a global network of factories, service outlets, and financial markets has also had consequences for the spatial organization of North American cities, resulting in situations that might be described as emergent urban apartheid, in which housing becomes more expensive, there are more and more homeless, and densities in low income areas increase. Those low-wage workers who take advantage of the opportunities afforded by the informal economy find it very difficult to afford to live in the cities that afford these opportunities (Sassen 1991b: 329). The deeper and deeper impoverishment of larger and larger sectors of the population is exacerbated in precisely those cities that contain increasingly affluent elites.

unlicensed gypsy cab driver who serves poor neighbourhoods, the craftsperson building furniture in an area not zoned for manufacturing activity, the immigrant woman reading pap smears or sewing teddy bears in a poorly lit suburban garage, and the unlicensed African street vendor are all participating in the burgeoning informal economy that characterizes a global city like New York. These are all new forms of "illegality" produced by the global restructuring of capital (Coombe 1994a).

The very definition of the informal sector presupposes a relationship to law as its fundamental referent, but surprisingly little attention has been paid to this phenomenon by scholars of law and society. Lauren Benton (1994) suggests that most analyses of the informal sector tend towards a structuralist dichotomy that divides legal structure and human agency. At best these studies advocate a legal pluralism that simply multiplies the levels of legal structure without attending either to the perceptions of those engaged in informal sector activities or to the way their very practices transform the legal and illegal or formal and informal.[2] Furthermore, this dichotomy does not illuminate how such spheres are locally understood.

The regulatory frameworks in which people operate are far more nuanced than an examination of legal rules and official regulations would suggest. People bring other knowledges and other disciplines to bear upon their productive activities in informal sectors. A Songhay vendor in Harlem, for example, negotiates his sales in a multiplicity of jural landscapes. He parlays his place on the sidewalk with other West African traders using Islamic precepts of propriety, he expresses his sense of entitlement to local business associations, and arbitrates terms of supply with Asian wholesalers in Chinatown. He also masters a new vernacular of race, politics and property to articulate solidarity with local residents, who may see him (because of the Asian goods he sells) as but a black mask for yet another invasion of Asian capital into the African American community. To understand informal economic activities in the late-twentieth century it is necessary to move beyond concepts of legal pluralism to consider the means by which an interjuridical consciousness is forged.

Although the informal economy is acknowledged to be structurally related to flexible regimes of global capital accumulation and not simply an arena of residual cultural forms imported by immigrants, migrants without documentation are disproportionately represented there. This is certainly true of Songhay peoples who

---

2. See Coombe 1989 for a longer theoretical discussion of the relationship between legal structure and social practice.

engage in multiple informal sector activities such as unlicensed street vending, the selling of pirated, counterfeit, or grey market merchandise (in violation of copyright and trademark legislation and licensing agreements), gypsy cab operations, unlicensed import and export activities, and undocumented wage labour. All are forms of illegality produced by global regimes of power and knowledge, regulatory activity and bureaucratic inaction.

Avoiding a Particular Sense of Place

> Imagine for a moment that you are on a satellite, further out and beyond all actual satellites; you can see "planet earth" from a distance. . . . You can see all the movement and tune-in on all the communication. . . . Furthest out are the satellites, then aeroplanes, the long haul between London and Tokyo and the hop from San Salvador to Guatemala City. Some of this is people moving, some of it is physical trade, some is media broadcasting. There are faxes, e-mail, film distribution networks, financial flows and transactions. Look in closer and there are ships and trains, steam trains slogging laboriously up hills somewhere in Asia. Look in closer still and there are lorries and cars and buses and on down further somewhere in sub-Saharan Africa there's a woman on foot who still spends hours a day collecting water.
>
> DOREEN MASSEY (1993:61)

If globalization encompasses a complex array of processes, it must also be recognized as generating its own forms of ideology. Doreen Massey's critiques (1991, 1993) of David Harvey's *The Condition of Postmodernity* (1989) provide a provocative point of departure for considering the nexus of the global and the local that complicates our ethnographic engagement in Harlem and Niger. Massey points to the obvious—the uneven development of global capitalism and the relations of power it engenders—but, more subtly, to the character of the gaze that is capable of constituting the global globally. Too many theories of postmodernity or flexible accumulation speak from within an unquestioned Euro-American perspective that assumes the implosion of time and space to be a process equally accessible and appreciable, rather than one realized from distinct positions. The academic gaze focused on the condition of postmodernity in the singular, as a systemic process of capital restructuring is a particular and an interested one.

Massey cautions against conceiving of place statically, as a source of stability and the space of a single, essential, or integrated identity in a Heideggerian mode; place resists boundaries (1993:63–64):

> what gives place its specificity is not some long internalized history but the fact that it is constructed out of a particular constellation of relations, articulated together at a particular locus. . . . The uniqueness of a place, or a locality, in other words is constructed out of particular interactions and mutual articulations of social relations, social processes, experiences and understandings, in a situation of co-presence, but where a large proportion of those relations, experiences, and understandings are actually constructed on a far larger scale than what we happen to define for that moment as the place itself . . . this in turn allows for a sense of place which is extra-verted, which includes a consciousness of its links with the wider world. (1993:66)

Unfortunately, however, Massey's own spatial gaze tends to essentialize the African woman "on foot who still spends hours a day collecting water," imagining her as unconnected to global processes, except perhaps as their victim. There are other ways to imagine the African woman drawing water, recognizing her unique positioning without romanticizing her purported isolation or denying her agency. This woman might be receiving remittances from her husband who sells hats on the streets in New York City. This in turn might enable her to hire others to draw her water and engage in her own marketing of dry goods. Early this year, due to World Bank and IMF structural adjustment policies, the value of the African franc was cut in half overnight. Abruptly, the woman's costs of doing business doubled. Compared to her neighbours, whose incomes are generated solely from local livelihoods, the woman is still relatively well-to-do. Friends now pressure her for money to help pay for the escalating costs of drugs to treat malaria, which now hoarded, are increasingly difficult to find. For those men in New York who had sent funds recently converted into francs, the capital accumulated from a year's work had been cut in half, increasing the amount of time they felt they must stay in America. West African vendors in New York tell us that migration is now the most viable form of accommodation to devaluation; more and more women are left to cope with the needs of children and relatives alone.

Although necessary as a point of departure, the macrostructural approach to global capitalism cannot illustrate the complexities of the lives of those who engage it. The incorporation of people into transnational economies is a complex and dialectical encounter between multiple cultural worlds, all of which are transformed by their mutual engagement. Capitalism is always a local cultural process, even when its reach is global and all encompassing. This is no less true of the current stage of capital accumulation, which, for all its vaunted flexibility, finds itself difficultly confronting and accommodating local cultural realities: spirit possessions on factory floors (Ong 1987); blessings of legal tender (Taussig 1980); ritual sacrifices to gold and copper mines believed to be the source of illness from Bolivia to Papua New Guinea (Taussig 1980; Nash 1979; Clark 1984); and devil possession rumours surrounding consumer trademarks (Coombe 1993a; Crain 1991, 1994; Hirschkind 1994).

The cultural study of global processes involves explorations of place, "a confrontation of signs and practices along the fault lines of power" (Comaroff and Comaroff 1992: 18), where polysemy in images and icons brings into relief the intercultural politics of contemporary public spheres. A confrontation of commodified images and commercial practices along fault lines of state and corporate power will be explored on the sidewalks at 125th Street and Lenox Avenue in New York City. As a cultural crossroads in an African American commercial marketplace, this place situates many of the ironies and ambiguities that currently animate the black public sphere in the United States.

Operating within a context forged by local entrepreneurial responses to global processes of capitalism, a group of Nigerian street vendors live amongst others who have been socially marginalized by these same processes. Shaped by juridical flows that are both religious and secular, international, national, state and municipal, the "juridiscapes"[3] the vendors negotiate contain conflictual images and contested meanings, many of which are commodified by laws of copyright and trademark. Songhay vendors cater to an African American community with whom their relations are strained. They are both subjects and objects of the publicity and counterpublicity that characterizes contemporary African American life; they contribute to the postmodern and postcolonial flows of exchange that increasingly complicate the politics of the black public sphere. To articulate these ambiguities, it is necessary to venture from the Sahel to Harlem, and back again, for only in such movements across the "Black Atlantic" (Gilroy 1993) do some of the multiple meanings of Black, America, Africa, and their commerce emerge. By maintaining

---

3. This neologism is offered to add legal or juridical dimension to those coined by Appadurai (1990, 1991) for an anthropological consideration of the transnational. Juridiscapes crosscut and often play a constitutive role in the mediascapes, ethnoscapes, technoscapes, finanscapes, and ideoscapes of global flows.

a commitment to mobile positionings some of the nuances of the global and the local may be evoked while avoiding the tendency to universalize or particularize any single perspective.

Signifiers for Sundry Spirits

With respect to Malcolm X in particular, his pervasive presence in the lives of young Black people today has begun to be reduced to the letter he chose to replace "Little," his last name. The "X" was a sign indicating refusal to accept names accorded to Africans by the white families (although there were a few Black ones as well) who asserted ownership of our ancestors as slaves. Now, it seems, the X etched on baseball caps, jackets, and medallions strives to represent the essence of Malcolm X, the quintessential X . . . that X is invested with an abstract affirmation of Black identity, Black dignity, Black resistance, Black rage. I wonder whether young people feel that by wearing the X, they are participating in the experience of something that cannot be defined once and for all: freedom – the freedom of African Americans and, thus, human freedom.

ANGELA DAVIS (1992:43)

Songhay peoples in West Africa have no indigenous script. There are, therefore, no sounds associated with the roman letter X. It does, however, mark a spot in Songhay ritual: X is one sign for a crossroads, considered a point of power in the Songhay cosmos. It marks the spot of sacrifice during spirit possession rituals and is articulated as a target for power in sorcerers' rites. In these ceremonies, deities occupying the bodies of human mediums draw an X on the sand dance grounds. This marks the point where the priest will slit a chicken or a goat's throat. Blood soaks into the earth where X marks the spot; it nourishes the land and makes it fertile for planting. In sorcerers' rites X also serves as a point of articulation. When sorcerers prepare *kusu*, the food of power, they mark an X on the dirt floor of their huts where a clay pot will sit. Only then will power infuse the millet paste and enable it to do its work – to make one impervious to sorcerous attack, and reinforce the sorcerer's embodied integrity (Stoller 1989).

Shifts in social contexts, however, transform cultural significations. Although most Songhay people today live in northeastern Mali, western Niger and northern Benin, like most West African peoples of the Sahel they have a longstanding tradition of migration. There have been communities of Songhay in Ghana, Togo,

Sierra Leone, and Nigeria for over a century. During the French colonial period in Niger, thousands of Songhay migrated seasonally to escape conscription into forced labour; wage labour was a necessary evil related to the imposition of colonial head taxes (Rouch 1956; Stoller 1992). Indigenous cultural forms were transformed to interpret and incorporate these new domains of transcultural experience. New deities in the Songhay spirit pantheon appeared. These horrific spirits parodied the forms of wage labour and the excesses of government with which colonial regimes made the Songhay all too familiar (Stoller 1989, 1994). Songhay people re-enchanted the rationalized forces of colonial power and satirized the iron cages in which they found themselves. The Hauka spirits — often big blustering military men obsessed with procedure, profit and rates of productivity — are not, however, immune to the greater powers of the Songhay cosmos. Despite their pomp and circumstance they too are ultimately compelled to pay homage to Dongo, the Songhay god of thunder who is attracted to the X that marks the spot of sacrifice.

Local practices of Songhay spirit possession do not operate in sociocultural isolation; they are always juxtaposed to and sometimes in conflict with national practices of Islam. Islam is the state religion in Niger, which means that the state officially discourages, but more often regulates publicly performed non-Islamic ritual activities. Spirit possession priests must obtain permits from the local police to stage a possession ceremony, but sorcery is more often denied, and certainly never countenanced by authorities in their official capacities. The spots that X marks are thus legally ambiguous ones, occupying juridiscapes defined by what Saskia Sassen has called "regulatory fractures" (1994a).

The globalization of the economy has encouraged Songhay men from Niger to expand their migratory horizons to Europe, and, more recently, North America. Global communications and transportation systems enable information and misinformation about opportunities available in North American cities to travel to even the most remote villages in the Sahel, prompting ambitious youth to leave desert compounds and seek their fortunes abroad. In New York City, X marks a very different kind of site for Songhay men; it configures the place occupied by Songhay traders who sit behind small aluminum card tables "no more than two feet from the curb" (as stipulated by local vending regulations). The tables of Songhay-speaking vendors and those of other Francophone West Africans line 125th Street where it meets Malcolm X Boulevard, a crossroads of African culture in the Americas. For these Songhay men, X is no longer only the point at which the powers of the cosmos may be contained and compelled for social purposes. It is also the sign that marks an anxious intersection of social, cultural, political and economic currents made possible by global capital restructuring, American corporate property interests, African American cultural politics and the juridiscapes in which these forces coalesce in the spaces Songhay occupy.

Since the mid-1970s New York City has become an ever more frequent destination for transnational migrants. Prior to the 1980s, the number of West African immigrants to New York was insignificant. The first Francophone West Africans in New York City's informal economy were Senegalese men who arrived in the early 1980s and set up tables to sell goods in midtown Manhattan. As West African predecessors to the Songhay and early participants in informal sector building, their experiences merit comment. In 1982 only two Senegalese street pedlars had obtained vending licenses from New York City's Consumer Affairs Board. In short order, they had discovered the monetary and bureaucratic headaches associated with regulatory compliance. City officials routinely fined them for insignificant infractions; locating a table a few inches too close to the curb resulted in fines of $300. After one year of operation, each of the two licensees had amassed fines of $11,000 (Ebin and Lake 1992:35). Other Senegalese simply remained unlicensed, quickly discovering which times of the day and month officials would be least likely to accost them. Some Senegalese positioned themselves as translators and assisted the local court system to prosecute their compatriots while simultaneously contributing to the coffers of the most important Senegalese Muslin brotherhood, the Mourides, which subsidizes the legal costs of their more unlucky brethren.[4]

The Senegalese have since become the aristocracy of African merchants in the city. With the financial power of the Mourides behind them, they dominate the street markets that cater to more affluent clienteles, consumers who have benefited from New York's emergence as a global city. They may well have passed their local knowledge to newly arriving Francophone Africans, but, lacking their organizational power, these more recent migrants have been less fortunate. With the Senegalese closely controlling midtown, newer arrivals from West Africa set up their tables in Harlem and Brooklyn where they cater to others, who like

4. The great majority of Senegalese vendors in New York City are Mourides (Ebin and Lake 1992). Rumours in the African American community circulate that the Mourides were sent to New York by Asian manufacturers to undercut African American economic livelihoods. Coombe has considered the political importance of rumour elsewhere (1993a). Although we have been unable to trace this rumour sufficiently to speculate upon its origins or significance, the purported relationship between Africans in African American communities and alleged Asian sponsorship is clearly one that needs to be addressed in a larger consideration of the commerce of publicity in the black public sphere.

themselves are marginalized by processes of globalization. Here they sell beads, fabric, leather goods and African art; Africans selling "African pride" to African Americans have become a visible presence at the People's Market in Harlem.

Songhay men came to America hoping to eventually find paid employment so they could send regular remittances home. They discovered little space for themselves in New York City's formal economy. Most of them spoke little, if any, English and many of them were illiterate. At that time all of them were undocumented, overstaying the terms of their tourist visas. In the summer of 1992, X marked a site of value, contradiction and contention for Songhay traders and for the African American community in which they lived. Although the sale of Malcolm X goods is no longer so ubiquitous in the People's Market, his iconographic presence marks ironies and ambiguities that continue to be salient.

An Honourable Sanctuary

To understand the reemergence of Malcolm we begin by considering his iconic power. In these hostile times, many African Americans are hungry for an honourable sanctuary, and Black spirit fits the bill. . . . But are the buyers, African American or not, angry or not, Black believers? Not necessarily, because Black spirit has never meant one thing, or anything concrete, which is its great power *and* failure. Spirit has no spine; it bends easily to the will of its buyer. Black spirit has many faces — it can mean anything from "angry" to "kindhearted" to "cool." Even for those who purchase Malcolm with the spirit's current militance in mind, the meaning of the possession is very uncertain. . . . Doesn't American spirit, backed by ideologies such as consumerism, have the upper hand? So whom does the icon serve most?

JOE WOOD (1992:6–7)

X marks one of the largest merchandising agreements and most controversial marketing campaigns of the twentieth century. The image, likeness, name and meaning of Malcolm X has been an ongoing site of political and legal controversy. The choice of Spike Lee to direct a film about the late black nationalist fuelled ongoing disputes over his legacy; it also consolidated forces promoting the commodification of his persona. Dr. Betty Shabazz, Malcolm X's widow, began the first round of legal battles with a copyright infringement suit against publishers of the book, *Malcolm X for Beginners*. Accused of violating Malcolm's own ethics by prohibiting wider access to progressive black political ideas, Shabazz downplayed her financial interest and shifted emphasis to the propriety of acknowledging and affirming her copyright as proper guardian of the Malcolm X legacy. She was less reticent about asserting her proprietary rights when the publicity for the Warner Bros. film accelerated the value of the Malcolm X persona. In 1992, *Forbes Magazine* suggested that "[R]etail sales of licensed Malcolm X products, all emblazoned with a large 'X' could reach $100 million this year (The estate would then collect as much as $3 million in royalties)" (Sullivan 1992:136). A licensing manager was retained when a proliferation of X merchandise began to appear on the sidewalks of New York. By October, there were thirty-five licensees under contract, and seventy more in negotiation (136). One of the more protracted negotiations was the ongoing work of determining the position of Spike Lee's own merchandising company, 40 Acres and a Mule®, whose efforts began the retail trade. His use of the X was called a blatant trademark infringement by the estate, a legally questionable proposition, but one that raised the stakes, multiplied the legal rights at issue, and further compelled a negotiated settlement. Worldwide sales of unlicensed X merchandise for 1992 were estimated in the range of $20 million (136).

Dozens of parties and a phalanx of highly paid legal talent were engaged in the negotiation of the copyright, trademark, publicity rights and merchandising rights to the iconographic presence of Malcolm X, as these were multiplied, divided up and licensed out. The unabashed conflation of X as a political symbol with X as an internationally circulating property with immense commercial value has created ambivalence amongst many African Americans, who see the proliferation of Malcolm X's iconographic presence as concomitantly diluting its political import.

Talking Black

As used today, Malcolm the icon is principally a form of Black mask. Like dreadlocks and kente cloth, Malcolm X worn on a T-shirt is an African American cultural form; as such it "speaks" African American culture. But it is also a political signifier—it is also an icon of Blackness, and consequently, a Black mask. No matter how much disagreement there is among African Americans about Malcolm X. . . you're talking Black when you wear these things.

JOE WOOD (1992:8)

In 1992, Songhay traders benefitted from the publicity of the Warner Bros. film and its spin-off industries. They bought and sold unlicensed Malcolm X hats and clothing, goods that intellectual property lawyers describe as counterfeit, pirated or knockoff merchandise. The *New York Times* recently referred to many of these goods as "cyberfakes" (Levy 1994b), alluding to new digital modes of copyright and trademark infringement which enable computers to quickly and accurately copy the logos, labels, and tags of merchandise bearing famous marks, and imprint the same insignia of authenticity onto other, allegedly inferior merchandise. The merchandise itself is often produced in Asia or in the many garment shops and illegal factories that have sprung up in Chinatown and New Jersey with the expansion of the informal sector. Those who mark these goods may well be immigrants, indentured to those who own the increasingly expensive and efficient technology that imitates the real thing. Those who make and sell such goods risk fines, searches and seizures. They are periodically raided by zealous FBI agents, contemporary guardians of the increasingly commodified cultural worlds of post-modernity (Coombe 1991, 1992).

For Songhay vendors, the idea that a man's name might be exclusively controlled as a source of continuous revenue is both foreign and strange. The mark of the X might call forth propitious powers if human rituals are properly performed, but in North America X returns a steady flow of royalties into the coffers of those whose No Trespassing signs look most likely to be legally legitimated. For Malcolm Little himself, X re-marked his unknown African family of origin; it replaced the name of the slavemaster. Capitalizing upon the market for things African, and the heightened awareness of Islam, Songhay found themselves the perfect props for peddling Malcolm X merchandise — unknown Muslim Africans conveying signs of a reified and alienated Islam, newly revalued in the African American community where they found themselves.

Michael Dyson suggests that the resurgent racism of American society and the increased economic marginalization that the forces of globalization have visited upon the inner city poor, "precipitate the iconization of figures who embody the strongest gestures of resistance to white racism": "the destructive effects of gentrification, economic crisis, social dislocation, the expansion of corporate privilege, and the development of underground political economies, along with the violence and criminality they breed mean that X is even more a precious symbol of the self-discipline, self-esteem, and moral leadership necessary to combat the spiritual and economic corruption of poor black communities" (1993: 51). The self-discipline, self-esteem and moral leadership that Islam provides the Songhay in a new and still foreign environment offers these black men little safety in the streets. In the summer of 1992, observant Songhay traders—unknown Africans purveying the multiply mediated and commodified sign of black Muslim resistance—turned away from their tables, opened the street's fire hydrants and performed ritual ablutions prior to afternoon prayer. During these ritual acts, they found themselves vulnerable to theft, insult and assault. For months they were laughed at and their Muslim piety was denigrated.

Asked what they knew about Malcolm X in 1992, some Songhay vendors claimed he was a former neighbourhood resident, whereas others had heard about his particular, and to them, peculiar, variant of Islam. Everyone in this group of thirty pragmatists recognized that Malcolm X marked a site of economic opportunity under the street sign that bore his name. In 1994, the Nation of Islam is well known through the figure of Louis Farrakhan, who personifies it for Songhay vendors. Malcolm X has become the political celebrity whose angry voice booms from a video playing constantly on a television mounted upon a nearby car. These are just two more of the famous that mark the multiple facades that figure as America in Songhay imagination.

Songhay vendors know from their cultural experience that X, the crossroads, marks a point of power. They know that points of power are spaces both of opportunity and danger, sources of potential security and inextricable violence. Today, when they venture into the bush (the Songhay description for places like Indianapolis, Oklahoma City and Dallas), their familiarity with Harlem and their commercial base on Malcolm X Boulevard provides them with a source of cultural legitimacy in black America, a form of goodwill and security for their national operations. X then, also operates for Songhay vendors as a form of trademark, a sign that symbolically carries established custom and goodwill in a wider African American market.

Still, many Songhay vendors have been mugged, some have been hospitalized, and at least one badly beaten merchant returned to Niger, leaving the space that X had marked for him to a more determined compatriot. Others have only had their economic security threatened by local authorities who periodically confiscate their merchandise. Most of them simply accept police actions, raids and fines as the price of doing business at the crossroads that X provides for them in America. Neither the vendors nor the police seriously believe that the periodic crackdowns on "scofflaws" (the new city administration's term for those who run informal enterprises) will curtail African vending.

Elusive Cultural Politics

Malcolm left the brothers their first revolutionary pop icon. . . . And when you dealing with American superstars, baby, all you need to

know is he lived fast and died young, a martyr who went out in a blaze
of glory. . . . We celebrate the death of Malcolm X for what it is—the
birth of a new black god. X is dead, long live X. He's like the Elvis of
black pop politics—a real piece of Afro-Americana. That's why Spike's
X logo is branded with an American flag. Malcolm couldn't have happened anywhere else.

GREG TATE (1992:185)

Today Songhay merchants vend two forms of goods—unmarked goods that represent a reified Africana and counterfeit trademarked goods for an African American
market. The African goods, ersatz kente cloth scarves, combs, trade beads, leather
goods and the occasional sculpture, are unmarked by any authorial signature or
point of origin. Those men with the necessary papers go back to Mali and Niger,
and have goods specially made for Harlem and the Black Expo circuit. Knowing
what forms Africa must take for an African American market, they produce
generic items that are marked neither by artist, village, cultural area nor region.
Their distinction lies in their being African—a monolithic cultural whole in the
Afrocentric imaginary that Songhay recognize as providing their own space in
the American market. Meanwhile, the American goods they sell are largely
manufactured in Asia and are all marked with famous names: Ralph Lauren, Polo,
Hugo Boss, Guess, Fila and dozens of sports team logos. The goods themselves are
indistinguishable. They include baseball caps and knit hats, sweatshirts and other
cheaply manufactured goods whose only allure is the fame of their trademark.
These are the goods Songhay vendors know as the American merchandise that
sells most quickly in African American communities.

Songhay vendors find themselves both catering to and resisting a stereotypical image of themselves (as Africans they say that they are seen as more "primitive"
intellectually by some of their clientele) that both benefits them economically
and denies their cultural specificity. They, however, may have less at stake in
maintaining a Songhay cultural identity than we, as scholars whose disciplinary
authority still rests upon such distinctions, might presume. Knowing something
about the history and plight of African Americans, a few Songhay-speaking
migrants accept the fact that the "Africa" African Americans "need" is not the
Africa they know. In the Harlem market context they are prepared to renounce
recognition of the complexities of the Africa from which they come, and make a
gift of the more unencumbered significance it has acquired in the local community.
Most of them easily engage in marketing the fetishes of an imaginary Africa and

the signs of a utopian America—learning to read their market, media culture and the marks of fame that appeal to African Americans.

Although the significance of commodities and commodified media signifiers in contemporary public spheres and subaltern counterpublics has been asserted (Garnham 1993; Lee 1993; Polan 1993; Warner 1993), its material details are seldom explored. For example, the popularity of goods that ostentatiously bear their trademarks in poor black neighbourhoods is often marked, but the politics of this semiotics is opaque. The role of the commodity's publicity in the black public sphere draws our attention to the fashions in which mimesis and alterity are articulated (Coombe 1994b) in inner-city contexts. Some trademarks have become so popular amongst minority youth that their owners have protested the association of their mark with inner-city black youth, and by implication, with crime. In other parts of the country, local law enforcement officials use particular brand names as indicia of gang membership; wearing such goods becomes the basis for refusing youth entry into public places of amusement (Russell 1992). In New York City, newspapers report the trademarks on clothing worn by young black men upon arrest (Levy 1994a), and the trademarks on items requested by minority youth in a guns-for-merchandise exchange sponsored by a chain of national toy stores (Jones 1994). The publicity of the trademark serves to mark black bodies in the national imaginary as they simultaneously invest it with unanticipated and unintended significations.

In 1993, the proliferation of Timberland® goods in inner-city neighbourhoods vastly improved the company's sales (Marriott 1993). The company, however, reacted to the growing publicity of their mark by reducing distribution networks to avoid inner-city venues. This strategy might be related to the unique demands made upon them. When an inner-city market becomes publicly known, it is sometimes suggested that manufacturers benefitting from such sales put some of their revenue back into social programs for those youth from whom they profit. The corporate fear of "dilution" (Coombe 1991), however, is also apparent. By the time today's fashion trend is dead and buried in hip hop culture, tomorrow's middle class Americans may have indelibly associated the mark with a racialised Other.

These examples suggest that the trademark figures significantly in the flows of publicity and counterpublicity that complicate categories of commerce and politics in the black public sphere. But when a Muslim cleric from a desert village extends spiritual solace to a local homeless man, and both are wearing a Timberland® cap in the asphalt and concrete jungle they know as the United States, the promise of America that Timberland® marks is ironically exposed, and the hypocrisy of attempting to maintain the purity of the commodity-form is betrayed. Within the inner city, the trademarks of such companies become obvious targets for bootleggers. The allure of Timberland® boots, which cost over a hundred dollars (inducing one youth to trade in his revolver to obtain a pair), can be possessed for the price of a knit cap with the company logo richly embroidered in gold thread across its brim.

The insignia of corporate ownership loom large on the streets of Harlem. But if the trademark form is densely instantiated as a form of publicity in the black public sphere, it may also be taken up and countered from within. In the fall of 1993, Songhay vendors had another hat upon their tables. This one was burdened by a heavy metal tag on which the signature Karl Kani was engraved. The attached card read:

> Inspired by the vitality of the streets of Brooklyn, New York Karl Kani the young African-American owner/designer of Karl Kani jeans encourages you to follow your dreams to accomplish your goals. Wear the clothing that represents the knowledge of African-American creativity and determination. Recognize the signature that symbolizes African-American unity and pride... Peace, Karl Kani.

Huge poster advertisements for Karl Kani® jeans appeared. Posing with pelvis thrust, crotch provocatively revealed, and accompanied by a muzzled pit bull, Kani or the model representing him exemplifies that masculinist, individualist hero-worship that many see as distorting black political life (Davis 1992; Simmons and Riggs 1992). The adoption of the trademark's publicity to proclaim a politics of pride from within the community also, however, asserts a potential counterpublicity. It proffers an affirmation and embrace in contrast to the seductive teasing and withdrawal, promise and betrayal, offer and rebuke that characterize the corporate trademark's signifying dance in African American communities.

Black Masks

> We seek, as Malcolm did, to name ourselves, and we begin, as Malcolm did, with the Black mask given us. We take the baton from Malcolm: we take our humanity for granted, and we realize that our community is made up of people of all sorts of colours, genders, classes, ethnicities, sexualities, etc. We have always known that African Americans weren't the only niggers on this earth, and now we invite all other

people who are oppressed to join us. . . We will seize the day and make a new Blackness.

JOE WOOD (1992:15)

The blackness of the black public sphere is potentially challenged and transformed by the questions posed by the entrepreneurial presence of Africans in African American communities. Is their participation in the commerce of the black public sphere, however defined, a part of or outside of black politics? Are they blacks to be included or excluded by other blacks, who can more authentically claim the integrity of African American culture as their own? To whom should such questions be addressed? Are the commercial struggles around the use of vending space issues of black politics or simply issues of American competition?

Relationships between originals and their copies, mimesis and alterity, authenticity and value are ironically twisted by African engagement in local markets. On one axis of the crossroads African Americans sell handmade jewelry that inscribes Malcolm's black nationalist X on a map of Africa colonized by the tripartite Garveyite flag. On the other, West African vendors sell a counterfeit version of Malcolm's X embroidered on Asian goods marked by immigrants who produce the signs of American commercial possibility in hidden factories. Are Songhay inauthentic purveyors of one of the authentic spirits of African American culture or authentic conveyors of an unlicensed and unauthorized image of an authentic spirit? Are they mere vehicles for the American spirit of consumerism or appropriate props to project images of militant Islam? The impossibility of a cultural politics of black authenticity in such circumstances is, at least, clear.

Joe Wood asks how Malcolm's image works, and points to the necessarily reductive character of all iconography: the abstractions that make an image widely attractive and accessible enable it to be grasped, domesticated and transformed. All trademarks and other commodified texts have the capacity to engender the authorship of Others (Coombe 1991, 1992, 1993a, 1994b), and Malcolm's X is no exception. When Songhay vend Malcolm's X they momentarily capture some of the authority of the black community and thereby risk resentment. They may also insert their Malcolm (who, due to his militance, gaze, bearing and rage, ironically resembles a Hauka spirit) behind the X. Songhay author and authorize an alternative Malcolm even as they retail his unauthorized likeness and pose questions that he recognized but could not resolve in the final year of his life.

Black activists and scholars complain both of Malcolm X's dilution throughout his mimesis in commerce and of the effacement of questions of alterity he embraced at the end of his life. Malcolm's X is replicated in the image markets of postmodernity in a fashion that obscures the postcolonial issues his legacy might encourage us to embrace. If the commodified iconization of his X distorts and dilutes black politics such that relations of production and distribution and the economic marginalization of black peoples is obscured, the Songhay sale of such goods serves as a challenge and a reminder of the need to continually reconsider the character of black political solidarity that a global economy demands:

> During most of his time with the Nation of Islam, Malcolm X saw race as a biological reality instead of a socially constructed, historical phenomenon. This assumption of biological essentialism coloured his Black nationalist philosophy. Relinquishing this biological essentialism in the last year of his life opened the doors for a greatly reformulated Black nationalism, one encompassing different notions of Black political consciousness and the types of political coalitions that Blacks might forge with other groups. . . . [This is] increasingly important to an African-American community situated in today's complex multiethnic, multinational political economy. . . . Malcolm's increasing attention to global structures of capitalism and imperialism led him to begin to consider the influence of global capitalism as a major structure affecting African Americans. The principal Black struggles of Malcolm's time were against colonialism. But in our postcolonial era, the need to incorporate analyses of global capitalism in any Black nationalist philosophy becomes not only more noticeable, but more important. (Hill Collins 1992:61–2)

The postcolonial and the postmodern confront each other in practices of trademark counterfeiting and the vending of knockoff merchandise. Such practices are usually considered simple acts of piracy, but in this instance, a political subtext might be discerned. The black market in illicit goods challenges the capitalist appropriation of Malcolm X and his control by the corporate forces of postmodernity, implicitly raising the postcolonial claims of Others. As migrants and workers in the informal economies of global cities, these Others reveal the myth of a postindustrial society and challenge the proprietorship over imagery and texts that defines the condition some call postmodernity.

When a Songhay vendor dons a hat made in Bangladesh, emblazoned with the slogan "Another Young Black Man Making Money" while greeting his customers as "Brother" on the streets of Harlem, the cross-cutting significations of this performative add new dimensions to an understanding of the black public sphere. Not only does he echo and refract an ironic African American response to the racism of white America, he also adopts a competitive posture and questions the parameters of the Blackness that defines the Man, marking his own difference as potentially "An Other Young Black Man." He is also complicit with the subtextual tensions of ethnicity, gender and class that reverberate from this phrase. The ironies of its traffic through export processing zones in Asia, factories in New Jersey, wholesalers in Chinatown, West African vendors in Harlem and the African American cultural community do not enable any singular conclusion. Neither the global nor the local can be understood unless we acknowledge and address the full range of ambiguities produced at their nexus in the commerce of emergent black public spheres.

Rosemary J. Coombe teaches in the Faculty of Law at the University of Toronto. She has written extensively on legal history, legal theory and the politics of intellectual property laws. Her book, *Cultural Appropriations: Authorship, Alterity, and the Law* is forthcoming from Routledge. She is currently working on two projects—a book on English copyright laws, colonialism, and the evangelical imaginary and another on the history of American trademark law, imperialism, incorporation, and citizenship.

Paul Stoller teaches in the Department of Anthropology at West Chester University. He is the author of numerous books and articles on the Songhay of Niger. Recent books include *Fusion of the Worlds* (University of Chicago Press, 1989), *The Cinematic Griot* (University of Chicago Press, 1992) and *Embodying Colonial Memories* (Routledge, 1994).

Literature Cited

Appadurai, Arjun. 1990. "Disjuncture and Difference in the Global Cultural Economy." *Public Culture* 2(2): 1–24.

———. 1991. "Global Ethnoscapes: Notes and Queries for a Transnational Anthropology." In Richard G. Fox, ed., *Recapturing Anthropology: Working in the Present*. Santa Fe: School of American Research Press, 191–210.

Benton, Lauren. 1994. "Legal Structure and Economic Restructuring: The Institutional Context of Law in the Informal Sector." *Studies in Law and Society* (in press).

Callaghy, Thomas M. and John Ravehill, eds. 1993. *Hemmed In: Responses to Africa's Economic Decline*. New York: Columbia University Press.

Castells, Manuel and Alejandro Portes. 1989. "World Underneath: The Origins, Dynamics and Effects of the Informal Economy." In Portes, et al., eds. *The Informal Economy.* Baltimore: The Johns Hopkins University Press, 11–37.

Clark, Jeffrey. 1994. "Gold, Sex, and Pollution: Male Illness and Myth at Mt. Kare, Papua New Guinea." *American Ethnologist* 20: 742–757.

Comaroff, Jean and John Comaroff. 1992. *Ethnography and the Historic Imagination.* Boulder: Westview Press.

Coombe, Rosemary J. 1989. "Room for Manoeuver: Towards a Theory of Practice in Critical Legal Studies." *Law and Social Inquiry* 14: 69–121.

_____. 1991. "Objects of Property and Subjects of Politics: Intellectual Property Laws and Democratic Dialogue." *Texas Law Review* 69: 1853–1880.

_____. 1992. "Publicity Rights and Political Aspiration: The Celebrity Image, Mass Culture, and Democracy." *New England Law Review* 26: 1221–1280.

_____. 1993a. "Tactics of Appropriation and the Politics of Recognition in Late Modern Democracies." *Political Theory* 21: 411–433.

_____. 1993b. "The Properties of Culture and the Politics of Possessing Identity: Native Claims in the Cultural Appropriation Controversy." *Canadian Journal of Law and Jurisprudence* 6: 249–286.

_____. 1994a. "The Cultural Life of Things: Globalization and the Anthropological Approaches to Commodification." *American Journal of International Law and Politics* 18: (forthcoming).

_____. 1994b. "Embodied Trademarks: Mimesis and Alterity on American Commercial Frontiers." Paper presented to the Society for Cultural Anthropology Annual Meeting, Chicago, May 13–15, 1994.

Crain, Mary. 1991. "Poetics and Politics in the Equadorian Andes: Women's Narratives of Death and Devil-Possession." *American Ethnologist* 18: 67–90.

_____. 1994. "Opening Pandora's Box: A Plea for Discursive Heteroglossia." *American Ethnologist* 21: 205–210.

Davis, Angela Y. 1992. "Mediations on the Legacy of Malcolm X." In Joe Wood, ed., *Malcolm X: In Our Own Image.* New York: St. Martin's Press, 36–47.

Dickens, Peter. 1992. *Global Shift: The Internationalization of Economic Activity.* New York and London: Guilford Press.

Dyson, Michael Eric. 1993. "X Marks the Plots: A Critical Reading of Malcolm's Readers." *Social Text* 35: 25–53.

Ebin, Victoria. 1990. "Commercants et Missionaires: Une Confrerie Musulmane Senegelaise a New York." *Hommes et Migrations* 1132: 25–31.

Ebin, Victoria and Rose Lake. 1992. "Camelots a New York: Les Pionniers de l'Immigration Senegelaise." *Hommes et Migrations* 1160: 32–37.

Garnham, Nicholas. 1993. "The Mass Media, Cultural Identity, and the Public Sphere in the Modern World." *Public Culture* 5(2): 251–265.

Gates, Henry Louis, Jr. 1988. *The Signifying Monkey.* New York: Oxford University Press.

Gilroy, Paul. 1993. *The Black Atlantic: Modernity and Double Consciousness.* Cambridge: Harvard University Press.

Harvey, David. 1989. *The Condition of Postmodernity.* Oxford: Basil Blackwell.

Hill Collins, Patricia. 1992. "Learning to Think for Ourselves: Malcolm X's Black Nationalism Reconsidered." In Joe Wood, ed., *Malcolm X: In Our Own Image.* New York: St. Martin's Press, 59–85.

Hirschkind, Lynn. 1994. "Bedevilled Ethnography." *American Ethnologist* 21: 201–204.

Jones, Charisse. 1994. "All Kinds of People Arrive Bearing Guns." *New York Times* January 1, A-1 and A-30.

Lee, Benjamin. 1993. "Going Public." *Public Culture* 5(2): 165–178.

Levy, Cliford J. 1994a. "Youth Held in Baby Death in a Car Seat." *New York Times,* February 10, B-1 and B-7.

———. 1994b. "Cyberfakes: The Latest in Knock-Offs: computer-made counterfeits." *New York Times,* February 20, 9-1 and 9-8.

Marriott, Michael. 1993. "Out of the Woods: The Inner City Loves Timberland: Does Timberland love the inner city?" *New York Times,* November 7, 9-1 and 9-11.

Massey, Doreen. 1991. "Flexible Sexism." *Environment and Planning D: Society and Space* 9(1): 31–57.

———. 1993. "Power-geometry and a Progressive Sense of Place." In Jon Bird, Barry Curtis, Time Putnam, George Robertson and Lisa Tickner, eds., *Mapping the Futures: Local Cultures, Global Change.* New York: Routledge, 59–69.

Mittelman, James. "Global Restructuring of Production and Migration." In Yoshikazu Sakamoto, ed., *Global Transformation.* Tokyo: United Nations University Press (forthcoming).

Mitter, Swatsi. 1987. *Common Fate, Common Bond: Women in the Global Economy.* London: Pluto Press.

Mollenkopf, John, ed. 1991. *Dual City: Restructuring New York.* New York: Russell Sage Foundation.

Nash, June. 1979. *We Eat the Mines and the Mines Eat Us.* New York: Columbia University Press.

Ong, Aihwa. 1987. *Spirits of Resistance and Capitalist Discipline: Factory Women in Malaysia*. Albany: State University of New York.

Polan, Dana. 1993. "The Public's Fear: or, Media as Monster in Habermas, Negt, and Kluge." In Bruce Robbins, ed., *The Phantom Public Sphere*. Minneapolis: University of Minnesota Press, 33–41.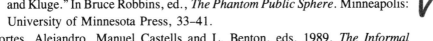

Portes, Alejandro, Manuel Castells and L. Benton, eds. 1989. *The Informal Economy*. Baltimore: The Johns Hopkins University Press.

Reed, Adolph. 1992. "The Allure of Malcolm X and the Changing Character of Black Politics." In Joe Wood, ed., *Malcolm X: In Our Own Image*. New York: St. Martin's Press, 203–232.

Rouch, Jean. 1956. "Migrations au Ghana," *Journal de la Societe des Africanistes* 26(1–2): 33–196.

Russell, Margaret. 1992. "Entering Great America: Reflections on Race and the Convergence of Progressive Legal Theory and Practice." *Hastings Law Journal* 43:749–767.

Sassen, Saskia. 1991a. "The Informal Economy." In J. Mellonkopf, ed., *Dual City: Restructuring New York*. New York: Russell Sage Foundation, 79–101.

_____. 1991b. *The Global City: New York, London, Tokyo*. Princeton: Princeton University Press.

_____. 1993. "Rebuilding the Global City: Economy, Ethnicity, and Space," *Social Justice* 20: 32–50.

_____. 1994a. "Regulatory Fractures in the Global City." A paper presented at the American International Law Society conference "Interdisciplinary Perspectives on International Economic Law," Washington, DC, February 25–27.

_____. 1994b. *Cities in a World Economy*. Thousand Oaks, CA: Pine Forge Press.

Simmons, Ron and Marlon Riggs. 1992. "Sexuality, Television, and Death: A Black Gay Dialogue on Malcolm X." In Joe Wood, ed., *Malcolm X: In Our Own Image*. New York: St. Martin's Press, 135–154.

Stoller, Paul. 1989. *Fusion of the Worlds: An Ethnography of Possession Among the Songhay of Niger*. Chicago: University of Chicago Press.

_____. 1992. *The Cinematic Griot: The Ethnography of Jean Rouch*. Chicago: University of Chicago Press.

_____. 1994. "Embodying Colonial Memories." *American Anthropologist* 96(3).

_____. 1994. *Embodying Colonial Memories: Spirit Possession, Power and the Hauka in West Africa*. New York: Routledge.

Sullivan, R. Lee. 1992. "Spike Lee versus Mrs. Malcolm X (Licensed Product Merchandising)." *Forbes Magazine* 150 (October 12): 136.

Tate, Greg. 1992. "Can This be the End for Cyclops and Professor X?" In Joe Wood, ed., *Malcolm X: In Our Own Image*. New York: St. Martin's Press, 183–189.

Taussig, Michael. 1980. *The Devil and Commodity Fetishism in South America*. Chapel Hill: University of North Carolina Press.

Wallace, Michelle. 1990. *Invisibility Blues*. New York: Routledge.

Warner, Michael. 1993. "The Mass Public and the Mass Subject." In Bruce Robbins, ed., *The Phantom Public Sphere*. Minneapolis: University of Minnesota Press, 234–256.

Wood, Joe. 1992. "Malcolm X and the New Blackness." In Joe Wood, ed., *Malcolm X: In Our Own Image*. New York: St. Martin's Press, 1–17.

Culture versus Commerce: The Marketing of Black Popular Music

Reebee Garofalo

> *Despite all of the trappings and veils, the unnecessary interventions, the blockages that culture and society have interposed between us and reality, something in us responds to black music and it will not be denied.*
>
> JERRY WEXLER, producer, 1971

Like any popular music that originates outside the mainstream, African American popular music has long been faced with trying to negotiate a path between the joint dangers of isolation and exclusion on the one hand, and incorporation and homogenization on the other. Despite the wellspring of creativity that African American artists have brought to popular music, they have historically been relegated to a separate and unequal marketing structure which has tended toward ensuring one unacceptable outcome or the other for their music. Because of industry and audience racism, black personnel have been systematically excluded from positions of power within the industry and the audience has been artificially fragmented, in part along racial lines. Against this backdrop, black popular music has not only nourished African American culture internally, but has also managed to exert a disproportionate influence on mainstream culture as well. These related social functions have not always existed in easy harmony, as the one has often acted to undercut the other. As a result, the poles of the debate surrounding strategies for African American culture have been marked by a nationalist impulse to preserve its purity versus an integrationist push to broaden its appeal.

In this essay, I will argue that, in broad historical strokes, the overall trajectory of black popular music has been progressive and that, faced with the tension

Public Culture 1994, 7: 275–287

between preservation and expansion, it has managed to accomplish both—not to the complete satisfaction of either side and certainly not without other contradictions—but both nonetheless. This discussion contains three parts. First, I will offer a brief history of official mainstream designations for African American popular music as illustrative of the complexity of the cultural terrain it must traverse and the forces that work to keep it circumscribed. Second, I will analyze three periods in popular music history—the ascendance of Tin Pan Alley, the rock 'n' roll rupture, and the current hip hop moment—which show qualitative, if contradictory, gains for black music. Finally, I will explore the globalization of the music industry in terms of its impact on changes in the domestic marketing structure.[1]

Conflating Culture and Commerce

When the music industry accidentally discovered that there was a substantial market for blues recordings in the early 1920s, Ralph Peer, an enterprising young white recording engineer who assisted at the earliest recording sessions, dubbed it "race" music. This was probably not a conscious attempt by Peer to demean the music. Prominent African Americans were referred to as race leaders at the time. This was particularly true in black newspapers like the *Chicago Defender* where race records were advertised. It is likely that this was simply Peer's attempt to make an intelligent marketing decision, but it was still a marketing decision. Race was a code word that identified the recording artist as African American for the record-buying public. It served to keep the music isolated from the mainstream. The term stuck and remained the official industry designation for working-class, African American musics until 1949.

When race records began to become popular in the mainstream market in the late 1940s, the (white) music industry became embarrassed by the term; it was decided that a more palatable term was needed. Record companies toyed with labels like "ebony" and "sepia" for a while, but these were obviously distinctions of color, not musical style. By the end of the decade, rhythm and blues—a catch-all phrase for a number of African American performance styles—had become the accepted term.

1. This essay was delivered as a paper at the "A to the K" conference sponsored by the American Studies Program, New York University on April 16, 1994. It draws on research undertaken previously and published elsewhere. See footnotes below for specific references.

At this time, the conventional marketing strategies of the music industry were based on three product categories: pop for the mainstream audience, country and western for the regional audience, and rhythm and blues for the black audience. *Billboard*, the leading trade magazine, developed separate listings or charts that reflected these divisions. On those rare occasions when a recording became popular in more than one market, it was said to "crossover." While the term can be used to indicate simply the simultaneous appearance on more than one chart, its most common usage in popular music history connotes movement from margin to mainstream. For a rhythm and blues release to become a pop hit, it had to "crossover" from the rhythm and blues charts to the pop charts, which is to say, it had to first sell well in the black community. This is the essence of the concept of crossover; by and large African American artists must first demonstrate success in the black market before gaining access to the mainstream. It is a process which holds black artists to a higher standard of performance than white and it is only recently that it has been successfully circumvented in any systematic way.[2]

African American popular music was charted as rhythm and blues through the early 1960s. In the context of the integrationist phase of the early civil rights movement, the rhythm and blues singles charts were actually discontinued altogether from the end of 1963 until the beginning of 1965. This period coincided with the first wave of the British Invasion when the Beatles led dozens of British acts to the United States in early 1964. It is also a period when a new product category called blue-eyed soul was coined following the success of the Righteous Brothers among black consumers. For African American artists, the results were disastrous. Nearly one-third of the Top Ten releases for that year belonged to British artists; one year earlier there had been none. Further displacing African American acts, the blue-eyed soul category included not only the expected artists like the Righteous Brothers, whose material was heavily influenced by rhythm and blues, but artists as diverse as Bob Dylan, Tom Jones and Brenda Lee. Even the Beatles' "Yesterday" was tagged with this label. As a result African American artists showed a sharp decline on the pop singles charts from an all-time high of forty-two percent in 1962 to twenty-two percent in 1966, their lowest point since the initial surge of rock 'n' roll in the mid-1950s. Only three of the top fifty albums for the years 1964 and 1965 were by black artists. If forcing African American artists to jump the rhythm and blues hurdle seemed punitive, eliminating

---

2. For a more developed discussion of the merits of crossing over see Reebee Garofalo, "Black Popular Music: Crossing Over or Going Under," in Tony Bennett, et al., eds., *Rock and Popular Music: Politics, Policies, Institutions* (New York: Routledge, 1993), 231–248.

it proved even more problematic. In this instance, African American artists were simply swept away in the wash of more marketable (read white) performers.

In the context of the growing militancy of the black power movement in the late 1960s, the rhythm and blues charts were reinstated and replaced with the term soul in 1969. The designation soul reflected the growing influence of the rootsy, hard-driving rhythm and blues called Southern soul (Aretha Franklin, Wilson Pickett, James Brown). As the radical movements of the 1960s were destroyed, this grittier rhythm and blues sound experienced a corresponding decline in popularity. It was gradually supplanted by the soft soul being produced out of Philadelphia (Stylistics, Spinners, O'Jays), which prepared the way for disco. In some ways, the industry came full circle when the soul charts were renamed black music in 1982. At the time *Billboard* felt that soul was too limited a term to define the diversity of musical styles appearing on the chart, and that black was "a better tribute to the music's cultural origins."[3] Applied to African American artists, the term black music was vulnerable to the same criticisms as the term race music four decades earlier. Stranger yet, the term was no longer limited to African Americans; it looked particularly odd when British-born George Michael won the 1989 American Music Award for the Best Black Male Vocal. Thus in 1990, *Billboard* returned to the logic of 1949 and retitled the chart, once again, rhythm and blues, explaining that it was "becoming less acceptable to identify music in racial terms."[4]

The industry's apparent confusion arises from its market-driven failure to distinguish between African American popular music as a collection of musical genres complete with a cultural context and a history, and African American popular music as a succession of race-based marketing categories. Manning Marable distinguishes between "racial identity, a category the Europeans created and deliberately imposed on us for the purpose of domination, and Black cultural identity, which we constantly reinvent and construct for ourselves. But for many white Americans, their understanding of Blackness is basically one definition only, racial identity."[5] This tendency is at the heart of the music industry's difficulty in coming to grips with the shifting cultural sands of black popular music. It is the difference between thinking culturally and thinking only in commercial terms.

---

3. *Billboard*, October 27, 1990, 35.
4. Ibid., 6.
5. Manning Marable, "Race, Identity, and Political Culture," in Gina Dent, ed., *Black Popular Culture* (Seattle: Bay Press, 1992), 295–296.

If we look at black popular music as a music which grows from a shared history and particular cultural heritage — from participation in the African American experience — then we are viewing it through the lens of culture. Says Stuart Hall: "'Good' black popular culture can pass the test of authenticity — the reference to black experience and to black expressivity."[6] Such a definition presents us with a basis for making aesthetic judgments that go beyond a simple consideration of market demographics. But the music industry represents commerce; it is organized according to market demographics. As such, the industry takes account of societal divisions in developing its product categories. Peering only through the lens of racial identity, black popular music becomes operationally defined either as what African American artists play or as what African American consumers buy. While such definitions may make it easier for advertisers to target potential buyers, they present double-edged dilemmas for many African American artists and complicate the search for cultural continuity.

There is no question that the rich musical tradition which grows out of the African American experience should be accorded a special cultural status. However, problems arise because defining black popular music as what African American artists play can be used to slot black artists, at least initially, into a limited market no matter what the category is called. It can also be needlessly confining for African American artists who want to explore other genres. Does it make sense to impose such a definition on Jackie Wilson singing the traditional Irish classic "Danny Boy" in as operatic voice as ever hit the popular market? The breadth of Paul Robeson's repertoire would present an even bigger dilemma. If we define black popular music as what the African American audience buys, where do we position African American artists like, say, Jimi Hendrix whose music clearly derived from African American sources but didn't sell to the African American community? Where do we place classic Motown hits which sold about seventy percent white to thirty percent black? Conversely, how would we define hits by white artists, from the Righteous Brothers and Mitch Ryder and the Detroit Wheels to Madonna and George Michael, which have sold to both audiences in roughly the same proportions?

As long as racism dominates social relations among the races, the structure of the music industry will tend to reflect the divisions it creates. Audiences will be fragmented accordingly. African American artists who sell primarily to an African American audience are more likely to be signed to labels or subsidiaries

6. Stuart Hall, "What is this 'Black' in Black Popular Culture?" in Gina Dent, ed., *Black Popular Culture*, 28.

that operate with inferior production, marketing and promotion budgets. This, of course, ensures the inferior treatment of such artists throughout the infrastructure of the industry, from the size of a record pressing, the breadth of distribution, the quality of in-store displays, and access to quality performance venues, to exposure on radio and television, and coverage in the trade and popular press.

During a four year period from 1978 to 1982, which included the height of the disco craze, *Rolling Stone* pictured only one black musician on its cover — vocalist Donna Summer. Publisher Jann Wenner made clear the racial dimension of this practice when his magazine finally ran a cover story on Prince. "My circulation department certainly wasn't asking me to put Prince on the cover," explained Wenner. "They know the issue of color works against him. It's a fact of life that the stars of 'The Jeffersons' aren't going to sell as well as Tom Selleck."[7]

If the popular music press provided limited access for black artists, the practice of excluding them almost completely was elevated to a full-blown policy in the creation of the most powerful music outlet ever to be developed, MTV. Two years after the channel was launched, *People* magazine reported in 1983 that only sixteen of MTV's roster of 800 videos were by black artists.[8] MTV executives tried to defend their racist programming by splitting the musical hairs between rock 'n' roll, funk and rhythm and blues. Prince was rock 'n' roll (he was also signed to Warner, MTV's parent company); Michael Jackson and Rick James were not. Such thin explanations could not paper over the statistics that *Rock and Roll Confidential* reported based on a tally of *Billboard*'s MTV listings for the week of July 16, 1983: there were no African American artists in heavy rotation, none in medium rotation, none with new vidoes added and none with concerts or specials in the history of the channel. There was only Donna Summer, in light rotation.[9] Given this level of isolation as late as 1983, it is a wonder that black popular music has made any inroads into the mainstream at all. Interestingly, its influence has increased more or less steadily for the better part of this century. A look at three periods in recent music history illustrates the point.

Three Periods of Change

Tin Pan Alley centralized the popular music business in the United States at a time when European high culture was considered the hallmark of taste. Opera stars

7. Jann Wenner, quoted in *Los Angeles Times* Calendar Section, September 4, 1983, 3.
8. *People*, April 4, 1983, 31.
9. *Rock and Roll Confidential*, January 1984, 2.

were international sensations who occupied the highest rung on the entertainment ladder. European art music was considered far superior to U. S. pop music. Tin Pan Alley toppled that dominance and brought U.S. popular music out from under the shadow of European high culture. In this transition to a more popular aesthetic, however, it is important to note that European sensibilities remained central.

The ascendancy of Tin Pan Alley was coincident with the emergence of a number of African American genres: ragtime, blues, boogie woogie, jazz and swing. As with any popular enterprise, the Tin Pan Alley songwriters were open to outside influences, drinking in New York's cultural diversity from their Broadway and 28th Street cubicles. Beginning with ragtime, they borrowed superficially from African American influences for what critic Gilbert Seldes once referred to as a touch of "dash and energy."[10] "A pattern was established with the ragtime song," writes musicologist Charles Hamm, "that was to recur time and again in the twentieth century: white popular music skimmed off superficial stylistic elements of a type of music originating among black musicians, and used these to give a somewhat different, exotic flavor to white music."[11] Tin Pan Alley incorporated such influences into a "much more homogeneous style than had ever before been the case in the history of song in America."[12]

Where blues and jazz lured audiences towards Africa at the grassroots, mainstream interpretations quickly pulled them back to Europe. This, of course, was reassuring to the custodians of "good taste." It slowed the displacement of high culture, preserved the centrality of Western civilization and kept upstart African American artists in check. Conservative culture critic H. F. Mooney, for example, considered it fortunate that the influence of African American music was "limited by compromises with middle class conventions,"[13] noting that it was "'polished' . . . so as to conform to the standards of European rendition."[14] Revealing his bias toward high culture, Mooney asserted: "The highest compliment most of the public could pay to big-band jazz between 1928 and 1950 was 'symphonic' or 'advanced.'"[15] Regarding African American artists, he observed:

10. Gilbert Seldes, *The Seven Lively Arts* (1924) (New York: A. S. Barnes, 1957), 71.

11. Charles Hamm, *Yesterdays: Popular Song in America* (New York: W. W. Norton, 1983), 321.

12. Ibid., 290.

13. H. F. Mooney, "Popular Music since the 1920s: The Significance of Shifting Taste," in Jonathan Eisen, ed., *The Age of Rock* (New York: Vintage Books, 1969), 10.

14. Ibid., 11.

15. Ibid., 10–11.

Middle-class Negroes who desired to "come up," as they put it, during the 1930s and the 1940s responded to the smoothly harmonized arrangements of a white Jimmy Dorsey's watered-down jazz. Duke Ellington himself was influenced by Guy Lombardo's "sweetest music this side of heaven," and brought something of the sound of the Roosevelt Hotel ballroom to Harlem. Commercial orchestras of the period around 1920–50 followed more or less the "safe bet"—the aesthetic aspirations of the middle-class market—as did, indeed, most of the big Negro bands."[16]

Not just "white" but also "watered-down" were unabashedly positive values for Mooney. Tin Pan Alley's music was described as bland and inoffensive not by its detractors but by its advocates. These too were positive values. At the same time, in moving popular music out of the shadows, Tin Pan Alley opened the door to influences from the grassroots, the most important of which were African American. Therefore, in the first period we see the emergence of popular culture as dominant, we see an awareness of African American influences, but these are safely incorporated into European stylistic patterns. It would be left for rhythm and blues and its emergence as rock 'n' roll to precipitate the next disruption.

By all accounts, the eruption of rock 'n' roll was marked by a profound shift in cultural values on the part of mainstream youth away from European sensibilities and toward African sensibilities. This can be seen in a cursory look at rhythmic structure, the call and response style, the use of blue notes, and improvisation.[17] Moreover, African American elements were no longer regulated by the constraints of white middle class decorum. Whereas before, African American influences were incorporated into a European paradigm, now African American style became the standard. A performer's authenticity was determined by how well he measured up. Peter Wicke explains:

> Elvis Presley or Bill Haley were no longer merely taking set pieces from blues and rhythm & blues and imposing them as superficial effects on quite different musical categories. Their popularity was founded precisely on the fact that they were copying Afro-American music with all its characteristic features, including the performance style of black musi-

16. Ibid., 10.

17. For a more complete discussion of these elements see Reebee Garofalo, "Crossing Over, 1939–1989," in Jannette L. Dates and William Barlow, eds., *Split Image: African Americans in the Mass Media*, 2d ed. (Washington, D. C.: Howard University Press, 1993), 75–79.

cians, as closely as possible. What was happening was a complete reversal of the earlier situation. Whereas before, white musicians had adapted elements of the Afro-American musical tradition to their own aesthetic ideas, now they were trying to suit their performance to the aesthetics of Afro-American music.[18]

Even with this degree of cultural conversion there still existed a societal need for white interpreters to make the music more acceptable. This is precisely why Elvis Presley was so complex and so controversial a character. Elvis represented both the triumph of African American culture and its vulnerability to the power of white supremacy. The second period, then, can be seen as one in which African American cultural sensibilities become dominant, but still with a need for white interpreters. It is in this area that rap has taken the next step.

Rap, writes David Toop, "was the new music by virtue of its finding a way to absorb all other music."[19] In this sense rap turned the Tin Pan Alley practice of skimming African American music on its head. Rap has incorporated everything from James Brown to Kraftwerk, from heavy metal to television theme music into a genre that preserves the dominance of its African American heritage. Just as bebop subverted individual Tin Pan Alley standards, rap inverts the entire Tin Pan Alley formula.

The progressive voices in rap seem, almost invariably, to be nourished by an Afrocentric impulse. Indeed, one of the things that makes rap so interesting is that it is perhaps the only form of African American popular music that has become more Afrocentric as it has gained mainstream acceptance. "It's a fresh approach," explains Public Enemy producer Bill Stephney. "Instead of seeking to produce crossover products that sometimes dilute the black experience, this posse embraces its own culture and makes that the basis of its success. It's about people coming over to *us*."[20] In this way, rap has avoided the usual pattern in which mainstream success is linked to an increase of white performers in the genre. The Beastie Boys and Vanilla Ice, for example, have tallied huge record sales, but have been largely incidental to the cultural trajectory of rap. Thus, in the third period, we see an Afrocentric genre that has achieved overwhelming

18. Peter Wicke, *Rock Music: Culture, Aesthetics, and Sociology* (New York: Cambridge University Press, 1990), 16–17.

19. David Toop, *Rap Attack 2: African Rap to Global Hip Hop* (New York: Serpents Tail, 1991), 154.

20. Bill Stephney, quoted in *Entertainment Weekly*, May 15, 1992, 34.

mainstream success, but this time without the necessity for (or the intrusion of) white interpreters.

This should not be taken to be the completion of the cultural dialectic, however. Externally, there are the dangers of censorship and repression which seek to force rap back into isolation. Against these forces, rap asserts itself with a vengeance. But there are internal tensions as well. The same aggressiveness that encourages rap's boldness also seems to privilege a male heterosexist posturing, to the detriment of other progressive urges. Stuart Hall comments: "certain ways in which black men continue to live out their counter-identities as black masculinites . . . are, when viewed from along other axes of difference, the very masculine identities that are oppressive to women, that claim visibility for their hardness only at the expense of the vulnerability of black women and the feminization of gay black men."[21] Filmmaker Isaac Julien puts the matter even more starkly: "The rise of rap as signifier of hetero black masculinity . . . has made it difficult for more complex representations of blackness. . . . Even Afrocentrism's privileging of a new black aesthetic is not dialogic enough to think through the 'hybridity of ethnicity,' let alone liberated enough to include 'queerness' in its 'blackness.' "[22]

While there is certainly cause for celebrating the overall progress of African American popular music, we cannot afford to be blind to its internal shortcomings any more than we can afford to be less than vigilant regarding the potential for repression. The gains of African American popular music must be seen as part of a complex and contradictory dialectical struggle which is far from over. In the current period, global forces must also be added to the dialectical mix: the local and the global are now inextricably bound in a way that adds another dimension to the foregoing discussion.

The Global and the Local

The 1980s marked a new period in the history of the music business—one that clearly defined it as global—both because technological wonders like the blanket coverage of satellite transmission and the incredible portability of cassette technology made the world a much smaller place, and because the industry was beset by a recession which forced it to look to international markets as a condition of

21. Stuart Hall, "What is this 'Black' in Black Popular Culture?" p. 31.

22. Isaac Julien, "Black Is, Black Ain't: Notes on De-Essentializing Black Identities," in Gina Dent, ed., *Black Popular Culture* (Seattle: Bay Press, 1992), 258.

further growth.[23] In all of these developments, African American artists figured prominently. None more so than Michael Jackson.

Despite his own ambiguous relationship to blackness, the path of Jackson's career has had important implications for the treatment of African American artists. After a struggle in which his videos of "Beat It" and "Billy Jean" played the pivotal role in breaking the color line on MTV, his *Thriller* album, which achieved international sales of some 40 million units, pointed the way out of the recession for the industry. Jackson then enabled the industry to put its best international foot forward by taking the first American giant step in developing the phenomenon that would come to be known as "charity rock." "We Are the World," co-written by Jackson and Lionel Richie, produced by Quincy Jones, with organizational input from Harry Belafonte, was clearly a product of African American leadership. As the U. S. companion to Bob Geldof's Band Aid project in Britain, it helped provide the basis for the Live Aid concert, the largest single event in human history in terms of audience size. Just as *Thriller* occasioned a new generation of international superstars, Live Aid ushered in an era of mega-events which made maximal use of the new technology.[24]

From a political point of view, charity rock was a paradoxical phenomenon. On the one hand, it enabled the music industry to put on a humanitarian face even as it exploited a veritable goldmine of untapped markets. Live Aid was simultaneously broadcast to an international audience of 1.5 billion people. On the other hand, these projects focused international attention on Africa in a way that was simply unprecedented. In the process, they created a climate in which musicians from countries all over the world felt compelled to follow suit with African famine relief projects of their own. A partial list illustrates the point: Band Aid, "Do They Know It's Christmas?" (Great Britain, thirty-seven artists); USA for Africa, "We Are the World" (U. S. A., thirty-seven artists); Northern Lights, "Tears Are Not Enough" (Canada); Band fur Ethiopia, "Nackt im Wind" (West Germany); Chanteurs sans Frontieres, "Ethiopie" (France, thirty-six artists); "Leven Zonder Honger" (Belguim); "Samen" (The Netherlands); "E.A.T.," East African Tragedy (Australia); "Tam Tam pour l'Ethiopie" (Africa, fifty artists

23. For a more in-depth discussion of these developments, see Reebee Garofalo, "Whose World What Beat: The Transnational Music Industry, Identity, and Cultural Imperialism," *World of Music* 2(1993):16–32.

24. See Reebee Garofalo, "Understanding Mega-Events: If We Are the World, Then How Do We Change It," in Reebee Garofalo, ed., *Rockin' the Boat: Mass Music and Mass Movements* (Boston: South End Press, 1992), 15–36.

including Youssou N'Dour, Hugh Masakela, Manu Dibangu, and King Sunny Ade.)[25]

While this initial burst of projects could easily be accused of trivializing starvation, it also opened up possibilities for cultural politics that were previously unthinkable. The themes for subsequent projects like Farm Aid, "Sun City," the Amnesty International Tours, and the Nelson Mandela Tributes took a decidedly more political turn, while still reaching audiences in the hundreds of millions. Recognizing the power of such events, Nelson Mandela delivered his first international address outside South Africa at a rock concert in London's Wembley Stadium celebrating his release from prison.

The global stage of mega-events also provided a moment of opportunity, albeit a limited one, where globalization itself was a two-way process. While Anglo American music was disproportionately broadcast to a worldwide audience, the international sounds of artists like Youssou N'Dour, Aswad, and Sly and Robbie also gained greater access to the world market. It is more than a coincidence that the development of charity rock, with its primary focus on Africa, paralleled the emergence of "world beat," a marketing category dominated by African and African-influenced sounds.

To bring the discussion back home, I would note that the internationalization of the music industry also had a curious effect on its domestic marketing structure. As *Thriller* paved the way for a limited number of international superstars, a surprising number of these new artists turned out to be African American. In addition to Michael Jackson, there were Lionel Richie, Prince, Diana Ross, Tina Turner and Whitney Houston, among others. This was perhaps the first hint that the greater cosmopolitanism of a world market might produce some changes in the complexion of popular music at home. I suggest that there is a connection between the acceptance of a greater diversity of artists in the international arena and the fact that the promotional clout that can lead to superstardom at home has become that much more available to African Americans. Nineteen of the top fifty albums for 1985 were by black artists.

Recently a number of other African American artists, not only black pop superstars like Michael Jackson and Whitney Houston, but also so-called alternative black artists like Living Colour, Tracy Chapman and Robert Cray, and gold and platinum selling rappers such as Public Enemy, D.J. Jazzy Jeff and the Fresh Prince, Queen Latifah, Ice T and Snoop Doggy Dogg, have also begun

25. Stan Rijven, "Rock for Ethiopia," presented at the Third International Conference on Popular Music Studies, Montreal, July, 1985, 3–7.

to transcend the confines of second-class marketing. Employing a variety of styles which can be traced back through various strands of the African American experience, these artists have been successfully marketed through pop outlets without losing a connection to the black audience. The recent pairings of rap artists with grunge and heavy metal groups in the annual Lollapalooza tours is a concept that would have been unimaginable just a decade ago. One might speculate that such direct marketing may have had some effect on why rap has been able to succeed in the mainstream without white interpreters.

While these advances may be cause for cautious optimism, it is necessary not to lose sight of how far we still have to go. Marable correctly argues that "blackness" should be defined "as a political category for the mobilization of several different ethnic groups. . . . We must find new room in our identity as people of color to include all other oppressed national minorities—Chicanos, Puerto Ricans, Asian/Pacific Americans, Native Americans, and other people of African descent. We must find the common ground we share with oppressed people who are not national minorities—working class people, the physically challenged, the homeless, the unemployed, and those Americans who suffer discrimination because they are lesbian or gay."[26] If our current fascination with multiculturalism is to be more than just a short-lived flirtation with the fashion of the moment, it must account not only for differences of race and ethnicity but also for differences of age, gender, sexual orientation and class.

Reebee Garofalo teaches in the College of Public and Community Service at the University of Massachusetts, Boston. He is the editor of *Rockin' the Boat: Mass Music and Mass Movements* (Boston: South End Press 1992). His current reseach concerns censorship and social responsibility in popular music and he is writing a social history of popular music since the invention of the phonograph.

---

26. Manning Marable, "Race, Identity, and Political Culture," 302.

Check Yo Self, Before You Wreck Yo Self: Variations on a Political Theme in Rap Music and Popular Culture

Todd Boyd

Rap music has clearly been established as the most visible form of African American cultural expression in contemporary society in the United States. This emergence of rap music also marks a change in African American popular culture specific to the late 1980s and early 1990s. The recent proliferation of African American film and televisual representation, with rap music as a strong influence, offers a touchstone for conversations that define contemporary African American popular culture, both in the academic and public domain.[1] One of the most interesting discussions engendered by this contemporary cultural nexus is the resurgence of a politically charged voice, which these forms provide a perfect venue for expressing. The articulation of cultural politics in contemporary society, using a visually sophisticated hip-hop culture as the cipher is the focus of this article.

The rise and decline of this political discourse in popular culture are also closely tied to the public presentation of popular forms. The political dimensions

---

1. Recently works devoted to analyzing rap music and contemporary culture have appeared with increasing regularity, especially in light of past omissions. For instance, academic texts such as Houston A. Baker, Jr.'s *Rap Music, Black Studies, and the Academy* (1993), Tricia Rose's *Black Noise: Rap Music and Black Culture in Contemporary America* (1994), and a large segment of Gina Dent's edited volume *Black Popular Culture* (1993) are devoted to the subject. In addition, former *Village Voice* writers Nelson George through his work on rap, largely chronicled in *Buppies, B-Boys, Baps, and Bohos* (1993) and Greg Tate through his *Flyboy in the Buttermilk* (1992), have gained increased attention as authorities on rap. Also, the popularity of magazines like *The Source* and *Vibe* add to this recent phenomenon.

Public Culture 1994, 7: 289–312

of popular culture reached an apex with the release of Public Enemy's second album *It Takes a Nation of Millions to Hold Us Back* (1988), but failed to create sustained movement which connected both cultural artifacts and political events as did similar movements in the late 1960s and early 1970s.[2]

The emergence of gangsta rap is associated with an open rejection of politics. Dr. Dre's ever popular "Dre Day" expressed a complete disregard for "medallions, dreadlocks, and black fists," obvious markers for the more politically minded aspirations of those interested in Black nationalism, commonly called Afrocentricity. This rejection of a political agenda is consistent with Spike Lee's mainstreaming of the most important figure of Black nationalism in his 1992 film, *Malcolm X*. These events mark the end of a political flirtation in rap music and by extension, African American popular culture.

The highs and lows of political discourse in rap music — similar to what Cornel West calls the "new cultural politics" — and the gradual displacement of this agenda by gangsta rap can be found in the meteoric rise of 1993 Grammy award-winning best new act, Arrested Development. Using images of critical spirituality, southern existence, stylized forms of dress and an overall ideology of Afrocentrism, Arrested Development engaged an empowered critique of both external racism and internal neglect, a critique which set it apart from other rap acts in the early 1990s. This overtly political stance endeared the group to many as the contemporary embodiment of a progressive discourse surrounding culture, society and politics.

My analysis concerns the "new cultural politics" of Arrested Development as it pertains to the opening up of discussions surrounding conflicts between race and class identity, youth culture, violence and the compromising influences of commercialism on political content. In relation to these broader issues, this critique looks at the contentious relationship between modernity and postmodernity in contemporary African American culture and the perception of an overall cultural decline brought about by urbanization throughout African American society. This analysis is also informed by an examination of Ice Cube, who as the antithesis to Arrested Development, combines both political images and icons of gangsta culture. Though focused on Arrested Development, attention to Ice Cube — his objection to nihilism, discussion of cultural assimilation as form of class critique

2. For an extended explanation regarding the "death of politics" relative to popular culture see my analysis (1993) of Spike Lee's *Malcolm X*, "Popular Culture and Political Empowerment," in the *Cineaste* critical symposium on the same subject.

and embrace of the Nation of Islam—discloses the strengths and limitations of political discourse in popular culture as it functions in contemporary society.

Rap and the New Cultural Politics of Difference

Rap as a cultural artifact has the ability to analyze the mutually illuminating yet divergent categories of race, class and gender in African American society. More often than not, questions of race dominate both popular and critical discussions about rap music. Though this discussion of race is undoubtedly important, contemporary society, especially in the post-Reagan-Bush era, forces one to address the influence of the class struggle in African American society. At the same time, an empowered female voice that fuses the issues of race, class and gender also opens up the possibilities for understanding the nuances of contemporary African American culture. As Tricia Rose points out, "through their lyrics and video images, black women rappers form a dialogue with working-class black women and men, offering young black women a small but potent culturally-reflexive public space" (1990:114). Although the female voice in rap has gained significant momentum over the last few years there remains much to be desired, both artistically and in terms of intellectual response.[3]

The cultural and economic base of this music emphasizes African presence in American society, which foregrounds race and class struggle and makes them paramount for understanding this cultural practice. Thus, certain elements of rap music have the potential to exemplify what Cornel West has called the "new cultural politics of difference":

> The new cultural politics of difference are neither simply oppositional in contesting the mainstream for inclusion, nor transgressive in the avant-gardist sense of shocking conventional bourgeois audiences. Rather, they are distinct articulations of talented contributors to culture who desire to align themselves with demoralized, demobilized, depoliticized and disorganized people in order to empower and enable social action, and, if possible, to enlist collective insurgency for the expansion of freedom, democracy, and individuality. (1993:19–20)

3. In addition to female rappers like Salt n Pepa, Queen Latifah and MC Lyte, whom Rose (1990) discusses extensively in her article, the recent emergence of female gangsta rappers like Yo Yo and Boss offers interesting possibilities for the continued exploration of gender issues in rap music.

African American culture is replete with examples that demonstrate this new cultural politics of difference, particularly in regard to the importance of lower class politics for understanding race.[4] By the late 1980s and the early 1990s discourse about "authentic" African American culture revolved around the exploits and endeavors of the lumpen proletariat. In this construction race and class consistently informed one another.

The most overt demonstration of this desire for cultural authenticity was white rapper Vanilla Ice's claim that he had grown up amongst African American poverty and was once a victim of gang violence. Although he was white, he claimed that he could identify with blackness because he himself had experienced its poverty-stricken lifestyle. His claim to being black was not based on his race, but on the extent of his association with lower-class African American existence: his class status made him black. Similarly the all-white rap group Young Black Teenagers, asserts that blackness is a "state of mind," undoubtedly a ghetto mindset. The impetus for forming the rock band in the Irish film *The Commitments* (1991) offers another example. According to the main character, the group can identify with African American music due to its multiple oppression as Northern Irish working-class Catholics: "The Irish are the Blacks of Europe, and the Dubliners are the Blacks of Ireland, and the Northsiders are the Blacks of Dublin. So say it loud, I'm Black and I'm proud." In this film, race, as expressed through the specific cultural artifact—the music of James Brown—justifies an argument rooted in the political economy of class articulation in European society.

This emphasis on the working class, using the ghetto or the "hood" as the dominant metaphor, has been most vividly presented in rap music. Whereas the

4. Contemporary examples of African American cinema demonstrate the fusion of race and class politics in the artifacts which are produced. We have witnessed the popularity of the working-class African American male as cipher for racial consciousness in *Do The Right Thing* (Lee 1989), *Straight Out of Brooklyn* (Rich 1991), *Strictly Business* (Hooks 1992), *Livin Large* (Schultz 1992), *Boyz in the Hood* (Singleton 1992) and *Menace II Society* (Hughes 1993). Each of these films portrays the struggles of being an African American male in a society of oppression and restrictive opportunity. These films gain their cultural authenticity by foregrounding class struggle within the context of race. This is in contrast to public perception surrounding *The Cosby Show* (1984–1992), which was often thought of as being inauthentic since the program concentrated on an upper-middle-class African American family. I would argue that the vociferous public claims of being superficial on the issue of class eventually influenced the program's creator and producers to at least recognize the possibility of class conflict by the inclusion of the lower-class character Pam as a central family member in the last few years of the program's first-run existence. The influence of class consciousness as critical in defining authenticity also indirectly generates the need for situation comedies such as *Roseanne* (white-working class assertion) and *The Fresh Prince of Bel Air* (the conflict between the ghetto and bourgeois African American society).

earlier days of rap were dominated by macho posturing, "dick" grabbing and braggadocio carried to hyperbolic proportions, recently much of the thematic core of rap music has presented a recurring narrative of his life in the hood. With the advent of west coast (primarily, Los Angeles) rap, the life of a young African American male and his struggles to survive have become the recurrent theme in demonstrating one's firm entrenchment in the jungle-like setting known as the ghetto.[5] Rappers who resisted the plunge into this genre were considered imposters. Thus a concentration on class struggle has been central to defining the cutting edge of rap music during this phase.

The reliance on this now clichéd narrative and the media's eager embrace of this ghetto lifestyle as monolithic within African American society encouraged the eventual proliferation of the hood scenario from an initially sublime posture to the utterly ridiculous. Through an intense combination of media manipulation and artistic culpability, the issue of class struggle has been reduced to mere spectacle and has not received sustained critical interrogation of domination and oppression. This genre of rap is becoming the modern day equivalent of the 1970s "Blaxploitation" film; the early films, works of African American grass roots financial struggle, were turned into valuable products of the culture that were duplicated, depoliticized and ultimately devoid of all cultural significance.

Rap offers a strong representation of the emotional range of urban, mostly male, existence. At the same time, the commodifying impulses of the music industry have opened a space for selling cultural products, which in their very construction undermine the structure distributing them. It is well known that rap's massive popular audience is comprised of dominant and marginal audiences. It is also apparent that capitalistic courting of this massive audience at some level reifies the music's political message. The point where radical political discourse meets the demands of the marketplace and the two merge, however, remains an important issue. The space between the points where radical political discourse can critique dominant culture and dominant culture becomes financially viable through the selling of this oppositional discourse is the only available space for a reasoned understanding of contemporary political culture. West's notion of a politics of difference sees the current cultural situation as indicative of an "inescapable double bind." This bind involves the reality of financial dependence that defines the structural dimension of rap music as a metaphorical "escape" from

5. The following West Coast rappers exemplify thematically my argument for Black male angst: Snoop Doggy Dogg, Ice-T, Easy E, Niggas Wit Attitude (NWA), Compton's Most Wanted (CMW), Dr. Dre, King Tee, 2 Pac, Paris, Too Short and most notably, Ice Cube.

oppressive conditions, much like society's regard for African American professional athletics. The rapper, in this sense, is "simultaneously progressive and co-opted" (1990:20).

Although a thin theoretical line divides radical political discourse in rap and the commodifying impulses of the dominant culture, an understanding of popular culture requires critique of both sides. Thus, the contemporary spectacle of the ghetto primarily operates to reinforce the dominant society's view of African American culture as a deprived wasteland. "Gangsta" rap describes the music's original commentary on the horrific nuances of ghetto life. In many cases, what formerly was a radical critique of repressive state apparatuses, as in *Fuck tha Police*, has been transformed into a series of unapologetic retread demands openly calling for a "Gangsta Bitch" or emphatically stating that the "Bitch Betta Have My Money." Too often, class struggle, in this regressive trend, becomes a series of rhetorical catch phrases and visual signposts lacking political or social relevance.

Yet some resist the redundant "nigga in the hood" scenario. Instead of relying solely on this overworked and most manipulated of clichés, a small core of rappers continue to advance a progressive political agenda that analyzes race, class and in some cases, gender through rigorous cultural critique. As West states, "there can be no artistic breakthrough or social progress without some form of crisis in civilization" (1990:20), we must continually engage our analysis of rappers who reject the simplistic confines of spectacle-making and attempt to remain politically progressive beyond media reduction. In the words of Ice Cube: we must attempt to understand those who stay "true to the game."

Foremost in this group of political rappers concerned with cultural politics are Public Enemy, Sister Souljah, Ice Cube, KRS-One and Arrested Development. A certain Afrocentric theme runs consistently throughout all of them, yet their individual positions cover a spectrum of topics related to living in late-twentieth century American society. All of these acts need thorough critical scrutiny to further extrapolate their meaning. The discussion here analyzes varying notions of cultural politics as expressed through separate, but distinct examples and uses Arrested Development and Ice Cube to clarify and extend these examples.

Arrested Development

The Atlanta based rap group Arrested Development was a leading new rap act of 1992. The group's male and female members sing as well as rap: their image centers around dreadlocks and African style clothing. This is in opposition to both the "b-boy" image of the east coast and the image of the west coast gangsta.

Arrested Development suggests a strong stylistic exception to conventions determined by the prevalence of the more popular east and west coast images.

Arrested Development shares its context with a section of the contemporary African American college-age audience that uses African fashion and hair styles to demonstrate their political connection to Africa. In this sense, fashion and style function as both icon and commodity. This emphasis on an Afrocentric style is a response to the monotonous fashions of other rappers and a rejection of the conservative preppie image favored by some white college students which flourished throughout the Reagan-Bush era. This fashionable Afrocentricity is easily devalued as it is transformed into mass commodity. Kobena Mercer argues that hair styles like the afro and dreadlocks "counter-politicized the signifier of ethnic devalorization redefining blackness as a positive attribute, but on the other hand, perhaps not, because within a relatively short period both styles became rapidly depoliticized and, with varying degrees of resistance, both were incorporated into mainstream fashions in the dominant culture" (1990:251). This situation demonstrates, once again, the contradictory nature of political culture in the age of commodity fetishism. Signifiers of leftist political culture are easily corrupted as they are coopted by the fashion industry of dominant society.

Musically, Arrested Development challenges traditions of rap, particularly through its use of singing in conjunction with the traditional rapping over beats. The content of its songs addresses topics ranging from homelessness, the search for spirituality and African Americans' connection with Africa. The group's popular appeal is demonstrated by its appearance as opening act on the 1992-1993 En Vogue tour, the use of the song "Tennessee" as the theme for the short-lived NBC situation comedy *Here and Now*, its appearance as the only contemporary voice on the soundtrack for Lee's *Malcolm X* (1992) and its selection as both "Best New Artist" and "Best Rap Artist" during 1993 Grammy Awards.

Arrested Development benefits from other African American cultural practices that have foregrounded a leftist bohemian political agenda. Arrested Development belongs to the musical tradition that includes the 1970s band Sly and the Family Stone—this group is sampled on "People Everyday"—the multicultural rhythm and blues group War and most recently African American female folk singer Tracy Chapman. This combination of a derivative folk song content, politics associated with the peace movement and rap is probably best exemplified by the rap organization Native Tongues, of which groups like De La Soul and A Tribe Called Quest, are notable members.[6]

6. As an example, De La's first single, "Me, Myself, and I" critiqued how many rappers imitate a monolithic rap posture as opposed to being oneself. Thus, they rejected the b-boy style of wearing gold chains, Kangol caps, and lambskin coats for their own stylized attire of uncombed hair and

A close analysis of Arrested Development's "People Everyday" song and video assists in revealing their political agenda. Using the sample from Sly Stone's track, "Everyday People," Arrested Development argues for a kind of cultural innocence or purity. This notion of purity is exemplified through a juxtaposition of the harsh urban realities of the street prominent in contemporary rap and their embrace of the premodern "country," the simplicity of a rural landscape. At one level the group attempts to be all inclusive in its outlook, promoting an Afrocentric version of political correctness that critiques race, class and gender, as opposed to privileging the male dominated discourse often associated with rap. Yet in doing so the group offers a position that unintentionally erects a class hierarchy while simultaneously trying to destroy existing hierarchies.

The video's time frame spans one day which is marked by sunrise and sunset at the beginning and end of the video. This alerts viewers to the group's concern with time and the extent to which time and space define African American politics. The title of the album, *3 Years, 5 Months, and 2 Days in the Life of Arrested Development* further suggests the group's concern for time.

The video begins by calling on multiple dimensions of African oral tradition. Group member, Headliner, offers a verbal and visual greeting; this is followed by a close close-up of his lips. In American society lips have gone from a regressive stereotype that emphasized the excessive fullness of African American lips through numerous visual objects in American culture such as Sambo pictures and lawn jockeys, to the current trend that uses this fullness to visually celebrate Africanness. White models and actresses also appropriate these features through chemical treatment as a fashionable sign of beauty.[7] This contemporary example of exploitative appropriation is what bell hooks describes as "eating the other."

nondescript baggy clothes. As the title, "Me, Myself, and I" states, they were concerned with asserting their own identity, while simultaneously offering a plural definition of self and affirming that blackness contained multiple subject positions. This reaffirms that blackness can be defined from multiple perspectives. De La Soul assumes this posture for its first album *3 Feet High and Rising*. On its second album the group boldly declared that "De La is Dead," short-circuiting the continuation of this style of rap.

7. The function of African American lips in the larger culture can also be seen in two recent cinematic examples. Using the close-up and emphasis on the lips as a derogatory stereotype can be seen in the recurring shots of the African American female radio announcer in the Walter Hill film *The Warriors* (1979). Though the character offers exterior commentary on the plight of the main characters, the Warriors street gang, as they proceed throughout the narrative's mysterious path, this character has no identity, she is reduced to her function without recourse to any sustained narrative or visual involvement other than these repeated tight shots that emphasize her "nigger lips."

More recently and in contrast to the earlier example, this tight shot of the lips was utilized in Spike Lee's *Do The Right Thing* (1989) with the character of Mr. Senor Love Daddy. In this case this emphasis on lips becomes an example of the bodily vehicle for the oral tradition. While also

From this tight close-up, the camera moves to a series of rapidly edited shots that alternate between Headliner's reggae-style call and the group's response. This visually replicates the verbal call and response pattern. The video's camerawork and editing disrupts classical Hollywood cinema's shot, the reverse shot pattern. It also alternates between black and white and color images, and privileges the oral to motivate the visual direction of the iconography. Thus, oral culture is used in conjunction with the character's motivation of visuals to create a specifically African American music video.

Another series of rapidly edited shots depict the group's reliance on a strongly rural aesthetic. Riding on the back of a pick-up truck, the equally mixed group of male and female participants are shown in their loosely fitting cast-off style African clothing; their hair is either in knotty dreadlocks or shaved. This emphasis on the rural is supplemented by various shots of the wide open landscape, dirt roads, wooden porches, which create an idyllic series of visual icons and foreground the technologically untainted and morally empowered version of African American life which Arrested Development promotes throughout the entire album, and especially in the song "People Everyday."

Little children run, play and ride their bicycles, and older people relax and enjoy rural life; these images illustrate the political agenda that informs Arrested Development. This visual setting evokes a rejection of modernity that harkens back to the "pre-New Negro" ideals of Booker T. Washington. These ideals opposed the virtues of southern agrarian living to utopian images of the industrial-

---

functioning as the voice of exterior commentary, Love Daddy articulates the film's rational direction from his empowered position, and is also used as the voice of reason in relation to the societal conflicts presented in the film. In addition, Love Daddy connects the film to its oral roots when he enlists in the roll call of prominent African American musical figures, both past and present. This use of the lips as vehicle for the oral tradition is also referenced repeatedly throughout *Mo Better Blues* (1990). The film's main character, Bleek Gillam, is shown as being obsessed with his lips as they determine his professional and emotional stability, especially when connected with the jazz that emerges from his trumpet.

Arrested Development's use of this racial trope can be seen as an extension of Mr. Senor Love Daddy and Bleek's function as oral facilitators within the Spike Lee films. This racial trope is also an embrace of the Africanness of their bodily features and, in turn, a rejection of what had been thought of as the traditionally Eurocentric standards of beauty prevalent in American society. Much like the often-mentioned *griot* of African society the lips as visual metaphor, emphasized through the extreme close-up, in this case, becomes particularly useful in exemplifying the oral nature of African American culture. Also, the critique of dominant standards of beauty, at both white and African American levels, can also be seen in the group's most prominent female character, who sports a shaved head. While Irish female singer Sinead O'Connor is most visible with this style in popular white culture, the female participant in Arrested Development uses this stylistic device as an affirmation of the Afrocentric cultural project that the group pursues.

ized north. Washington's argument suggested that the virtues of autonomy made possible by this southern agrarian lifestyle and economy were superior to the urban lifestyle in the industrialized north. Washington's exhortation, "lay your buckets down where you are" expresses his desire to make the south, in all its simplicity, the preferred landscape of his contemporaries and future generations of African Americans as well. The angst associated with the dilemma of migrating north or staying in the south informs numerous other cultural forms, including blues singer Juke Boy Bonner's comically titled cut, "I'm Going Back to the Country Where They Don't Burn the Buildings Down," soul singer Gladys Knight's hit, "Midnight Train to Georgia," August Wilson's play, *The Piano Lesson*, Julie Dash's film, *Daughter of the Dust* and Charles Burnett's film, *To Sleep with Anger*.

Arrested Development updates this theme in its first single, "Tennessee." In a video similar to "People Everyday" the group rhetorically engages in a quizzical, and at times, cynical exploration of African American existence in contemporary society. As if praying, the group wonders aloud about its tenuous place in a modern but problem-filled America: "Lord I've been really stressed/Down and out, losing ground/Although I am Black and proud/Problems got me pessimistic/Brothers and sisters keep messin' up/Why does it have to be so damn tough?"

The song's refrain which is also used in the introduction to the sitcom *Here and Now*, suggests the possibility of freedom and understanding that lies ahead. Speech asks the Lord to "take me to another place/take me to another land/make me forget all the hurt/let me understand your plan." This spiritually informed intellectual journey using "Tennessee" as the metaphor of freedom is similar to the musical excursions of John Coltrane during the latter part of his life and career. On the ever popular *A Love Supreme* and all of his later albums, Coltrane spiritually expresses his intellectual and creative explorations.

In the same sense, Arrested Development sees "Tennessee" as the location of history and a site of struggle that informs both past and present: "walk the streets my forefathers walked/climb the trees my forefathers hung from/ask those trees for all their wisdom." According to Arrested Development, return to these roots of struggle is necessary for understanding contemporary society and the placement of the African American in these problematic circumstances: "now I see the importance of history/Why my people be in the mess that they be/Many journeys to freedom made in vain/By brothers on the corner playing ghetto games." Arrested Development offers, at one level, a political impossibility. Their nostalgia for an earlier African American culture romanticizes southern roots, premodernity and a better quality of life. This is not only simplistic, but also untenable given the demands of contemporary society. On another level, however, it offers an incisive critique of destructive elements in contemporary African American culture.

Arrested Development's intellectual posture foregrounds a globally leftist notion of Afrocentric discourse and takes rap music in a new direction. The group critiques how modernized society destroys positive aspects of the supposed earlier communal nature of African American culture, and exposes the self-inflicted problems associated with "brothers on the corner," a reference to the urge to romanticize urban Black male ghetto culture in other rap circles. A religiously self-critical orientation is strengthened by the presence of the group's spiritual advisor, Baba Oje whose intellectually empowered voice articulates guidance for the future by invoking the past and opposing it to the seductions of the present. As I have already asserted, the group's concern with time makes possible a radical critique of political and cultural space in rap music and contemporary African American culture.

Arrested Development's song and video for "People Everyday" extends the practice of self-critique within the African American community and in particular addresses the status of women. The group advocates progressive gender politics, especially given the usual agenda of male rap. Arrested Development includes both male and female rappers/singers. The female rappers have equal voice in defining the group's political project. This collaborative effort, like the critical academic endeavor undertaken by bell hooks and Cornel West in *Breaking Bread* (1991), demonstrates the possibilities of empowered political discourse that rejects misogyny and favors collective articulation.

During the extended call and response segment of "People Everyday," female rapper, Aerle Taree, responds to Speech's call. She often repeats the last portion of his dialogue in order to strengthen her point. The point where Speech refers to his passivity, "but I ain't Ice Cube," Aerle Taree replies with an ironic "Who?" This demonstrates the group's dialectical self-consciousness regarding Ice Cube's political struggles; it also indicates Arrested Development's reluctance to identify itself with the aggressively militant posture of African American masculinity of macho rappers like Ice Cube. The female voice again becomes significant during the video's conclusion when Montesho Eshe states the moral of the story and has the last word.

"People Everyday" also focuses on gender issues. Arrested Development, particularly Speech, is contrasted to what it defines as a "group of brothers." Throughout the video we see black and white shots of African American males who personify media stereotypes of macho, working-class behavior. This group of brothers holds forty-ounce bottles of malt liquor, grabs their crotches and laughs amongst themselves. When an African-attired Black woman approaches they encircle her. After one of the men grabs her buttocks, the other men reward him with a "dap" for displaying his masculinity. The lyrics emphasize this obvious sexual harassment: "My day was going great and my soul was at ease/Until a group of brothers started buggin out/Drinkin the 40 oz./Going the nigga route/Disrespecting my Black Queen/Holding their crotches and being obscene." Speech's reference to his Black Queen extends the group's valorization of women expressed through the lyrics.

This segment also clearly demarcates the distinction between the intellectual politics of Arrested Development and lower-class male rappers, who display their hostility towards African American women and other African Americans who do not fit into their lower class stereotypes. This is evident in the proclamation that they came to "test Speech cuz of my hair doo/and the loud bright colors that I wear, boo/I was a target cause I'm a fashion misfit/and the outfit that I'm wearing brothers dissin it." Speech's Afrocentric style, and by extension his politics, are rejected by the brothers as unwelcome in their small, ghettoized world. Much like the overpublicized Los Angeles gang culture of identification by "colors," the brothers in the video identify not only on the basis of race, but on the basis of distinctive class indicators, particularly clothing and appearance. Thus, like gangbangers, the brothers are presented as destroying their own African American community through debauchery and violence.

This distinction between the politically correct behavior of Arrested Development and the group of brothers is based on the difference, according to Speech, between a "nigga" and an "African." In numerous media interviews, Speech defines a nigga as someone who realizes that he/she is oppressed and wallows in it; the African realizes his or her oppression and attempts to overcome it through knowledge. The terms themselves have an extensive history in rap music. Nigga has often been the calling card of rappers who consider themselves products and practitioners of the ghetto life. The "hardest" and often the most confrontational rappers have defined themselves as niggas in opposition to the dominant society. For instance, NWA, having called their 1991 album *EFIL4SAGGIN* ("Niggas 4 Life", spelled backwards) proclaim that "Real Niggas Don't Die." Ice T boldly alerts his listeners that "I'm a nigga in America and I don't care what you are," and rejects "African American and Black" as inconsistent with his ghetto identity. Ice Cube has described himself as both "the nigga you love to hate" and "the wrong nigga to fuck wit." In each instance nigga indicates class and racial politics. This usage often involves a strong identification with the ghetto, but a hostile attitude toward women. "African" has recently been used to signify a spiritual connection with the continent and a political connection with Afrocentric politics. In this regard, Flavor Flav of Public Enemy has declared, "I don't wanna be called yo nigga" on the 1991 cut "Yo Nigga," which leads the way into Sister Souljah's assertion "African people, too scared to call themselves African" on her 1992 cut, "African Scaredy Cat in a One Exit Maze." Calling oneself African supposedly demonstrates an advanced state of consciousness that eliminates any connection to America and affirms links with an Afrocentric cultural, political and spiritual base. Souljah suggests that those, who reject this idea are "scared" to reject the ideological forces compelling them to see America as home.

Arrested Development expresses this notion of Africa by continually identifying themselves as African in "People Everyday." Speech states, "I told the niggas please/Let us past friend/I said please cause I don't like killing Africans/ But they wouldn't stop/And I ain't Ice Cube/Who?/But I had to take the brothers out for being rude!" Speech shows some sympathy to niggas by implying that they are ultimately Africans. He also sees their masculine lower class behavior as part of their definition as niggas. Speech suggests that if they reject this class-based behavior then they can then be seen as Africans. Yet, they can rise no higher than their lower-class status; Speech declares, "that's the story yaw'll/of a Black man/acting like a nigga/and get stomped by an African!" This final statement emphasizes opposition between nigga as defined by offensive behavior and African as defined by intellectual and political sophistication.

Similar to the confrontation scene in Spike Lee's *School Daze* (1988) — between the "fellas" and the men from the neighborhood at Kentucky Fried Chicken — Arrested Development acknowledges class difference within the African American community, but does not critically analyze it. Representations of class positions are reproduced through the reliance on stereotyped behavior. Foregrounding this incident increases the possibility for this scene to replicate a dominant view on lower-class African American males and their menacing qualities.

Arrested Development brings an important intellectual and critical dimension to rap music and culture. It breaks away from the redundant "boy'n the hood" scenario that has become almost counterproductive through the dominant media's overwhelming reliance on it, and the rap community's willingness to participate in the exploitation of this narrative. Arrested Development's female members are central to determining and articulating the group's political position. Though their collaborative effort has its limitations, it provides an empowered position for female speakers, without necessarily privileging the male voice. Unfortunately, compared to the rest of the rap community the group's gender politics is uncommon.

Arrested Development's critical Afrocentricity involves an unconscious co-optation of regressive class politics. Its sophisticated and at times, self-righteous political position can critique modernity, capitalism and gender, yet it does not articulate an empowering voice for lower-class Blacks. Much like W.E.B. Du Bois's notion of the "talented tenth," Arrested Development, attempts to close the societal gap on race, but widens it on class and fails to initiate a political dialogue that could strengthen both areas. Although Arrested Development does not blame the victim, it does intensify class divisions with its intellectually elitist argument on the ghetto and African American male culture. While it claims to be concerned with everyday people it locates the "group of brothers" that it critiques somewhere else. Yet as I have asserted earlier, my interest in Arrested Development relates to how it opens up the dialogue on politics and rap culture through the invocation of its gendered Afrocentric position. My analysis of Arrested Development's politics in turn suggests how multiple levels of political discourse are juxtaposed within contemporary African American culture.

Arrested Development is clearly linked to a revisionist southern history which locates the problems of contemporary African American existence in the destructive effects of urbanization. This critical posture, in light of most other rap music, appears progressive and somewhat liberating. Yet, when extrapolated to the larger political themes, this position seems uncomplicated and mainstream. With conservative media manipulation of the popular term "political correctness" all but cutting it off from its progressive aspirations, Arrested Development can be easily coopted as being aligned with this weakened position. This dynamic is apparent in the group's public acceptability across race and gender lines. Arrested Development indicates in many ways the mainstreaming of Afrocentricity and the death of an earlier revolutionary agenda.

But I Ain't Ice Cube!

This limited political agenda, furthered by an inability to address class inequities that define much of contemporary society, is best understood when comparing Arrested Development to Ice Cube, who packages his political agenda in icons of gangsta culture and the modernized landscape of a racialized urban America, namely South Central Los Angeles. Ice Cube and the world he represents motivates much of Arrested Development's critical posture. Ice Cube not only functions as an extension of the political argument in rap music, but also as a critical interlocutor that exposes the limitations of Arrested Development.

Ice Cube's persuasive power relates to his agility in moving between the general and specific, simultaneously analyzing individual actions and societal oppression. Arrested Development can be seen in the same tradition as advocating an empowered version of religion, much like James Cone's idea of "Black Liberation Theology" or Albert Cleage's theory of the "Pan-African Orthodox." However, Ice Cube embraces the controversial tenets of Louis Farrakhan and the Nation of Islam. Unlike Arrested Development, who advocate a return to southern tradition as the solution to the problems of contemporary African American existence, Ice Cube's focus is the inner city in all its blighted glory.

Ice Cube's politics of location is clearly conversant with Burnett's *To Sleep With Anger*. Instead of focusing on the deep south and migration northward, the migration pattern of the early part of this century so often discussed in popular versions of African American history, Ice Cube, like Burnett, finds critical solace in a neglected segment of African American migration—the westward migration of southwestern (Arkansas, Louisiana, Texas) Blacks to Los Angeles primarily after World War II. Thus, Ice Cube's concerns with history are more current, and in a sense, better able to engage aspects of contemporary culture. Whereas Arrested Development is interested in issues surrounding modernity, Ice Cube addresses issues of postmodernity.

This postmodern urban agenda is visually underscored through scenes of the burnt-out remains of post-uprising Crenshaw Boulevard in the "True to the Game" video. This is in direct opposition to the rural landscapes that dominate Arrested Development's videos. Ice Cube sees the pathology of self-destruction as perpetrated by many African Americans themselves and the propensity towards assimilating into mainstream society, thus losing one's identity, as the social hindrances that deny self-empowerment. Though this agenda is not radically different from that advocated by Arrested Development, it is the urban setting, the embrace of the Nation of Islam, a postmodern criticism of societal institutions and a rigorous critique of class politics that allow for a clear distinction between the two rap acts.

A good example of Ice Cube's fusion of these ideas into a coherent critical position appears on the album *Death Certificate* which brings together the Nation of Islam's notion of race and a concern for the problems within African American society resulting from late commodity culture and the neoconservatism of the Reagan-Bush era. The album is equally divided between what Ice Cube describes as the "Death" and the "Life" sides. With the "Death" side, Ice Cube documents the violently destructive mentality that flourishes throughout lower-class African American culture. Gangbanging, sexism, wanton violence and other abusive behaviors are presented without the usual saccharine justification or uninformed rejection, but as harsh realities. This is what Ice Cube wants to "kill." The "Life" side concerns revitalization and understanding the roots of these societal problems, dealing with them efficiently and moving on to more concrete solutions.

The "Death" side begins with the funeral of another of Ice Cube's long line of "dead homiez." Minister Khallid Muhammad of the Nation of Islam eulogizes the victim and sets the album's critical posture in place. Muhammad concludes by stating that the person being eulogized, which by this time we know is Ice Cube, is "the wrong nigga to fuck wit." It is at this point that Ice Cube begins his verbal assault on the racism, conformity and the overall lack of self-expression of contemporary society. Still seeing himself as the ultimate rebel who exists outside of varying sectors of both black and white society, Ice Cube goes on a verbal rampage that attacks everything from contemporary African American popular music to police brutality. Much like his opening declaration on *Amerikka's Most Wanted*, "The Nigga You Love to Hate," Ice Cube revels in his utter disgust with American culture. African American complacency is as detrimental to progress as the most vile forms of white supremacy. Ice Cube's unrelenting attack on these cultural manifestations becomes the core of his identity: the angry black man, the enraged lyricist.

At the conclusion of the "Death" side we are slowly transformed from being sympathetic, yet passive listeners, to unconscious perpetrators of the very acts and attitudes that reinforce oppressive behavior. Once again, Ice Cube's critical cipher treats both African Americans and the dominant society as equal culprits in the continual destruction of African American culture. Yet, as the "Life" side begins with sounds of a newborn baby, we are given a glimpse of hope as to the future undoing of the shackles of oppression. Ice Cube implies through the metaphor of life that a strong critical, and at times self-critical posture, is necessary in order to fully understand the dynamics that continually restrict African American progress and ultimate empowerment in the larger society. The "Life" side proceeds with a critical analysis of sexual harassment, forced patriotism, assimilation, the self-destructive nature of gang violence and the unwitting rejection of one's culture and soul for financial gain. The "Life" side takes Ice Cube's project to the next level, as he has successfully found a way to neither romanticize nor unequivocally reject the societal problems facing African Americans. Instead, he seems to have found a much needed ground of critical scrutiny with useful extrapolation for the future. As underscored below by Khallid Muhammad's sermon, the implications of life for future directions, becomes the source of potential empowerment:

No longer dead, deaf, dumb, and blind/Out of our mind/Brainwashed with the white man's mind/ No more homicide!/No more fratricide, genocide, or suicide!/Look the goddamn white man in his cold blue eyes/Devil don't even try/We like Bebe's kids/We don't die/We multiply/You've heard the death side/So open your Black eyes to the resurrection, rebirth, and rise.

In Ice Cube's use of Muhammed's oratorical qualities, Nation of Islam icons ("blue-eyed devil") are fused with icons of the gang subculture ("we don't die, we multiply") and popular African American media culture (Robin Harris's "Bebe's kids") in order to create an empowered rhetorical articulation that points towards the possibility of a future free of these restraints. Muhammed also relies on a liberatory notion of freedom as expressed through popular religious icons ("resurrection, rebirth, and rise"), giving new meaning to the at times constraining position that organized religion has occupied throughout history for African Americans. Thus, the "Life" side places contemporary African American culture under a critical microscope, while refusing to relinquish the ever present nature of dominant culture and its capacity to separate and destroy African American society.

Central to Ice Cube's political agenda is an ongoing critique of the nihilism that exists throughout lower-class African American society. In conjunction with Cornel West's argument in *Race Matters*, which sees this nihilism in the form of "psychological depression, personal worthlessness, and social despair" (1993: 13), in the provocative tune "Us," Ice Cube vividly extends this argument by discussing the contradictory nature of African American culture as it often assumes a victimized posture of helplessness. Most telling in this regard is his declaratory line that "sometimes I believe the hype, man/we mess it up ourselves and blame the white man."

In a society where conservative political criticism of African Americans is abundant and encourages a defensive posture that romanticizes societal problems, Ice Cube rejects the idea of the "airing of one's dirty laundry in public" or to use the more succinctly Black phrase, "putting one's business in the street." He favors instead exposing the problems of the community for public debate. This rejection of victimization for an empowered critical agenda goes against the popular grain of African American public etiquette. But unlike conservative African American critics such as Clarence Thomas, Stanley Crouch or Shelby Steele, Ice Cube's position cannot be easily coopted. He uses this self-critical posture as an instance of cultural empowerment. His analysis of race and emphasis on class opens up the dialogue on the problems of contemporary culture, as opposed to closing off this debate through a needed, but often uninformed cultural deconstruction.

This self-critical duality is exemplified through Ice Cube's commentary on drugs and the subculture within which drugs circulate:

> And all ya'll dope dealers/You as bad as the police/Cause you kill us/ You got rich when you started slingin' dope/But you ain't built us a supermarket/So we can spend our money with the Blacks/Too busy buying gold and Cadillacs.

Any regular or irregular glimpse at the television news describes at length the entrenched presence of drugs in the African American community and the ghettoized culture that perpetuates this behavior. Conservative arguments repeatedly suggest that localized dealers be treated as felons and be punished with the death penalty. It is also no surprise to find many African Americans who live in the midst of what amounts to open air drug markets corroborate elements of this conservative argument out of sheer necessity, as their daily lives are in constant danger. However, in the gangsta rap community from which Ice Cube originally emerged, many advocate the glamorized lifestyle and economic independence of a drug dealer. For instance, rapper Scarface has even rejected the usual accompaniment of female sexual subservience by stating "fuck the bitches/I want money and the power," to demonstrate his complicity with the excesses of late commodity capitalism within the drug culture.

Ice Cube is careful not to fall into either ideological trap as he turns his critique of the drug culture into a positive vision for the community. The drug dealer's vigorous embrace of the fetishized commodity – gold and Cadillacs – is seen as a hindrance to an economically informed Black nationalism that allows African Americans the opportunity to spend their capital within their own self-sufficient communities. Drug dealing is not condemned in terms of "family values," but, as in the case of Gordon Parks, Jr.'s *Superfly* (1972), it is seen as an imposed necessity that if properly utilized can be turned into an economic base for one's own cultural empowerment.

Ice Cube goes on in "Us" to enumerate the contradictory nature of many elements within the African American community:

> Us gonna always sing the blues/Cause all we care about is hair styles and tennis shoes/If you mess with mine/I ain't frontin'/Cause I'll beat

you down like it ain't nothin'/Just like a beast/But I'm the first nigga to
holler out, peace/I beat my wife and children to pulp/When I get drunk
and smoke dope/Gotta bad heart condition/Still eat hog mauls and chit-
tlins/Bet my money on the dice or the horses/Jobless/So I'm a hoe for
the armed forces/Go to church but they tease us/With a picture of a
blue-eyed Jesus/Use to call me negro/After all this time I'm still bustin'
up the chiferow.

From the very beginning of this passage, Ice Cube points out contradictions
inherent in various activities. His claim that African Americans engage with
oppressive economic and cultural forces by an overemphasis on style and commodity culture reflects how corporations target African Americans as prime markets for their products. The Nike/Michael Jordan advertisements are probably
the most popular, with the Gatorade slogan "I want to be like Mike," adding to
the increased awareness that links stylish commodity consumption with African
American culture. As other athletic shoe companies have entered the fray, ads
for athletic shoes are located in an urban environment dominated by African
Americans. Thus the massive proliferation of these products and others in most
music videos make increasingly apparent how mediated slices of African American life have become oversaturated with stylish commodities.

Ice Cube argues that the suturing effects of commodity culture has caused
those who are oppressed to lose sight of their oppression due to this willing, yet
uncritical relationship with elements of the dominant society. The "singing of
the blues" is a direct result of this uneasy identity with popular elements of
the dominant culture. African American identity is depoliticized as possessing
commodities becomes superior to knowing the political dynamics fueling consumption. The fashion for "X" on baseball caps and clothing is another example
of this process of depoliticization. Originally created as an endorsement for Spike
Lee's film about Malcolm X, the letter has become a vulgar postmodern reification
of what Jean Baudrillard described as simulation, where signs are detached from
all referents and exist simply as signs. A knowledge of Malcolm X, his life, and
his philosophies is no longer required. The presence of the "X" stands for all of
the above and simultaneously allows the person wearing the sign to demonstrate
cultural hipness and a stylish political agenda. Ultimately, the "X" loses all association with Malcolm and simply becomes the sign of popular commodity culture,
as the increased visibility on a wide variety of people, regardless of their politics,
becomes the moment's most fashionable statement.

Ice Cube continually points out the many contradictions of African American life and he offers several examples of ruptures in relation to the dominant society. Ice Cube's political agenda stresses rigorously public self-criticism that forces African Americans to deal with internal problems and not use racism to answer all questions of oppression. While he is careful to acknowledge that racism exists and should not be ignored, he goes further to suggest that racism is often exacerbated through an uncritical relationship with commodity culture and other self-destructive activities. Ice Cube moves between both conservative and liberal positions in making this assertion. What is most useful about his position is the fact that an African American popular figure, albeit a self-proclaimed nationalist, has taken this stance through a strong cultural product. It is the opening up of the dialogue on African American culture that allows for the possibility of solutions to the difficulties imposed by the white supremacist culture of late capitalism.

Besides opening up the dialogue on culture through public self-criticism of the nihilism permeating the community, Ice Cube identifies another problem facing African American empowerment: attempts to assimilate into mainstream society, which entail compromising one's cultural identity. As a sophisticated class critique, assimilation into a tenuous middle-class existence is portrayed as consistent with oppression. This argument is clearly articulated through the song and video, "True to the Game." Ice Cube's most informative arguments about compromising one's identity appear through the metaphor of musical assimilation. Ice Cube here refers to the tendency of many rappers to reject tenets of rap music's hard political edge in exchange for success in mainstream culture. This has been a recurrent theme throughout recent rap music, but Ice Cube's video gives it visual emphasis. A rapper dressed in what is coded as hard-core clothing — a skull cap, sweatshirt and work khakis — slowly dissolves into a red-sequin attired entertainer who smiles repeatedly and performs elaborate dance moves. While the immediate reference is pop star Hammer, who in his recent comeback has contradicted his earlier self by embracing gangsta culture, the video uses this well known example to implicate all those who use the ghettoized trappings of hard-core rap to facilitate their transition into the more lucrative musical mainstream.

The transition from hard-core rapper to pop star is at the expense of one's cultural and class identity. The musically assimilative rapper attempts to change his style for the sake of mainstream culture, yet he is only to be exploited and ultimately rejected.

On MTV/But they don't care/They'll have a new nigga next year/Out in the cold/No more white fans and no more soul/And you might have a heart attack/When you find out Black folks don't want you back/And you know what's worst?/You was just like the nigga in the first verse/ Stop sellin' out your race/And wipe that stupid ass smile off your face/ Nigga's always gotta show they teeth/Now I'm gonna be brief/Be true to the game.

Repeated presentation and embrace on cable network MTV is seen as the ultimate mark of crossover success, especially when compared to the African American venue Black Entertainment Television (BET) and the Miami-based video jukebox, The Box, both of which have long been associated with playing African American music videos. Yet this is also ironic since after much initial hesitation, MTV has only recently begun playing rap or other forms of African American music on a regular basis. Although programs like *Yo MTV Raps* and *MTV Jams* are quite popular, it is the cable station's early association with rock and roll and heavy metal, at the expense of African American music, that makes MTV a lasting symbol of mainstream white culture in the music industry.

Ice Cube's assertion that "they don't care" directly comments on the exploitative nature of the music industry, as personified by MTV, and how it has historically used African American culture as trendy and disposable material: "they'll have a new nigga next year." MTV is only a recent example of a longstanding exploitative trend. Ice Cube also suggested that after the assimilative rapper has been rejected by trendy mainstream culture, the African American community has no further need for him. In this sense these rappers, and by extension, the desire to assimilate in any form, are complicit in their own oppression.

Ice Cube has demonstrated through both "Us" and "True to the Game" that he can consistently bring an empowered class critique to bear on both nihilistic individuals and societal institutions. This ability is underscored by his continual use of Nation of Islam ideology in his critique. Historically, the Nation of Islam has been a solid avenue of empowerment for individuals who exist outside of mainstream society, in African American society and in the society as a whole. Their focus on convicts, ex-convicts and reformed drug abusers is without equal, especially as it relates to African American males with these backgrounds. Nation of Islam patriarch, Elijah Muhammed, highlights this focus in the title to his popular book, *Message to the Black Man*. It is no coincidence that Ice Cube's manipulation of this ideology, with the trappings of L.A. gang culture, can forward an empowered critique of that which entraps the lower-class black male. Thus, the gaps in Arrested Development's elitist critical agenda are here fully exposed. Ice Cube's class critique, however, leaves no stone unturned.

Yet the limitations to Ice Cube's project lie in the same arena as its strengths. The Nation of Islam can critique bourgeois black society but it cannot empower those outside of the underclass, who it so effectively targets. The xenophobic anti-intellectualism and the overall passive approach to critically engaging mainstream society while existing in it, is the point at which the form of critique loses its usefulness. These are the limitations that forced Malcolm X, a true intellectual, to leave the Nation of Islam and search for wisdom elsewhere. And while Ice Cube's clever fusion of Nation of Islam ideology with gangsta iconography is an important form of class critique, it cannot raise questions of race and class to the next level of understanding. The strength of the Nation of Islam has always been its ability to erect a solid image of defiance. While this is a useful tool for raising consciousness, defiance is not the embodiment of all political understanding. If in contemporary society, an embrace of the Nation of Islam, which has always been misunderstood as an empowered expression of Black Nationalism, is the extent of our historical knowledge, then we have reached an intellectual impasse. Ice Cube and the Nation of Islam both refuse to properly engage a gender critique, and their reductive class critique leaves much to be desired.

Much of the political dimension that briefly had defined rap music and by extension African American popular culture, has been effectively killed off. Discussions of the resurgence of Black nationalism or attempts to define the elusive term Afrocentricity have subsided. In their place are discussions about rights to linguistic property: "niggas," "bitches," "hoes." Repeated denouncements concerning the hyper-violent atmosphere that circulates throughout gangsta culture became increasingly common and prompted Congressional hearings on the social impact of this nihilism.

That these issues moved from the rap world into the United States Congress attests to the importance of rap culture for the larger society. Yet this move also wrongly reasserts what I have often called the "moral imperative" of African American criticism, which supports problematic censorship under the guise of "what's good for our children," as in the critical rejection of a film like Melvin Van Peebles *Sweetsweetback's Badass Song* (1971). These moralistic cries do not address the real issues that underlie a systematic suturing of self-hatred which African Americans have been forced to identify with. Rap music, however, in this sense of a new cultural politics, has been a consistent vehicle for multiple voices – Arrested Development and Ice Cube – that have always had difficulty being heard. The critical question remains: when can there be a sustained movement that examines this historical self-hatred, while linking both politics and culture in a way that truly empowers all who subscribe to a liberated notion of existence in an otherwise oppressive society? All these concerns clearly prompt Ice Cube's self-critical imperative to "check yo self, before you wreck yo self."

Todd Boyd teaches in the Division of Critical Studies at the School of Cinema-Television, University of Southern California. His recent publications include "Jazz and the Abstract Truth" (*Rap Sheet* March 1994), "Popular Culture and Political Empowerment" (*Cineaste* 19:4, 1993), and "The Wrong Nigga to Fuck Wit: Sweetback and the Dilemma of the African American Avant Garde" (*Filmforum* 1994). He is author of *True to the Game: Black Men and Popular Culture* and coeditor of *Sports, Masculinity and American Culture*, both forthcoming from Indiana University Press.

Literature Cited

Baker Houston, A. J. 1993. *Black Studies, Rap, and the Academy*. Chicago: University of Chicago Press.

Baudrillard, Jean. 1993. *Simulations*. New York: Semiotext(e).

Boyd, Todd. 1993. "Popular Culture and Political Empowerment." *Cineaste* 19 (4): 12–13.

Dent, Gina (ed.) 1993. *Black Popular Culture*. Seattle: Bay Press.

George, Nelson. 1993. *Buppies, B-boys, Baps, and Bohos*. New York: Harper Collins.

hooks, bell. 1992. *Black Looks*. Boston: South End Press.

hooks, bell and Cornel West. 1991. *Breaking Bread: Insurgent Black Intellectual Life*. Boston: South End Press.

Mercer, Kobena. 1990. "Black Hair/Style Politics." In *Out There: Marginalization and Contemporary Culture*, edited by Russell Ferguson, et al., 247–264. Cambridge: MIT Press.

Rose, Tricia. 1990. "Never Trust a Big Butt and a Smile." *Camera Obscura* 23: 105–120.

_____. 1994. *Black Noise: Rap Music and Black Culture in Contemporary America*. Boston: University Press of New England.

Tate, Greg. 1992. *Flyboy in the Buttermilk*. New York: Fireside Press.

West, Cornel. 1990. "The New Cultural Politics of Difference." In *Out There: Marginalization and Contemporary Culture*, edited by Russell Ferguson, et al., 19–38. Cambridge: MIT Press.

———. 1993. *Race Matters*. Boston: Beacon Press.

University Presses and the Black Reader

Elizabeth Maguire

L ike long skirts, wispy shag hairstyles and tweezed eyebrows, the big buzz in book publishing throughout 1992 and 1993 seemed to be a replay of something we'd already learned in the early 1970s: many of this country's 30 million plus Black citizens read books. Many of those readers actually buy books. Good books by Black writers sell across racial and cultural lines. The most visible sign of this phenomenon was the Sunday of June 21, 1992 when three Black women writers — Alice Walker, Toni Morrison and Terry McMillan — appeared simultaneously on *The New York Times Book Review* bestseller list for hardcover fiction. Morrison did double duty. Her Harvard University Press book, *Playing in the Dark*, also appeared on the nonfiction bestseller list, where it spent six weeks, followed by Marian Edelman's *Measure of Our Success* and Cornel West's *Race Matters*. Thanks in part to Spike Lee, the *Times* paperback bestseller list included Malcolm X's autobiography. Maya Angelou's *I Know Why the Caged Bird Sings* has been on the list since Clinton's inauguration. Inside the industry, it was considered newsworthy that none of this was limited to Black History Month, when publishers usually play up their books on Black themes.

Back in February 1991, Edwin McDowell's article in *The New York Times* noted the increased visibility of Black writers and audiences. In a special 1992 report, "Blacks and the Book World," *Publisher's Weekly* analyzed the "explosive" growth of independent Black publishers, distributors and bookstores (January

Public Culture 1994, 7: 313–320

20, 1992). To media-watchers it seemed that miles of precious column space were devoted to books by Black writers that included not only the holy trinity of Walker, Morrison and McMillan, but also Darryl Pinckney, Caryl Phillips, Henry Louis Gates, Jr., Patricia Williams, Anthony Appiah and Cornel West. The *Voice Literary Supplement* organized an issue around the theme of "Black Talk." Derek Walcott won the Nobel Prize, as has Toni Morrison since this essay was first written. Reminding us that money is to be made in all this, that arbiter of middlebrow culture *The New York Times Magazine* ran an article titled "McMillan's Millions," (August 9, 1992) with the slightly surprised subtitle "Publishers agreed that blacks don't buy books. Author Terry McMillan is making a fortune by proving them wrong." Yet the article neglected to mention that her publisher is making a fortune too. Meanwhile, university presses with longstanding commitments to African American studies struggled to retain authors, both promising newcomers and seasoned scholars, while editors at commercial houses raided our backlists with glee. In the relatively low-stakes world of scholarly publishing, where customers' resources diminish by the month, reprints of African American texts, critical works and journals remain one of the only sure bets left in the humanities.

The readership for any or all of these publishing ventures is not exclusively a *Black* readership. However, it has become impossible to imagine the success of any of these books without the commitment of Black readers. For years Black writers seeking the backing of major houses needed to prove that their books were not "too Black," not only for the eyes of Black readers. Now, publishers readily admit that those readers are crucial.

Like many institutions that combine culture and commerce, book publishing has traditionally been a (White) gentlemen's profession. Though editors of vision have worked to promote Black writing, mainstream publishers help create and serve mainstream culture. For an author, the gold ring is artistic and intellectual legitimacy, as well as economic remuneration. This legitimacy long carried a special burden for Black writers, who had to endure an ongoing critical discussion of whether or not their work appealed just to Black readers. In 1952, *The New Yorker* commended Ellison's *Invisible Man* by saying, "What gives it its strength is that it is about being colored in a white society and yet manages not to be a grievance book; it has not got the whine of a hard-luck story about it, and it has not got the blurting, incoherent quality of a statement made in anger." This critical rhetoric changed along with the culture, with the fervor of the Black Arts movement in the 1960s, and the success of Black women writers in the 1970s. But even in 1981, the year that Toni Morrison appeared on the cover of *Time* after the publication of *Tar Baby*, *The New York Times Book Review* said of the novelist, "Morrison's greatest accomplishment is that she has raised her novel above the social realism that too many black novels and women's novels are trapped in."

Publishing is an inexact business, and it is nearly impossible to make exact claims about who is buying what. Editors constantly invoke a mythical "educated general reader" when trying to pitch their books to their colleagues in sales and marketing. When it comes to books by or about African Americans, there has been tension – commercial, intellectual, creative – between the notion of this ideal universal readership, and an equally idealized, universal, *Black* readership. Now we see tensions about exactly who this ideal Black reader is. Even at the venerable Oxford University Press, where we all know that the idea of race is socially constructed, a marketing colleague recently asked me, "Is this author Black? Because if she is, then we should definitely put her picture on the jacket."

Although an essentialist notion of a monolithic Black readership is problematic, the fact remains that there is a socioeconomically and regionally diverse Black reading community that is *hungry* for books that deal with African American experiences, in genres as varied as history, religion, philosophy, fiction; at levels as distinct as children's, educational, reference, trade. The special needs and buying habits of this hungry readership have given rise to an explosion within the publishing industry: more independent Black publishers such as Just Us Books, Third World Press, Noble Press, as well as special commercial imprints such as One World at Ballantine; over 200 bookstores that define themselves as Black compared to only a dozen ten years ago; a proliferation of middlemen/distributors channeling books from publishers to the Black community; an African American Booksellers Association and a related African American bestseller list put out by Blackboard, Inc. If mainstream publishers learned anything from the Terry McMillan phenomenon, it is that grassroots promotion and publicity can make a book's success with those Black readers who do not base their reading habits on the indicators of mainstream publishing: the *Publisher's Weekly* advance review, *The New York Times Book Review* and other newspaper reviews, the serious magazines and academic journals.

◆◆◆

What do university presses have to with any of this? Especially since one might more reasonably ask if university presses have any readers at all? University presses did play a special role in the development of African American Studies and African American publishing. Although it seems unlikely that the esoteric world of the university press—a gentlemen's preserve if ever there was one—could act as a creative and positive force in such a politically-charged field, that is, in fact, what happened. A strange blend of idealism and entrepreneurship was at play.

The relationship between the university press and its primary audience is an unusually direct one. University presses exist to publish and disseminate scholarship; they rely on scholars to advise them on what to publish. Most of them also publish in varying proportions trade, college and reference books, but their *raison d'etre* is professional publishing for academic professionals. Of course, Black biologists, medievalists, classicists and philosophers read university press books in their respective disciplines; yet from the outset, African and African American Studies had a large potential readership beyond the scholars working in these fields. Academic publishers and scholars worked together to create and develop that readership, resulting in one of the genuine success stories in book publishing.

This success is not simply presses and authors selling books and making money, but rather setting in motion a profound change. University presses, with their standardized procedures of peer review and their imprimaturs of academic quality, helped to legitimize the field of Afro-Am (as it used to be called), and to gain job security for scholars within the academic establishment. Afro-Am scholars moved from toeholds in the university to firmly entrenched positions. In a related and even more dramatic development, leading books in the field became crucial college texts. Tens and even hundreds of thousands of students came into contact with them. This new course market insured a growing student readership. Today, Black intellectuals are moving outside the academy to write books for a wider audience that includes those members of the Black middle class who took the first Afro-Am courses. Basic scholarship continues to flourish, and new textbooks proliferate, but there are now far more provocative books aimed at a larger readership. You can see this at many university presses—Chicago, Harvard, Oxford, Rutgers, Minnesota—and similar houses such as Routledge and Beacon. It also accounts for the current frenzy for Black books at the big commercial houses.

The growth of this reading audience, which began thirty years ago, has gained momentum in the past fifteen years. In the 1960s and 1970s, the civil rights movement, open admissions, and what now seems like the luxury of university life in an era of well-funded expansion, provided fertile ground for the growth of publishing in African American Studies. It's quite unusual that college textbooks, not usually considered a cutting-edge branch of publishing, provided the most important avenue for early Afro-Am books from university presses; publishers and scholars worked together to help create a new market. People were eager to teach these books and students were eager to study them. The development of Oxford's program in African American Studies offers a mini-narrative of what was happening in the university at large.

After the Brown vs. Board of Education decision, Oxford published its first major book in African American history in 1955: C. Vann Woodward's *The Strange Career of Jim Crow*. In three editions it has sold nearly a million copies in paperback. In the 1960s, my colleague Sheldon Meyer, pursuing his passion for jazz, Black history and southern history, began to lay the groundwork for a list that would help to shape the field. Among the books he published were Richard Wade's *Slavery in the Cities* (1964), Weinstein and Gatell's *American Negro Slavery* (1968), John Blassingame's *The Slave Community* (1972), Nathan Huggins' *Harlem Renaissance* (1972), Winthrop Jordan's *The White Man's Burden* (1974) and Leon Higgenbotham's *In the Matter of Color* (1978). What's fascinating from a publisher's point of view is that all these books began as trade hardcovers, yet continue to sell in paperback in large quantities to the college market. Although not all students in African American courses are Black, it's inconceivable that this publishing boom could have happened without the increased presence of and pressure from Black students and Black scholars.

As the field broadened to include the study of literature and culture in the late 1970s and early 1980s, Oxford's list expanded in those directions. Arnold Rampersad's biography of Langston Hughes (1986, 1988), Henry Louis Gates, Jr.'s *The Signifying Monkey* (1988) and Hazel Carby's *Reconstructing Womanhood* (1987) are among works that continue to sell to scholars, students and general readers. Enriched by feminist scholarship and the blossoming of Black women creative writers (Naylor, Walker, Shange, Morrison, et al.), women's writing provided some of the liveliest work in African American Studies. What might have seemed like mundane textual archaeology has actually been fruitful publishing, e.g., at Oxford, the *Schomburg Library of 19th Century Black Women Writers* showed how an audience could be created at every possible level: libraries; scholars; students; general readers. This second wave resulted in the canon expansion that conservative critics abhor. It's also created a new wave of college readers for reclaimed literary works such as Hurston's *Their Eyes Were Watching God* selling several hundred thousand copies a year for HarperCollins, or one of the Schomburg paperbacks selling a few thousand a year for Oxford.

Fortunately for publishers, many students grow up into adult bookbuyers. We see not only more scholars and more courses, but also more general readers. This is reflected in the projects editors including myself are supporting – new textbooks, scholarly works that use the tools of cultural studies and trade books pitched for a general readership. Of these, the most exciting and most difficult is the last: working with Black intellectuals to address a wider audience. This is the next great wave of readership, and one we've just begun to ride.

◆◆◆

African American intellectuals from Du Bois to bell hooks have wrestled with the complicated role of the Black intellectual in American society. Is there an audience? Is that audience Black? The burden of representation is heavy and even well-intentioned publishers, always in search of that perfect typical reader, might not entirely appreciate its weight. There is a sizable though diverse Black readership for books by Black intellectuals, and the importance of that audience should not be obscured by the presence of equally serious readers who are White or Asian or Native American.

Last summer, a leading Black scholar of African American studies said, as if letting me in on a big secret, "You know, Liz, Terry McMillan's book is selling to *real Black women*. Toni Morrison's stuff is read mostly by upper middle-class White women." Now, I'd like to put aside one of the few accepted demographic factoids in the publishing industry, which is that women with college degrees with disposable incomes comprise the main audience for what is called "literary" fiction; men seem to prefer history books. I have no doubt that Toni Morrison sells a lot of books to upper–middle class White readers. I've remained troubled by this scholar's statement, because it relates to an anxiety I see among my authors about the Black readership for their books. It also speaks to a flawed notion of Blackness that I've heard articulated by many publishers – all White – and also by Black scholars. It's the idea that once you are thinking and writing fancy thoughts, your audience automatically becomes White, liberal and largely female. (In this context female carries derogatory connotations.)

Are Black readers of popular fiction more real than Black readers of serious fiction? Are Black readers of serious fiction not really Black? Is a book less Black when White people read it too? Therefore, are the "realest" Black women those who have to wait for the paperback, rather than buy a twenty–two dollar hardcover book? Are they those who have to borrow the book from their local public library, which may or may not be open, much less have the book? Was the comment one of those rare moments of self-reflection in the life of an intellectual, when one voices a nagging doubt about the value of the work of the mind in relation to the real world? Or did the comment speak to the specific burdens of the Black intellectual or writer today?

I negotiate this intellectual-at-large-in-a-society-hostile-to-intellectuals stuff all the time. It's what I do for a living. All my instincts and experience as a publisher tell me that we have a substantial Black readership for our books. But, while writing this essay, I thought, Who the hell am I to be so upbeat? How can I be sure that Black readers want to read books by scholars and intellectuals that are published by university presses and other serious publishers? What if I'm just part of this small bookish community, and all thirty of us are reading the same articles, books, journals? So, I got up from my wordprocessor and went to Black Books Plus, on 94th and Amsterdam Avenue, and looked around.

There they all were! Cornel West and Pat Williams and Houston Baker, Jr., and Martin Bernal and bell hooks and Valerie Smith and Henry Louis Gates, Jr., ... Little Schomburg paperbacks – and lots of the Oxford backlist classics. I asked Glyn Johnson, who opened the store four years ago, if Black customers buy university press books, and she said, "Oh, yes." She showed me a huge file of orders to university presses, and we talked about some of the problems she faces as an independent bookseller: trying to get books quickly, keeping stock, being hounded to pay bills as if she were one of the chains, needing to nag university and independent presses to ship stock in a timely way. We talked about what really helps her: book signings, cooperative ads with publishers, more books by and about women, books that are written in what she calls "readable English." Her message was clear. Black readers come in knowing what they want, and they buy aggressively. By the time I left I was so excited that I was telling her how I had wanted to join the Black Panthers when I was in eighth grade at St. Gregory the Great grammar school, and she probably thought I was just another crazy White girl who took a wrong turn off Broadway.

So, I conclude on an upbeat, though cautious note. People who buy books can read, and have money to spare. Unfortunately, these two criteria do not describe most people in this country, whether or not they are Black. Book buying is a middle-class luxury; book reading is not, though the current state of our public libraries makes it seem like one. People who buy serious books have to be especially committed to reading something that might be difficult. But the strength of that commitment – professional or personal – is especially powerful among Black readers. These readers witness and experience racism, the effects of diminishing educational resources and an ongoing backlash from factions of the right. Black intellectuals who want to write for a wider audience will find one: students and general readers, Black and White. But in book publishing everything is a fight for public space, be it review space in a magazine, or shelf space in a book store. As would be the case with any academic writer, Black intellectuals reaching into that public space will often have to let go of the language that legitimizes scholarly discourse, and it's a good thing, too.

Interested White, Asian American, Native American and Latino readers will always buy good books by Black intellectuals. But Black writers can work with publishers to make sure that the nonacademic Black community also knows about their books and has access to them. As commercial publishers merge into fewer and more powerful media empires, it seems likely that university presses and similar publishers will remain an important haven for independent thinking and mid-list books that are aimed at a serious readership. As with the first college books of the 1960s and 1970s, it is a matter of creating new audiences, rather than responding to the existing marketplace—envisioning Black people as active reading subjects, not just objects of scholarly inquiry.

Elizabeth Maguire is senior editor, Literary and Cultural Studies at Oxford University Press in New York City.

Afterword:
Mapping the Black Public Sphere

Thomas C. Holt

The occasion for this collection of essays is the amazing eruption and transformation of black "publicity" in the latter half of the twentieth century.[1] Between 1980 and 1992, especially, the black public sphere expanded in reach and complexity, despite the fact that progressive black political agendas were being shattered and significant social programs gutted by the policies and ideologies of the Reagan-Bush era. Indeed, the simultaneity of these developments has contributed to, if not largely produced, the profound paradoxes of contemporary America: African Americans find themselves more highly integrated into American life than ever before, and yet, in many ways, still as thoroughly segregated as at any time during this century; wealthier than at any time in our history, yet increasingly economically isolated and impoverished; more visible in public life, yet more alienated and angry. The analytical and political utility of the concept of a black public sphere will depend on its relevance to resolving such paradoxes, and whether it proves a fruitful starting point from which to reexamine the interrelationships among African-American political, cultural, and intellectual agendas.

The notion of a "public sphere," popularized by the work of Jürgen Habermas, has stimulated over the past decade a wide-ranging and sometimes contentious inquiry into theoretical matters of immediate political valence. Habermas defined the public sphere historically as that arena — emerging and interdependent with the transition to capitalism — constituted by autonomous, individual men (rather

---

1. This afterword was originally written as a statement of purpose for the "Black Public Sphere in the Reagan-Bush Era Conference" sponsored by the Chicago Humanities Institute at the University of Chicago in October 1993.

than feudal estates), who within a private (i.e., non-state) *discursive* space determined the rules and norms that governed political relations. Habermas has been criticized, of course, for the idealized, programmatic framing of his discussion; for romanticizing or not taking sufficient account of the exclusionary agendas of his "democratic" regimes, for privileging the bourgeois over oppositional "counter-publics." Yet, as the papers here attest, the notion of *a* public sphere, or spheres, can provide a powerful entry into the interrelatedness of matters that—within the disciplinary fragmentation of the academy's normal science—might appear disparate and unconnected. Economics, politics, cultural politics, racial identity, gender, popular music, religion, reading: all these play a role in creating speech communities, "publicity," and the material and power relations in which these are grounded. Moreover, this rubric, which is theoretically a space defined equally by speakers and listeners, leaders and followers, material resources and discursive performances, might recast the stubborn tensions between structure and agency that burden so much of contemporary social theory.

Indeed, the theoretical explication of how majority norms and conventions are generated is crucial to a more powerful examination of the processes and significance of minority and oppositional cultures. When applied to the black public, such analysis might provide more sophisticated approaches to matters previously and historically consigned to such inadequate and fragile discursive rubrics as "the Negro problem," "subcultures," "minorities," "inner city," and "multicultural." Each of the latter has proven less an analytic framework than a sphere of containment, flattening black life into monolithic stereotypes. Of course, if we are not cautious, the notion of a black public sphere will not be immune to a similar fate. Its analytical vitality can be sustained only if we cleave firmly to its historicity, its materiality, its plurality, and its political relevance.

The bourgeois public sphere, it must be remembered, had a historically specific provenance and development; it cannot be simply mapped onto contemporary African-American lifeworlds. Emblematic of the historical distance is the fact that the same coffee houses that nurtured Habermas's seventeenth and eighteenth century bourgeois version gave birth as well to Lloyd's of London and other underwriters of the Atlantic slave trade. Among our first questions then is how—by what processes and with what limitations and resources—has the black public sphere been constituted historically? What have been and are the conditions of possibility for a separate black counter-public in America? And how have those conditions changed over time? Our appreciation of the contemporary black public sphere must begin with recognition that separate institutional life, media, and discourse have long characterized African-American experience, at least since churches, newspapers, mass political rallies, and mutual aid societies flowered in the years after slavery emancipation. Moreover, these media have always existed in an uneasy and complex relationship to the institutions of the white majority as well as to the ideology of democratic community, an ideology and value claimed by both whites and blacks but interpreted differently. The ensuing struggles over such competing meanings and values gave shape to the separateness of black publicity even as they forged intrinsic and inescapable links between the spheres of dominance and of opposition.

Such linkages reflect the fact that the material and political environments we inhabit are central elements for defining the "conditions of possibility" for black publics. Historically, a black public could only come into existence after slavery emancipation or in communities of freed slaves. There were slave communities, to be sure, but the conditions of slavery precluded the existence of institutions which could sustain politically viable speech communities. The exponential growth of churches, newspapers, mutual aid associations, political organizations, literary societies, and other elements of organizational life after the Civil War underscores the vital difference between the speech and informational networks that could be sustained by slaves, and the complex institutional infrastructure of the freedpeople's public sphere. Similar differences, ruptures, and transformations can be traced across the changing political-economic terrain of sharecropping, urbanization, and the global networks of post-industrial society. If we are to understand the conditions of possibility for historically specific black publics, it makes a difference where people lived, how they lived, and what was happening in the world(s) in which they lived. For example, neither the content and means by which rap music challenges mainstream culture nor its commodification and cooptation can be understood outside the cultural processes that typify the global capitalist hegemony configuring contemporary life.

Some of the essays here also suggest the crucial role played in the evolution of contemporary black publicity by the conditions of political repression during the 1980s. Many of the incidents that have exacerbated the schisms between whites and blacks and among blacks themselves had their origins in the racial politics of the Reagan-Bush regime. Of these the Anita Hill-Clarence Thomas controversy is perhaps the most striking, but the sustained attack on social welfare, unions, public employment, taxation, and the very notion of claiming redress for racial injustice shaped cultural politics as well as urban electoral politics. Ironically, then, it may be that the phenomenal recent growth of separate black public spheres owes a great deal to the policies of the Reagan-Bush era.

If institutional and material conditions matter, then we should not speak of *the* black public sphere but of a plurality of spheres. Despite sharp disagreements about how to interpret the phenomenon, it is undeniable that economic transformations since World War II have had differential impact on African Americans, intensifying their institutional and economic diversity. Greater class differentiation, institutional fragmentation, and spatial isolation had to have affected black public life and publicity. One need only compare the experience of viewing a "black" film at a downtown moviehouse and then in "the hood" to appreciate the impact of that diversity of habitus.

Finally, our inquiries into the development and functioning of black public spheres must recognize the inherent political significance of and impetus behind the concept. Theoretically, speech communities are democratic forums in which public opinion takes shape, opinion aimed at directing or influencing public policy, norms of behavior, or political consensus. Although these are idealistic and perhaps unrealistic goals for counter-publics, which are by definition publics divorced from substantial control over how public power is deployed, they define the point of the analytic exercise nonetheless: not only speech but also action. In the case of an oppositional public, the goal quite simply is oppositional action. This, then, is the standard, the gauge of the relevance, value, and importance of various forms of contemporary publicity. Whether it is new media heroes, an expanded black press, rap music, or a Supreme Court justice that is the subject of our inquiry, its ultimate significance is determined by whether that phenomenon facilitates democratic values and justice for all. Does it represent not simply resistance but positive change? Does our better understanding of it help us see how such change might be effected? True, the contemporary black public sphere is partly the creature of the political economy of a global, advanced capitalist order, but in the past it has offered — and may yet again offer — space for critique and transformation of that order. If not, then all this is only idle talk.

Index

flexible accumulation of capital, 212–13, 255, 259
flight. *See* exodus; migration
Florida State A & M Marching Band, 21–22
Flory, Thomas, 176
"Flying' Home," 50
Foner, Eric, 120
40 Acres and a Mule, 266
Fourteenth Amendment, 121
Fourth Baptist Church, 133
Franklin, Aretha, 282
Franti, Michael, 220
Fraser, Nancy, 14–15, 201–3, 210, 215
fraternal societies, 137, 142, 240
Frazier, Franklin, 159
freedmen, 66–67, 76, 175–76
freedom, 53–80, 262
    political life in transition from slavery, 111–50
Fresh Prince, 290
Freyre, Gilberto, 175, 177
Funkenstein, Dr., 59
funk music, 284

gangs, 162, 240–41
    "colors," 240
    Los Angeles gang culture, 313–14
    membership, 270
    subculture, 309
    violence, 296
gangsta rap and rappers, 306, 312
    Black counterpublic, 221
    iconography, 314
    marketing of Black popular music, 294
    political theme, 61, 77, 298, 310
Garofalo, Reebee, 279–91
Garvey, Marcus, 51, 204, 206
Garvey movement, 211
Gates, Henry Louis, Jr., 55, 318, 321, 323
gays and gay rights, 218, 240, 288

Geldof, Bob, 289
gender issues. *See also* feminism; women
    bio-politics and etho-poetics, 55–56, 70–71
    Black counterpublic, 201, 203–4, 216–17
    critique, 314
    differences, 146
    political life in transition from slavery to freedom, 111–50
    politics of gender, 303, 306
    rap music, 288, 295, 303–5
    roles, 79
generational issues, 26, 30
Gerima, Haile, 90
ghettos
    identity, 304
    life, 304
    Malcolm X, 42, 45
    popular culture, political theme, 296, 298, 303, 306, 310
    poverty, 153
    rioting, 32
    trappings of hard-core rap, 312
Gibson, E.L., 125
Gilbert and Sullivan, 9
Gillespie, Dizzy, 51
Gilroy, Paul, 53–80, 261
globalization, 254–59
    economy, 263
    music industry, 288–91
Goetz, Bernard, 214
Golgatha Community Baptist Church, 76
Grand Fountain, 136
Gray, Susan, 111
The Greatest, 93
Greek sororities and fraternities, 240
Green, Jane, 111, 131
Gregory, Steven, 151–70
guns, 126–27